HARCOURT **HORIZONS**

The Pledge of Allegiance

I pledge allegiance to the Flag

of the United States of America,

and to the Republic

for which it stands,

one Nation under God, indivisible,

with liberty and justice for all.

HARCOURT HORIZONS

Indiana

Harcourt

Orlando   Austin   Chicago   New York   Toronto   London   San Diego

Visit *The Learning Site!*
www.harcourtschool.com

HARCOURT HORIZONS

INDIANA

General Editor

Dr. Michael J. Berson
Associate Professor
Social Science Education
University of South Florida
Tampa, Florida

Contributing Author

Dorothy W. Drummond
Department of Geography, Geology,
 and Anthropology (retired)
Indiana State University
Terre Haute, Indiana

Series Consultants

Dr. Robert Bednarz
Professor
Department of Geography
Texas A&M University
College Station, Texas

Dr. Asa Grant Hilliard III
Fuller E. Callaway Professor
 of Urban Education
Georgia State University
Atlanta, Georgia

Dr. Thomas M. McGowan
Chairperson and Professor
Center for Curriculum and Instruction
University of Nebraska
Lincoln, Nebraska

Dr. John J. Patrick
Professor of Education
Indiana University
Bloomington, Indiana

Dr. Cinthia Salinas
Assistant Professor
Department of Curriculum and Instruction
University of Texas at Austin
Austin, Texas

Dr. Philip VanFossen
Associate Professor,
 Social Studies Education,
 and Associate Director,
 Purdue Center for Economic Education
Purdue University
West Lafayette, Indiana

Dr. Hallie Kay Yopp
Professor
Department of Elementary, Bilingual, and
 Reading Education
California State University, Fullerton
Fullerton, California

Content Reviewers

Dr. Darrel E. Bigham
Professor of History,
University of Southern Indiana
Director, Historic Southern Indiana
Evansville, Indiana

Dr. Robert L. Beck
Department of Geography
Indiana University–Purdue University
Indianapolis, Indiana

Dr. Margo J. Byerly
Assistant Professor
Social Studies Education
Ball State University
Muncie, Indiana

Dr. Stephen L. Cox
Vice President
Indiana Historical Society
Indianapolis, Indiana

Dr. Michael William Doyle
Assistant Professor
Department of History
Coordinator of Public History
 Internship Program
Ball State University
Muncie, Indiana

Dr. William H. Wiggins, Jr.
Acting Chairperson and Professor
Afro-American Studies and Folklore
Indiana University
Bloomington, Indiana

Maps
researched and prepared by

MAPQUEST.COM

Readers
written and designed by

TIME FOR KIDS

Acknowledgments appear in the back of
this book.

Printed in the United States of America

ISBN 0-15-321348-5

2 3 4 5 6 7 8 9 10 032 10 09 08 07 06 05 04 03

Contents

· UNIT · 1

The Land and Early People

· UNIT ·

2

Europeans Settle Indiana

· UNIT ·

3

Progress as a State

· UNIT ·

Into the Twenty-First Century

Reference

Features You Can Use

Skills

Citizenship

Music and Literature

Primary Sources

Biography

Geography

Heritage

Science and Technology

Charts, Graphs, and Diagrams

Maps

Time Lines

Reading Your Textbook

Getting Started

Your textbook is divided into four units.

Each unit has a Unit Preview that gives facts about important events. The Preview also shows where and when those events took place.

Each unit begins with a song, poem, story, or other special reading selection.

Each unit is divided into chapters, and each chapter is divided into lessons.

The Parts of a Lesson

This statement gives you the lesson's main idea. It tells you what to look for as you read.

This statement tells you why it is important to read the lesson.

These are the new vocabulary terms you will learn in the lesson.

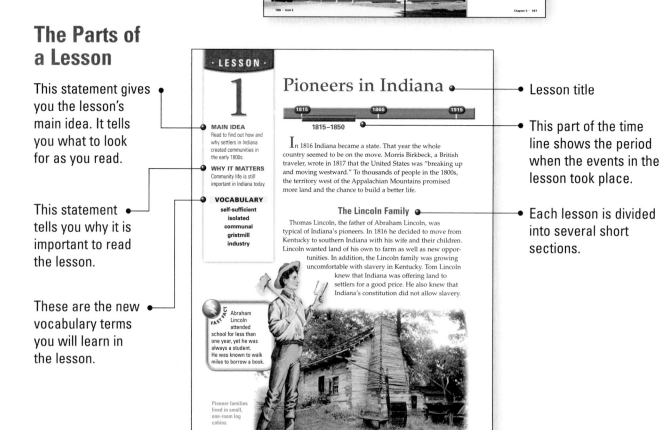

Lesson title

This part of the time line shows the period when the events in the lesson took place.

Each lesson is divided into several short sections.

Each new vocabulary term is highlighted in yellow and defined.

Each lesson, like each chapter and each unit, ends with a review. There may be a Summary Time Line that shows the order of the events covered in the lesson. Questions and a performance activity help you check your understanding of the lesson.

Each short section ends with a REVIEW question that will help you check whether you understand what you have read. Be sure to answer this question before you continue reading the lesson.

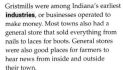

Gristmills were among Indiana's earliest **industries**, or businesses operated to make money. Most towns also had a general store that sold everything from nails to laces for boots. General stores were also good places for farmers to hear news from inside and outside their town.

As settlements grew, Native Americans were forced to leave the area. In 1838 more than 800 Potawatomi were forced to march from northern Indiana to what is now Kansas. This forced march was called the Trail of Death because more than 150 Native Americans died along the way.

Indiana's towns continued to grow. By 1850 Indiana had eight towns with populations of more than 2,500.

REVIEW What kinds of communal activities did early Indiana pioneers participate in?

General stores sold all sorts of goods.

LESSON 1 REVIEW

Summary Time Line

1815 — 1850

• 1816 The Lincoln family moves to Indiana
• 1825 Robert Owen begins New Harmony
• 1838 Native Americans march the Trail of Death
• 1850 Indiana has eight towns with populations of 2,500 or more

1. **MAIN IDEA** How did Indiana's settlers establish communities in the early 1800s?

2. **WHY IT MATTERS** How are communities important to Hoosiers today?

3. **VOCABULARY** Sort the following vocabulary words into two groups on the basis of their meanings. Then give each word's meaning. **self-sufficient, gristmill, isolated, industry**

4. **TIME LINE** How many years after the Lincoln family moved to Indiana did the state have eight towns with populations of 2,500 or more?

5. **READING SKILL—Compare and Contrast** How were early pioneer farms different from the first communities in Indiana? How were they similar?

6. **GEOGRAPHY** From which regions of the United States did most Indiana pioneers come? How did they travel?

7. **ECONOMICS** How did Indiana pioneers in the early 1800s get the goods and services they needed?

8. **CRITICAL THINKING—Synthesize** Why did so many people choose the hard life of a pioneer?

PERFORMANCE—Write a Letter Imagine what it must have been like to move to Indiana in the early 1800s. Write a letter to a friend describing life on a pioneer farm. Include three things you like about life on your farm and three things you miss about your old home.

Chapter 5 ■ 163

Skills

Your textbook has lessons that will help you build your reading, citizenship, chart and graph, and map and globe skills.

SKILLS **Read a Double-Bar Graph**

VOCABULARY double-bar graph

▶ **WHY IT MATTERS**

A good way to compare statistics, or facts shown with numbers, is to make a graph. A bar graph is a good way to compare statistics for several different time periods. If you want to compare and contrast two statistics during the same time period, you can use a double-bar graph. A double-bar graph makes it possible to compare and contrast information not only for different time periods but also within the same time period.

▶ **WHAT YOU NEED TO KNOW**

The double-bar graph on page 175 shows how much corn and wheat Indiana farmers grew between 1850 and 1900. The years covered by the graph are shown horizontally. The scale on the left of the graph shows the number of bushels of corn and wheat grown each of the six years. The vertical bars show the two statistics for each year. The red bars show the amount of wheat. The blue bars show the amount of corn grown.

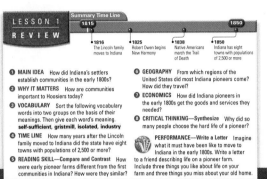

To find out how much corn was grown during a year shown on the graph, locate the year at the bottom of the graph. Then, with your eyes or your finger, follow the orange bar from the bottom up. Notice where the bar ends. The number on the left scale closest to the end of the bar is the number of bushels (in millions) of corn harvested that year. Follow the same process with the blue bar to find out how much wheat was grown by Indiana farmers. Compare and contrast the information shown to learn more about Indiana's changes in farming in the nineteenth century.

1. Which crop decreased in the number of bushels grown between the years of 1880 and 1900?
2. What crop increased the most in the number of bushels between 1850 and 1900?
3. Were farmers growing more wheat in 1880 or in 1900?
4. In what year did wheat production come closest to corn production?

▶ **APPLY WHAT YOU LEARNED**

For the next seven days, keep track of how much time you spend playing or exercising and how much time you spend watching television. Make a double-bar graph to show your findings. Be sure to title and label your graph and supply a legend. Display your completed double-bar graph in the classroom.

▶ **PRACTICE THE SKILL**

Study the double-bar graph on this page. Then use the information in the graph to answer these questions.

CHART AND GRAPH SKILLS

Chapter 5 ■ 175

SKILLS **Compare Maps with Different Scales**

▶ **WHY IT MATTERS**

Many battles in the Civil War were fought in the eastern United States in states such as Pennsylvania, Maryland, and Virginia. One such battle, the Battle of Gettysburg, fought in Pennsylvania in 1863, was a major turning point in the war.

If you wanted to learn more about the battles of the Civil War, you could use maps with different scales. Scale refers to the size of the area shown on a map. Most maps have a scale bar, a line with numbers showing a unit of measurement (usually inches or centimeters) and the number of miles or kilometers this unit represents.

Map scales differ in size depending on how much area is shown on a map. This means that different maps are drawn to different scales. Maps that show a large area must use a small scale because places must be drawn small enough for all the information to fit. On the other hand, maps that show only small areas can use a large scale. Using a large scale allows mapmakers to show more detailed information.

▶ **WHAT YOU NEED TO KNOW**

The maps on page 183 are maps with different scales. The scale used for a map depends on the kind of information to be shown. Map A is a small-scale map. It shows the locations of Civil War battles in the East. Map B is a large-scale map. It is drawn to a larger scale, so it shows many more details about Gettysburg than Map A can. The map scale on each map compares the distance in the map to the distance in the real world.

Use a ruler to measure the length of the map scale on Map A. You can see that 1 inch (2.5 cm) stands for 100 miles (161 km). Next measure the map scale on Map B. You can see that on this map, 1 inch (2.5 cm) equals 1 mile (1.6 km). By using your ruler and the map scale you can measure distances on the maps and figure out the distances in the real world. You also can use a piece of paper to measure distances on a map. Place the paper below the map scale. With a pencil mark the distances either in miles or kilometers. Then use the piece of paper as you would a ruler and convert your measurements using the map scale.

Map A: Civil War Battles in the East

Map B: Battle of Gettysburg

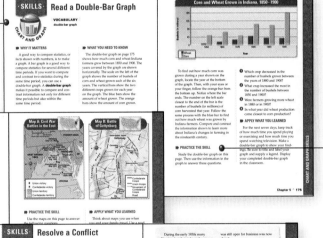

★ Union victory
★ Confederate victory
  Union territory
  Confederate territory

  Confederate troops
  Union troops
  Movement of Confederate troops
  Road

▶ **PRACTICE THE SKILL**

Use the maps on this page to answer the following questions.

▶ **APPLY WHAT YOU LEARNED**

Think about maps you use when resolving your family travel. Use a map

182 ■ Unit 3

You will be able to practice and apply the skills you learn.

SKILLS **Resolve a Conflict**

VOCABULARY resolve compromise

▶ **WHY IT MATTERS**

Most people work well together when they agree. Sometimes, however, people have different ideas about how things should be done. That can lead to conflict. It is important to learn how to handle conflict with civility, or politeness. Knowing how to **resolve**, or settle, conflicts with other people is an important life skill.

There are many ways to resolve conflict. You can explain your ideas and try to get others to change their minds and agree with you. Sometimes resolving conflict involves talking about and listening to different points of view. It may mean making a compromise. In a **compromise** both sides in a conflict give up something they want so they can reach an agreement.

▶ **WHAT YOU NEED TO KNOW**

To resolve a conflict, you can use these steps.

Step 1 Before you begin talking to the person with whom you disagree, understand that you may have to give up some of the things you want.

Step 2 Tell the other person clearly what you want.

Step 3 Listen carefully to what the other person wants.

Step 4 Decide which part is most important to you and what you are willing to give up. Present a plan for a compromise.

Step 5 Let the other person present his or her plan.

Step 6 Talk about the differences. Keep talking until you can agree on a compromise. You may need to change your plans several times before you reach an agreement.

Step 7 If you begin to feel angry or frustrated, take a break to calm down before you go on talking.

President Franklin D. Roosevelt addresses people on the radio during the Great Depression.

During the early 1930s many Hoosiers lost their jobs and many had borrowed from banks. Some banks in Indiana and in other states were forced out of business. When banks began to close, many depositors, or people who had saved money in banks, wanted to get their money back. They had placed, or deposited, money in a bank account. They no longer trusted the banks with their money. These depositors grew angry when bank owners refused to return their money.

President Franklin D. Roosevelt came up with a compromise to resolve this conflict between depositors and bank owners. During a 1933 radio address, Roosevelt declared a "bank holiday." Any bank that

was still open for business was now closed.

During the brief "holiday" that followed, Roosevelt made most banks stronger. He made money available to banks. As a result, most banks reopened after a few days or weeks, and depositors were able to get their money if they wanted it. President Roosevelt encouraged depositors to keep what money they did not need in banks. Roosevelt said, "I can assure you that it is safer to keep your money in a reopened bank than under the mattress."

Hoosiers would face more hard times and economic challenges during the 1930s. Still, Roosevelt's ability to reopen banks quickly gave many people a reason to believe that things would get better.

▶ **PRACTICE THE SKILL**

Read the passage on this page. Then use what you have learned about resolving conflicts to answer these questions.

1. How did economic hard times in the 1930s create a conflict between bank owners and their depositors?
2. What kind of compromise did President Roosevelt suggest to resolve the conflict?

▶ **APPLY WHAT YOU LEARNED**

With your classmates, choose an issue that you do not all agree on. You might select an issue that affects your neighborhood, your school, or your community. Or you might choose an issue that has an impact on all people in the United States. After you have selected an issue, form two groups to discuss it. Both groups should follow the steps outlined on page 206 to resolve the conflict.

CITIZENSHIP SKILLS

206 ■ Unit 3

Chapter 6 ■ 207

This section tells you why it is important to learn the skill.

Special Features

The feature called Examine Primary Sources shows you ways to learn about different kinds of objects and documents.

The Visit feature lets you "visit" many interesting places.

Atlas

The Atlas provides maps and a list of geography terms with illustrations.

For Your Reference

At the back of your textbook, you will find the reference tools listed below.

- Almanac
- Biographical Dictionary
- Gazetteer
- Glossary
- Index

You can use these tools to look up words and to find information about people, places, and other topics.

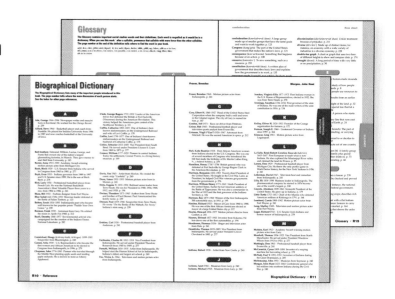

Atlas

Read a Map

VOCABULARY

grid system	map title	intermediate direction
inset map	compass rose	map scale
locator	cardinal direction	map key

➡ WHY IT MATTERS

Maps help you see where places are located in the world. They show the locations of cities, states, and countries. They also show where mountains, valleys, rivers, and lakes are found. Knowing how to read a map is an important skill for learning social studies.

➡ WHAT YOU NEED TO KNOW

A map is a drawing that shows some or all of Earth on a flat surface. Mapmakers often include features to help people use maps more easily. Mapmakers sometimes include lines that cross one another to form a pattern of squares called a **grid system**. Look at the map of Indiana on the next page. Around the grid system are letters and numbers. The columns, which run up and down, have numbers. The rows, which run left and right, have letters. Each square on the map can be identified by its letter and number. For example, the top row of squares on the map contains square A-1, square A-2, square A-3, and square A-4.

Mapmakers sometimes also include smaller maps called **inset maps** within larger maps. Inset maps usually show a larger view of a small area of the main map. They can also show areas that do not appear on the main map. Many times, maps of the United States show inset maps for Alaska and Hawaii.

Look at the map of Indiana. The inset map allows you to see the Indianapolis area more clearly than on the main map.

➡ PRACTICE THE SKILL

Use the map of Indiana to answer these questions.

1. What cities are located in square C-3?
2. In what direction would you travel to go from Fort Wayne to Muncie?
3. Find the map key. What symbol is used to show the state capital?
4. About how many miles is it from Terre Haute to Richmond?
5. Look at the inset map of the Indianapolis area. What is the distance between Speedway and Greenfield?

➡ APPLY WHAT YOU LEARNED

Write ten questions about finding places on the Indiana map. You might ask the distance between places, the direction for traveling from one place to another, or the grid location of a place. Then exchange questions with a classmate. See if you can answer all your classmate's questions.

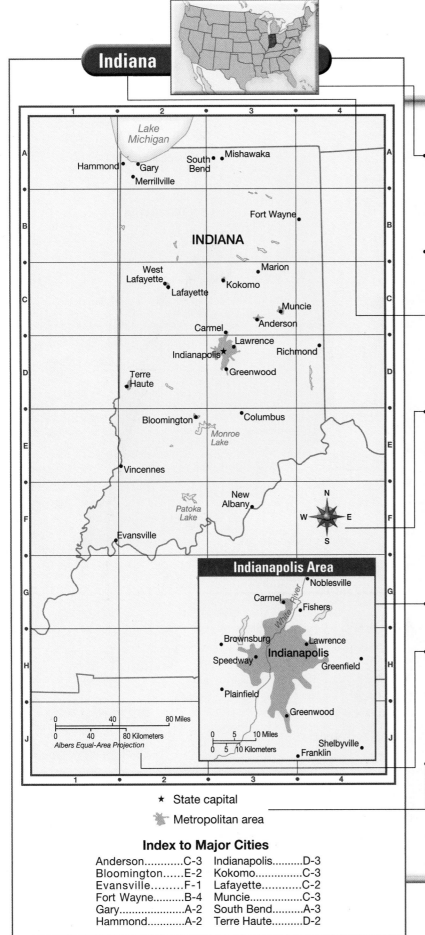

Indiana

INDIANA

Lake Michigan

Hammond • Gary • Merrillville • South Bend • Mishawaka

Fort Wayne

West Lafayette • Lafayette • Kokomo • Marion • Muncie • Anderson

Carmel • Lawrence • Richmond
Indianapolis ★ Greenwood

Terre Haute

Bloomington • Columbus
Monroe Lake

Vincennes

Patoka Lake • New Albany

Evansville

N
W • E
S

0   40   80 Miles
0   40   80 Kilometers
Albers Equal-Area Projection

Indianapolis Area

Noblesville
Carmel • Fishers
White River

Brownsburg • Lawrence
Speedway • **Indianapolis**
Greenfield

Plainfield

Greenwood

Shelbyville
Franklin

0   5   10 Miles
0   5   10 Kilometers

★ State capital

🗺 Metropolitan area

Index to Major Cities

Anderson............C-3	Indianapolis..........D-3
Bloomington......E-2	Kokomo..............C-3
Evansville.........F-1	Lafayette............C-2
Fort Wayne.........B-4	Muncie................C-3
Gary...................A-2	South Bend..........A-3
Hammond............A-2	Terre Haute..........D-2

- **The locator** is a small map or a picture of a globe that shows where the place shown on the main map is located.

- **The map title** tells the subject of the map. It may also tell the kind of map it is.
  - **Physical maps** show kinds of land and bodies of water.
  - **Political maps** show cities, states, and countries.
  - **Historical maps** show places as they were in the past.

- **The compass rose,** or direction marker, shows directions.
  - **The cardinal directions,** or main directions, are north, south, east, and west.
  - **The intermediate directions,** or directions between the cardinal directions, are northeast, southeast, southwest, and northwest.

- **The inset map** shows greater detail of a small area.

- **The map scale** compares a distance on the map to a distance in the real world. It helps you find the real distance between places shown on the map.

- **The map key,** or legend, explains what the symbols on the map stand for. Symbols may be colors, patterns, lines, or other special marks.

The World
POLITICAL

180° 160°W 140°W 120°W 100°W 80°W

80°N

60°N

Greenland
(DENMARK)

ALASKA
(U.S.)

CANADA

NORTH
AMERICA

40°N

UNITED STATES

Azores
(PORTUGAL)

ATLANTIC
OCEAN

Midway
Islands
(U.S.)

Bermuda
(U.K.)

20°N

Tropic of Cancer

Area of inset

MEXICO

HAWAII
(U.S.)

CAPE VERDE

PACIFIC
OCEAN

VENEZUELA GUYANA
SURINAME

COLOMBIA

FRENCH GUIANA
(FRANCE)

Equator

ECUADOR

Galápagos
Islands
(ECUADOR)

BRAZIL

Tokelau
(N.Z.)

KIRIBATI

SOUTH
AMERICA

PERU

SAMOA

American
Samoa
(U.S.)

Cook
Islands
(N.Z.)

French
Polynesia
(FRANCE)

BOLIVIA

20°S

PARAGUAY

TONGA

Tropic of Capricorn

Pitcairn
(U.K.)

Easter Island
(CHILE)

CHILE

Niue
(N.Z.)

URUGUAY

ARGENTINA

40°S

PACIFIC
OCEAN

Falkland
Islands
(U.K.)

South
Georgia
(U.K.)

60°S

Antarctic Circle

80°S

180° 160°W 140°W 120°W 100°W 80°W

Central America and the Caribbean

100°W

30°N

N
W   E
S

Gulf of Mexico

ATLANTIC
OCEAN

60°S

Tropic of Cancer

BAHAMAS

20°N

CUBA

Turks and
Caicos (U.K.)

20°N

Cayman
Islands
(U.K.)

HAITI

DOMINICAN
REPUBLIC

Puerto
Rico
(U.S.)

Anguilla (U.K.)
St. Martin (FRANCE AND NETH.)

ANTIGUA AND BARBUDA
Montserrat (U.K.)
Guadeloupe (FRANCE)

BELIZE

JAMAICA

Virgin Islands
(U.S. AND U.K.)

ST. KITTS
AND NEVIS

DOMINICA
Martinique (FRANCE)

GUATEMALA

HONDURAS

Caribbean Sea

ST. LUCIA

BARBADOS

EL SALVADOR

NICARAGUA

Aruba
(NETH.)

Netherlands
Antilles
(NETH.)

ST. VINCENT AND
THE GRENADINES

| | National
border |
| --- | --- |

PACIFIC OCEAN

10°N

GRENADA

TRINIDAD AND
TOBAGO

10°N

0   200   400 Miles
0 200 400 Kilometers
Azimuthal Equal-Area Projection

COSTA
RICA

Panama
Canal

PANAMA

90°W   80°W   70°W   60°W

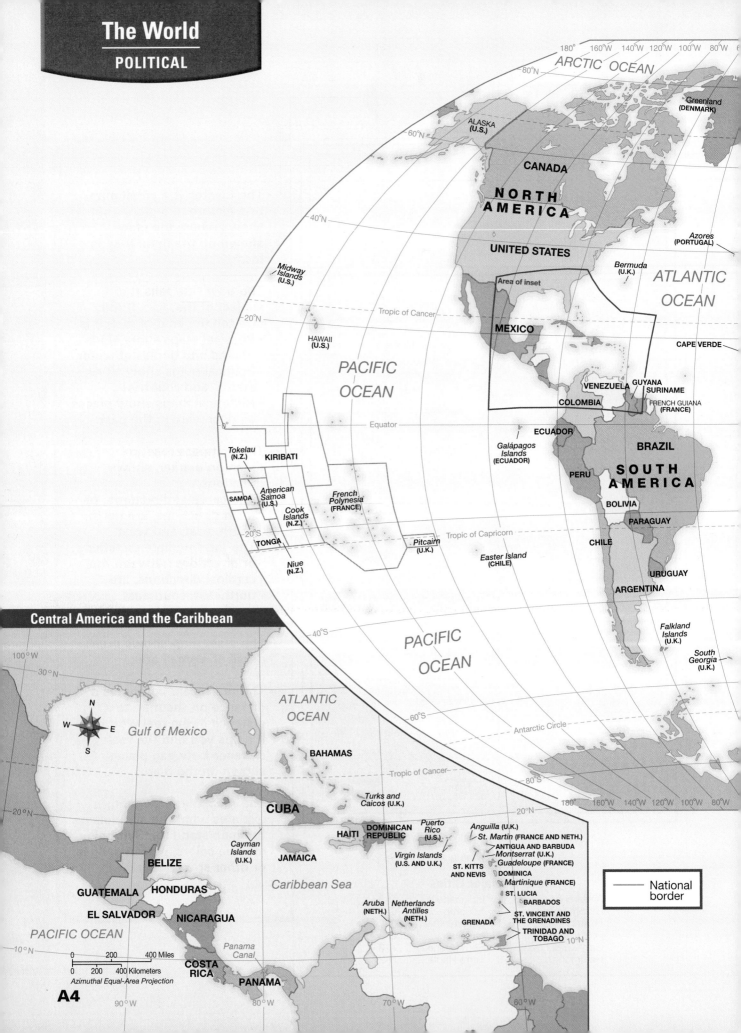

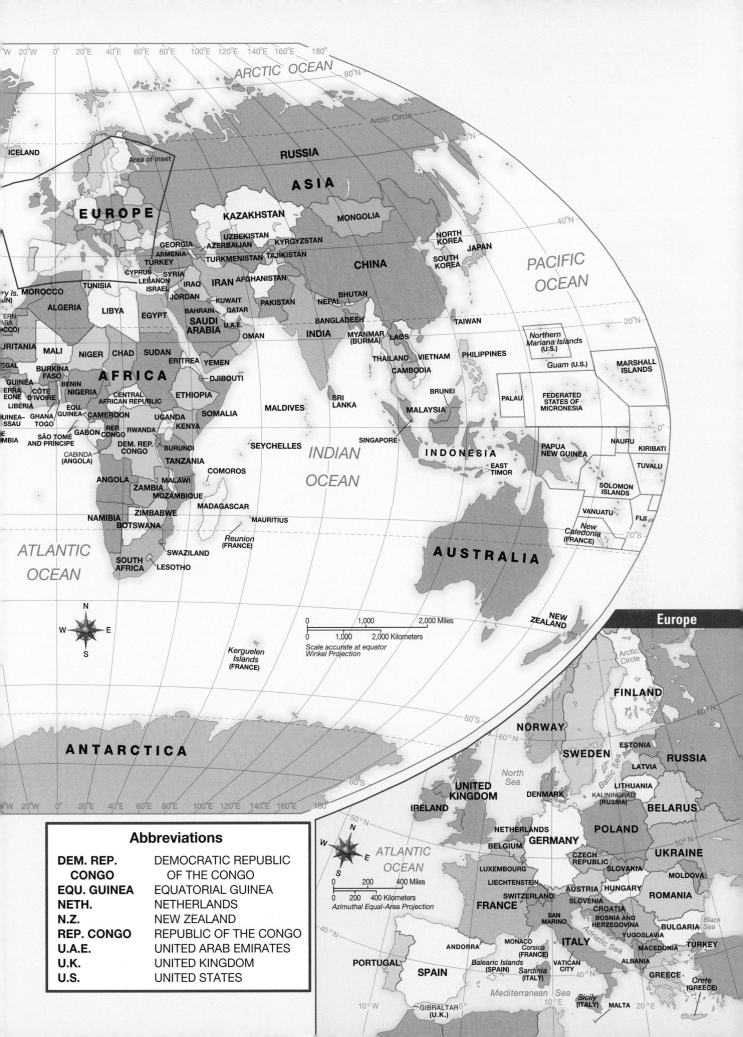

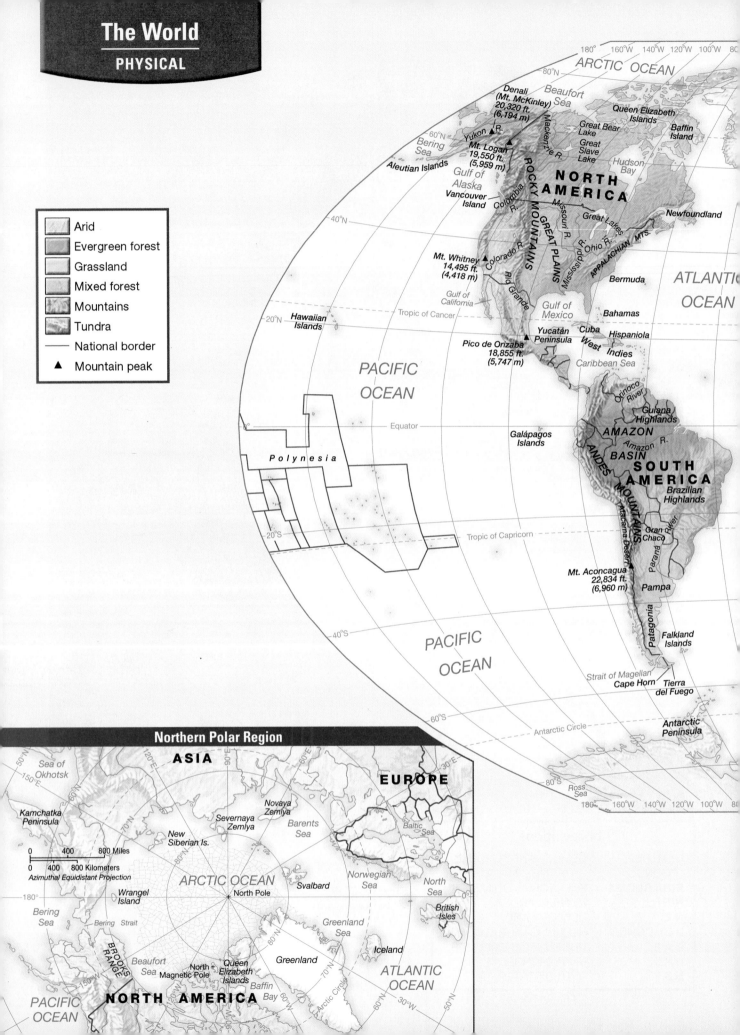

The World
PHYSICAL

Legend:
- Arid
- Evergreen forest
- Grassland
- Mixed forest
- Mountains
- Tundra
- National border
- ▲ Mountain peak

North America / Labels:
ARCTIC OCEAN
Beaufort Sea
Queen Elizabeth Islands
Baffin Island
Denali (Mt. McKinley) 20,320 ft. (6,194 m)
Yukon R.
Great Bear Lake
Great Slave Lake
Hudson Bay
Mt. Logan 19,550 ft. (5,959 m)
Aleutian Islands
Gulf of Alaska
Vancouver Island
Columbia R.
ROCKY MOUNTAINS
GREAT PLAINS
NORTH AMERICA
Missouri R.
Great Lakes
Newfoundland
Mt. Whitney 14,495 ft. (4,418 m)
Colorado R.
Ohio R.
Mississippi R.
APPALACHIAN MTS.
Bermuda
ATLANTIC OCEAN
Gulf of California
Rio Grande
Tropic of Cancer
Gulf of Mexico
Bahamas
Hawaiian Islands
Pico de Orizaba 18,855 ft. (5,747 m)
Yucatán Peninsula
Cuba
Hispaniola
West Indies
Caribbean Sea

PACIFIC OCEAN
Polynesia
Equator
Galápagos Islands
Orinoco River
Guiana Highlands
AMAZON
Amazon R.
BASIN
SOUTH AMERICA
Brazilian Highlands
ANDES MOUNTAINS
Atacama Desert
Tropic of Capricorn
Gran Chaco
Paraná River
Mt. Aconcagua 22,834 ft. (6,960 m)
Pampa
PACIFIC OCEAN
Patagonia
Falkland Islands
Strait of Magellan
Cape Horn
Tierra del Fuego
Antarctic Circle
Antarctic Peninsula

Latitude/Longitude labels: 180°, 160°W, 140°W, 120°W, 100°W, 80°N, 60°N, 40°N, 20°N, 20°S, 40°S, 60°S, 80°S

Northern Polar Region

ASIA
EUROPE
Sea of Okhotsk
Kamchatka Peninsula
Novaya Zemlya
Severnaya Zemlya
Barents Sea
Baltic Sea
New Siberian Is.
ARCTIC OCEAN
Norwegian Sea
North Sea
Wrangel Island
North Pole
Svalbard
British Isles
Bering Sea
Bering Strait
Greenland Sea
Iceland
BROOKS RANGE
Beaufort Sea
North Magnetic Pole
Queen Elizabeth Islands
Greenland
ATLANTIC OCEAN
Baffin Bay
NORTH AMERICA
PACIFIC OCEAN

Ross Sea

0   400   800 Miles
0   400   800 Kilometers
Azimuthal Equidistant Projection

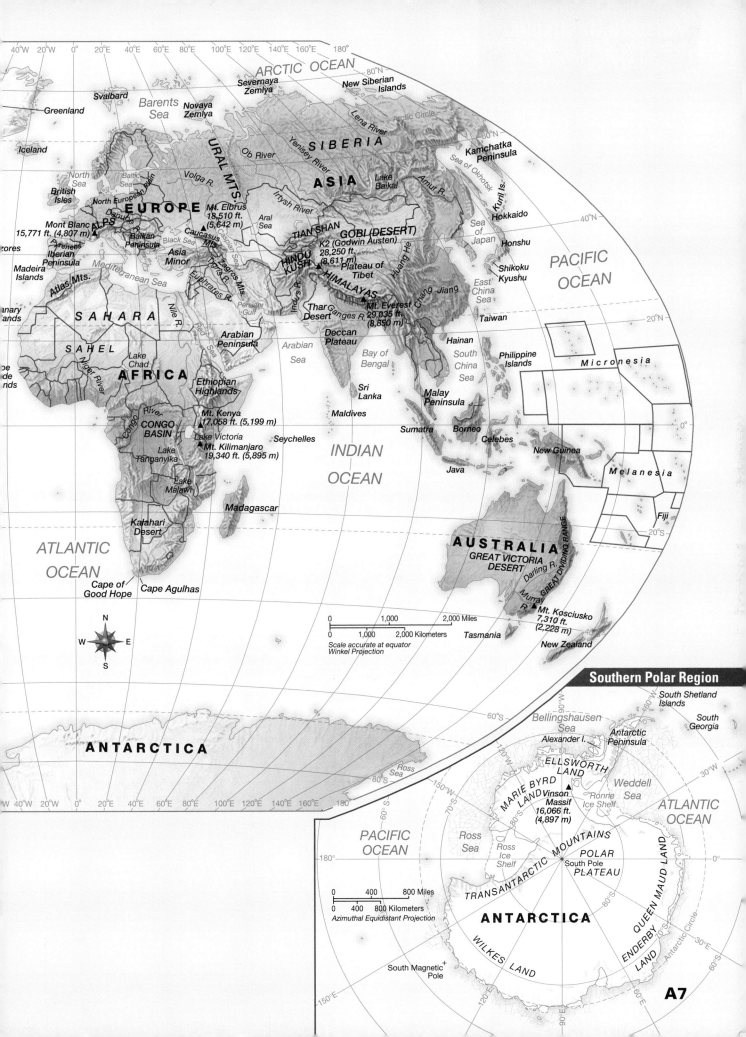

Western Hemisphere
POLITICAL

ARCTIC OCEAN

Beaufort Sea

Viscount Melville Sound

Baffin Bay

Greenland
(DENMARK)

Bering Strait

ALASKA
(U.S.)

Fairbanks

Yukon River

Anchorage

Whitehorse

Great Bear Lake

Yellowknife

Great Slave Lake

CANADA

Foxe Basin

Arctic Circle

Davis Strait

60°N

Gulf of Alaska

Juneau

Mackenzie River

Liard River

Peace River

Athabasca R.

Lake Athabasca

Hudson Strait

Labrador Sea

Bering Sea

Edmonton

Calgary

Vancouver

Saskatchewan R.

Saskatoon

Regina

Lake Winnipeg

Winnipeg

James Bay

Hudson Bay

St. John's

Seattle

Portland

Puget Sound

UNITED STATES

Thunder Bay

St. Lawrence River

Quebec

St. John

Gulf of St. Lawrence

Halifax

Columbia R.

Boise

Snake R.

Great Salt Lake

Salt Lake City

Missouri R.

Chicago

Ottawa

Toronto

Detroit

Albany

Montreal

Boston

Reno

San Francisco

Las Vegas

Denver

Colorado R.

St. Louis

Cleveland

Indianapolis

New York City

Philadelphia

Washington, D.C.

Los Angeles

San Diego

Phoenix

Tucson

El Paso

Dallas

Rio Grande

Houston

Memphis

Richmond

Atlanta

Norfolk

Raleigh

Charleston

30°N

ATLANTIC OCEAN

Hermosillo

Gulf of California

Chihuahua

San Antonio

New Orleans

Mississippi R.

Savannah

Jacksonville

Tampa

Orlando

BAHAMAS

Nassau

MEXICO

Durango

Monterrey

Gulf of Mexico

Miami

Havana

CUBA

HAITI

Port-au-Prince

Santo Domingo

Tropic of Cancer

Honolulu

HAWAII
(U.S.)

León

Tampico

Guadalajara

Mexico City

Puebla

Veracruz

JAMAICA

Kingston

BELIZE

Puerto Rico (U.S.)

DOMINICAN REPUBLIC

PACIFIC OCEAN

Acapulco

Guatemala City

GUATEMALA

Belmopan

HONDURAS

San Salvador

Tegucigalpa

EL SALVADOR

Managua

Caribbean Sea

San José

NICARAGUA

Maracaibo

COSTA RICA

Panama City

Caracas

GUYANA

SURINAME

PANAMA

Medellín

Georgetown

Paramaribo

Cayenne

Cali

Bogotá

VENEZUELA

FRENCH GUIANA (FRANCE)

0°

COLOMBIA

Quito

Equator

Galápagos Islands
(ECUADOR)

Guayaquil

Iquitos

Manaus

Rio Negro

Amazon R.

Belém

Fortaleza

ECUADOR

Recife

Trujillo

PERU

Tapajós River

Xingu R.

Tocantins R.

Lima

Cuzco

São Francisco R.

BRAZIL

Salvador

Lake Titicaca

La Paz

Brasília

Arequipa

BOLIVIA

Goiânia

Belo Horizonte

French Polynesia
(FRANCE)

Sucre

Rio de Janeiro

Papeete

Antofagasta

Campo Grande

Tropic of Capricorn

PARAGUAY

Salta

Asunción

São Paulo

Curitiba

Paraguay R.

Paraná R.

San Miguel de Tucumán

Córdoba

Pôrto Alegre

30°S

CHILE

Valparaíso

Santiago

Concepción

Rosario

Buenos Aires

La Plata

URUGUAY

Montevideo

Rio de la Plata

Mar del Plata

Valdivia

Bahía Blanca

0   1,000   2,000 Miles

0   1,000   2,000 Kilometers

Miller Cylindrical Projection

ARGENTINA

N
W   E
S

Falkland Islands
(U.K.)

South Georgia
(U.K.)

A8

Punta Arenas

— National border

⊛ National capital

• City

150°W   120°W   90°W   60°W   30°W

ARCTIC OCEAN

Ellesmere Island

North Magnetic Pole +
Queen Elizabeth Islands

Melville Island

Devon Island

Baffin Bay

Greenland

Bering Strait
Point Barrow

Beaufort Sea

Banks Island

Viscount Melville Sound

Victoria Island

Brooks Range

Mt. McKinley
20,320 ft.
(6,194 m)

Yukon

Mackenzie Mts

Mackenzie River

Great Bear Lake

Great Slave Lake

Baffin Island

Foxe Basin

Arctic Circle

Alaska Range

Yukon River

Yukon Plateau

Liard R.

Peace River

CANADIAN

Hudson Strait

Hudson Bay

60°N

Gulf of Alaska

Mt. Logan
19,550 ft.
(5,959 m)

Coast Mountains

ROCKY

Athabasca R.

Lake Athabasca

James Bay

Labrador Sea

Cape Farewell

Kodiak Island

Alaska Peninsula

Bering Sea

Aleutian Islands

Queen Charlotte Islands

Vancouver Island

Puget Sound

Cascade Range

Coast Ranges

Snake R.

MOUNTAINS

GREAT PLAINS

Saskatchewan River

Lake Winnipeg

SHIELD

Newfoundland

Gulf of St. Lawrence

NORTH AMERICA

St. Lawrence R.

Great Lakes

Nova Scotia

Bay of Fundy

Cape Cod

Long Island

Sierra Nevada

Great Salt Lake

GREAT BASIN

Black Hills

Missouri R.

Platte

Mississippi

APPALACHIAN MTS.

Mt. Whitney
14,495 ft. (4,418 m)

Colorado R.

Arkansas

Ozark Plateau

Ohio R.

Cape Hatteras

Death Valley
(lowest point in N.A.)
-282 ft. (-86 m)

Sonoran Desert

Rio Grande

COASTAL PLAIN

ATLANTIC OCEAN

30°N

Baja California

Sierra Madre Occidental

Gulf of California

Sierra Madre Oriental

Gulf of Mexico

Bahamas

Tropic of Cancer

Hawaiian Islands

Cuba

Greater Antilles

Hispaniola

Puerto Rico

Lesser Antilles

PACIFIC OCEAN

Pico de Orizaba
18,855 ft.
(5,747 m)

Yucatán Peninsula

Caribbean Sea

Lake Maracaibo

Lake Nicaragua

Isthmus of Panama

Llanos

Orinoco R.

Guiana Highlands

Chimborazo
20,702 ft.
(6,310 m)

Galápagos Islands

Equator

ANDES

Rio Negro

Amazon R.

AMAZON BASIN

Cape São Roque

Line Islands

Marquesas Islands

Huascarán
22,205 ft.
(6,768 m)

Tapajós River

Xingu River

Tocantins R.

São Francisco River

Cook Islands

Society Islands

Tuamotu Archipelago

Lake Titicaca

Altiplano

Mato Grosso Plateau

Brazilian Highlands

SOUTH AMERICA

Tropic of Capricorn

Atacama Desert

Gran Chaco

Paraguay R.

Paraná R.

Iguazú Falls

30°S

MOUNTAINS

Uruguay R.

0   1,000   2,000 Miles

0   1,000   2,000 Kilometers

Miller Cylindrical Projection

Mt. Aconcagua
22,834 ft.
(6,960 m)

Pampa

Rio de la Plata

Valdés Peninsula
(lowest point in S.A.)
-131 ft. (-40 m)

▲ Mountain peak

▼ Point below sea level

— National border

≈ Waterfall

N
W   E
S

Patagonia

Falkland Islands

A9

Strait of Magellan

Tierra del Fuego

Cape Horn

South Georgia

150°W   120°W   90°W   60°W   30°W

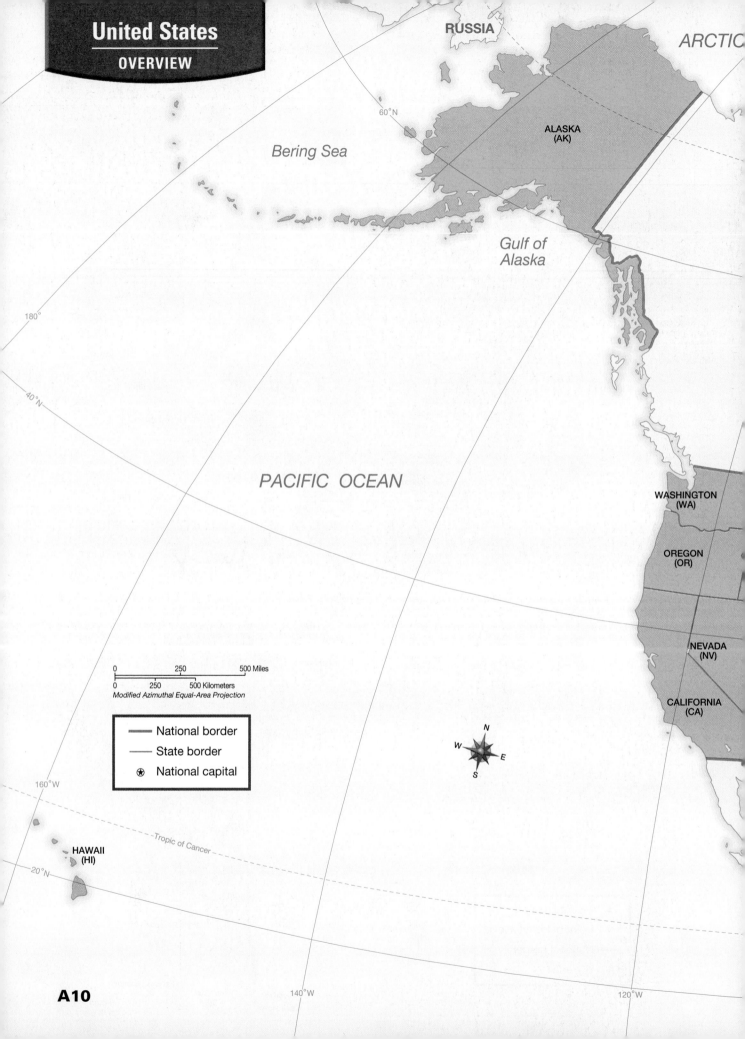

RUSSIA

ARCTIC

60°N

Bering Sea

ALASKA
(AK)

Gulf of
Alaska

180°

40°N

PACIFIC OCEAN

WASHINGTON
(WA)

OREGON
(OR)

250   500 Miles

0   250   500 Kilometers
Modified Azimuthal Equal-Area Projection

NEVADA
(NV)

National border
State border
National capital

CALIFORNIA
(CA)

N
W   E
S

160°W

Tropic of Cancer

HAWAII
(HI)

20°N

140°W   120°W

OCEAN

ICELAND

Baffin
Bay

Greenland
(DENMARK)

40°W

60°N

Labrador
Sea

Hudson
Bay

CANADA

James
Bay

MONTANA
(MT)

NORTH
DAKOTA
(ND)

MINNESOTA
(MN)

Lake Superior

MICHIGAN

VERMONT
(VT)

MAINE
(ME)

IDAHO
(ID)

SOUTH
DAKOTA
(SD)

WISCONSIN
(WI)

Lake Huron

NEW
YORK
(NY)

NEW HAMPSHIRE
(NH)

60°W

WYOMING
(WY)

Lake Michigan

Lake
Ontario

MASSACHUSETTS
(MA)

40°N

Great
Salt Lake

NEBRASKA
(NE)

IOWA
(IA)

Lake Erie

PENNSYLVANIA
(PA)

RHODE ISLAND (RI)

CONNECTICUT
(CT)

UTAH
(UT)

COLORADO
(CO)

ILLINOIS
(IL)

INDIANA
(IN)

OHIO
(OH)

Washington,
D.C.

WEST
VIRGINIA
(WV)

NEW
JERSEY
(NJ)

DELAWARE
(DE)

MARYLAND
(MD)

KANSAS
(KS)

MISSOURI
(MO)

KENTUCKY
(KY)

VIRGINIA
(VA)

ARIZONA
(AZ)

NEW MEXICO
(NM)

OKLAHOMA
(OK)

ARKANSAS
(AR)

TENNESSEE
(TN)

NORTH
CAROLINA
(NC)

SOUTH
CAROLINA
(SC)

MISSISSIPPI
(MS)

ALABAMA
(AL)

GEORGIA
(GA)

ATLANTIC OCEAN

TEXAS
(TX)

LOUISIANA
(LA)

FLORIDA
(FL)

BAHAMAS

Gulf of California

MEXICO

Gulf of Mexico

CUBA

DOMINICAN
REPUBLIC

PUERTO
RICO
(U.S.)

HAITI

100°W

80°W

A11

United States
POLITICAL

RUSSIA

ARCTIC OCEAN

170° E

180°

170° W

160° W

150° W

140° W

130° W

120° W

70° N

60° N

50° N

40° N

ALASKA

Arctic Circle

Yukon River

Fairbanks

Anchorage

Yukon River

CANADA

Bering Sea

Gulf of Alaska

Juneau

PACIFIC OCEAN

0   250   500 Miles

0   250   500 Kilometers

CANADA

130° W

120° W

110° W

PACIFIC OCEAN

30° N

	Legend		
Northeast	⊛	National capital
South	★	State capital
Middle West	•	Major city
West	▬	National border
	▬	State border

Seattle
Tacoma
Olympia
WASHINGTON
Spokane
Portland
Columbia River
Salem
Eugene
OREGON

Great Falls
Helena
MONTANA
Billings
Yellowstone R.

IDAHO
Boise
Snake River
Pocatello

WYOMING
Casper
Cheyenne

NEVADA
Lake Tahoe
Reno
Carson City

Great Salt Lake
Ogden
Salt Lake City
Provo
UTAH

Sacramento
San Francisco
Oakland
San Jose
Fresno
CALIFORNIA
Bakersfield

Las Vegas

Colorado River

Denver
Colorado Spring
COLORADO
Puebl

Los Angeles
San Bernardino

Flagstaff
ARIZONA
Phoenix
Tucson

Santa Fe
Albuquerque
NEW MEXICO
Roswell

San Diego

El Paso
Rio Grande

MEXICO

130° W

120° W

110° W

20° N

N
W   E
S

160° W   155° W

PACIFIC OCEAN

Honolulu
HAWAII
Hilo

20° N

0   100   200 Miles

0   100   200 Kilometers

0   250   500 Miles

0   250   500 Kilometers

Albers Equal-Area Projection

A12

United States
PHYSICAL

CANADA

RUSSIA

ARCTIC OCEAN

Brooks Range

Seward **ALASKA** Yukon River
Peninsula

St. Lawrence
Island

Mt. McKinley
20,320 ft.
(6,194 m) △ Alaska Range

CANADA

Yukon River

Bering
Sea

Gulf of
Alaska

| 0 | 250 | 500 Miles |

| 0 | 250 | 500 Kilometers |

Aleutian Islands

Kodiak
Island

Legend

	Arid
	Evergreen forest
	Grassland
	Mixed forest
	Mountains
	Tundra
▬	National border
—	State border
▲	Mountain peak
△	Highest point
▼	Lowest point

**PACIFIC
OCEAN**

Cape
Mendocino

Point
Conception

Channel
Islands

Coast Ranges

Cascade Range

WA

Mt. Rainier
14,410 ft. (4,392 m)

Mt. St. Helens
8,366 ft. (2,550 m)

Columbia River

Mt. Hood
11,237 ft.
(3,425 m)

OR

Columbia Plateau

Bitterroot Range

ID

Salmon
River
Mountains

Snake River

MT

Fort Peck
Lake

Yellowstone River

Bighorn Mts.

WY

Teton Range

Wind River Range

Great Divide
Basin

R O C K Y

Pyramid
Lake

Donner Pass

Lake
Tahoe

Sierra Nevada

Sacramento River

Central Valley

San Joaquin R.

NV

**G R E A T
B A S I N**

Great
Salt
Lake

Wasatch Range

Uinta Mts.

UT

Mt. Whitney
14,495 ft.
(4,418 m)

Death
Valley
-282 ft.
(-86 m)

CA

Mojave

Desert

Salton
Sea

Imperial
Valley

Sonoran
Desert

Lake
Mead

Grand
Canyon

Lake
Powell

Colorado River

**Colorado
Plateau**

AZ

Baldy Peak
11,403 ft.
(3,476 m)

Mt. Elbert
14,433 ft.
(4,399 m)

San Juan Mts.

CO

M O U N T A I N

NM

Guadalupe Pea
8,749 f
(2,667 m

Rio Gra

M E X I C O

N
W E
S

| 0 | 250 | 500 Miles |

| 0 | 250 | 500 Kilometers |

Albers Equal-Area Projection

Kauai PACIFIC OCEAN

Niihau Oahu

Molokai

HAWAII Lanai Maui
Kahoolawe

Hawaii

Mauna Kea
13,796 ft.
(4,205 m)

| 0 | 100 | 200 Miles |

| 0 | 100 | 200 Kilometers |

100°W · 90°W · 80°W · 70°W

50°N

CANADA

Lake of
the Woods

Upper
Red Lake

Lower
Red Lake

Mesabi
Range

Isle
Royale

Lake Superior

Keweenaw
Peninsula

Moosehead
Lake

▲ Mt. Katahdin
5,269 ft.
(1,606 m)

ME

St. Lawrence River

Lake Sakakawea

ND

Leech
Lake

Mille
Lacs
Lake

MN

Upper   Peninsula

Lake Huron

Lake
Champlain

VT

Green Mts.

White Mts.

▲ Mt. Washington
6,288 ft.
(1,917 m)

Cape Ann

Lake
Oahe

SD

Black
Hills

Missouri River

WI

Wisconsin River

Lake
Winnebago

Lake Michigan

Lower Peninsula

MI

Lake
St. Clair

Lake Erie

Lake Ontario

Niagara
Falls

NY

Adirondack
Mountains

Finger
Lakes

Hudson R.

Connecticut R.

NH

MA

Cape
Cod

CT

RI

40°N

North Platte R.

Sand Hills

NE

South Platte R.

Platte River

IA

INTERIOR

Mississippi River

Illinois River

IL

PLAINS

CENTRAL PLAINS

Wabash River

IN

OH

Ohio River

WV

Allegheny Mts.

PA

MD

Potomac R.

DE

Delaware
Bay

70°W

G R E A T

Smoky Hills

KS

Red Hills

Missouri River

MO

Lake of
the Ozarks

Harry S. Truman
Reservoir

Ozark Plateau

Lake
Barkley

Lake
Barkley

KY

Cumberland
Gap

Mississippi   River

Cumberland R.

▲ Mt. Mitchell
6,684 ft.
(2,037 m)

VA

James R.

Roanoke R.

PIEDMONT

APPALACHIAN   MOUNTAINS

Cape
Charles

Chesapeake
Bay

Albemarle
Sound

P L A I N S

OK

Canadian River

Arkansas

River

Ouachita
Mountains

Lake
Texoma

AR

Red River

TN

Tennessee R.

Cumberland R.

NC

Cape Fear River

Cape
Fear

Cape
Hatteras

Llano

Estacado

Pecos River

TX

Edwards

Plateau

Colorado River

Brazos River

Sabine River

Toledo
Bend
Reservoir

Sam
Rayburn
Reservoir

LA

MS

Tombigbee R.

AL

Alabama R.

Stone
Mountain ▲

Chattahoochee R.

Clark
Hill Lake

Oconee R.

Ocmulgee R.

GA

SC

Savannah River

Altamaha R.

Okefenokee
Swamp

C O A S T A L

ATLANTIC

OCEAN

30°N

Rio Grande

Galveston
Bay

C O A S T A L

P L A I N

Lake
Maurepas

Lake
Pontchartrain

Mobile
Bay

**Mississippi
Delta**

Tampa
Bay

St. Johns River

Lake
Okeechobee

FL

Cape
Canaveral

BAHAMAS

Gulf of Mexico

Everglades
Cape
Sable

Florida Keys

Straits of Florida

CUBA

100°W · 90°W · 80°W

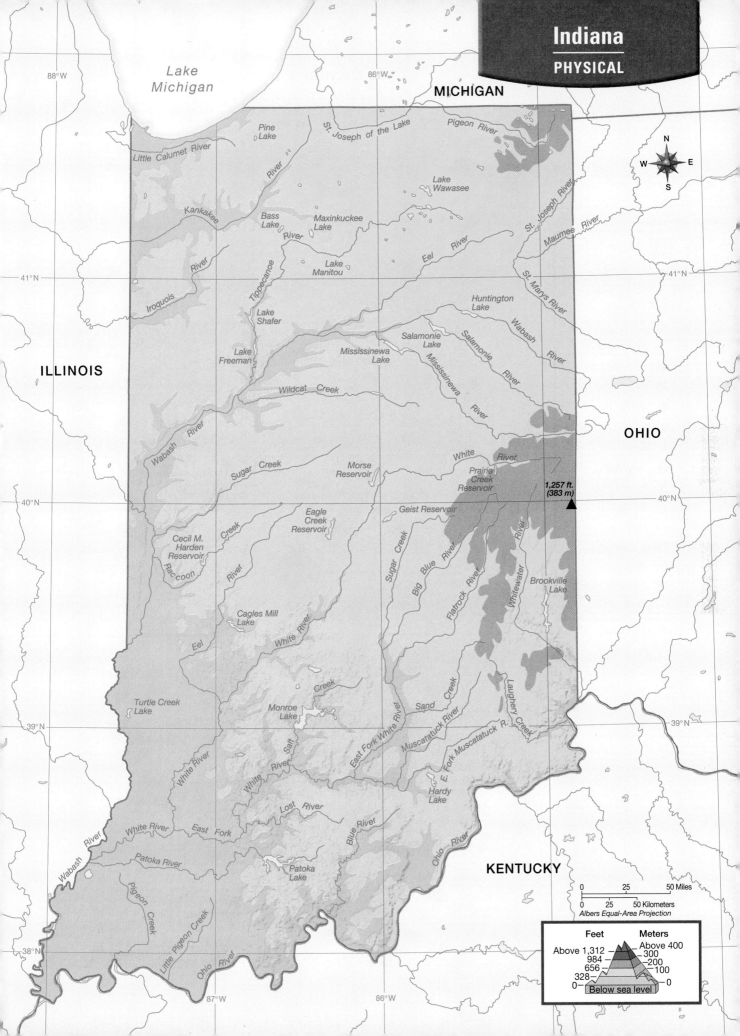

Indiana
PHYSICAL

Lake Michigan

88°W

86°W

MICHIGAN

N W E S

Pine Lake

Little Calumet River

St. Joseph of the Lake

Pigeon River

River

Kankakee

Bass Lake

Maxinkuckee Lake

Lake Wawasee

Lake Manitou

Eel River

St. Joseph River

Maumee River

41°N

Tippecanoe

River

Iroquois

Lake Shafer

Huntington Lake

St. Marys River

41°N

ILLINOIS

Lake Freeman

Mississinewa Lake

Salamonie Lake

Salamonie River

Wabash River

Wildcat Creek

Mississinewa River

Wabash River

OHIO

Sugar Creek

Morse Reservoir

White River

Prairie Creek Reservoir

1,257 ft. (383 m) ▲

40°N

Creek

Eagle Creek Reservoir

Geist Reservoir

Sugar Creek

40°N

Cecil M. Harden Reservoir

River

Big Blue River

Flatrock River

Whitewater River

Brookville Lake

Raccoon

Cagles Mill Lake

White River

Eel

Turtle Creek Lake

Monroe Lake

Creek

Salt River

East Fork White River

Sand

Creek

Muscatatuck River

Laughery Creek

39°N

White River

E. Fork Muscatatuck R.

39°N

White

East Fork

Lost River

Hardy Lake

Wabash River

White River

East Fork

Blue River

Ohio River

KENTUCKY

Patoka River

Patoka Lake

Pigeon Creek

Little Pigeon Creek

Ohio River

38°N

87°W

86°W

0 25 50 Miles

0 25 50 Kilometers
Albers Equal-Area Projection

Feet	Meters
Above 1,312	Above 400
984	300
656	200
328	100
0	0
Below sea level	

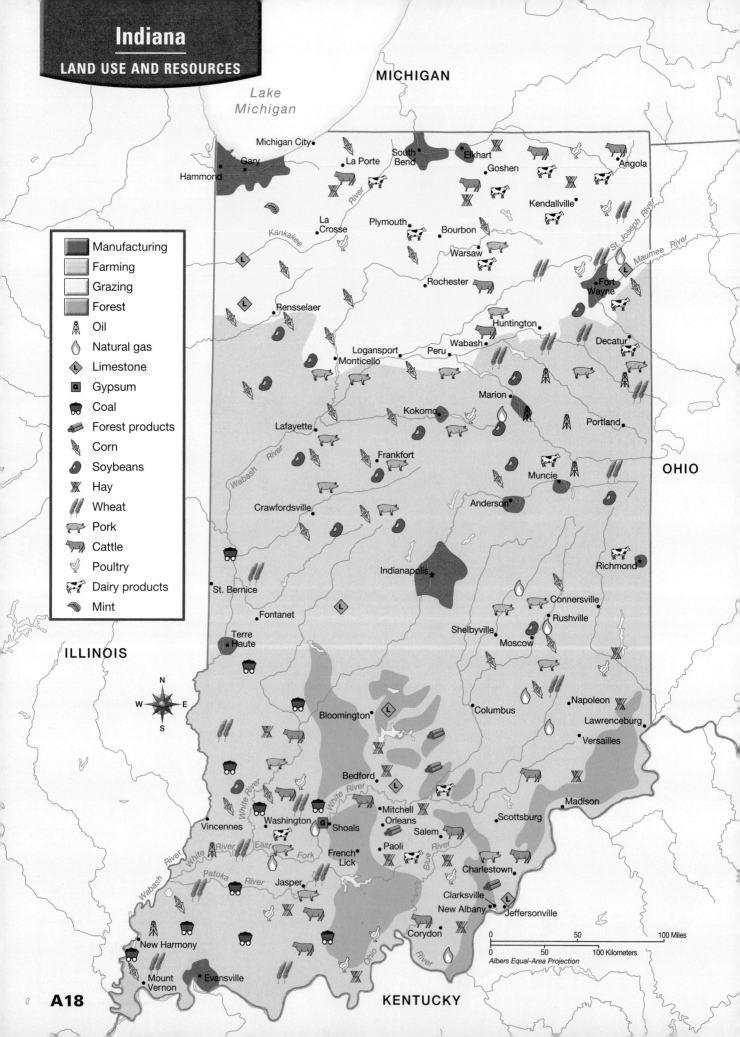

Indiana
LAND USE AND RESOURCES

MICHIGAN

Lake Michigan

Legend:
- Manufacturing
- Farming
- Grazing
- Forest
- Oil
- Natural gas
- Limestone (L)
- Gypsum (G)
- Coal
- Forest products
- Corn
- Soybeans
- Hay
- Wheat
- Pork
- Cattle
- Poultry
- Dairy products
- Mint

Michigan City · Gary · Hammond · La Porte · South Bend · Elkhart · Goshen · Angola

Kankakee · La Crosse · Plymouth · Bourbon · Warsaw · Rochester · Kendallville · St. Joseph River · Maumee River · Fort Wayne

Rensselaer · Logansport · Peru · Wabash · Huntington · Decatur

Wabash River · Monticello · Marion · Portland

Lafayette · Kokomo · Muncie

Frankfort · Anderson

Crawfordsville

St. Bernice · Fontanet · Indianapolis · Richmond · Connersville · Rushville · Shelbyville · Moscow

Terre Haute · Bloomington · Columbus · Napoleon · Lawrenceburg · Versailles

ILLINOIS

Bedford · Madison

White River · Vincennes · Washington · Shoals · Mitchell · Orleans · Salem · Scottsburg · Charlestown

New Harmony · Mount Vernon · Evansville · Jasper · French Lick · Paoli · Patoka River · Blue River · Clarksville · New Albany · Jeffersonville · Corydon · Ohio River

OHIO

KENTUCKY

0   50   100 Miles
0   50   100 Kilometers
Albers Equal-Area Projection

A18

Indiana
CITIES AND HIGHWAYS

Lake Michigan

Chicago
Michigan City
Gary
Hammond
Joliet
La Porte
South Bend
Elkhart
Sturgis
Goshen
Angola
Bryan
Defiance
Kendallville
Kankakee
La Crosse
Plymouth
Bourbon
Warsaw
Rochester
Fort Wayne
Rensselaer
Van Wert
Huntington
Decatur
Watseka
Logansport
Monticello
Peru
Wabash
ILLINOIS
Marion
Celina
Hoopeston
Kokomo
Portland
Lafayette
OHIO
Frankfort
Muncie
Champaign
Danville
Crawfordsville
Anderson
Greenville
Indianapolis
Richmond
Dayton
St. Bernice
Connersville
Fontanet
Rushville
Middletown
Terre Haute
Moscow
Marshall
Shelbyville
Napoleon
Robinson
Bloomington
Columbus
Lawrenceburg
Cincinnati
Versailles
Olney
Bedford
Madison
Washington
Mitchell
Scottsburg
Carrollton
Vincennes
Shoals
Orleans
Salem
Paoli
French Lick
Charlestown
Jasper
Clarksville
Jeffersonville
New Albany
Corydon
Frankfort
New Harmony
Carmi
Evansville
Mount Vernon
Owensboro
KENTUCKY

St. Joseph River
Maumee River
Kankakee
Wabash River
White River
East Fork
White River
Blue River
Patoka River
Wabash River
Ohio River

N W E S

	50	100 Miles
0 50 100 Kilometers
Albers Equal-Area Projection

──	State border	⟨70⟩ Interstate highway
★	State capital	⟨52⟩ U.S. highway
•	Other city	⟨37⟩ State highway

A19

Geography Terms

1. **basin**   bowl-shaped area of land surrounded by higher land
2. **bay**   an inlet of the sea or some other body of water, usually smaller than a gulf
3. **bluff**   high, steep face of rock or earth
4. **canyon**   deep, narrow valley with steep sides
5. **cape**   point of land that extends into water
6. **cataract**   large waterfall
7. **channel**   deepest part of a body of water
8. **cliff**   high, steep face of rock or earth
9. **coast**   land along a sea or ocean
10. **coastal plain**   area of flat land along a sea or ocean
11. **delta**   triangle-shaped area of land at the mouth of a river
12. **desert**   dry land with few plants
13. **dune**   hill of sand piled up by the wind
14. **fall line**   area along which rivers form waterfalls or rapids as the rivers drop to lower land
15. **floodplain**   flat land that is near the edges of a river and is formed by silt deposited by floods
16. **foothills**   hilly area at the base of a mountain
17. **glacier**   large ice mass that moves slowly down a mountain or across land
18. **gulf**   part of a sea or ocean extending into the land, usually larger than a bay
19. **hill**   land that rises above the land around it
20. **inlet**   any area of water extending into the land from a larger body of water
21. **island**   land that has water on all sides
22. **isthmus**   narrow strip of land connecting two larger areas of land
23. **lagoon**   body of shallow water
24. **lake**   body of water with land on all sides

26	**mesa** flat-topped mountain with steep sides
27	**mountain** highest kind of land
28	**mountain pass** gap between mountains
29	**mountain range** row of mountains
30	**mouth of river** place where a river empties into another body of water
31	**oasis** area of water and fertile land in a desert
32	**ocean** body of salt water larger than a sea
33	**peak** top of a mountain
34	**peninsula** land that is almost completely surrounded by water.
35	**plain** area of flat or gently rolling low land
36	**plateau** area of high, mostly flat land
37	**reef** ridge of sand, rock, or coral that lies at or near the surface of a sea or ocean
38	**river** large stream of water that flows across the land
39	**riverbank** land along a river

40	**savanna** area of grassland and scattered trees
41	**sea** body of salt water smaller than an ocean
42	**sea level** the level of the surface of an ocean or a sea
43	**slope** side of a hill or mountain
44	**source of river** place where a river begins
45	**strait** narrow channel of water connecting two larger bodies of water
46	**swamp** area of low, wet land with trees
47	**timberline** line on a mountain above which it is too cold for trees to grow
48	**tributary** stream or river that flows into a larger stream or river
49	**valley** low land between hills or mountains
50	**volcano** opening in the earth, often raised, through which lava, rock, ashes, and gases are forced out
51	**waterfall** steep drop from a high place to a

Introduction

❝ The origin of the term "Hoosier" is not known with certainty. But it is certain that . . . Hoosiers bear the nickname proudly. ❞

—Meredith Nicholson, from *The Hoosiers*, 1900

Learning About Indiana

The word *Hoosier* is a nickname for people who live in Indiana. Hoosiers are proud of the state of Indiana. As you read this book, you will find out why. You will learn about the state's interesting past. You will also learn about the land, water, and climate of Indiana. In addition, you will find out about the many different people of Indiana. All of these things will help you understand why people are proud to be Hoosiers.

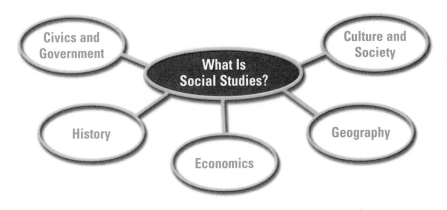

Civics and Government

Culture and Society

What Is Social Studies?

History

Economics

Geography

Why History Matters

VOCABULARY

history	historian	oral history	analyze
chronology	evidence	point of view	

History, or what happened in the past, is very important to the people of Indiana. In this book you will read about people, places, and events of the past. You will learn about the ways of life of the people of Indiana long ago. You will also find out how Indiana has changed over the years.

Learning About Time

Understanding history requires knowing when events took place. The order in which events take place is called **chronology** (kruh•NAH•luh•jee). **Historians**, or people who study the past, look closely at the chronology of events. This helps them better understand how one event affects another. They can also discover how the past and the present connect.

Finding Evidence

How do historians find out about the past? One way is to find **evidence**, or proof, of when, why, where, and how things happened. Historians read books and newspapers from long ago. They study old diaries, letters, and post-cards. They look at paintings and photographs from the past. They also listen to oral histories. An **oral history** is a story of an event told aloud. Historians use these different kinds of evidence to piece together the history of a place.

The Eiteljorg Museum of American Indians and Western Art (above) and the new Indiana State Museum (below), both in Indianapolis, are good places to study the history and art of the state.

Identifying Points of View

Historians think about why people of the past said or wrote what they did. They try to understand different people's points of view. A person's **point of view** is how he or she sees things. It can depend on a person's beliefs and ideas. It can be affected by whether a person is young or old, male or female, rich or poor. Background and experiences also affect point of view. People with different points of view may have different ideas about the same event.

To understand points of view about an event, historians learn about the people who took part in the event. They find out as much as possible about how people lived long ago. This helps them get a better idea of the actions and feelings of people of the past.

Drawing Conclusions

After historians have identified the facts about a historical event, they still have work to do. They need to analyze the event. To **analyze** an event is to examine each part of it. Analyzing an event allows historians to draw conclusions about how and why it happened.

REVIEW What is history?

Background and experience help determine point of view. Above are some of the many faces of Indiana. Historians study artifacts, or objects made by people. This artifact (left) is a quilt made by a young woman from Indiana.

·SKILLS· READING

Compare Primary and Secondary Sources

VOCABULARY

primary source

secondary source

▶ WHY IT MATTERS

People who study the past look for evidence, or proof. They want to be sure they know what really happened. They look for evidence in two different kinds of sources—primary sources and secondary sources.

▶ WHAT YOU NEED TO KNOW

Primary sources are records made by people who saw or took part in an event. They may have written their thoughts in journals or diaries. They may have told their stories in letters, poems, or songs. They may have given speeches. They may have painted pictures or taken photographs. Objects made or used during an event can also be primary sources. All these primary sources are direct evidence from people who saw what happened.

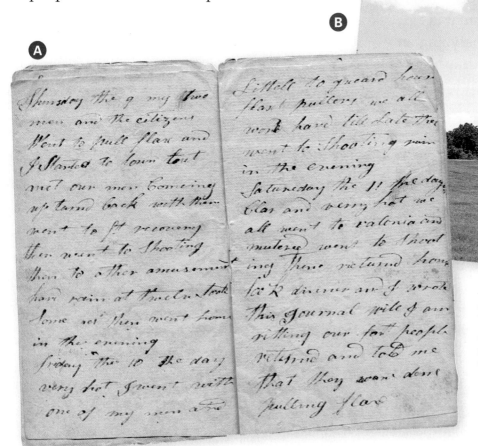

A page from the journal of John Tipton, a soldier in the Battle of Tippecanoe Ⓐ, and Fort Ouiatanon Historical Park in Tippecanoe County, Indiana Ⓑ.

Secondary sources are records of an event that were made by people who were not there. Books written by authors who only heard about or read about an event are secondary sources. So too are magazine articles and newspaper stories written by people who did not take part in the event. Paintings or drawings by artists who did not see the event are also secondary sources.

The sources on pages 4 and 5 tell about the Battle of Tippecanoe that took place in Prophetstown in 1811. One is a primary source and the other is a secondary source. Can you tell which is which?

➡ PRACTICE THE SKILL

Look at the photographs and printed materials that give information about the Battle of Tippecanoe. Then answer these questions.

1 Which source was written by someone who took part in the Battle of Tippecanoe?

2 Which sources are primary sources? Which sources are secondary sources? Explain how you know.

3 What are the advantages and disadvantages in using each source to understand the Battle of Tippecanoe?

➡ APPLY WHAT YOU LEARNED

Work with a partner to find examples of primary and secondary sources in your textbook. Discuss why you think each source is either a primary source or a secondary source.

D

C

Tippecanoe and the Internet Too!

You can learn more about the Battle of Tippecanoe on some Web sites **C**. This obelisk stands as a monument at the Tippecanoe Battlefield **D**.

Why Geography Matters

The study of Earth and the people who live on it is called **geography**. People who study geography are called **geographers**. Geographers do much more than find places on maps. They learn all they can about places and the people who live there.

The Five Themes of Geography

Geographers sometimes divide geography into five themes, or key topics. Most of the maps in this book focus on one of the five themes. Keeping the themes in mind will help you think like a geographer.

Location
Everything on Earth has its own **location**—the place where it can be found.

Human-Environment Interactions
Humans and their surroundings **interact**, or affect one another. The actions of people change the environment. The environment also affects people.

Place
Every location on Earth has features that make it different from all other locations. Features formed by nature are called **physical features**. Physical features include landforms, bodies of water, and plant life. Features created by people are called **human features**. Human features include buildings, roads, and people themselves.

GEOGRAPHY THEME

Movement
People, things, and ideas move every day. Each movement affects the world in some way.

Regions
Areas on Earth whose features make them different from other areas can be called **regions**. A region can be described by its physical features or by its human features.

Essential Elements of Geography

Geographers use six other topics to understand Earth and its people. These topics are the six essential elements, or most important parts, of geography. Thinking about the six essential elements of geography will help you learn more about the world and your place in it.

GEOGRAPHY ESSENTIAL ELEMENTS

• GEOGRAPHY •

The World in Spatial Terms

Spatial means "having to do with space." Every place on Earth has its own space, or location. Geographers want to know where places are located and why they are located where they are.

Places and Regions

Geographers often group places into regions. They do this to show that all the places in a group have a similar physical or human feature.

Physical Systems

Geographers study the physical parts of the Earth. For example, they look at climate, landforms, and bodies of water.

Human Systems

Geographers study where people have settled, how they earn their livings, and what laws they have made.

Environment and Society

People's actions affect the environment. The environment also affects people's activities.

The Uses of Geography

Knowing how to use maps, globes, and other geographic tools helps people in their day-to-day lives.

REVIEW What is geography?

Why Economics Matters

VOCABULARY

economy   economics

Banks, farms, hospitals, and stores—these are just a few of the many places where Hoosiers work. Most people work to be able to buy what they need or want and to save for the future. By working, buying, and saving, they are taking part in the Indiana economy. An **economy** is the way people use resources to meet their needs. The study of how people do this is called **economics**.

In this book you will read about how Hoosiers in the past made, bought, sold, and traded goods to meet their needs. You will also discover how the economy of Indiana changed over time and how it came to be what it is today.

REVIEW What name is given to the study of how people meet their needs and wants?

Money plays an important role in today's economy. People earn, spend, and save money (above). People work at a variety of jobs. At right, a worker in Fairmount, Indiana, is helping to make a new fire truck.

Why Civics and Government Matter

To live together peacefully, people form governments. A **government** is a system of leaders and laws that helps people live safely together in a community, a state, or a country. As a citizen of Indiana, you follow the laws of your city or town, the state of Indiana, and your country— the United States of America. A **citizen** is a member of a country, state, city, or town.

Harcourt Horizons: *Indiana* tells about the role of Hoosiers in community, state, and national governments. It also tells how Indiana's government came to be and how it changed over time. As you read this book, you will learn about leaders and laws in Indiana history.

Government and civics go together. **Civics** is the study of citizenship. As you read this book, you will learn about the rights and responsibilities of citizens.

REVIEW **How are *government* and *civics* different?**

Indiana's state government is based in Indianapolis, the capital city of Indiana. Below is the Indiana State House.

Why Culture and Society Matter

VOCABULARY

culture   society

heritage

As you read this textbook, you will find out how people in the past helped make Indiana what it is today. You will learn about where the early people came from, how they dressed, and what they believed in. You will learn about their families and communities. You will also find out about how they made a living. You will learn about the languages they spoke and the foods they ate. All these things make up a **culture**, or way of life.

Indiana is made up of several cultural groups. These groups of people share common languages, religions, and customs.

These Amish children (above) use a buggy to get around. Amish people in Indiana live simple lives. The Feast of the Hunter's Moon in West Lafayette celebrates Indiana's French and Native American cultures (left).

Each human group, or **society**, has a culture. Many groups of people have contributed to Indiana's culture. There are different types of social groups to which people belong. This book gives information about the different cultures that have come together in Indiana. Some of these social groups have religious, recreational, educational, service, or political functions.

Lieutenant Governor Joseph Kernan presents Sheriff Oatess E. Achrey with the Governor's Award for Excellence in Public Safety at the Black Expo Summer Celebration in Indianapolis.

Many Hoosiers go to Indianapolis to visit the Indiana State Fair each year. The Indiana State Fair is one way Hoosiers join together to celebrate and share their customs.

This book also describes Indiana's **heritage**, or the ways of life that have been passed down through history. People celebrate their heritage by keeping their customs and traditions alive.

Some of Indiana's festivals celebrate the products of the area. Others celebrate the heritage of the city or county. People from other countries who settled in Indiana share their heritage with others.

REVIEW How are the terms *culture* and *society* related?

This popcorn person symbolizes the spirit of the Valparaiso Popcorn Festival (top). This Highland dancer (above) and bagpipe players (above right) celebrate their Scottish heritage at the Columbus Scottish Festival. The community of Berne gathers at the annual Swiss Days festival (right).

The Land and Early People

A compass

Brown County, Indiana

CD 1
Track 2

1

The Land and Early People

66 **This is Indiana,
the place that I love—
with wide open spaces
and stars above.** 99

—Rebecca Kai Dotlich, "This Is Indiana," 2000

Preview the Content

Read the lesson titles. Then fill in the first two columns of the chart with information about the land and early people of Indiana. After you have read the unit, fill in the last column.

K (What I Know)	W (What I Want To Know)	L (What I Have Learned)

Preview the Vocabulary

Multiple Meanings A word can often have several meanings. For each word below, write what you think the word means. Use the Glossary to look up each term. Then draw pictures to show the social studies meanings.

mouth   **fork**   **band**   **till**   **plain**

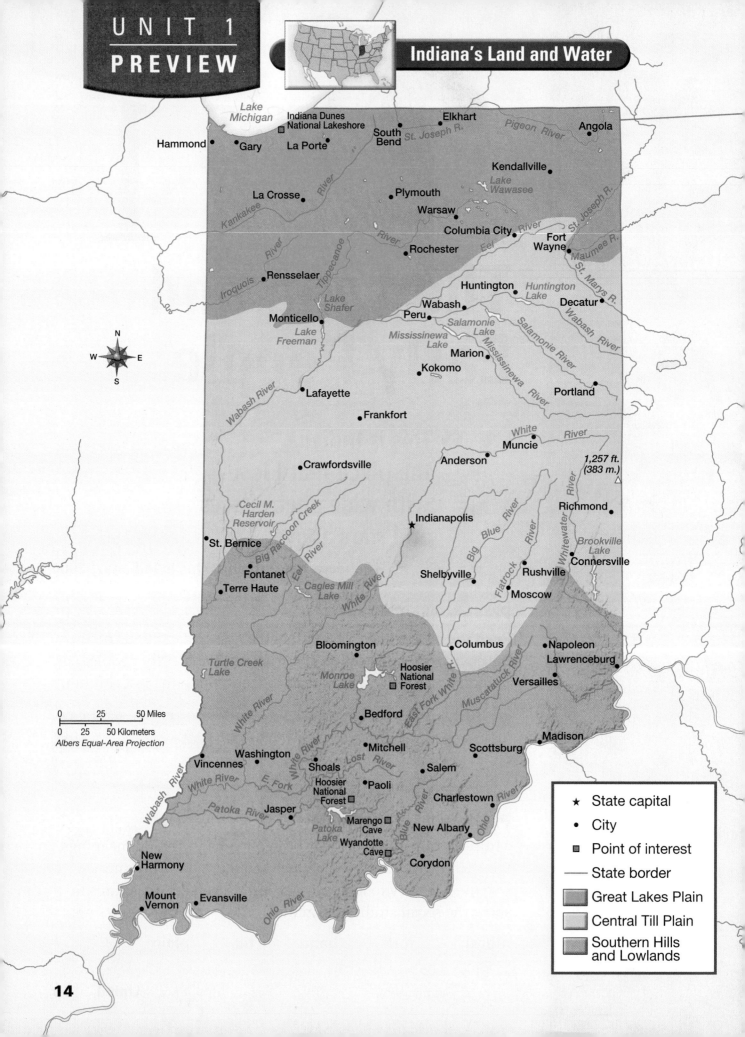

Lake Michigan

Indiana Dunes National Lakeshore

Hammond
Gary
La Porte
South Bend
Elkhart
St. Joseph R.
Pigeon River
Angola

Kendallville

La Crosse
Kankakee River
Plymouth
Warsaw
Lake Wawasee

Columbia City
Eel River
St. Joseph R.
Fort Wayne
Maumee R.

Rochester

St. Marys R.

Iroquois River
Rensselaer
Tippecanoe River
Huntington
Huntington Lake
Decatur

Monticello
Lake Shafer
Wabash
Peru
Salamonie Lake
Salamonie River
Wabash River

Lake Freeman
Mississinewa Lake

Marion
Mississinewa River
Portland

Wabash River
Kokomo

Lafayette

Frankfort

White River
River

Crawfordsville
Muncie
Anderson
1,257 ft. (383 m.)

Richmond

Cecil M. Harden Reservoir
Big Raccoon Creek
Indianapolis
Big Blue River
Flatrock River
Whitewater River
Brookville Lake

St. Bernice
Eel River
Connersville

Fontanet
Cagles Mill Lake
White River
Shelbyville
Rushville
Moscow

Terre Haute

Turtle Creek Lake
Bloomington
Columbus
Napoleon
Lawrenceburg

Monroe Lake
Hoosier National Forest
East Fork White R.
Muscatatuck River
Versailles

Bedford

White River
Madison

Washington
Mitchell
Scottsburg

Vincennes
Shoals
Lost River
Salem

White River
E. Fork
Hoosier National Forest
Paoli
Charlestown
Ohio River

Jasper
Patoka River
Blue River
New Albany

Marengo Cave
Patoka Lake
Wyandotte Cave
Corydon

New Harmony

Mount Vernon
Evansville
Ohio River

Wabash River
White River

Compass: N, S, E, W

Scale:
0 25 50 Miles
0 25 50 Kilometers
Albers Equal-Area Projection

Legend

★ State capital
• City
▪ Point of interest
— State border
▨ Great Lakes Plain
▨ Central Till Plain
▨ Southern Hills and Lowlands

Population of Indiana Cities

CITY	POPULATION
Anderson	🧍🧍🧍
Bloomington	🧍🧍🧍
Evansville	🧍🧍🧍🧍🧍
Fort Wayne	🧍🧍🧍🧍🧍🧍🧍
Gary	🧍🧍🧍🧍🧍
Hammond	🧍🧍🧍🧍
Indianapolis	🧍🧍🧍🧍🧍🧍🧍🧍🧍🧍🧍🧍🧍🧍🧍🧍🧍🧍🧍🧍🧍🧍🧍
Muncie	🧍🧍🧍
South Bend	🧍🧍🧍🧍
Terre Haute	🧍🧍🧍

🧍 = 25,000 people

Indiana's Farm Production, 2000

Product or Crop	Rank Among 50 States	Total Sales
Tomatoes for processing	2nd	$19,261,000
Soybeans	3rd	$1,230,155,000
Cantaloupes	4th	$9,998,000
Peppermint	4th	$5,472,000
Corn	5th	$1,509,323,000
Eggs	5th	$262,214,000
Spearmint	5th	$960,000
Hogs	6th	$544,917,000
Watermelons	6th	$10,150,000

28,000 years ago

21,000 years ago

14,000 years ago

7,000 years ago

PRESENT

Key Events

28,000 years ago   Early people begin to come to North America p. 58

12,000 years ago   Early people arrive in what is now Indiana p. 58

1,000 years ago   Mound Builders live in what is now Indiana p. 62

300 years ago   Miamis become successful traders p. 67

200 years ago   Delawares settle in what is today central Indiana p. 71

On the Banks of the Wabash, Far Away

by Paul Dresser

"On the Banks of the Wabash, Far Away" was approved as the Hoosier state song by the Indiana General Assembly in 1913. It was written by Terre Haute native Paul Dresser, who described his home and happy childhood memories growing up on the banks of the Wabash River.

'Round my Indiana homestead wave
  the cornfields,
In the distance loom the woodlands clear
  and cool,
Often times my thoughts revert to scenes
  of childhood,
Where I first received my lessons—
  nature's school.

But one thing there is missing in the picture,
Without her face it seems so incomplete.
I long to see my mother in the doorway,
As she stood there years ago, her boy to greet.

Chorus:
Oh, the moonlight's fair tonight along
  the Wabash,
From the fields there comes the breath of
  new-mown hay,
Through the sycamores the candle lights
  are gleaming,
On the banks of the Wabash, far away.

homestead	a house and the land around it
loom	to rise in the distance
revert	to go back
new-mown	recently cut
gleaming	shining brightly

Analyze the Literature

1 What do you think the author means by the line
   "Where I first received my lessons—nature's school"?

2 Suppose you moved away from your home in Indiana.
   Do you think you would be homesick, as the author
   of this song seems to be? What scenes or images
   from Indiana would you remember most? Write a
   song expressing your feelings for Indiana.

READ A BOOK

START THE UNIT PROJECT

A Native American Festival
With your classmates, hold a Native
American Festival. As you read this
unit, take notes about Native American
culture. Your notes will help you decide
what parts of Native American culture
to include in your festival.

USE TECHNOLOGY

Visit The Learning Site at
www.harcourtschool.com/
socialstudies for additional
activities, primary sources,
and other resources to use in this unit.

RAVINE GARDEN AT THE INDIANAPOLIS MUSEUM OF ART

The Ravine Garden is part of the 26-acre country estate located on the grounds of the Indianapolis Museum of Art. The garden features thousands of flowers and plants as well as a stream that rushes down the hillside into three beautiful pools.

LOCATE IT

INDIANA

Indianapolis ★

Indianapolis Ravine Garden

CD1
Track
4

Indiana's Geography

❝ I see blue sky,
the sun rifting through
the leaves,
and . . . flowers . . . ❞

—from *Freckles*
by Gene Stratton-Porter, 1904

CHAPTER READING SKILL

Main Idea and Supporting Details

The **main idea** is the most important idea in a chapter, lesson, or paragraph. **Supporting details** are the facts, reasons, or examples that provide information to support the main idea.

As you read this chapter, list the main ideas and supporting details for each lesson.

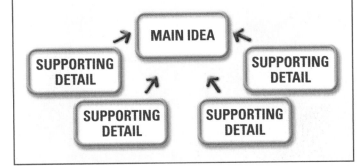

MAIN IDEA

SUPPORTING DETAIL

SUPPORTING DETAIL

SUPPORTING DETAIL

SUPPORTING DETAIL

1

Where on Earth Is Indiana?

MAIN IDEA
Read to learn how to describe the location of Indiana.

WHY IT MATTERS
Knowing the location of a place can help you better understand its history, geography, and economy.

VOCABULARY
region
landform
natural resource
relative location
continent
hemisphere

FAST FACT Indiana is ranked 38th in land area among the 50 states, yet it has the 14th largest population.

Where do you live? There are many ways to answer that question. You could give your street address or the name of your city or town. You also could tell the name of the state in which you live—Indiana.

Where is Indiana? If someone asked you to describe Indiana's location, you could say that it is in the United States.

A Middle Western State

You could add that Indiana is located in the Middle West region of the United States. A **region** is an area with at least one feature that makes it different from other areas. The Middle West is one of four regions that make up the United States. Another name for the Middle West is the Midwest. The other three regions are the Northeast, the South, and the West.

Ten states make up the Northeast region of the United States. The Northeast region stretches along the northern Atlantic coast from Maine to Delaware and west to the Great Lakes.

The region called the South reaches from the southern Atlantic coast of the country to Texas. The region extends south to the Gulf of Mexico and north to the Ohio River. Along the Atlantic and Gulf coasts, the land is mostly flat. Farther inland these low areas rise to the Appalachian Mountains.

The region called the West stretches from the Pacific Ocean to the Rocky Mountains. The West is the largest region of the United States. The West also is more mountainous than the other regions.

Like the other three regions of the United States, the Middle West takes its name from where it is in the country. The Middle West region stretches across the *middle* of the United States and is *west* of the Northeast region.

Regions of the United States

Northeast
South
Middle West
West

Regions The 50 states are often grouped into four large regions.

♦ Which states are in the Middle West region?

The land there is mostly flat or with rolling hills and is good for farming. Mighty rivers flow across the region. Four of the five Great Lakes border states in the Middle West.

The states within each geographic region of the United States are alike in many ways. For example, they may have the same kinds of **landforms**, or shapes that make up Earth's surface. They may have the same kinds of **natural resources**, or things found in nature that people can use. The people who live in those states often earn their living in similar ways.

To describe Indiana's location, you can say that it is west of Ohio, south of Michigan, east of Illinois, and north

of Kentucky, a state in the South region. When you describe Indiana's location in this way, you are describing its **relative location**, or its position in relation to other places.

Indiana is like the other Middle West states in many ways. It has flat and rolling land. Indiana is home to big cities. Many people in Indiana work in the cities or farm the rich soils of the region.

REVIEW What is Indiana's relative location?

The Ohio River forms the southern border of the state of Indiana.

A Region Within Regions

INDIANA

UNITED STATES

NORTH AMERICA

WESTERN HEMISPHERE

Analyze Diagrams Indiana is a state of the United States that is also on the continent of North America and in the Western Hemisphere.

◈ Which generally covers a larger area, a country or a continent?

Part of a North American Nation

Indiana is one of the 50 states that make up the nation of the United States of America. A nation includes all the territory, people, and the government of a place.

All the states of the United States except the island state of Hawaii are located on the continent of North America. A **continent** is one of the main areas of land on Earth. As part of the United States, Indiana also is located on the continent of North America.

The United States is just one of the countries in North America. The country of Canada borders the United States to the north. Canada is divided into provinces instead of states. The country of Mexico lies south of the United States. Like the United States, it is divided into states.

North America is one of the seven continents found on Earth. The other six are Antarctica, Africa, Asia, Australia, Europe, and South America. Of the seven continents, North America is the third largest in size. Only Asia and Africa are larger. Australia is the smallest continent.

REVIEW On which continent is Indiana located?

Indiana's Global Address

You can describe Indiana's location on Earth in another way. People often divide Earth into hemispheres as a way to locate places more easily. A **hemisphere** is half of Earth. *Hemi-* means "half." A line drawn around Earth through the North and South Poles splits it into two equal parts. The Western Hemisphere is one of these halves. The continents of North America and South America are in the Western Hemisphere.

Another imaginary line drawn around the middle of Earth midway between the North and South Poles splits it into equal northern and southern halves. North America is in the Northern Hemisphere, along with the continents of Europe, Asia, and part of Africa.

As part of North America, Indiana is located both in the Western Hemisphere and in the Northern Hemisphere. Now you have many answers to the question "Where on Earth is Indiana?" Indiana is located in the Middle West region of the country of the United States, on the continent of North America, in Earth's Western and Northern Hemispheres. Knowing the location of Indiana, or any other place, is important because it can help you understand its history, geography, and economy.

REVIEW In which two hemispheres is Indiana located?

• **HERITAGE** •

The Name "Hoosier"

For nearly 200 years the people of Indiana have been called Hoosiers. No one really knows what the word *Hoosier* first meant. Some say the word comes from pioneer days. At that time, people greeted one another along the trail with "Who's 'yere?" meaning "Who's there?" Others think Hoosier comes from *hoozer*, a word some Europeans used to describe people who settled the hills of southern Indiana. To those Europeans, *hoo* meant "hill." Many people in Indiana would agree with Indiana writer Meredith Nicholson, who noted, "The origin of the term 'Hoosier' is not known with certainty. But it is certain that . . . Hoosiers bear the nickname proudly."

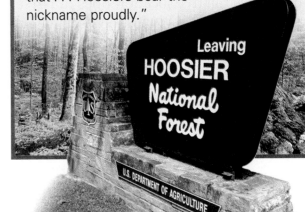

LESSON 1 REVIEW

1 **MAIN IDEA** How would you describe Indiana's location?

2 **WHY IT MATTERS** Why do you think it is important to know the location of a place?

3 **VOCABULARY** Use the words **continent** and **hemisphere** in a sentence that describes Indiana's location on Earth.

4 **READING SKILL—Main Idea and Supporting Details** What are two details that support the idea that it is important to know the location of a place?

5 **GEOGRAPHY** Why is the region in which Indiana is located called the Middle West?

6 **CRITICAL THINKING—Synthesize** Why might people living in a geographic region earn their livings in similar ways?

7 **CRITICAL THINKING—Analyze** How might Indiana differ from other states in the Middle West?

 PERFORMANCE—Make a Postcard On one side of an index card, draw a picture that illustrates Indiana's location. On the other side, explain the picture. Then write Indiana's global address as the address on the card and "send" the card to a classmate.

· SKILLS ·

MAP AND GLOBE

Use Latitude and Longitude

VOCABULARY

absolute location	equator	lines of longitude
lines of latitude	parallel	prime meridian

▶ WHY IT MATTERS

There are many ways to describe where you live. You might say that you live in a certain part of Indiana. If your house is in Fort Wayne, you might say that you live in northeastern Indiana. In this way you are describing your relative location. Sometimes relative location does not give enough information. Mapmakers have a more exact way to identify locations. You can describe the **absolute location**, or exact position on Earth, of a place by using a set of lines that mapmakers draw on maps and globes.

▶ WHAT YOU NEED TO KNOW

The sets of lines that mapmakers draw are lines that do not really appear on Earth, just on maps and globes. One set of lines runs east and west around Earth. These lines are called **lines of latitude**. The **equator** is a line of latitude. It is the imaginary line that runs around the middle of Earth. Other lines of latitude circle the globe north and south of the equator. Because they are all the same distance apart, they are called **parallels** (PAIR•uh•lelz). Lines of latitude are labeled in degrees (°), from 0° at the

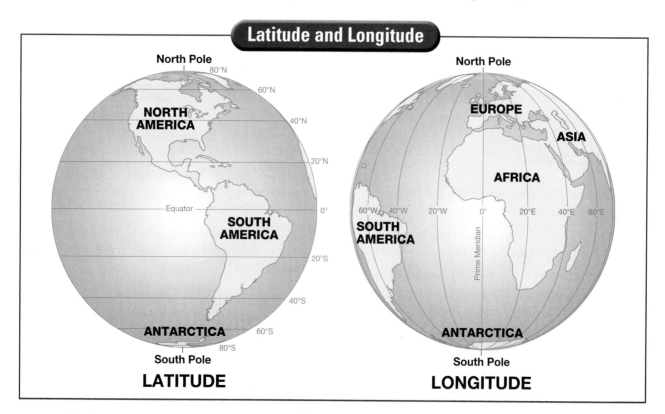

Latitude and Longitude

LATITUDE

North Pole
80°N
60°N
NORTH AMERICA
40°N
20°N
Equator — 0°
SOUTH AMERICA
20°S
40°S
ANTARCTICA 60°S
80°S
South Pole

LONGITUDE

North Pole
EUROPE
ASIA
AFRICA
60°W 40°W 20°W 0° 20°E 40°E 60°E
SOUTH AMERICA
Prime Meridian
ANTARCTICA
South Pole

equator to 90° at the North and South Poles. The lines of latitude north of the equator are labeled *N* for *North*. The lines south of the equator are labeled *S* for *South*.

Another set of lines runs from the North Pole to the South Pole. These north-south lines are called **lines of longitude** (LAHN•juh•tood), or meridians (muh•RIH•dee•uhnz). The **prime meridian**, an imaginary line that passes near London, England, is the starting point for labeling the lines of longitude. Lines of longitude are labeled from 0° at the prime meridian to 180°, halfway around the globe. The lines of longitude west of the prime meridian are labeled *W* for *West*. The lines east of the prime meridian are labeled *E* for *East*.

Together, the lines of latitude and lines of longitude form a grid. You can give the absolute location of a place by naming the line of latitude and the line of longitude closest to it. Find Fort Wayne on the map of Indiana. Near which lines of latitude and longitude is Fort Wayne? Always give latitude first and then longitude when describing absolute location. Fort Wayne's absolute location is 41°N, 85°W.

▶ PRACTICE THE SKILL

Answer these questions using the map of Indiana.

1 Find the lines of latitude and longitude that are near Richmond, Versailles, and Evansville.

2 Which city is located nearest 39°N, 87°W? nearest 40°N, 86°W?

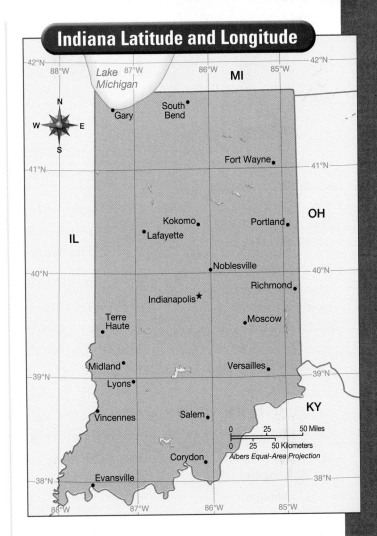

Indiana Latitude and Longitude

3 Most of Indiana lies between which lines of latitude?

▶ APPLY WHAT YOU LEARNED

Write a letter that you might send to a friend or relative in another state. Use latitude and longitude to tell where your city or town is located in Indiana. Also describe the location of the state of Indiana, using latitude and longitude.

Practice your map and globe skills with the **GeoSkills CD-ROM.**

MAP AND GLOBE SKILLS

2

MAIN IDEA
As you read, think about
what makes each of the
three natural regions of
Indiana different.

WHY IT MATTERS
Indiana's varied landscape
has shaped people's lives
in different ways.

VOCABULARY

glacier
natural region
fertile
plain
lithosphere
moraine
marsh
sand dune
till
sea level

Glaciers like those shown
below once covered much
of what is now Indiana.

The Land in Indiana

People who briefly pass through Indiana do not always
get a true picture of what its land looks like.

> **A flat land is what most [travelers through Indiana]
> remember, a flat land of rectangular fields planted
> mostly in corn. . . .**

Depending on where you live in Indiana, this description of
the state by historian William E. Wilson may or may not fit the
land that you know best.

Indiana's land shows great variety. Broad, flat areas of farmland make up a large part of the state. Yet in the southern part
of the state, both low hills and steep hills mark the land as
well. The land in Indiana varies the most from north to south.
Forces of nature long ago helped make the land in the northern
part of the state different from the land in the southern part.

Shaped by Ice

Many thousands of years ago, **glaciers**, huge masses of ice,
began to push into the Indiana area from the north. They
usually moved only a few feet each day. The first glacier
moved farther south than where the Ohio River is now. It covered all of what is Indiana today except for the central part of
southern Indiana. Later, thick ice from a second glacier covered
two-thirds of Indiana. A third glacier followed the second,
covering the northern half of the state. Warm periods lasting

thousands of years separated times of freezing cold.

In the northern part of Indiana, the glaciers flattened the land. They cut the tops off hills and carried them away in pieces. The glaciers ground much of the rock they carried into fine soil and scattered it. They left much of the soil behind in valleys, leveling the land.

The glaciers also shaped water and land features in and near Indiana. As they moved, the glaciers carved wide channels and dug deep holes in the land. As the glaciers melted, they dropped the materials they had been carrying onto the land. These mounds of soil and rock became low hills. The melting ice filled the wide channels and deep holes with water, making rivers and lakes. In this way, the glaciers helped form the Ohio River and the Great Lakes.

The movement of the glaciers greatly affected two of Indiana's three natural regions. A **natural region** is a part of Earth that has one major kind of natural feature, such as mountains, hills, or plains. The glaciers smoothed out the land that makes up what are now the Great Lakes Plain region and the Central Till Plain region of Indiana. In these regions the glaciers left behind a thick layer of fertile soil. **Fertile** means that the soil is good for growing crops. Today both regions are good places for farming.

The glaciers did not reach Indiana's third region, the Southern Hills and Lowlands. Because of this, the soil there is poorer. This region also has more ridges and hills than the other two because the glaciers did not flatten the land.

REVIEW What force of nature long ago greatly affected two of Indiana's natural regions?

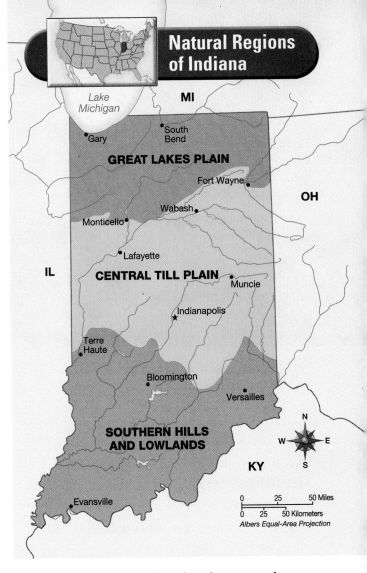

Natural Regions of Indiana

Regions **Indiana has three natural geographic regions.**

❖ Which region of Indiana is located farthest north?

The Great Lakes Plain

Today a broad **plain**, or flat area, covers the northern third of Indiana. This region is the Great Lakes Plain. This natural region is part of a large lowland area that stretches along much of the shoreline of the Great Lakes. In Indiana the Great Lakes Plain extends south from Lake Michigan and Indiana's border with Michigan to the Wabash River valley in the north-central part of the state.

Marshes and wetlands such as this one in the Indiana Dunes National Lakeshore contain hundreds of kinds of plants and wildlife.

LOCATE IT

Indiana Dunes National Lakeshore

INDIANA

Glaciers formed the main features of this region, including its lithosphere. The **lithosphere** (LIH•thuh•sfeer) is the soil and rock that form Earth's surface. Besides leaving behind fertile soil, the glaciers left piles of soil and rock in some places. These piles of stony earth became low hills called **moraines** (muh•RAYNZ).

The glaciers also scraped out holes in the land in this region. Later, water from melting glaciers filled the holes, creating lakes. Today hundreds of lakes dot the Great Lakes Plain region, including Lake Wawasee (wah•wah•SEE), Indiana's largest lake. Many **marshes**, or lowland areas with wet soil and tall grasses, can be found there as well. These features explain why this part of the state is also called the Northern Lake and Moraine region. Yet these features alone do not define the region.

In addition, tall sand dunes rise in the northwest corner of the region, near Lake Michigan. A **sand dune** is a hill built up from sand that the wind has swept from beaches. The sizes and shapes of the dunes shift with the wind. The highest sand dune, Mount Tom, sometimes reaches a height of nearly 200 feet (61 m).

Where the sand dunes are today, forests once stood. As the dunes shift, parts of these ancient woods are sometimes uncovered. Businesses and homes have been built over large parts of the dunes area. The United States government created the Indiana Dunes National Lakeshore to protect these dunes and allow everyone to enjoy this special area.

REVIEW What are some of the natural features of the Great Lakes Plain region?

The Central Till Plain

South of the Great Lakes Plain is the Central Till Plain. This region takes its name from the **till**, or thick layer of soil, that the glaciers left on the land. Till is a fertile mix of sand, small stones, and clay.

The soil in this region is excellent for growing corn, soybeans, and many other crops. These crops are sometimes called cash crops because farmers earn their living from them. The till makes this region the best farmland in Indiana. It also provides grasslands that are good for grazing livestock.

Glaciers made the land in the Central Till Plain fairly level. Even so, the land in this part of Indiana is not entirely flat. Shallow valleys break up the land here and there. Large rocks in fields and yards mark places where glaciers once cut through this part of Indiana. Moraines make the land hilly, especially in the south.

The highest point in Indiana is located in the Central Till Plain. Along the Indiana–Ohio border in Wayne County, the land reaches 1,257 feet (383 m) above sea level. **Sea level** is the same height as the surface of the oceans. The height of landforms is measured starting from sea level.

REVIEW How would you describe the land in the Central Till Plain region?

Indiana's fertile soil has made it the third-largest producer of soybeans in the United States.

The Indiana Dunes National Lakeshore extends for nearly 25 miles (40 km) along southern Lake Michigan. The park contains about 15,000 acres and includes sand dunes, beaches, wetlands, and forests. Many people have long been concerned about protecting this area of northwest Indiana. Other people felt that the land should be used for businesses. In 1966 the United States government made the area a national lakeshore.

CHESTERTON TRIBUNE, 1916

66 Part of the [lake] front should be set aside for park purposes and the rest should be reserved for industry [business]. 99

JENS JENSEN, landscape architect, 1916

66 If this wonderful dune country should be taken away from us and on it built cities . . . it would show us to be in fact a people who only have dollars for eyes. 99

Analyze the Viewpoints

❶ What was the *Chesterton Tribune*'s point of view on the use of the land along Lake Michigan? What was Jensen's point of view?

❷ What does Jensen mean by "people who only have dollars for eyes"?

❸ **Make It Relevant** Do you feel strongly about an issue relating to the environment? Write a letter that you might send to the editor of your local newspaper. First, describe the issue. Then explain your point of view.

The Southern Hills and Lowlands

To the south of the Central Till Plain lies the Southern Hills and Lowlands region. This region makes up the southern third of the state. Although the earliest glacier pushed into the region, later glaciers did not. As a result, the land in this region kept its hills when most of the land in the rest of the state was flattened.

As its name shows, the Southern Hills and Lowlands region has both high and low land. As you travel from east to west, you cross a strip of upland, or high land, followed by a strip of lowland. Another strip of upland follows, and then a strip of lowland, and so on. Between the high and low areas, the land often drops sharply down rocky slopes. The land stands high along the Ohio border in the east, but the westernmost part of the region is very low. In fact, the lowest point in Indiana is located in this region. The land dips to 320 feet (98 m) above sea level in Posey County, where the Wabash and Ohio Rivers meet.

Many unusual features are found in this region. Streams and small rivers cut through the land. Waterfalls tumble down cliffs into narrow canyons called gorges. Water and wind have shaped tall rock masses, which stand on their own next to cliffs and hills. Jug Rock, in Martin County, and Pompey's Pillar, near Napoleon in Ripley County, are examples of these standing rocks. Streams have worn rounded hills, known as The Knobs, near New Albany in Floyd County. These scenic wood-covered hills can rise to more than 600 feet (180 m) in some areas.

Caves and caverns are other special features of this part of the state. Marengo and Wyandotte Caves in Crawford County took thousands of years to form.

Charlestown State Park (right) and Hoosier National Forest (below) are in the Southern Hills and Lowlands.

Indiana's Lost Rivers
Understanding Physical Systems

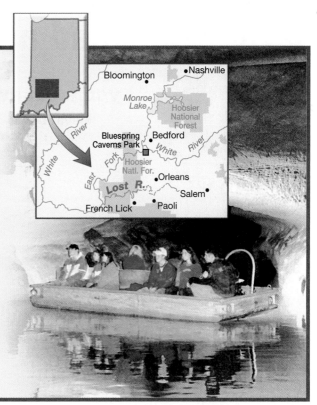

The Southern Hills and Lowlands region has many "lost" rivers. They are "lost" because they disappear below the surface of the land and flow mostly underground. Lost rivers enter underground areas through sinkholes. A sinkhole is an opening in the land that develops when the rock above a cavern collapses. The Lost River, which begins near Orleans, is one of the longest underground rivers in the United States. After about 15 miles (about 24 km), it vanishes through sinkholes. It reappears miles away to flow on the surface.

One "lost" river in Indiana flows through Bluespring Caverns, near Bedford.

Water carved them out of rock deep inside some of the region's hills. As water flowed through these openings, more of the rock broke away. Then chambers, or rooms, opened up. Hoosier George Cottman toured Wyandotte Cave in the late 1800s. He described being "filled with wonder at the power that could thus invade the foundations of the earth and hollow out vast chambers in the very heart of the living rock." Today, many visitors share his feelings.

REVIEW What are some natural features of the Southern Hills and Lowlands?

LESSON 2
REVIEW

1 MAIN IDEA Why is the Southern Hills and Lowlands different from other regions in Indiana?

2 WHY IT MATTERS How has fertile land affected people's lives in the Central Till Plain?

3 VOCABULARY Use the word **fertile** to explain the meaning of the word **till**.

4 READING SKILL—Main Idea and Supporting Details What details support the idea that the Great Lakes Plain is also called the Northern Lake and Moraine region?

5 GEOGRAPHY What are the three natural regions of Indiana? In which natural region do you live?

6 CIVICS AND GOVERNMENT Why was Indiana Dunes National Lakeshore created?

7 GEOGRAPHY Where is the highest point in Indiana located?

8 CRITICAL THINKING—Hypothesize How would Indiana be different if the glaciers had moved through all of the state?

 PERFORMANCE—Make a Map Map the natural regions of Indiana, and identify the natural features found within the state.

Read an Elevation Map

VOCABULARY

elevation

relief

▶ WHY IT MATTERS

As you travel south from Indianapolis, the **elevation** (eh•luh•VAY•shuhn), or height of the land, begins to rise. You begin to see more hills. How high is the land in the southern part of the state? How does its elevation differ from that of northern Indiana? You cannot answer these questions just by looking at the land. You need to study an elevation map.

▶ WHAT YOU NEED TO KNOW

The elevation map of Indiana on page 33 uses color to show **relief** (rih•LEEF), or differences in elevation. To find elevation on the map, use the map key to learn what each color stands for.

Elevation is measured from sea level, usually in feet or in meters. The elevation of land at sea level is zero. On the map a triangle marks the highest point in Indiana. The map gives the elevation of this point as 1,257 feet (383 m) above sea level.

The map does not give exact elevations for other places in the state. Each color on the map matches a range of elevations given in the map key, or stands for an area's highest and lowest elevations and all the elevations in between.

For example, the area along the shoreline of Lake Michigan is colored green. The map key tells you that the land near the lake is from 0 to 328 feet (0 to 100 m) above sea level.

▶ PRACTICE THE SKILL

Study the map key to understand elevations in Indiana. Then use the key to answer these questions.

1. What is the elevation of the land near the highest point in the state?

2. What is the elevation of the land in the part of the state where the Ohio and Wabash Rivers meet?

3. What is the elevation of the area where you live?

▶ APPLY WHAT YOU LEARNED

Prepare a travel brochure that tells visitors what parts of the state would be best for the following activities—hiking, biking, and a scenic car trip. Use elevation to suggest areas for these activities. Write one paragraph for each activity. Explain why you made each suggestion.

Practice your map and globe skills with the **GeoSkills CD-ROM.**

42°N

88°W 87°W 86°W 85°W 84°W

MI

Lake Michigan

IL

Little Calumet River

St. Joseph R.

Pigeon River

Kankakee River

Lake Wawasee

41°N

Tippecanoe River

Lake Shafer

Eel River

St. Joseph River

Maumee River

St. Marys River

Lake Freeman

Wabash River

Huntington Lake

OH

Mississinewa Lake

Salamonie Lake

Salamonie River

Wabash River

Wildcat Creek

Mississinewa River

Morse Reservoir

White River

0 25 50 Miles
0 25 50 Kilometers
Albers Equal-Area Projection

40°N

Eagle Creek Reservoir

1,257 ft. △ (383 m)

River

Big Blue River

Whitewater River

Brookville Lake

△ Highest point
▽ Lowest point

Cagles Mill Lake

White River

Eel

Flatrock River

Feet   **Meters**
Above   Above
   400
1,312   300
984   200
656   100
328
0   0
Below sea level

39°N

Turtle Creek Lake

Monroe Lake

East Fork White River

Muscatatuck River

Hardy Lake

White River

Lost River

East Fork

Blue River

Patoka River

Patoka Lake

Wabash River

White River

Ohio River

38°N

▽
320 ft. (98 m)

Ohio River

KY

88°W 87°W 86°W 85°W 84°W

N
W E
S

CD 2 Track 2

3

Indiana's Rivers and Lakes

Waterways and bodies of water always have been an important part of life in Indiana. Take a look at a map of Indiana, and you can see why. Water is everywhere in Indiana. Rivers wind through every part of the state. They even help form Indiana's borders in the west and south. Lakes also dot the land. One of the Great Lakes—Lake Michigan—makes up part of Indiana's northern border.

The people of Indiana and the rest of the world depend on Earth's hydrosphere (HY•drih•sfeer). The **hydrosphere** is all the water on Earth's surface. People use water in many ways. In Indiana, rivers and lakes supply fresh water to homes, farms, and businesses. Rivers and lakes also offer places for people to fish, swim, and boat. All through Indiana's history, bodies of water—both natural and human-made—have been important to trade and settlement.

FAST FACT
The name *Wabash* comes from a Miami Indian word meaning "shining white" or "water over white stones."

LOCATE IT

INDIANA

Wabash River

The mighty Wabash River is Indiana's longest river.

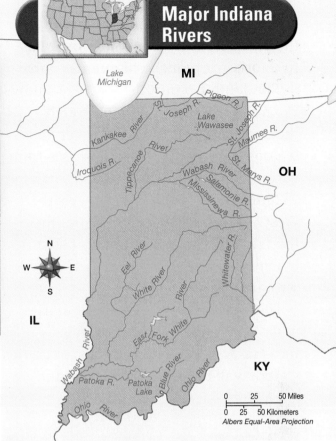

Major Indiana Rivers

Location Many rivers flow through and around Indiana.

❖ What river forms part of the western border of Indiana?

The Wabash River System

The Wabash River is probably the best known of all Indiana's rivers. At 475 miles (764 km), it is also the state's longest river. The **source**, or beginning, of the Wabash River is in western Ohio. The river enters Indiana in the east, near where the Great Lakes Plain and the Central Till Plain meet. Near Huntington the river heads west and passes through the cities of Wabash, Peru, and Logansport. Then it turns southwest, flowing through Lafayette. About 60 miles (97 km) past Lafayette, the Wabash turns south.

Near Terre Haute, the Wabash River becomes the border between Indiana and Illinois. The river winds between the two states for 200 miles (322 km). In Indiana's southwestern corner is the end, or mouth, of the Wabash River. The **mouth** of a river is the place where it empties into a larger body of water. The Wabash River flows into the Ohio River where

the states of Indiana, Illinois, and Kentucky meet.

Many tributaries (TRIH•byuh•ter•eez) join the Wabash River as it makes its way across Indiana. A **tributary** is a river or creek that flows into another river or creek that is larger. The Tippecanoe (tih•pee•kuh•NOO) River is the main tributary of the Wabash in the northern part of the state. The Tippecanoe is about 200 miles (320 km) long. It flows through the city of Monticello and meets the Wabash near Lafayette. Other tributaries in the north include the North Eel, Mississinewa (mih•sih•SIH•nuh•wuh), and Salamonie (SA•luh•moh•nee) Rivers.

In central and southern Indiana the White River is the main tributary of the Wabash River. The White River has two **forks**, or branches. From its source in Randolph County, the West Fork flows 255 miles (410 km), cutting through Indianapolis. The South Eel River joins it along its way. The East Fork rises from various streams in Henry County. It runs 282 miles (454 km) before it meets the West Fork, near Petersburg. From there the White River flows 52 miles (84 km) to join the Wabash on Indiana's border with Illinois.

The Wabash River and its tributaries make up the largest river system in Indiana. A **river system** drains, or carries water away from, the land around it.

The Wabash River and its tributaries drain about two-thirds of Indiana and a large part of Illinois. When you consider the size of this river system, it is easy to understand why Indiana historian William E. Wilson said, "The Wabash is Indiana."

In times past, the Wabash River and its tributaries were important transportation routes. Canoes, flat-bottomed boats, and steamboats carried people and goods on these waterways. Later, railroads and other means of transportation largely replaced river travel and trade. Today, people enjoy boating and other activities on the Wabash and its tributaries.

REVIEW What is the longest river in Indiana?

The Wabash River joins the Ohio River near Mt. Vernon, in southwestern Indiana. The lowlands in this area sometimes are flooded when heavy rains or melting snow cause the rivers to overflow their banks.

LOCATE IT

INDIANA

Mt. Vernon

LOCATE IT

INDIANA
Madison

Clifty Falls

Dropping 70 feet (about 21 m), Clifty Falls in Clifty Falls State Park is one of Indiana's tallest waterfalls. Big Clifty Creek empties into the Ohio River near Madison, Indiana.

Other Indiana Rivers

Other rivers besides those of the Wabash River system are important to Indiana's people. The Ohio River is Indiana's main water link with much of the rest of the United States. From its source at Pittsburgh, Pennsylvania, the Ohio River flows 981 miles (1,579 km) to its mouth at Cairo, Illinois. There it joins the Mississippi River. The Ohio is the second-busiest river in the United States. Only the Mississippi is busier. Hundreds of millions of tons of raw materials and factory goods are shipped on the Ohio River each year.

The Ohio River forms Indiana's southern border with Kentucky. Here the river passes by the cities of Madison, Jeffersonville, New Albany, Evansville, and Mount Vernon, Indiana.

Two of the state's largest rivers are tributaries of the Ohio. The Whitewater River joins the Ohio River where it enters Indiana in the east. The Wabash River empties into the Ohio in the southwestern corner of the state. The Ohio then carries the waters of these rivers west to the Mississippi River.

The waters of Indiana's Kankakee River also reach the Mississippi. This river starts near South Bend in northwestern Indiana. A traveler in the late 1800s noted that near Culver, "the Kankakee River oozes and creeps sluggishly westward." About 135 miles (217 km) from its source in Indiana, the Kankakee joins the Illinois River. Like the Ohio River, the Illinois empties into the Mississippi River.

Although some of Indiana's rivers flow west toward the Mississippi, others flow east to the Great Lakes.

Two of these rivers share the name St. Joseph River. Both start in south-central Michigan. One St. Joseph River flows into northern Indiana. At South Bend it turns, or bends. After passing through Elkhart, the river flows back into Michigan. There it drains into Lake Michigan. The other St. Joseph River flows into Indiana from Ohio. At Fort Wayne it joins the St. Marys River to form the Maumee River. The Maumee flows northeast across Ohio to Lake Erie.

REVIEW What rivers in Indiana flow into the Great Lakes?

Lakes and Reservoirs

Northern Indiana is a land of lakes. Most of these are natural lakes, which means they were made by nature.

LOCATE IT

INDIANA
Versailles

Versailles State Park

Fishing is a popular sport at Indiana's lakes and reservoirs.

Lake Wawasee is the largest natural lake in the state. It spreads over more than 4 square miles (10 sq km) in northeastern Indiana. Lakes Manitou, Maxinkuckee, and Bass are other large lakes in the area. Many smaller lakes are scattered across the northern half of the state as well.

Southern Indiana also has many lakes. However, many of these lakes were made by people. People often make lakes to help keep rivers from flooding.

· SCIENCE AND TECHNOLOGY ·

Dams and Reservoirs

Human settlement in Indiana and other parts of the world depends on having enough water to meet people's demands. At first, settlers built dams of earth, rocks, and shrubs for storing small amounts of water. People then learned to build larger and more permanent dams. Later, people built reservoirs and used the energy of the water spilling over a dam to produce electricity.

Water that flows down the spillway, or passageway, of a dam continues on the path of the river or stream. Pipes take in some of the water from the spillway. This water rushes through turbines and spins them. The turbines in turn drive generators, or machines that produce electricity. Electric power passes through transformers and travels along power lines to homes and businesses.

To make a new lake, people build a **dam**, or wall, across a river or creek. The dam protects against flooding by not letting too much water flow through the river at one time. When a dam is built across a waterway, it causes water to back up behind the dam. This backup of water forms a lake. This kind of human-made lake is called a **reservoir** (REH•zuh•vwar).

People have built many reservoirs in southern Indiana because flooding often is a problem there. A dam built across Salt Creek near Harrodsburg created Lake Monroe, Indiana's largest reservoir. This lake covers an area more than three times the size of Lake Wawasee. Other reservoirs in the southern part of the state include Patoka (puh•TOH•kah) Lake on the Patoka River east of Jasper and Cecil M. Harden Reservoir on Raccoon Creek between Crawfordsville and Fontanet. Mississinewa Lake and Salamonie Lake are reservoirs on rivers with the same names in northern Indiana.

The people of Indiana use reservoirs and natural lakes in many ways. Both kinds of lakes supply fresh water to nearby communities. Reservoirs and lakes are also places of recreation. People enjoy boating and other water sports, such as waterskiing and swimming, on Indiana's reservoirs and lakes. Fishing is popular all year. In the winter some people even go ice fishing. People also camp, hike, and picnic in the wooded areas around the state's lakes and reservoirs.

REVIEW What is the difference between a natural lake and a reservoir?

LESSON 3
REVIEW

① **MAIN IDEA** How is water important to people?

② **WHY IT MATTERS** What are the important waterways and bodies of water in Indiana?

③ **VOCABULARY** Explain the difference between a river's **source** and its **mouth**.

④ **READING SKILL—Main Idea and Supporting Details** What details support the idea that "the Wabash is Indiana"?

⑤ **HISTORY** Why did the Wabash and other rivers become less important for transportation?

⑥ **CRITICAL THINKING—Apply** What is the main use of the rivers or lakes near where you live?

⑦ **CRITICAL THINKING—Analyze** Many of Indiana's largest cities are located near rivers or lakes. Why do you think this is so?

PERFORMANCE—Design a Stamp Imagine that you have been asked to create a sketch for a postage stamp. The stamp will be part of a new series about important bodies of water in Indiana. Choose one of Indiana's rivers or lakes. Find out more about the river. Then draw a scene that includes the river. Next, write a paragraph that explains your drawing.

4

MAIN IDEA
Read to discover how people in Indiana use the state's many natural resources.

WHY IT MATTERS
People often change the environment when they use natural resources.

VOCABULARY
product

mineral

fuel

pollute

nonrenewable resource

quarry

renewable resource

biosphere

habitat

prairie

Indiana's rich, fertile soil is ideal for growing many crops.

Indiana's Natural Resources

Water is one of many natural resources that have always made Indiana a good place in which to live. Hundreds of years ago, a European explorer in what is now Indiana noted that "one can find there, in abundance with very little trouble, everything necessary" for people to live. The same holds true today. Now, as in the past, people in Indiana make use of the state's many natural resources.

Fertile Soil

The soil left behind by the glaciers is one of the state's most valuable natural resources. The glaciers ground stone and rock into soil as they moved. When the glaciers melted, they left a deep layer of this rich soil on the land. Novelist Thomas Wolfe, while traveling through Indiana, once described the soil as "fat as a hog and so fertile you felt that if you stuck a fork in the earth the juice would spurt. . . ." Two-thirds of the state of Indiana is farmland. Most farming is done in northern and central Indiana. Farms are also common in southern Indiana, even though the soil there is less fertile.

Farmers in Indiana grow a variety of crops. Corn and soybeans are Indiana's most important farm products. A **product** is something people make or grow, usually to sell. Farmers use some of the corn and soybeans they grow to feed their cattle, hogs, or chickens. People, too, eat Indiana's corn and soybeans. Mint from farms in the northwestern part of the state is another important product. One-tenth of all the peppermint and spearmint produced in this country comes from Indiana. Indiana farmers also sell many livestock products.

REVIEW What are the two most important farm products grown in Indiana?

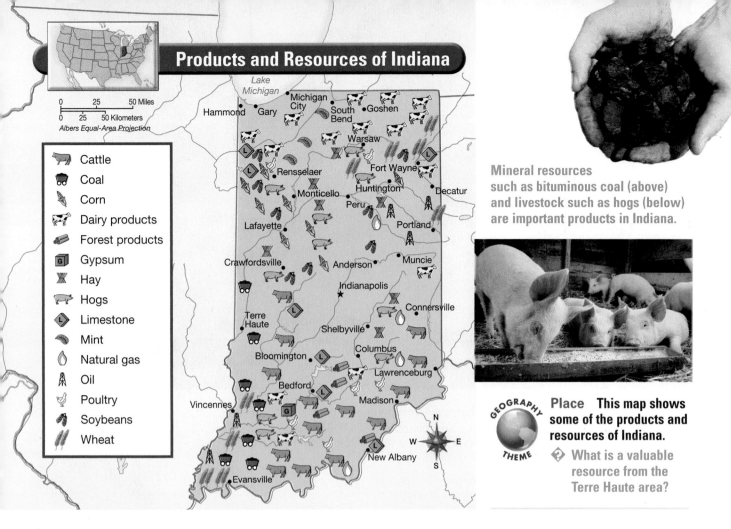

Products and Resources of Indiana

Legend:
- Cattle
- Coal
- Corn
- Dairy products
- Forest products
- Gypsum
- Hay
- Hogs
- Limestone
- Mint
- Natural gas
- Oil
- Poultry
- Soybeans
- Wheat

0   25   50 Miles
0   25   50 Kilometers
Albers Equal-Area Projection

Lake Michigan

Hammond, Gary, Michigan City, South Bend, Goshen, Warsaw, Rensselaer, Fort Wayne, Monticello, Huntington, Decatur, Peru, Lafayette, Portland, Crawfordsville, Anderson, Muncie, Indianapolis, Connersville, Terre Haute, Shelbyville, Columbus, Bloomington, Lawrenceburg, Bedford, Madison, Vincennes, New Albany, Evansville

Mineral resources such as bituminous coal (above) and livestock such as hogs (below) are important products in Indiana.

GEOGRAPHY THEME

Place This map shows some of the products and resources of Indiana.

❓ What is a valuable resource from the Terre Haute area?

Rich Natural Resources

Although the richest farmland is located in north-central Indiana, southern Indiana is rich in another way. It holds many of Indiana's minerals. A **mineral** is a natural substance found in the ground. Like the fertile soil of Indiana, many of the state's mineral resources were formed thousands of years ago.

Coal is Indiana's most valuable mineral resource. Large deposits of coal lie close to Earth's surface in southwestern Indiana. The kind of coal found there is bituminous (buh•TYOO•muh•nuhs), or soft coal. Coal deposits are the remains of ancient plants. When the plants died, minerals such as sand covered them. These materials piled up on top of the plants and pressed on them. Some of the material turned to rock, and the plants underneath became coal.

People mine coal, or take it out of the ground, to use as a fuel. A **fuel** is a natural resource that is used to make heat or energy. At one time people burned coal to heat buildings. Today coal is mainly used to make electricity.

There are two main problems with using coal as a fuel. First, Indiana's coal contains a great deal of sulfur. Sulfur **pollutes**, or harms, the air when it is burned. The other problem with coal is that it is a **nonrenewable resource**. Once it is used it cannot be made again by nature or people. Indiana's coal supplies will not last forever.

Limestone is Indiana's second-most valuable mineral resource. It is a hard rock formed from sea-animal skeletons.

Limestone mined from Indiana quarries has been used for many famous buildings all over the United States, including state capitols, churches, and the Empire State Building (right), in New York City, New York.

Long ago a huge sea covered much of North America. When sea animals died, their shells and bones piled up at the bottom of the sea. Over time, the weight of the water and sand pressed the animal skeletons into layers of rock called limestone. Today a band of this rock stretches south from Monroe County to Lawrence County, between Bloomington and Bedford. This area is known for its limestone quarries. A **quarry** is a place where stone is cut or blasted out of the ground.

Limestone has several uses. When crushed, it can be used to pave roads and highways. Indiana limestone is also a strong and beautiful building material. Indiana is a leading supplier in the United States of limestone for building. Limestone from Indiana covers the United States Holocaust Memorial Museum in Washington, D.C. Limestone was also used to construct the Indiana state capitol building and those of Nebraska, Tennessee, and West Virginia.

Indiana's other natural resources are oil, natural gas, clay, sand, gravel, and gypsum (JIP•sum). Oil and natural gas, like coal, are nonrenewable resources. They are found mostly in southwestern Indiana. Clay, sand, and gravel are found in many parts of the state. These materials are used in road construction. Gypsum, a kind of rock similar to limestone, is found in LaPorte, Martin, and Owen counties. When ground, gypsum is used in paint and in building products such as plaster and wallboard.

REVIEW What are Indiana's two most valuable mineral resources?

Valuable Forests

One of Indiana's most precious resources is its trees. Forests cover about one-sixth of the state. Most of this wooded land is in the Southern Hills and Lowlands region. Hoosier National Forest alone spreads over more than 190,000 acres near Bedford.

At one time trees covered almost all of what is now Indiana. J. Richard Beste, a traveler in Indiana less than 200 years ago, remarked, "I never saw more magnificent timber than shaded the valleys through which we passed. . . . At times, partial clearings . . . opened vistas into the lands beyond, and still the same noble timber everywhere arose." Over time, people cleared much of this timber to make room for their farms. They also used trees for fuel and lumber, or boards cut from logs.

Today, Indiana's forests are used for both lumber and recreation. Wood from trees is also used to make paper and to cut into chips for gardens. However, the people of Indiana also enjoy activities such as camping and hiking in the state's woodlands. To save this valuable resource, they have created parks and other protected forest areas. Because they can be replanted, trees are a **renewable resource**. By replanting trees, people can create new woodlands.

The Hoosier National Forest—one of the state's most valuable natural resources—covers almost 200,000 acres in south-central Indiana.

LOCATE IT

INDIANA

Hoosier National Forest

Gene Stratton-Porter 1863–1924

Character Trait: Individualism

"From the earliest moment that I was allowed to wander at will, I made friends with the birds, with the flowers, with the trees, with anything and everything with which I came in contact." As a young girl in Wabash County, Gene Stratton-Porter preferred being outdoors on her own rather than playing with other children. Stratton-Porter became one of Indiana's best-loved authors. She began her career by photographing and writing about the birds and animals of Limberlost Swamp. Limberlost is a wetlands habitat near Geneva, Indiana. Her home near the marsh—Limberlost Cabin, which Stratton-Porter, her husband, and daughter lived in—is an Indiana State Historic Site today.

MULTIMEDIA BIOGRAPHIES
Visit The Learning Site at **www.harcourtschool.com/biographies** to learn about other famous people.

Two main kinds of trees make up Indiana's forests: broadleaf trees and needleleaf trees. Most of the trees in Indiana are broadleaf trees. They have wide, flat leaves that fall off each year before winter. Before they fall, the green leaves change color. When autumn comes, Indiana's forests display brilliant shades of orange, yellow, and red. By contrast, needleleaf trees have thin, sharp leaves like needles that stay green all year. For this reason, people call these trees evergreens. Red cedar and pine are two common kinds of needleleaf, or evergreen, trees in Indiana.

REVIEW How do people use Indiana's forests today?

A Place for Animals

Forests and other natural areas are part of Indiana's biosphere. The **biosphere** includes all the plants and animals in the environment. Many kinds of animals have their **habitats**, or places where they find food and shelter, in Indiana's marshes and forests.

Beavers, muskrats, river otters, and water birds such as ducks, herons, and sandhill cranes live in the marshes and other areas around rivers and lakes. Deer, raccoons, opossums, skunks, squirrels, rabbits, and game birds such as quail and wild turkeys make their homes in Indiana's forests.

The yellow poplar, or tulip tree, is Indiana's state tree.

Different kinds of birds are found across the state. Yellow-winged sparrows and prairie larks live on the edges of the wetlands. Wood thrushes and various warblers sing in the trees in southern Indiana near the Ohio River. Sparrows, larks, blue jays, orioles, robins, swallows, and cardinals can be seen throughout most of the state.

Animals have been an important natural resource since people first arrived in Indiana. The earliest settlers hunted animals for food. They also used animal skins, furs, and bones to meet their needs for clothing, shelter, tools, and weapons. Even today, people depend on animals for some of these purposes.

Animal habitats can easily be damaged or destroyed. Two hundred years ago, herds of buffalo roamed the **prairies**, or grasslands, of western Indiana. These and other animals were hunted until no more of them could be found. Others disappeared when people built settlements and farms. Cities and towns continue to grow and spread into animal habitats. Today an important issue for many people in Indiana is the protection of animal habitats.

REVIEW **What are two animal habitats in present-day Indiana?**

Indiana's state flower—the peony—and the state bird—the red cardinal—are colorful symbols of the Hoosier state.

LESSON 4
REVIEW

1 **MAIN IDEA** How do people in Indiana use the state's many natural resources?

2 **WHY IT MATTERS** How do people change the environment when they use Indiana's natural resources?

3 **VOCABULARY** Explain the difference between **nonrenewable** and **renewable resources**.

4 **READING SKILL—Main Idea and Supporting Details** What are Indiana's most important natural resources?

5 **GEOGRAPHY** How did Indiana's coal develop?

6 **HISTORY** How did early people use Indiana's natural resources?

7 **CRITICAL THINKING—Analyze** In what ways are coal and limestone the same? How are they different?

8 **CRITICAL THINKING—Evaluate** What are some ways people can protect Indiana's forests?

 PERFORMANCE—Write "What Am I?" Riddles Prepare four "What Am I?" riddles about the natural resources of Indiana. Each riddle should include a short description followed by "What am I?" For example: "I was left behind by glaciers long ago. What am I?" Ask your classmates your riddles and answer theirs.

Indiana's Climate and Weather

CD 2
Track
IX

MAIN IDEA
As you read, discover what gives different parts of Indiana different weather.

WHY IT MATTERS
Weather and climate affect people's activities.

VOCABULARY
precipitation
climate
drought
humid
lake effect
tornado

How would you describe this morning's weather in your community? You might describe how hot or cold it is by mentioning the temperature (TEM•pruh•chuhr). You could talk about whether any precipitation has fallen. **Precipitation** (pri•sip•uh•TAY•shuhn) is water in the form of rain, snow, sleet, or hail that falls to Earth's surface. You also might describe how windy it is. The temperature, precipitation, and wind in a place on a particular day make up the weather. The weather today in the area where you live can be very different from the weather in other parts of Indiana. Weather also can be different in your community from day to day.

A Climate in Between

How would you describe the climate where you live? To answer this question, you have to know the difference between weather and climate. Weather describes the day-to-day conditions in a place. **Climate** is the kind of weather a place has over a long period of time. No matter where you live in Indiana, the climate is temperate, or moderate. That means that year after year the weather in Indiana is not extreme. Most of the time it is not too hot or too cold. Several factors help explain Indiana's temperate climate.

One factor affecting Indiana's climate is its location between the equator and the North Pole. Earth gets all its heat from the sun. Some places on Earth, however, get more heat than other places do. Direct rays from the sun give more heat than indirect rays do. Places close to the equator get more of the sun's direct rays than places farther away. That means that places

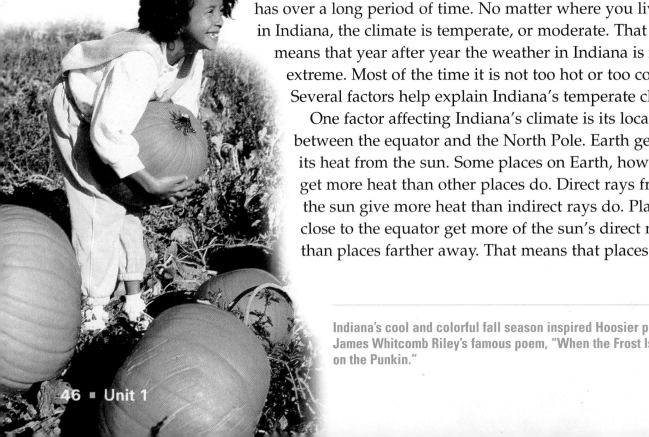

Indiana's cool and colorful fall season inspired Hoosier poet James Whitcomb Riley's famous poem, "When the Frost Is on the Punkin."

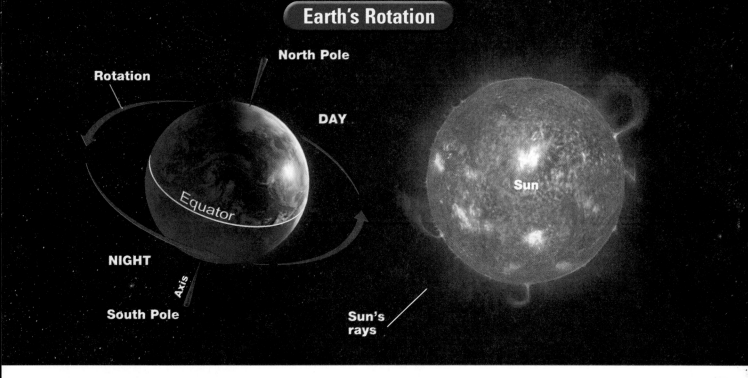

Earth's Rotation

Rotation

North Pole

DAY

Equator

NIGHT

Axis

South Pole

Sun

Sun's rays

Analyze Diagrams   **As Earth rotates, parts of it are always moving into the sun's light.**

❖ Why is it nighttime on the side of Earth tilting away from the sun?

near the equator also get more heat. These places usually have the warmest climates on Earth. Places far from the equator—to the north and south—get the indirect rays of the sun. They get less of the sun's heat.

Indiana is about halfway between the equator and the North Pole. It is in between the places that get the most heat and the places that get the least heat from the sun. Like Indiana, much of the United States has a temperate climate. Many places in western Europe—such as Paris, France, and London, England—enjoy a temperate climate for the same reason.

The state's closeness to water also affects Indiana's climate. Places near an ocean or a large lake usually have a milder climate than places far from water. Water heats up and cools off more slowly than land does. For this reason,

the temperature of the water does not vary much from winter to summer. Air temperatures over bodies of water also do not vary as much as air temperatures over land do. In the summer, air blowing off an ocean or a large lake keeps nearby land cooler than land that is far from water. In the winter, land near water stays warmer. Temperatures in parts of the state near Lake Michigan are cooler in summer and warmer in winter than temperatures farther from the lake.

Elevation usually has an effect on climate. Places at high elevations often are colder than places at lower elevations. Indiana has high hills, but it does not have any mountains. Temperatures in Indiana's hills and valleys do not differ much.

REVIEW How does Indiana's location affect its climate?

Highs, Lows, and When to Grow

Indiana poet James Whitcomb Riley described some of the differences between summer and fall in Indiana when he wrote:

> 66 **They's something kindo' harty-like about the atmusfere**
>
> **When the heat of summer's over and the coolin' fall is here.** 99

Temperatures in Indiana vary with the changing seasons. Earth's position in relation to the sun and its movement around the sun cause the change in seasons. Earth spins around its axis (AK•suhs) as it moves around the sun. An axis is an imaginary line that runs through Earth from the North Pole to the South Pole. Earth tilts, or slants, on its axis. Because of this tilt, places on Earth get different amounts of sunlight and heat at different times of the year. In the summer the Northern Hemisphere tilts toward the sun, so Indiana and other places in the Northern Hemisphere are warmer and get more of the sun's direct rays. In the winter the Northern Hemisphere tilts away from the sun, causing cooler temperatures for Indiana and other places in the northern half of Earth.

Indiana summers are warm. Average daytime temperatures range from about 80°F (27°C) in southern Indiana to 73°F (23°C) in the north. On some, but not many summer days, temperatures may rise above 100°F (38°C). The highest

Analyze Diagrams   As Earth moves around the sun, the seasons change.

◈ When does winter begin in the Northern Hemisphere?

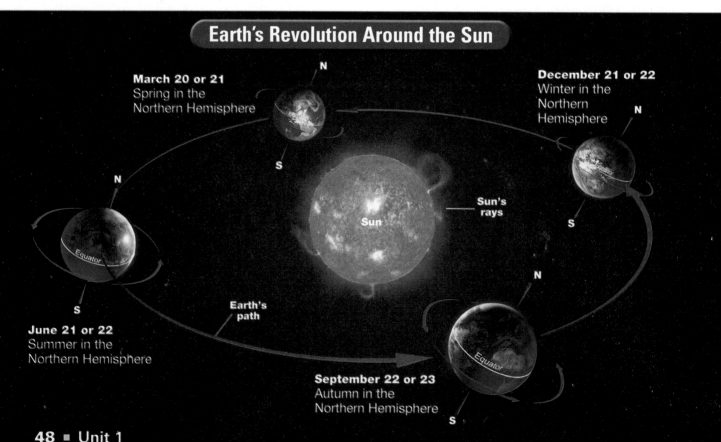

Earth's Revolution Around the Sun

March 20 or 21
Spring in the
Northern Hemisphere

December 21 or 22
Winter in the
Northern
Hemisphere

Sun's
rays

Sun

Earth's
path

June 21 or 22
Summer in the
Northern Hemisphere

September 22 or 23
Autumn in the
Northern Hemisphere

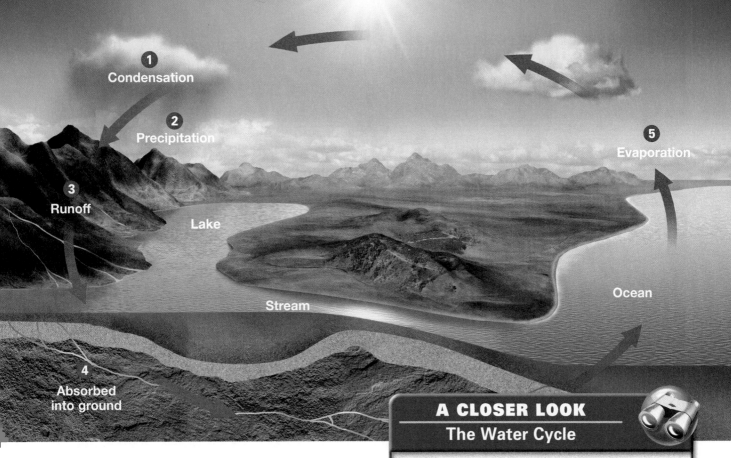

1 **Condensation**

2 **Precipitation**

3 **Runoff**

Lake

5 **Evaporation**

Stream

Ocean

4 **Absorbed into ground**

temperature ever recorded in Indiana was 116°F (47°C) at Collegeville on July 14, 1936.

Winters can be cold in Indiana. Temperatures average about 25°F (⁻4°C) in northern Indiana to 37°F (3°C) in the south. Some winter temperatures stay below 32°F (0°C), the temperature at which water freezes. The lowest temperature ever recorded in Indiana was ⁻36°F (⁻38°C), on January 19, 1994, in New Whiteland.

REVIEW Which part of Indiana generally has warmer temperatures, the north or the south?

Plenty of Precipitation

Of course, crops and other plants need more than warm temperatures to grow. They also need plenty of rain.

Amounts of precipitation vary from north to south in Indiana. Southern Indiana usually receives more rain than

A CLOSER LOOK
The Water Cycle

Earth's water supply is always being cleaned and recycled through the hydrologic (hy•druh•LAH•jik) cycle, or water cycle.

1 Water changes through condensation to form clouds. Condensation (kahn•den•SAY•shun) changes water from a gas to a liquid, causing precipitation to fall to Earth.

2 Precipitation falls into rivers, lakes, or oceans.

3 Runoff, or extra water from precipitation, flows into oceans, streams, or lakes.

4 Some precipitation is absorbed into the ground.

5 Other precipitation evaporates. Evaporation (ih•va•puh•RAY•shun) happens when the sun heats the water, turning some of it into gas that rises and then condenses to form clouds.

❓ What would happen if any of the stages of the water cycle did not occur?

northern Indiana does. Average rainfall in the south is about 45 inches (114 cm) a year, while the north receives an average of about 35 inches (89 cm). In the south, when too much precipitation falls, flooding can be a problem.

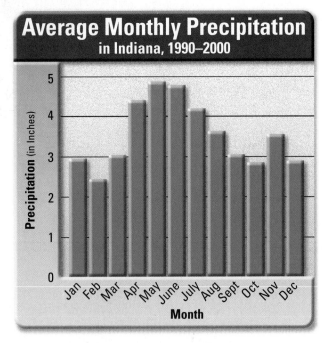

Average Monthly Precipitation
in Indiana, 1990–2000

Precipitation (in inches) vs. **Month**

Jan, Feb, Mar, Apr, May, June, July, Aug, Sept, Oct, Nov, Dec

Analyze Graphs Indiana's precipitation, on average, is highest during the late spring and early summer.

◆ According to the graph, which month is driest in Indiana?

Rivers such as the Ohio often overflow their banks with water from melting snow and spring rains. Now and then the south also has dry periods, or droughts. A **drought** is a long period of time with very little or no precipitation. During a drought crops can dry up and soil may blow away.

In summer, winds in Indiana usually come from the south. This warm air carries moisture from the Gulf of Mexico. It makes the Indiana summers humid. **Humid** air has a lot of moisture in it.

In winter, precipitation patterns in the state change. The northern part of Indiana gets much more snow than the southern part. More than 40 inches (102 cm) of snow usually fall in the north each year. Southern Indiana receives only about 10 inches (25 cm) a year. Northern Indiana gets more snow because part of it is located on Lake Michigan. Cold, dry

winds blow from the north. As this air passes over Lake Michigan, it picks up moisture. When the air moves over land, it drops the moisture in the form of snow. This snow, like the mild temperatures near the lake, is part of what is called the lake effect. The **lake effect** is the effect bodies of water such as Lake Michigan have on the weather in places near them.

REVIEW How is precipitation different in northern and southern Indiana?

Whirling Winds

Severe storms happen in Indiana when cold, dry air from the north meets warm, humid air from the south. These strong and often sudden storms sometimes strike Indiana and other Middle West states in the spring and summer. They bring thunder, lightning, heavy rains,

FAST FACT Lightning can heat the surrounding air to temperatures of 50,000°F (27,760°C)!

and high winds. They can also cause tornadoes. A **tornado** is a funnel-shaped column of spinning air that can cause serious damage.

Tornadoes usually form under the clouds of severe thunderstorms. The winds in a storm cloud often spin at different speeds and in different directions. This can cause the storm cloud to turn in a circle. The center of the storm cloud spins the fastest. It becomes a swirling funnel-shaped column of air and moves under the storm cloud. Then it may drop to the ground.

Although they usually last only a few minutes, tornadoes can do much damage. Tornadoes can reach speeds of up to 300 miles (480 km) an hour. They can blow apart buildings and uproot trees. Tornadoes tear off roofs, turn over mobile homes, and often pick up cars and trucks.

Scientists can often predict tornadoes by using a kind of radar called Doppler radar. The radar's computers can tell in which direction a storm or tornado is moving and how fast it is moving.

REVIEW At what time of year do tornadoes happen in Indiana?

LESSON 5
REVIEW

1. **MAIN IDEA** Why do different parts of Indiana have different kinds of weather?

2. **WHY IT MATTERS** What part of Indiana's weather affects the crops that are grown?

3. **VOCABULARY** Use the words **precipitation** and **drought** in a sentence about farming.

4. **READING SKILL—Main Idea and Supporting Details** What damage can tornadoes cause?

5. **GEOGRAPHY** What other places in the world have a climate similar to Indiana's?

6. **GEOGRAPHY** How does Lake Michigan affect the weather in parts of Indiana?

7. **CRITICAL THINKING—Synthesize** Why does the Northern Hemisphere have warmer temperatures in the summer than in the winter?

8. **CRITICAL THINKING—Evaluate** How does the climate where you live affect the way you live?

 PERFORMANCE—Make a Weather Chart Chart the daily average temperature and precipitation level in your community for a week. Do the same for a city in another part of the country. What conclusions can you make about the climates in the two places? Share your findings with your classmates.

Use a Table to Group Information

VOCABULARY

classify

▶ WHY IT MATTERS

People gather information for many reasons. They organize it in different ways to make it easier to understand. For example, when you need to compare information, a table is a good way to organize it.

Suppose that you and your family would like to visit one of the many beautiful lakes or reservoirs found throughout the southern part of Indiana. You have gathered information about several of these reservoirs and lakes. Now you need to compare the details about them to make a choice.

Lake Monroe (below), near Bloomington, is Indiana's largest reservoir. Wilcox Lake (right), in Clark State Forest, is one of the state's smallest reservoirs.

Table A: Five Indiana Reservoirs

RESERVOIR	SIZE (in acres)	LOCATION
Monroe	10,750	Bloomington
Patoka	8,800	Birdseye
Mississinewa	3,210	Peru
Salamonie	2,855	Andrews
Cecil M. Harden	2,060	Rockville

SOURCE: Indiana Department of Natural Resources

Table B: Five Indiana Reservoirs

RESERVOIR	SIZE (in acres)	LOCATION
Cecil M. Harden	2,060	Rockville
Mississinewa	3,210	Peru
Monroe	10,750	Bloomington
Patoka	8,800	Birdseye
Salamonie	2,855	Andrews

SOURCE: Indiana Department of Natural Resources

▶ WHAT YOU NEED TO KNOW

Tables can provide many kinds of information. For example, tables let you compare information about two or more people, places, or things. Before you put information in a table, however, you must decide how you want to **classify**, or group, the information. When you classify information, you group it according to a pattern. The pattern makes it easier to compare information. Tables have columns and rows. Each column contains a certain kind of information. Each row includes all the different kinds of information for each person, place, or thing.

▶ PRACTICE THE SKILL

The two tables on this page give information about some of Indiana's reservoirs. Both tables give the same information, but they classify it in different ways.

1 Study Table A. Which reservoir is the largest? How large is it? Which reservoir is the smallest? As you can see, Table A lists the reservoirs in order from largest to smallest.

2 Now study Table B. Table B gives the same information as Table A but classifies it differently. How are the reservoirs classified in Table B?

3 Which table makes it easier to find information about a certain reservoir? Explain your answer.

4 Which table makes it easier to compare the size of the reservoirs? Explain your answer.

▶ APPLY WHAT YOU LEARNED

Make a table in which the same information about the reservoirs is grouped by location. Then explain how this table would be useful in comparing information. Share your table with members of your family.

CD2 Track

Review and Test Preparation

USE YOUR READING SKILLS

Complete this graphic organizer to show that you understand how to identify the main ideas and supporting details. A copy of this graphic organizer appears on page 16 of the Activity Book.

The Land in Indiana

MAIN IDEA: Tall sand dunes rise in the northwest corner of the Great Lakes Plain region along Lake Michigan.

↓ ↓ ↓

DETAIL: Wind built the dunes with beach sand.

DETAIL: _____

DETAIL: _____

MAIN IDEA: The best farmland in Indiana is found in the Central Till Plain region.

↓ ↓ ↓

DETAIL: _____

DETAIL: _____

DETAIL: _____

MAIN IDEA: _____

↓ ↓ ↓

DETAIL: Hills, ridges, and valleys break the land.

DETAIL: _____

DETAIL: Waterfalls tumble into gorges.

THINK  & WRITE

Write a Newspaper Headline Think about a weather event in Indiana such as a flood, drought, tornado, or snowstorm that might be big news. Write a newspaper headline about the event and its effect on people's lives.

Make Up a Slogan Suppose that you have been asked to make up a slogan to persuade people to visit Indiana. Think about the natural features in the state and reasons to visit Indiana. Then write a paragraph to share with your classmates.

USE VOCABULARY

Identify the term that correctly matches each definition.

landform (p. 21)

moraine (p. 28)

fork (p. 36)

quarry (p. 42)

humid (p. 50)

1 having lots of moisture

2 low, stony hill

3 place where stone is cut from the ground

4 shape that makes up Earth's surface

5 branch of a river

RECALL FACTS

6 What does Indiana have in common with other states in the Middle West region?

7 How did glaciers make Indiana's soil fertile?

8 What are Indiana's two most valuable farm products?

9 What is coal? How is it formed?

10 What kind of climate does Indiana have?

Write the letter of the best choice.

11 **TEST PREP** Indiana's highest point is located—
  A in the southern part of the state.
  B near the Indiana-Ohio border.
  C in the northwest corner of the state.
  D near the Illinois border.

12 **TEST PREP** Land in the Southern Hills and Lowlands is—
  F flat.
  G fertile.
  H uneven.
  J level.

13 **TEST PREP** Because of the lake effect—
  A snow can be heavy in northern Indiana.
  B sand dunes pile up along Lake Michigan.
  C farming near Lake Michigan is good.
  D there could be a drought in northern Indiana.

THINK CRITICALLY

14 Why might some people not want to put a dam across a river?

APPLY SKILLS

Use Latitude and Longitude

15 Use the map on page A16 to identify the latitude and longitude of Indiana cities. Compare the latitudes and longitudes you found with those a classmate found. Did he or she arrive at the same latitude and longitude for each city?

Read an Elevation Map

16 On the map on page 33, study how elevation at the source of a river differs from elevation at its mouth. Explain your findings.

Use a Table to Group Information

17 Make two different tables that show the same information about tributaries of the Wabash River. Tell how you classified the information in each table. Explain the purpose of each table.

ANGEL MOUNDS STATE HISTORIC SITE

Angel Mounds State Historic Site offers visitors a chance to see how early people called Mound Builders lived in what is today Indiana. Angel Mounds, near Evansville, is one of the largest Mound Builder settlements in the Middle West. Native Americans first settled this area about 1,000 years ago. It is believed that they lived there for about 300 years. Angel Mounds became a religious, political, and economic center.

LOCATE IT

INDIANA

Evansville

Angel Mounds
State Historic Site

CHAPTER

2

The Early People of Indiana

> " Indiana, the land of Indians "
>
> —Name first applied to the region, 1800

CHAPTER READING SKILL

Summarize

To **summarize**, restate the most important ideas or key points in your own words.

As you read this chapter, think about the key points of each lesson. Then write them down in your own words.

KEY POINTS → SUMMARY

1

CD3 Track 2

The Land and People Long Ago

12,000 years ago   6,000 years ago   **PRESENT**

12,000 years ago–1,000 years ago

MAIN IDEA
Read to find out how changes in the land and climate of Indiana affected how early people lived.

WHY IT MATTERS
People today change their ways of life as the world around them changes.

VOCABULARY

migrate
band
cooperate
extinct
specialize
tribe
earthworks

The story of Indiana's people begins thousands of years ago. Long ago, no people lived in North America. Glaciers covered much of the land. Because some of the world's ocean water froze, ocean levels dropped. Then dry land appeared above sea level. A strip of this land joined Asia and North America. Many scientists believe that people began to follow the animals they hunted across this land bridge. The first people to **migrate**, or move, to North America may have arrived between 40,000 and 12,000 years ago. People probably reached what is now Indiana about 12,000 years ago.

Hunting Large Animals

The land that is now Indiana was very different when people first arrived. Summers were cooler and winters were warmer than they are today. Glaciers stretched across most of the land in northern Indiana, and densely wooded forests grew in the south. The forests and nearby plains provided food for many very large animals.

FAST FACT   Mastodons had up to four rows of short but strong teeth, which they used to grind up plants.

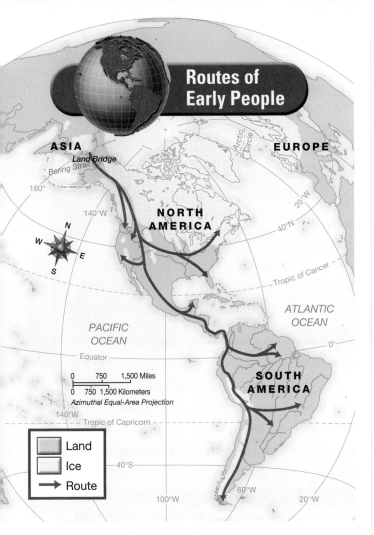

Routes of Early People

ASIA

EUROPE

Land Bridge
Bering Strait

NORTH AMERICA

PACIFIC OCEAN

ATLANTIC OCEAN

Equator

0   750   1,500 Miles
0   750 1,500 Kilometers
Azimuthal Equal-Area Projection

SOUTH AMERICA

Tropic of Cancer

Tropic of Capricorn

Land
Ice
Route

Movement The first people to migrate to North and South America came from Asia.

❖ What may have allowed the people to travel from Asia to North America?

Mammoths and mastodons wandered across the land, towering over all the other animals. Some mammoths were as tall as 14 feet (4 m). Mastodons were only slightly smaller. With their trunks, long tusks, and woolly hair, mammoths and mastodons looked like huge, shaggy elephants.

The earliest people to enter what is now Indiana were most likely hunters searching out these giant animals as sources of

food. The early people traveled in **bands**, or small groups of families that lived and worked together. They were always on the move, hunting the animals they needed for food. They camped in caves, rock shelters, or tents made of animal skins instead of making lasting shelters.

Hunting large animals was too big a job for one person to do alone. To hunt large animals, people needed to **cooperate**, or work together. One group of hunters might surprise an animal as it drank from a stream or pond. Then another group might rush in with spears to attack the animal.

Hunting large animals was hard work, but it was worth the effort. Dried meat from one mammoth could feed a band all winter. People also made clothing and shelters from animal skins and fur. They made weapons and tools from animal tusks and bones.

REVIEW How did the early people in what is now Indiana meet their needs for food, clothing, and shelter?

Mastodons provided early people with a source of food, clothing, shelter, tools, and weapons.

The Atlatl, or Throwing Stick

Early people used heavy spears to hunt giant animals, such as mammoths and mastodons. These spears were especially good for thrusting from a short distance. To hunt smaller animals, people turned to lighter spears. They also developed a tool for throwing them. The new tool was the atlatl (AT•lat•uhl), or throwing stick. The atlatl was a long piece of wood with a hook at one end. The hunter put a spear on the stick and slid the pole end into the hook. Then, he used the stick to fling the spear. The atlatl helped early hunters throw spears farther. By putting stone weights on the stick, they also could hurl their spears faster.

An atlatl made it easier to hunt animals from greater distances.

Meeting Basic Needs

For hundreds of years people hunted giant animals through the forests and across the plains in the area that is known today as Indiana. This way of life changed when the environment changed. Beginning about 10,000 years ago, glaciers started to melt. Summers became hotter. Winters became warmer and drier.

These changes affected both animals and people. Many of the plants that the large animals ate could not grow in this climate. Without a source of food, the mammoths, mastodons, and other giant animals began to become **extinct**, or to die out.

Without giant animals to hunt, people needed other sources of food. They began to rely more on plants. They gathered seeds, nuts, fruits, and berries and dug up roots. They also began hunting smaller animals. To do this, they used new kinds of stone tips on their spears. At rivers and lakes they sank hooks and nets into the water to catch fish and shellfish.

People learned that different kinds of plants were ready to eat during different seasons. They also learned the movement patterns of animals throughout the year.

REVIEW How did early people change their way of life when the giant animals died out?

Early Farmers

People gathered plants for food long before they learned to grow them. In time, they discovered that they could grow food instead of having to search for it. People in what is today Indiana probably began growing plants, or farming, about 3,000 to 2,000 years ago.

The best places for farming had fertile soil and plenty of water. People grew beans, squash, and maize, or corn, along the Ohio River, the Wabash River, and smaller rivers and streams.

Farming required that people stay in one place to care for their crops. Near their crops they built shelters close together. These groups of houses became settlements, or communities.

Early farmers grew maize near many riverbanks.

As farmers, people did not have to spend all their time looking for food. They could develop other skills. Soon people began to specialize. **Specialize** means to work at one job and do it well. While some people farmed, hunted, or gathered food, others made pots or did weaving. This separation of jobs, or division of labor, helped communities meet people's needs more easily.

As populations in these early communities grew, bands formed together into larger groups called **tribes**. These groups of bands shared land and ways of life.

Each tribe developed its own culture. A tribe's culture included its beliefs and ways of speaking, dressing, and behaving. Its culture united, or brought together, the people in the tribe.

REVIEW How did farming change the way some people lived?

Mound Builders

After people in North America started farming, some tribes began to build **earthworks**, or large human-made mounds of dirt. Some of these mounds of earth were about 4 feet (1.3 m) high. Others rose as high as 70 feet (21 m) and covered a wide area. Today the different groups of people who built earthworks in Indiana and other parts of North America are known as Mound Builders.

Scientists believe that the Mound Builders first built earthworks as burial places. A single mound might contain one or more log tombs. Later, people made flat-topped mounds. On these they built important buildings. A temple, community center, or leader's home might stand on top of a mound.

The Mound Builders who lived in settlements across the Middle West were part of a culture called Mississippian.

Mound Builders often built their religious temples on top of large mounds with flat tops. Mound Builders' temples usually stood in the center of the settlement, such as this one at Angel Mounds.

These Native Americans lived in large towns.

The largest Mound Builder town in North America was Cahokia (kah•HOH•kee•uh), in what is today Illinois. Between 20,000 and 40,000 people lived in Cahokia. The largest Mound Builder settlement in Indiana was found near the location of present-day Evansville. About 1,000 people lived at the settlement known today as Angel Mounds.

Mound Builders in Indiana farmed large pieces of land. They made crafts and set up long-distance trade systems. The Mound Builders traded with people as far away as the Rocky Mountains in the West and the Appalachian Mountains in the East. Indiana's Mound Builders had

A small figure, such as this one, was often placed in the burial mounds of Native Americans.

tools, pottery, and jewelry to trade. In return, they received items not found in Indiana, such as freshwater pearls, sea turtle shells, and sharks' teeth.

For reasons that are still not clear, sometime between 1,000 and 500 years ago, the Mound Builders stopped trading. They also no longer built earthworks.

The Mound Builders seem to have disappeared. Yet what remains of their culture—the pottery, art, and earthworks—are clues to understanding Indiana's rich past.

REVIEW How did Mound Builder life differ from that of earlier people?

LESSON 1 REVIEW

Summary Time Line

12,000 years ago	6,000 years ago	PRESENT

12,000 years ago
Native Americans arrive in what is now Indiana

3,000 to 2,000 years ago
Farming begins in Indiana

1,000 years ago
Mound Builders are active in Indiana

① **MAIN IDEA** What changes in the environment led people to rely more on plants?

② **WHY IT MATTERS** How might ways of life in Indiana be different today if glaciers still covered most of the land?

③ **VOCABULARY** Write a sentence that uses the word **band** to explain the meaning of the word **tribe**.

④ **TIME LINE** How many years after the arrival of the first Native Americans did farming begin in what is now Indiana?

⑤ **READING SKILL—Summarize** How would you summarize the information in this lesson that tells about Mound Builder trade?

⑥ **ECONOMICS** How did division of labor change the way Indiana's Native Americans lived?

⑦ **CULTURE** Why did Mound Builders build earthworks?

⑧ **CRITICAL THINKING—Evaluate** Would you prefer to have lived the life of a hunter or a farmer? Explain your answer.

PERFORMANCE—Draw a Book Cover Imagine that you have written a book called *The Mound Builders of Indiana*. Draw an illustration for the cover of your book. Show that you understand the kind of lives these Native Americans led. Display your cover in your classroom.

Identify Cause and Effect

VOCABULARY

cause

effect

WHY IT MATTERS

A **cause** is an action that makes something else happen. An **effect** is what happens because of an earlier action. Many events in life are linked to other events. Understanding causes and their effects can help you understand why certain things happened.

WHAT YOU NEED TO KNOW

Word clues in your reading can help you identify causes and effects. Terms such as *because, since, then, led to,* and *as a result* often connect causes and effects. Read the sentences that follow and look closely at the signal words.

Because some of the world's ocean water froze, ocean levels dropped. *Then* dry land appeared above sea level.

Which events in the two sentences above are causes? Which are effects?

Sometimes events have more than one cause. Likewise, some events have more than one effect. The diagram below shows how the change in climate about 10,000 years ago caused other kinds of changes in the way animals and humans behaved. Each was an effect of the climate change.

PRACTICE THE SKILL

Study the diagram below. Then answer these questions.

1. What caused giant animals to become extinct?
2. What were the effects of the giant animals dying out?
3. Why did people develop new spear tips?

APPLY WHAT YOU LEARNED

Write a paragraph that explains the causes and effects shown in the diagram. In your paragraph, include words that show connections between the causes and the effects. Compare your paragraph with a classmate's paragraph.

Cause and Effect

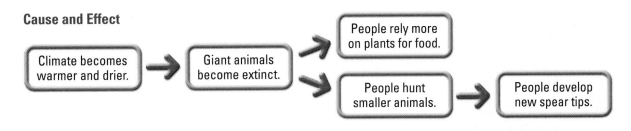

READING SKILLS

Chapter 2 ■ 63

CD 3
Track 2

Mound Builders Artifacts

Since the Mound Builders left no written records, the artifacts they left behind are the only clues about their way of life. Beginning in the early 1800s, archaeologists began to find tools and pieces of pottery from the Mound Builder sites. They offer our only clues about the Mound Builders, but some of the unusual shapes are hard to explain.

Archaeologists use a scale to determine the size of the artifacts they find. The artifacts they found at the Mound Builder sites are all different shapes and sizes.

FROM THE INDIANA STATE MUSEUM AND BALL STATE UNIVERSITY

Mound Builders were mostly hunters and gatherers. They carved arrowheads and spear points from stone.

Analyze the Primary Source

❶ **Which of these artifacts was used for hunting?**

❷ **What do you think the carved figures called birdstones were used for?**

❸ **What do these artifacts tell about the Mound Builders' way of life?**

Many burials included a carved figure called a birdstone.

This collar was used to protect the throat.

Bracelets were made from animal bones.

This piece of pottery was shaped to look like a bear.

ACTIVITY

Write a Story Imagine that you are a Mound Builder. Choose two artifacts from these pages, and write a story about them. Include information about how you use these items in your life. You may want to tell how and why you made the items. Share your story with a classmate.

RESEARCH

Visit The Learning Site at **www.harcourtschool.com/ primarysources** to research other primary sources.

MAIN IDEA
Read to find out how the
Miamis used the natural
resources around them
to support large and
successful settlements.

WHY IT MATTERS
Much like the Miamis,
people in Indiana today
depend on natural
resources.

VOCABULARY
headwaters
portage
longhouse
hereditary
council
clan

Native Americans used
the bark of birch trees to
make both canoes and
storage containers.

The Miami People

| 12,000 years ago | 6,000 years ago | PRESENT |

500 years ago—300 years ago

By about 500 years ago, the Mound Builder settlements in what are now Indiana and nearby states had become nearly empty. New groups of Native Americans began to move into the area. Together these groups of native people are known as the Indians of the Eastern Woodlands. They lived on the lands between the Atlantic Ocean and the Mississippi River. The Indians of the Eastern Woodlands found that the land around them provided most of the things they needed to survive. They hunted animals, gathered plants, and farmed. They sometimes traded with other people to get what they could not grow or make. Some of their settlements were as large as those built by the Mound Builders.

Miami Settlements

The Miamis were one of the first Eastern Woodlands groups to settle in what is now Indiana. Around 1600 they migrated to Indiana from what are today the states of Wisconsin and Illinois. Different Miami bands chose different places to live. Two bands settled along the Wabash River and its tributaries. They built villages at what are today Lafayette and Vincennes. They also settled near the **headwaters**, or beginning, of the Maumee River, where the city of Fort Wayne stands today. There they built a settlement called Kekionga (kee•kee•ohn•GUH). It became an important village of the Miami people. From it they controlled the **portage**, or overland route, between the Wabash and Maumee Rivers. Various buildings made up each Miami village. The Miamis built dome-shaped houses called wigwams.

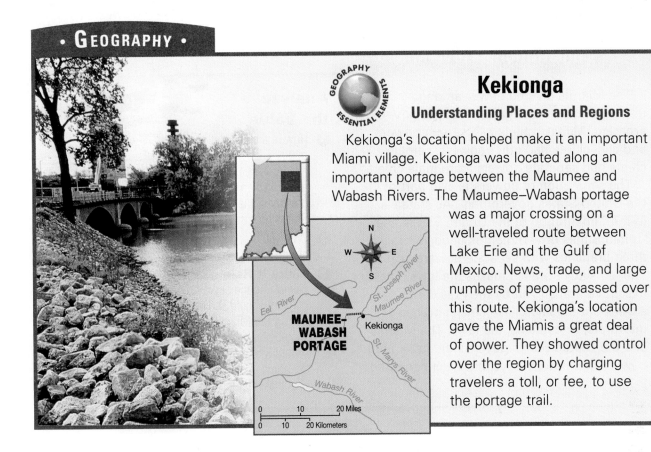

Kekionga

Understanding Places and Regions

Kekionga's location helped make it an important Miami village. Kekionga was located along an important portage between the Maumee and Wabash Rivers. The Maumee–Wabash portage was a major crossing on a well-traveled route between Lake Erie and the Gulf of Mexico. News, trade, and large numbers of people passed over this route. Kekionga's location gave the Miamis a great deal of power. They showed control over the region by charging travelers a toll, or fee, to use the portage trail.

First, they bent the trunks of young trees to form an arched frame. Then they covered the frame with bark or mats woven out of grass. They left an opening in the roof to let out smoke from the fire built in the center of the shelter. Although small, wigwams had sleeping platforms and room for storage. Miami Indians also built a long wooden building called a **longhouse**, for ceremonies.

The Miamis farmed in fields near their settlements. In the fields the Miami women raised beans, squash, melons, pumpkins, and several kinds of corn. Miami corn was famous for its soft white kernels and sweet taste. Other Native American groups traded for Miami corn.

While the women farmed, Miami men hunted deer, bear, and smaller animals, such as porcupines and raccoons. In the late fall they headed to the nearby prairies to hunt buffalo. Miamis dried the meat of the animals so that it would keep over the winter months. They made warm clothing for cool weather out of the animal skins and fur.

REVIEW What kind of houses did the Miamis have? How did they build them?

Government and the Miamis

Groups of Miamis continued to build new settlements in the area that is now Indiana. In time, the Miami people formed the largest group of Native Americans in what is now central Indiana.

Miami Indians used clay pots like this one for cooking food.

DEMOCRATIC VALUES
Constitutional Government

The Miamis divided power among different leaders and groups in their government. Military chiefs had certain powers, and civil chiefs had other powers. Female chiefs had separate powers from male chiefs.

The separation of powers is also part of the United States government. As stated in the Constitution of the United States, the United States government is divided into three branches with separate powers. The legislative branch makes the laws. The executive branch, led by the President, carries out the laws. The judicial branch interprets, or explains, the laws. The Miamis and the United States government separated powers in different ways, but each benefited from the same good idea.

Analyze the Value

❶ How is the separation of powers in Miami government similar to the separation of powers in the United States government?

❷ Why is the separation of powers a good idea?

United States Constitution

❸ **Make It Relevant**   Make two diagrams illustrating the separation of powers. The first diagram should show the separation of powers among the Miami chiefs. The second diagram should show the separation of powers in the United States government. Share your diagrams and compare them with those of your classmates.

Like other large groups of people, the Miamis had a government, or a system for deciding what is best for a group. A government sets up ways to protect its citizens from other groups. It also sets up ways to settle disagreements among the group's own members. A government makes rules. Leaders help make decisions in a government.

The leaders of the Miami people were called chiefs. The position of chief was **hereditary** (huh•REH•duh•tair•ee), or passed between family members. When important decisions needed to be made, such as whether to go to war, groups of advisers, or a **council**, formed to discuss the issue. Chiefs usually made up the councils.

Each Miami village had two kinds of chiefs, military chiefs and civil chiefs. Each chief had special jobs, or responsibilities. Military chiefs had jobs related to war. They planned when to fight and organized war ceremonies. Both men and women could become military chiefs. The women prepared supplies for those

System of Government
for the Miami Tribe

Council of Chiefs

Village Chiefs   Village Chiefs

Civil Chief   Military Chief   Civil Chief   Military Chief

Analyze Diagrams   The Council of Chiefs met to decide on important matters that affected the entire Miami people.

◆ What two kinds of chiefs did Miami villages have?

A CLOSER LOOK
A Miami Village

Miami villages were much like the settlements of many other Eastern Woodlands groups.

1. Miamis grew crops in fields near the village. Miami men cleared the land for the fields. Miami women planted, raised, and harvested the crops.

2. Miamis built houses called wigwams. The wigwams were placed all around the village. One or two families lived in each wigwam.

3. Forests supplied firewood and materials for building homes and making canoes. Miami men hunted in the woods. Miami women gathered nuts, berries, and other foods there.

4. The Miamis located their villages near water. Rivers and lakes provided fresh drinking water, fish, and a means of transportation.

What are some ways Miamis used natural resources in their villages?

going to fight. The men led the groups of warriors.

Civil chiefs took care of village business. The men helped keep the peace among Miami groups. Women chiefs helped settle disagreements among people within their tribe. The women were also in charge of feasts.

REVIEW What were the responsibilities of the civil chiefs?

Miami Culture

Miamis lived in clans. A **clan** is a group of closely related people. Some of the larger Miami villages had as many as three clans.

Miami families divided jobs between women and men. Women planted, raised, and harvested crops. They also cooked meals, sewed clothes, and took care of the children. Men cleared land, made tools and weapons, and fought their enemies. Many times, their responsibilities took them away from home. Men left their settlements, sometimes for long periods, to hunt and fight.

GEOGRAPHY THEME **Human–Environment Interactions** **Most Miamis who came to what is today Indiana settled near rivers.**

❖ What advantages did rivers offer the Miamis?

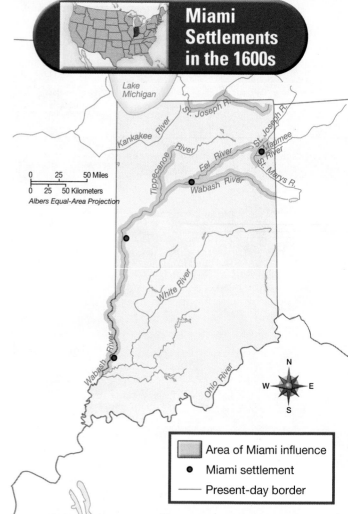
Miami Settlements in the 1600s

Lake Michigan
St. Joseph R.
Kankakee River
Tippecanoe River
Eel River
St. Joseph R.
Maumee River
St. Marys R.
Wabash River
White River
Wabash River
Ohio River

0 25 50 Miles
0 25 50 Kilometers
Albers Equal-Area Projection

N W E S

☐ Area of Miami influence
● Miami settlement
— Present-day border

Like many Native American groups, the Miamis believed that the world around them was full of spirits. They believed that spirits lived in animals, such as bears, snakes, and wildcats, as well as in natural events such as thunder, lightning, and wind. Miamis offered gifts of tobacco to an underwater spirit so they could catch many fish. They also offered gifts to spirits to have a successful hunt.

The Miami people gathered often for religious events. They held festivals to honor the spirits. They also had ceremonies to mark the harvesting of crops and the return of successful warriors.

REVIEW **Why did the Miami people offer gifts to the spirits?**

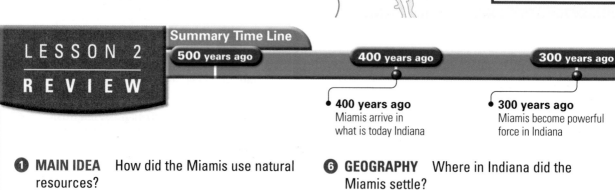

LESSON 2 REVIEW

Summary Time Line

500 years ago	400 years ago	300 years ago

400 years ago
Miamis arrive in what is today Indiana

300 years ago
Miamis become powerful force in Indiana

❶ **MAIN IDEA** How did the Miamis use natural resources?

❷ **WHY IT MATTERS** How are the ways we meet our basic needs today similar to Miami ways?

❸ **VOCABULARY** Use the terms **headwaters** and **portage** to describe the location of the Miami settlement of Kekionga.

❹ **TIME LINE** After the Miami people arrived in what is today Indiana, how many years did it take for them to become a powerful force in the area?

❺ **READING SKILL—Summarize** What were some of the Miamis' religious beliefs?

❻ **GEOGRAPHY** Where in Indiana did the Miamis settle?

❼ **CIVICS AND GOVERNMENT** Who was most likely to represent the Miamis at council meetings?

❽ **CRITICAL THINKING—Analyze** What were the benefits of having two kinds of chiefs in each Miami village?

 PERFORMANCE—Make a Diorama Use a shoebox to create a scene that shows how the Miamis lived. To complete your diorama, reread the information about Miami villages. Display your diorama in the classroom.

Other Native American Groups

| 12,000 years ago | 6,000 years ago | PRESENT |

400 years ago–200 years ago

MAIN IDEA
As you read, compare the cultures of different groups of Native Americans who came to live in what is today Indiana.

WHY IT MATTERS
Just as in the past, Indiana today is a place of many cultures.

VOCABULARY
immediate family
extended family
ancestor

After the Miami people settled in the Wabash River valley, other Indians of the Eastern Woodlands came to live in what is now Indiana. Many of these groups came from the eastern United States. For hundreds of years many Native Americans had hunted and farmed land along the Atlantic coast. When Europeans began building settlements there in the 1600s and 1700s, Native Americans had to find new places to live. They moved west. Many different groups of Native Americans eventually made their way to what is now Indiana.

Native American groups from the Great Lakes also moved into Indiana. European settlers and wars with other Native Americans drove them off their lands. These groups moved south into what is today western and northwestern Indiana.

The Delawares

In the 1770s the Delawares, also known as the Lenni Lenape (len•NAH•pay), or just Lenape, arrived in Indiana. They had slowly moved west from their homeland, located in what are today Pennsylvania, New Jersey, New York, and Delaware. In the early 1700s European settlers had forced the Delawares off their lands in the East. First they settled in what is today Ohio, near the Ohio River and its tributaries. Then the Miami people invited the Delawares to live south of them, along the White River in what is now central Indiana.

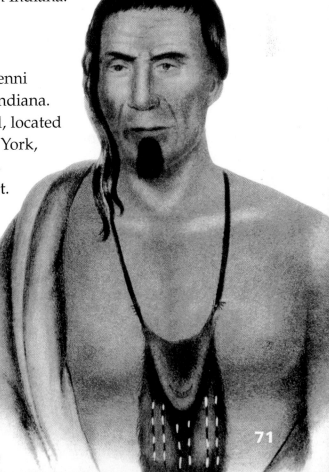

After the Delawares were driven from their homes in the eastern United States, they settled in what is today central Indiana.

71

The Delawares built longhouses 50 to 150 feet (15 to 46 m) in length. As many as 60 people might live in one of these buildings.

The Delawares set up many villages in their new location. Many of the Delaware people lived in villages along the west fork of the White River between what are now the cities of Muncie and Indianapolis. Near their villages they raised beans, squash, and corn in the rich soil. Men camped and hunted and harvested sugar from maple trees. Women cared for children, gathered firewood, made clothing, and raised crops. The Delawares traded maple sugar as well as fur and skins from deer, bear, and beaver.

The Delawares lived in wigwams as well as

Native Americans made arrowheads from a kind of rock called flint.

longhouses. Many Delaware villages also included a sweat lodge. Inside the lodge the Delawares poured cold water over heated stones to make steam. After sitting in this moist heat, they would jump into the cool water nearby. The Delawares believed this practice made a person's body pure, or clean.

The Delawares also had a special building called the Big House for one of their most important rituals. The Big House itself stood for the universe. For 12 days and nights, the Delawares prayed to their Creator of the universe and their spirits in the world around them. They gave thanks for their crops. They also thanked the spirits for protection from dangerous storms, floods, and earthquakes.

REVIEW What kinds of buildings were part of a Delaware village?

The Shawnees

Like the Delawares, the Shawnees came to what is now Indiana from the East. In the 1600s the Iroquois drove the Shawnees out of their homeland in the Ohio River valley. After moving to different places in the East and the Southeast, the Shawnees finally returned to the Ohio area. European settlers forced the Shawnees off that land in the late 1700s. A group of Shawnees moved to what is now Indiana when the Delawares invited them to settle on the White River.

In many ways Shawnee life was similar to that of other Eastern Woodlands groups, including the Delawares and the Miamis. The Shawnees lived in wigwams made of poles and bark or animal hides. Besides wigwams their villages included a council house for meetings and ceremonies.

For the Shawnees the village was important, but the family was even more important. The **immediate family**, made up of the father, mother, and children, was the most meaningful. The Shawnees shared their living space with only their immediate family. Like other Native Americans, they also valued their extended families. An **extended family** included the immediate family plus grandparents, aunts, uncles, and other relatives.

During most of the year, Shawnee women farmed and Shawnee men hunted. When it was time for the winter hunt, Shawnee families traveled as a group. Shawnee villages became empty when families spent the winter in hunting camps.

The Shawnees marked the other seasons with ceremonies. They held a ceremony before spring planting.

Shawnee women tended the crops in their villages (below). They used wooden hoes (right) to help them care for their crops.

This special event was called the Bread Dance. Before the dance Shawnee men and women played a ball game. They kept score with kernels of corn. The women chiefs planted the kernels after the game. When the ceremony was over, the Shawnees planted their entire corn crop for the season.

REVIEW Where did the Shawnees live in the winter?

The Potawatomi

The Potawatomi (pot•uh•WOT•uh•mee) came to the land now called Indiana from the area around the Great Lakes. They had lived between Lake Michigan and Lake Huron until the Iroquois pushed them west into Wisconsin. Later, the Potawatomi moved back into Michigan and south into Illinois. By the end of the 1700s, groups of Potawatomi had settled in the Indiana area. They set up villages along the St. Joseph River and the Tippecanoe River, as well as the upper part of the Wabash River. They also built settlements on the southern shore of Lake Michigan.

Like other Native American groups, the Potawatomi used their surroundings to meet their needs. They, too, lived in wigwams covered with bark or reed mats. The soil of the lake shores and river valleys where they settled was good for farming. They also fished, hunted, and gathered food. Potawatomi men and women divided these jobs much like other Native Americans did.

The clan, or dodem (DO•duhm), was the most important group among the Potawatomi. Every person belonged to a clan. According to the Potawatomi, clans included not only living people

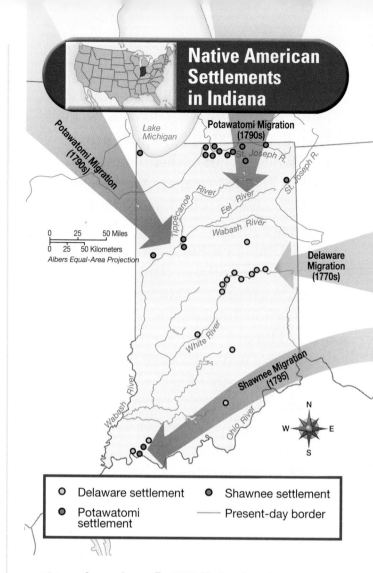

Native American Settlements in Indiana

Potawatomi Migration (1790s)

Potawatomi Migration (1790s)

Delaware Migration (1770s)

Shawnee Migration (1795)

0 25 50 Miles
0 25 50 Kilometers
Albers Equal-Area Projection

○ Delaware settlement   ● Shawnee settlement
● Potawatomi settlement   — Present-day border

GEOGRAPHY THEME

Location By 1800 Native Americans had settled in nearly every part of what is today Indiana.

? From what direction did the Potawatomi migrate to what is today Indiana?

but also the dead and people not yet born. A clan traced its beginnings to a common **ancestor**, or early family member. Membership in a clan was based on a person's male relatives.

Men lived in the same community with other members of their clan. Women went to live with their husband's clan when they married, but they remained members of their own clan. Clan members shared property. If any one clan was threatened, all the clans joined forces to protect one another.

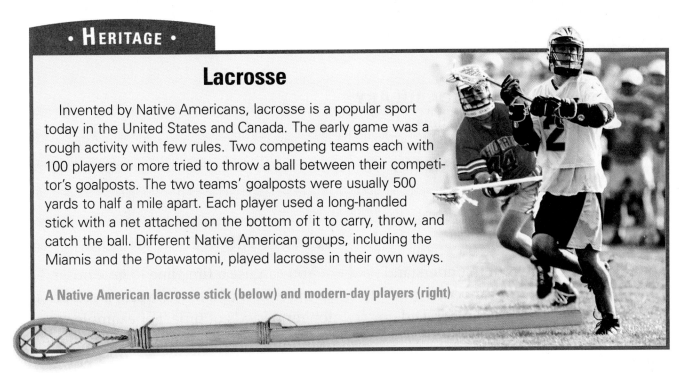

Lacrosse

Invented by Native Americans, lacrosse is a popular sport today in the United States and Canada. The early game was a rough activity with few rules. Two competing teams each with 100 players or more tried to throw a ball between their competitor's goalposts. The two teams' goalposts were usually 500 yards to half a mile apart. Each player used a long-handled stick with a net attached on the bottom of it to carry, throw, and catch the ball. Different Native American groups, including the Miamis and the Potawatomi, played lacrosse in their own ways.

A Native American lacrosse stick (below) and modern-day players (right)

No one person had authority, or power, over all the Potawatomi people. Each clan and village had a leader, or wkama (WAH•kah•maw). The leaders formed a council, or wkamek (WAH•kah•mek), that met to discuss matters that affected many Potawatomi clans and villages. The council did not give commands. Instead, it gave advice or suggestions that the Potawatomi people might follow.

REVIEW What was the most important group among the Potawatomi?

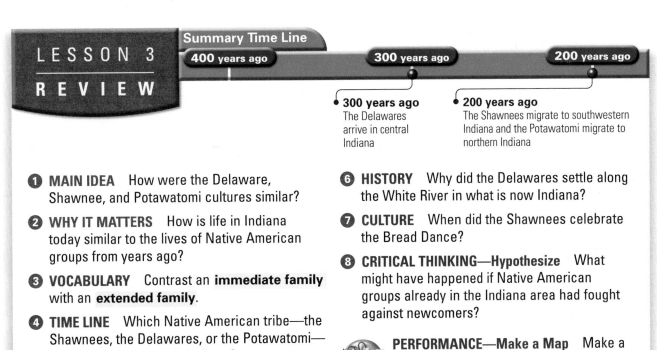

LESSON 3
REVIEW

Summary Time Line

400 years ago   300 years ago   200 years ago

300 years ago
The Delawares arrive in central Indiana

200 years ago
The Shawnees migrate to southwestern Indiana and the Potawatomi migrate to northern Indiana

1 **MAIN IDEA** How were the Delaware, Shawnee, and Potawatomi cultures similar?

2 **WHY IT MATTERS** How is life in Indiana today similar to the lives of Native American groups from years ago?

3 **VOCABULARY** Contrast an **immediate family** with an **extended family**.

4 **TIME LINE** Which Native American tribe—the Shawnees, the Delawares, or the Potawatomi—was the first to settle in Indiana?

5 **READING SKILL—Summarize** Why did other Native American groups come in the 1700s to what is now Indiana?

6 **HISTORY** Why did the Delawares settle along the White River in what is now Indiana?

7 **CULTURE** When did the Shawnees celebrate the Bread Dance?

8 **CRITICAL THINKING—Hypothesize** What might have happened if Native American groups already in the Indiana area had fought against newcomers?

PERFORMANCE—Make a Map Make a map of Indiana that includes major rivers. Use different color markers to show where the different Native American tribes settled. Display your completed map in your classroom.

Read a Time Line

VOCABULARY

time line
decade
century

▶ WHY IT MATTERS

Sometimes it is helpful to understand when important events happened and how events relate to one another. Did glaciers cover Indiana before or after mammoths lived there?

Time lines can help you find out when important events took place. A **time line** is a diagram that shows when events took place. It shows the order in which events happened and the amount of time that passed between events. Putting events in the order in which they took place can help you understand how one event relates to another.

▶ WHAT YOU NEED TO KNOW

You can use a time line to give order to the events of a day, a week, a year, or longer periods of time. For example, you could use a time line to list events in the order in which they happen on a normal school day. Such events might include doing homework, brushing your teeth before going to bed, eating your lunch, and riding or walking to school. Your time line should look somewhat like Time Line A, with the events added.

To complete the time line, mark the earliest event, riding or walking to school, on the left side of the time line, in between 7 A.M. and 12 noon. Mark the last event, brushing your teeth before going to bed, on the right side of the time line, between 5 P.M. and 10 P.M.

Time Line A

| 7:00 | 12:00 | 5:00 | 10:00 |
| A.M. | noon | P.M. | P.M. |

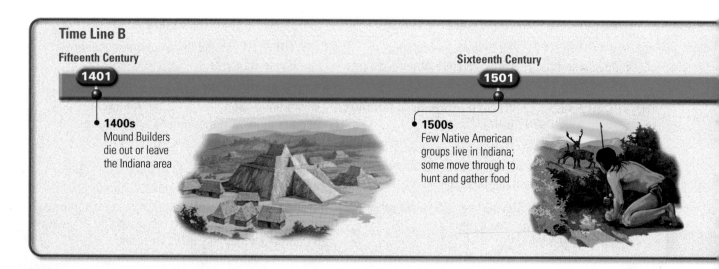

Time Line B

Fifteenth Century

1401

Sixteenth Century

1501

1400s
Mound Builders die out or leave the Indiana area

1500s
Few Native American groups live in Indiana; some move through to hunt and gather food

Sometimes time lines are organized by decades. A **decade** lasts for ten years. It begins with a year such as 1901, 1911, or 1921, and ends in a year such as 1910, 1920, or 1930. Most of you were probably born in the 1990s. Perhaps your parents were born in the 1960s. A time line could help you organize that information.

Time Line B shows when important events in the early history of Indiana took place. The marks on the line stand for points in time. On this time line, the space between two marks stands for one **century**, or 100 years. A century is a unit of time just as a day, week, month, or year is a unit of time. The earlier dates are near the left end of the time line. The dates near the right end of the time line are later.

The first event on Time Line B marks the time when the Mound Builders died out or left what is now the state of Indiana. This event took place sometime in the fifteenth century, or between the years 1401 and 1500.

▶ **PRACTICE THE SKILL**

Use Time Line B to answer these questions.

1 What important event happened in the 1500s?

2 When did the Miami Indians first arrive in what is now Indiana?

3 In what century did the Miamis settle near the Maumee River?

▶ **APPLY WHAT YOU LEARNED**

Make a time line that shows the end of the twentieth century and the beginning of the twenty-first century. The twentieth century began in 1901, and the twenty-first century began in 2001. Mark the current year. Mark important years of your life. Mark the year that you were born, the year that you started first grade, and the year that you will begin high school. Add pictures of the first two events you have marked. Then display your time line on a bulletin board in your classroom.

Seventeenth Century
1601

Eighteenth Century
1701

1600s
Miamis settle near the
Maumee River and build
the settlement of Kekionga

CD 3
Track 8

2 Review and Test Preparation

12,000 years ago
Native Americans
arrive in Indiana

USE YOUR READING SKILLS

Complete this graphic organizer to help you summarize
what you learned in Chapter 2 about early people in Indiana.
A copy of this graphic organizer appears on page 25 of the
Activity Book.

The Early People of Indiana

KEY POINTS	SUMMARY
Lesson 1: The Land and People Long Ago	Summary:
Lesson 2: The Miami People	Summary:
Lesson 3: Other Native American Groups	Summary:

THINK & WRITE

Write an Invitation Imagine you are a
Native American living in the 1700s in the
area that will become Indiana. You hear that
European settlers and the Iroquois are driving
many Native American groups off their lands.
Write an invitation to these groups to come
live near you. Give reasons you think they
should come. Provide facts and details to
support your reasons.

Describe a Place Think about what the
land in what is now Indiana was like when
the climate changed about 10,000 years
ago. Using what you have learned, write
a descriptive paragraph about the land
then. Include details that appeal to the
five senses—sight, hearing, smell, taste,
and touch. Share your paragraph with other
students in your class.

1,000 years ago
Mound Builders
live in Indiana

400 years ago
Miamis arrive
in what is today
Indiana

300 years ago
Delawares
come to central
Indiana

200 years ago
Shawnees migrate to southwestern
Indiana and Potawatomi
migrate to northern Indiana

USE THE TIME LINE

Use the chapter time line to answer these questions.

1 How long after the Miamis arrived in what is today Indiana did the Shawnees migrate to southwestern Indiana?

2 When did the Delawares come to central Indiana?

USE VOCABULARY

Fill in the blanks with the correct terms.

migrate (p. 58)

cooperate (p. 59)

extinct (p. 60)

hereditary (p. 68)

ancestor (p. 74)

3 Mastodons and mammoths are now _____.

4 To hunt large animals, people had to _____.

5 The Miami position of chief was _____.

6 People from Asia might have been able to _____ to North America across a strip of land.

7 Clan members had a common _____.

RECALL FACTS

Answer these questions.

8 Why did some of the early people in North America first make their way to the land that is now Indiana?

9 Where did the Miami Indians settle in what is now Indiana?

10 Which Native American groups came to the Indiana area from the East?

Write the letter of the best choice.

11 **TEST PREP**   The Miamis built the village of Kekionga at the headwaters of —
  A Lake Michigan.
  B the Maumee River.
  C the Ohio River.
  D the Atlantic coast.

12 **TEST PREP**   In the Big House ceremony, the Delawares gave thanks for —
  F a new place to live.
  G the return of warriors.
  H everything in the universe.
  J their crops.

THINK CRITICALLY

13 How did a system of government benefit the Miami tribe? Explain your answer.

14 How do you think the Miamis felt about other Native American groups moving into the Indiana area?

15 What do you think were the advantages of the Potawatomi wkamek, or council, which gave suggestions but not commands?

APPLY SKILLS

Identify Cause and Effect

16 Identify an event that is described in this chapter. Make a cause-and-effect diagram to show the causes that led to the event.

Read a Time Line

17 Look at the time line on pages 76–77. Which groups of Native Americans settled in what is today Indiana in the seventeenth century?

VISIT

THE INDIANA DUNES
NATIONAL LAKESHORE

GET READY

The Indiana Dunes National Lakeshore runs for nearly 25 miles (40 km) along the shore of Lake Michigan and covers more than 15,000 acres of land. It was created in 1966 to preserve the natural areas along Lake Michigan. Natural forces shape the dunes along the beach. The winds that blow across Lake Michigan sweep across the beaches, picking up grains of sand. As the winds are slowed by plants and hills, they drop the sand in new places. Wind, water, and waves form an ever-changing mountain of sand, more than 100 feet (30 m) high, known as Mount Baldy. Trees and grass cannot keep this huge, shifting sand dune in one place.

LOCATE IT

Indiana Dunes National Lakeshore

INDIANA

The shifting sand dunes cover trees and then, years later, uncover tree graveyards.

The Cedar Waxwing is one of more than 250 types of birds that have been spotted at the Indiana Dunes National Lakeshore.

More than 200 types of wildflowers can be found at the Indiana Dunes National Lakeshore.

The plant life found in the sandy lakefront and the island forests is quite different. To protect the area and prevent erosion, activities such as hiking are permitted only on marked trails.

TAKE A FIELD TRIP

GO ONLINE

A VIRTUAL TOUR
Visit The Learning Site at **www.harcourtschool.com/tours** to take virtual tours of other parks and scenic areas.

CD 3
Track 10

1 Review and Test Preparation

USE VOCABULARY

For each pair of terms, write a sentence or two that explains how the terms are related.

1 **natural resource** (p. 21), **product** (p. 40)

2 **tributary** (p. 35), **river system** (p. 36)

3 **band** (p. 59), **tribe** (p. 61)

4 **hereditary** (p. 68), **ancestor** (p. 74)

RECALL FACTS

Answer these questions.

5 What are Indiana's three natural regions?

6 Which crops are most important to Indiana?

7 What is Indiana's longest river?

8 How did the lives of early hunters change after the giant animals died out?

9 Before 1600, what groups lived in the region that became Indiana?

Write the letter of the best choice.

10 **TEST PREP** The natural region of Indiana that has the most fertile soil is the—
A Great Lakes Plain.
B Central Till Plain.
C Middle West.
D Southern Hills and Lowlands.

11 **TEST PREP** The largest reservoir in Indiana is—
F Patoka Lake.
G Lake Wawasee.
H the Cecil M. Harden Reservoir.
J Lake Monroe.

12 **TEST PREP** Indiana's most important mineral resource is—
A gypsum.
B limestone.
C coal.
D oil.

13 **TEST PREP** The Miami settlement at the headwaters of the Maumee River was called—
F Kekionga.
G Fort Miami.
H Delaware.
J Vincennes.

14 **TEST PREP** The Native American group that had both military chiefs and civil chiefs was the—
A Shawnees.
B Potawatomi.
C Delawares.
D Miamis.

THINK CRITICALLY

15 In what ways do landforms and water features affect how and where people live?

16 How do Earth and the sun affect the climate of Indiana?

17 How did the Miamis handle conflict and cooperation?

18 In what ways is your life similar to that of the early Native American groups in Indiana? In what ways is it different?

APPLY SKILLS

Read an Elevation Map
Use the elevation map on this page to answer the following questions.

MAP AND GLOBE SKILLS

19 What is the elevation of the land along the east coast of Canada?

20 Where is the highest point in North America? What is its elevation? What is the lowest point? What is its elevation?

21 Which mountains are higher, the Appalachian Mountains or the Sierra Madre Occidental? How do you know?

22 How would you describe the change in elevation in the middle of the United States?

Elevations of North America

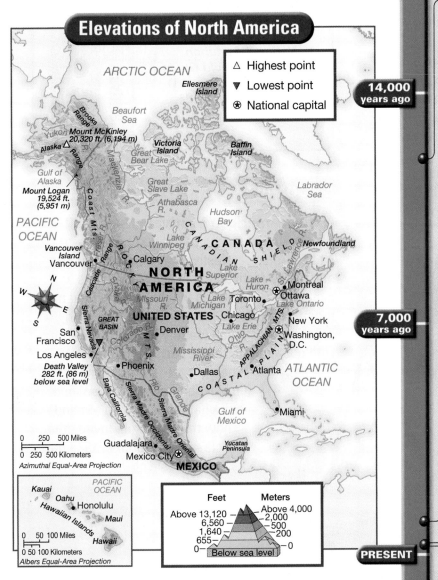

Legend:
△ Highest point
▼ Lowest point
✶ National capital

ARCTIC OCEAN
Ellesmere Island
Beaufort Sea
Brooks Range
Yukon
Mount McKinley 20,320 ft. (6,194 m)
Alaska
Victoria Island
Baffin Island
Great Bear Lake
Gulf of Alaska
Mount Logan 19,524 ft. (5,951 m)
Great Slave Lake
Athabasca R.
Labrador Sea
PACIFIC OCEAN
Mackenzie R.
Hudson Bay
Coast Mts.
Fraser R.
Lake Winnipeg
CANADA
Newfoundland
Vancouver Island
Vancouver
Rocky Range
Calgary
CANADIAN SHIELD
St. Lawrence R.
Snake R.
NORTH AMERICA
Lake Superior
Cascade Range
Sierra Nevada
Missouri R.
Lake Michigan
Lake Huron
Montreal
Ottawa
Toronto
Lake Ontario
GREAT BASIN
UNITED STATES
Chicago
Lake Erie
New York
San Francisco
Colorado R.
Denver
Ohio R.
APPALACHIAN MTS.
Washington, D.C.
Los Angeles
Death Valley 282 ft. (86 m) below sea level
Mississippi River
Phoenix
Dallas
Atlanta
COASTAL PLAIN
ATLANTIC OCEAN
Baja California
Rio Grande
Sierra Madre Occidental
Sierra Madre Oriental
Gulf of Mexico
Miami
N W E S
0 250 500 Miles
0 250 500 Kilometers
Azimuthal Equal-Area Projection
Guadalajara
Mexico City
Yucatan Peninsula
MEXICO

PACIFIC OCEAN
Kauai
Oahu
Honolulu
Hawaiian Islands
Maui
Hawaii
0 50 100 Miles
0 50 100 Kilometers
Albers Equal-Area Projection

Feet	Meters
Above 13,120	Above 4,000
6,560	2,000
1,640	500
655	200
0	0
Below sea level	

28,000 years ago Early people begin to come to North America p. 58

12,000 years ago Early people arrive in what is now Indiana p. 58

1,000 years ago Mound Builders live in what is now Indiana p. 62

300 years ago Miamis become successful traders p. 67

200 years ago Delawares settle in what is today central Indiana p. 71

21,000 years ago

14,000 years ago

7,000 years ago

PRESENT

Unit Activities

Visit The Learning Site at
www.harcourtschool.com/
socialstudies/activities
for additional activities.

Create a Brochure

Create a brochure to interest people in visiting Indiana. Make the brochure from a sheet of paper folded in thirds. Write a catchy slogan about Indiana for the front of the brochure. On the inside panels, provide illustrations and information about the geography of Indiana. On the back panel, draw a map that shows the state's natural regions and locates physical features of interest. Display your brochure in your classroom.

Make a Museum Display

With a small group, put together a museum display about the early peoples of Indiana. Focus on one of the following groups: the Mound Builders, the Miamis, the Delawares, the Shawnees, or the Potawatomi. Create copies of artifacts or objects the group might have used in daily life. Write descriptions that tell about the artifacts. Set up your display on a table or in a display case in your classroom or the school library.

VISIT YOUR LIBRARY

- **The Year of No More Corn** by Helen Ketteman. Orchard Books.

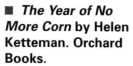

- **The Shawnees (People of the Eastern Woodlands)** by Laurie A. O'Neill. Millbrook Press.

- **National Audubon Society First Field Guide: Weather** by Jonathan D. Kahl. Scholastic Trade.

COMPLETE THE UNIT PROJECT

Native American Festival Work with classmates to complete the unit project—a Native American festival. As a class, organize and hold a festival that Native Americans might have celebrated in what is now Indiana. It can be a festival mentioned in the text or another festival you identify through research. Find out about different parts of the festival: special ceremonies, games, music, and dancing. Also, find out what foods people ate and how they dressed. Invite other classes to watch or take part in the festival.

Europeans Settle Indiana

General Anthony Wayne's
Peace Medal, 1795

Historic Fort Wayne, a reconstruction of the fort built in 1815

CD 4
Track 1

Europeans Settle Indiana

66 To put an end to a destructive war, to settle all controversies, and to restore harmony . . . 99

—Beginning of the Treaty of Greenville, 1795

Preview the Content

Read the lesson titles and the Main Idea statements for each lesson. Write a paragraph telling what you think each lesson is about. After reading each lesson, check your paragraph, and correct it if needed.

Preview the Vocabulary

Parts of Speech   Parts of speech include nouns, adjectives, and verbs. Use the Glossary to look up each word listed below. Then write a sentence that shows you understand each word's meaning and its part of speech.

UNITE	PERMANENT	CENSUS
↓	↓	↓
verb	adjective	noun

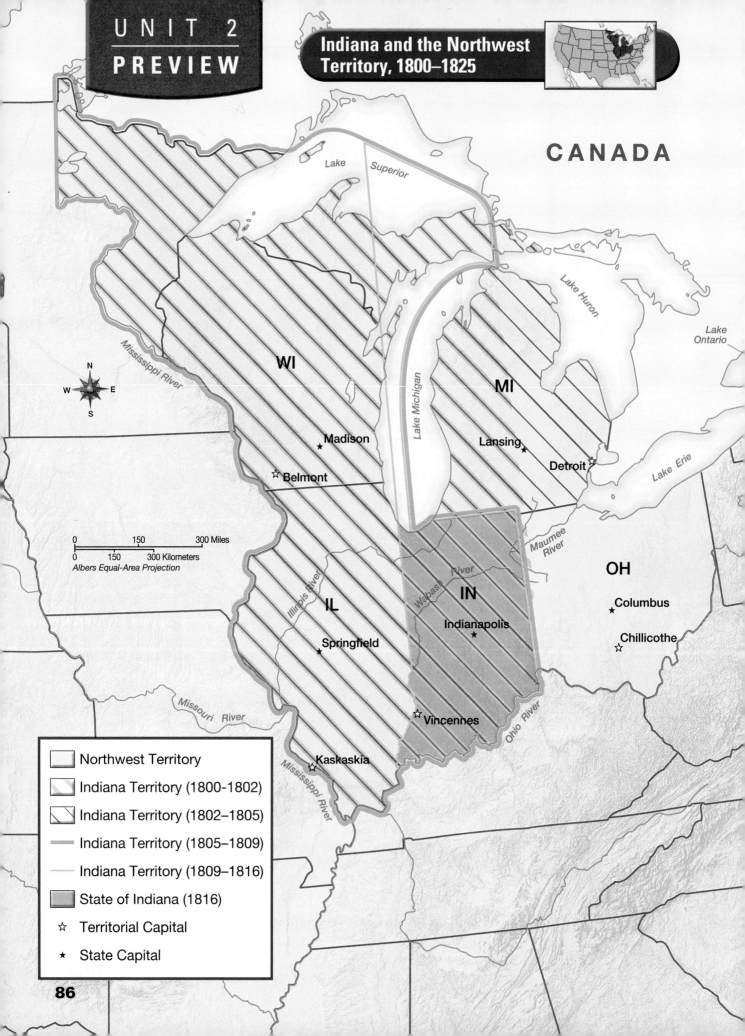

CANADA

Lake Superior

Lake Huron

Lake Ontario

Lake Michigan

Lake Erie

WI

MI

Mississippi River

★ Madison

☆ Belmont

Lansing ★

Detroit ☆

0   150   300 Miles
0   150   300 Kilometers
Albers Equal-Area Projection

Maumee River

OH

Wabash River

Illinois River

IN

★ Columbus

IL

Springfield ★

Indianapolis ★

Chillicothe ☆

Missouri River

☆ Vincennes

Ohio River

☆ Kaskaskia

Mississippi River

Legend:

	Northwest Territory
	Indiana Territory (1800–1802)
	Indiana Territory (1802–1805)
	Indiana Territory (1805–1809)
	Indiana Territory (1809–1816)
	State of Indiana (1816)
☆	Territorial Capital
★	State Capital

From Territory to Statehood, 1798–1848

Territory	State/Order of Admission to the Union	Date of Admission to the Union
Ohio Territory, 1798–1803	Ohio/ 17th state	March 1, 1803
Indiana Territory, 1800–1816	Indiana/ 19th state	December 11, 1816
Illinois Territory, 1809–1818	Illinois/ 21st state	December 3, 1818
Michigan Territory, 1805–1837	Michigan/ 26th state	January 26, 1837
Wisconsin Territory, 1836–1848	Wisconsin/ 30th state	May 29, 1848

Indiana's Population Growth, 1800–1820

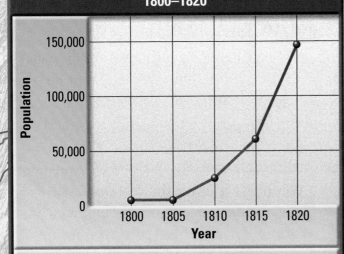

Reaching a population of 5,000 free men enabled Indiana to become a territory.

Reaching a population of 60,000 free adults enabled Indiana to become a state.

Key Events

1679   La Salle explores the Indiana area p. 95

1763   French and Indian War ends p. 104

1779   George Rogers Clark captures Fort Sackville pp. 113–114

1810   Tecumseh meets with William Henry Harrison at Vincennes p. 128

1816   Indiana becomes the nineteenth state p. 137

1675

1725

1775

1825

CD 4
Track 2

Ollie's Cabin in the Woods

by Robert and Katheryn Hessong

Young Oliver Johnson and his family moved from near Brookville, Indiana, to Indianapolis in 1822. Their homestead—mostly woods and wetlands—was located on the western banks of Fall Creek. Ollie and his family worked with their neighbors to set up a community on the north side of Indianapolis, near where the State Fairgrounds is located today. Read to find out more about pioneer life in early Indiana.

Digging the Well

Pap got busy finding an elm pole to use so he could dig our well for water. He used this elm pole for a sweep that he attached to a crotched tree located at the site of the future waterhole. On the end of the elm pole he fastened a rope tied to a wooden bucket brought from our former home. This apparatus would serve to lift the water out of the well after it was dug. For now Pap could use it to lift the dirt out as he dug the well. The water level in this place was only eighteen to twenty feet deep. After much dirt had been removed from the hole, his shovel hit a clean gravel bed with water. He built a three feet high box from puncheons, which were shaved slices of a tree. This box needed to fit around the top of the open well. I got many a good drink from that place!

The year's corn crop had to be planted as soon as the earth warmed from winter. Again the almost three acres would have to feed our family and animals that next season. So as soon as the well was done, it was planting time.

crotched	angled or forked intersection of tree branches
apparatus	an instrument designed for a specific use

Neighbors Help Build Our Barn

With the season of winter ahead, Pap knew the barn had to be built next. Our oxen, chickens, pigs, and milk cow provided us with either workpower or food. Thus a warm shelter from the unknown winters here was a necessity.

To begin with, Pap and his brothers, who were starting their own farms in the New Purchase area near our farm, gathered in some large logs to frame the barn. After the foundation logs were put into place, a barn-raising was called. At this time all of the neighbors came and the men put the barn together while the women brought their special dishes of food for the feast that was a part of these special days. Some of the children helped with the project while younger ones played and enjoyed themselves.

New Purchase   name given to newly opened land around Indianapolis

At times women and girls brought dishes for which they were famous or with which they hoped to secure a community reputation. Cooperative enterprises such as this barn raising were popular and needed among the pioneers; and they might also include log cabin raising, harvesting, and hog butchering for the men, as well as quiltings and apple parings for the women. These times, as I grew older, were some of the most memorable occasions of my youth. It was important that you took the time to help your neighbors after they had been generous with their time to help you.

enterprises   difficult or complicated projects
quiltings   get-togethers where quilts are made
apple parings   get-togethers where apples are prepared for cooking

Pap Clears More Land

All around us were endless trees. The forest was a problem for pioneers who needed to cultivate the land for food. With a growing family, Pap needed more than the three acres he cleared last year. He first cut trees that were small such as eighteen inches or less in diameter. After the trees were felled, the smaller trees were dragged and stacked against the larger trees. Oxen pulled bushes and grubs out by their roots. All of these unusable forest parts were fired and burned. As the trees burned, we had to continue to readjust the burning timbers and bushes so that all were turned to ash. Eyes of the pioneers stung from the constant wood smoke. Pap's objective was to get rid of as many trees as possible in a short time. The Johnson family's food supply of corn needed to be planted.

Larger trees had to wait until the third year of Pap's ownership of the land.

The largest trees were girdled when he had time before crop harvest. To girdle a tree, he used his adz to chop out the bark and make a ring around the oak, poplar, or ash trees. This injury to the tree would stop the flow of food to the leaves from the soil, and the tree would die. A dry, lifeless tree is easier to cut.

Pap Builds a Cabin Loft

Shortly after my first birthday, winter came. Pap's second harvest of corn was done, and he knew it was time to enlarge the eighteen-by-twenty-foot cabin. Since pioneer families had many children, he wanted to be ready.

Building a sleeping loft in the space overhead was a task for the cold season.

adz   (also adze) a cutting tool used for shaping wood

cultivate   to prepare, such as by plowing, for the raising of crops
diameter   the length of a straight line through the center of an object
felled   cut down
grubs   stumps
objective   goal

Pap placed wood planks on the cross-beams of the cabin. These crossbeams rest on the top logs of the cabin's side walls. When the planks were in tightly the room now had a flat ceiling over half of it. Steps to reach the loft were carved into a poplar log that had a diameter of two feet. This ladder was placed against a wall, and Pap added rails so that climbing into the loft was safer.

As I grew older, I slept in this warm loft with my brothers: Luther, Volney, and Newton. Always we were so tired by the time we crawled up to the loft, sleep came immediately. Since the fireplace heat rises, this place was very warm and comfortable.

Analyze the Literature

1. Why do you think that digging the family well was important to the Johnsons?

2. In what ways did pioneer families get together and help each other?

3. Imagine you are taking part in a barn-raising or other community event. Write a journal entry describing your day.

READ A BOOK

START THE UNIT PROJECT

A Historical Medal Work in a small group to create a medal marking a key event in the history of Indiana before it became a state in 1816. As you read this unit, take notes about the key people and events. Your notes will help you decide what to show in your historical medal.

USE TECHNOLOGY

Visit The Learning Site at **www.harcourtschool.com/ socialstudies** for additional activities, primary sources, and other resources to use in this unit.

GUILDIN PARK IN FORT WAYNE

Visitors to Guildin Park can see the reconstructed fort of General Anthony Wayne. Wayne's army defeated British soldiers during the Revolutionary War. This photograph shows actors recreating a ceremony honoring Veterans Day.

LOCATE IT

Fort Wayne

INDIANA

Claiming the Land

❝ **If a country is not worth protecting, it is not worth claiming.** ❞
—George Rogers Clark, 1775

CHAPTER READING SKILL

Cause and Effect

A **cause** is an event or action that makes something else happen. An **effect** is what happens as a result of that event or action.

As you read this chapter, list the causes and effects of key events.

What Caused the Event	→	Event
CAUSE	→	EFFECT

MAIN IDEA
Read to find out why the French started settlements in what is now Indiana.

WHY IT MATTERS
People today move to new places for a variety of reasons.

VOCABULARY

missionary

colony

fort

scarce

voyageur

permanent

rights

French Explorers and Traders

1550–1750

For thousands of years Native Americans were the only people living in North America. Then in 1492, Christopher Columbus became the first European to sail to what we now call the Americas, the continents of North and South America. After 1500, explorers, traders, and settlers came to North America from Spain, England, and France. Some were looking for new travel routes to Asia. Others wanted land. Still others desired the rich natural resources found in the Americas. The Europeans brought with them ways of life that were very different from those of the Native Americans.

The French Arrive

In the early 1500s French explorers sailed to North America. First, the French explored the northern Atlantic coast of the continent. Then they traveled inland on the St. Lawrence River into what is now Canada and claimed the land for France. They began trading with Native Americans there. French missionaries traveled throughout the region and taught the Native Americans they met about the Christian religion. A **missionary** is a person who teaches his or her religious beliefs to others. By the 1600s the French had founded a colony called New France in the St. Lawrence River valley. A **colony** is a place set up and ruled by another country.

FAST FACT
French explorer La Salle learned how to live off the land from the Native Americans he met. He ate only corn he carried with him and animals he trapped.

From New France the French traveled southwest around the Great Lakes and beyond. The first European known to have visited what is now Indiana was the French explorer René-Robert Cavelier (kah•vuhl•YAY), Sieur (SUHR) de La Salle (luh•SAL).

La Salle wanted to claim land for his native country of France and to expand the French fur trade. He also wanted to find a water route through North America from the Atlantic Ocean to the Pacific Ocean. La Salle made several trips to the region south of the Great Lakes and built forts there. A **fort** is a building that offers protection from an enemy attack.

In late 1679 La Salle set out toward the Mississippi River. With 30 men in eight canoes, he paddled up the River of the Miamis from its mouth on Lake Michigan. Today this waterway is known as the St. Joseph River. After two days La Salle and his group reached the southern bend in the river, where a large Miami village stood. This is where the city of South Bend, Indiana, stands today.

Local villagers told La Salle about a portage to the Kankakee River. He believed that the Kankakee led to the Mississippi River. White Beaver, La Salle's Native American guide, led the travelers to the St. Joseph–Kankakee portage. They carried their canoes and equipment about 5 miles (8 km) over land. Then they paddled down the Kankakee to the place where it empties into the Illinois River. La Salle built a fort there near where the city of Peoria, Illinois, stands today. The explorer then headed back to New France for supplies.

REVIEW Why did La Salle want to explore the Indiana area?

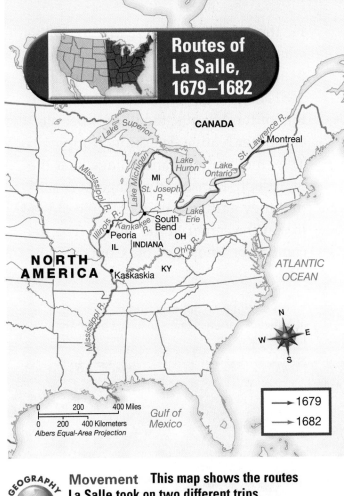

Routes of La Salle, 1679–1682

Movement **This map shows the routes La Salle took on two different trips.**

❓ In which year did La Salle travel through what is today northwestern Indiana?

The Meeting at Council Oak

Two years later, La Salle returned to the Indiana area. He found trouble among the Native Americans there. The Miamis were fighting with the Illinois people, their neighbors to the west. The Delawares and Shawnees were at war with Iroquois tribes from the east. The Iroquois wanted to stop the French from trading with other Native American tribes. They attacked French forts and trading posts as well as Native American villages.

La Salle wanted to protect French trade and land claims in the area.

He thought that the best way to do this was to help Native Americans make peace with one another. In the spring of 1681, La Salle called a council, or meeting, of the Miamis, the Illinois people, and other Native American groups. They met at the Miami village near the St. Joseph–Kankakee portage. It is said that they gathered under a huge old oak tree at the center of the village. The tree came to be known as the Council Oak.

In this drawing, La Salle encourages several groups of Native Americans to make peace under the Council Oak.

During the meeting La Salle urged the chiefs not to fight among themselves but to stand as one against the Iroquois. La Salle promised France's help in fighting their enemy. The Native Americans accepted La Salle's idea for peace. They agreed to come to one another's defense when the Iroquois attacked.

After the Native Americans made peace, La Salle again traveled down the Kankakee River to the Illinois River. Then he followed the Illinois to the Mississippi River. In 1682 La Salle canoed south on the Mississippi to its mouth on the Gulf of Mexico. He claimed the entire Mississippi River valley for France, including the lands drained by the river's tributaries. He named the area *Louisiana* to honor the French king Louis XIV. Indiana was part of this land.

REVIEW **What did La Salle promise the chiefs at Council Oak if they made peace?**

The Fur Trade Grows

After La Salle's death in 1687, the French continued to expand their fur trade. French fur traders traveled through the Wabash River valley, where there were many Native American villages and many fur-bearing animals.

Native Americans trapped animals such as beavers for their fur. The furs were sold in Europe, where beaver fur was **scarce**, or hard to find. Europeans valued beaver hats as a status symbol, or sign of importance or wealth. Because fur products sold for high prices in Europe, the fur trade grew in North America during this time.

Native Americans traded furs for goods made in Europe. European traders offered the Native Americans beads, knives, guns, blankets, shirts, mirrors, and metal pots. Native Americans sometimes used these goods in new ways. A Native American woman might unravel a blanket and use the yarn to make a bag. Some Native Americans cut metal pots into pieces. Then they used the metal pieces to make spearheads and decorations for their clothes. Of course, they also used some blankets for warmth and some metal pots for cooking.

When the French traders gathered a large number of furs, they hired **voyageurs** (voy•uh•ZHERZ) to carry the furs to be sold. *Voyageur* is a French word meaning "traveler."

The voyageurs took the furs by canoe to Montreal, a busy harbor in New France, where the furs were shipped to Europe. At Montreal the voyageurs picked up European goods to trade with Native Americans in what is now Indiana.

REVIEW What did Native Americans get for the furs they traded?

A CLOSER LOOK
A French Fort

In the early 1700s the French built forts in what is now Indiana to control the fur trade.

1. The French and the Native Americans exchanged goods at a trading post inside the fort. Traders and their families lived in cabins near the post. Soldiers and their families lived in the fort.

2. Guards kept watch from blockhouses, or towers, in the corners of the fort.

3. A stockade, or tall, strong fence made of pointed logs, surrounded the buildings in the fort and kept out enemies.

4. People living at the fort grew some of their own food in a nearby garden.

◆ Why do you think forts were sometimes located near waterways?

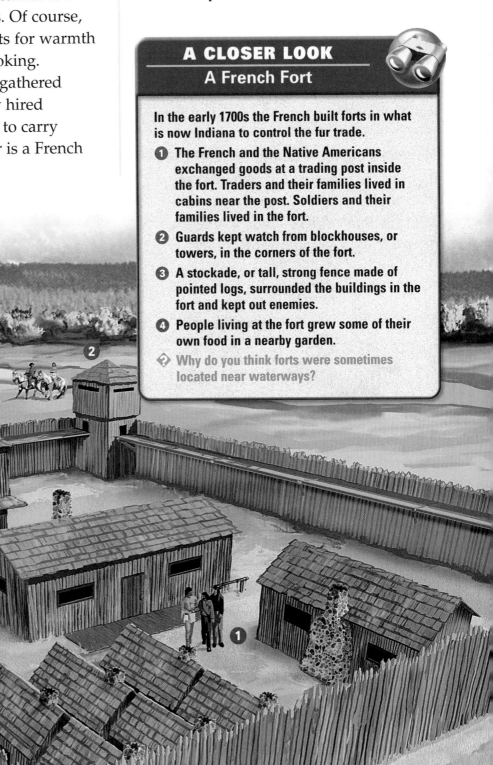

Protecting Trade and Land

The French controlled most of the fur trade in the Indiana area and beyond. French soldiers protected their trading posts and lands. The trading posts were similar to towns today.

The French built several trading posts in what is now Indiana. Fort Ouiatenon (wee•AHT•uh•nohn), on the Wabash River near present-day Lafayette, was built in 1717. The French hoped that the forts would stop the British from trading with the Native Americans and from taking French land.

In 1721 the French built another post at the portage between the Maumee and Wabash Rivers. This post was near the Miami village of Kekionga, where the city of Fort Wayne is today. The French called this post *Fort Miami*. Its location gave the French control of the important crossing between the Wabash and Maumee Rivers and control of the Wabash River valley.

The French built another post on the Wabash, closer to the Ohio River. French settlers started a community there in 1732. Later the settlers named their community Vincennes (vin•SENZ) after the French captain in charge of the post. Vincennes was Indiana's first **permanent**, or lasting, European settlement. The present-day city of Vincennes grew up on the site of this French community.

REVIEW How was Vincennes different from other trading posts?

Traders offered blankets, metal pots, beads, and other items in exchange for furs.

• HERITAGE •

La Porte, The Door to Trade

Many places in Indiana have French names. For example, the name *Terre Haute* means "high land" in French. That was how the French described the area midway along the course of the Wabash River, where the city of Terre Haute is today. French settlers also gave the present-day city of La Porte its name. *La Porte* in French means "the door." La Porte was the place where the forests of Indiana opened onto the prairies. It served as a door or gateway for trade and travel between the northern and southern regions of what is now Indiana.

The Gentle Invasion

Native Americans and the French got along well with each other. For this reason the coming of the French to the Indiana area is sometimes called "the gentle invasion." The French did not force the Native Americans off the land or build large settlements in the area. They respected the Native Americans' **rights**, or legal claims, to the land. They also treated the Native Americans as equal trading partners.

Although the arrival of the French was peaceful, it changed Native American life in many ways. As a result of trade with the French,

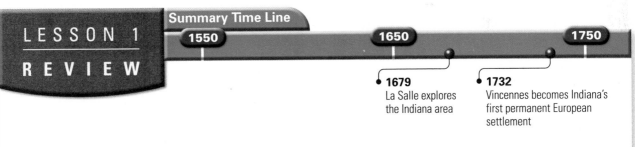

Copper kettles and other goods were traded for furs.

many Native Americans began using European goods. Some Native Americans started wearing woven cloth instead of animal skins. They used metal pots instead of clay pots. They began to hunt with guns instead of bows and arrows.

The arrival of the French also had harmful effects. As French settlers moved into Indiana, some Native Americans died in wars or were forced to move. The diseases Europeans brought, such as smallpox and measles, killed thousands of Native Americans. Missionaries questioned the beliefs of the Native Americans, while French leaders and soldiers threatened the authority, or power, of Native American chiefs.

REVIEW Why is the coming of the French called "the gentle invasion"?

LESSON 1 REVIEW

Summary Time Line

1550 — 1650 — 1750

1679 La Salle explores the Indiana area

1732 Vincennes becomes Indiana's first permanent European settlement

1 MAIN IDEA Why did the French start settlements in the Indiana area?

2 WHY IT MATTERS What reasons do people today have for moving to new places?

3 VOCABULARY Use the terms **voyageurs** and **scarce** in a sentence about the fur trade.

4 TIME LINE Which event took place first, La Salle's exploration of the Indiana area or the settlement at Vincennes?

5 READING SKILL—Cause and Effect What harmful effects did the arrival of the French have on the Native Americans?

6 GEOGRAPHY What were the names of three French trading posts in Indiana?

7 CRITICAL THINKING—Analyze Do you think "the gentle invasion" is an accurate term to describe French settlement in North America? Explain.

PERFORMANCE—Draw a Diagram Make a diagram to show how the fur trade worked. Include both pictures and words in your diagram. Use your completed diagram to explain the steps in the fur trade to a classmate.

CD*
Track 5

Fur Trade

When the French came to North America, they began to trade for animal furs with the Native Americans who lived nearby. The Native Americans trapped and traded deer, raccoon, fox, and beaver for their fur. Beaver was the most highly prized because its fur was made into hats that were popular in Europe. The Native Americans traded for European goods, such as iron tools, pots, pans, jewelry, and decorative items.

FROM THE INDIANA STATE MUSEUM, MUSEUM OF FUR TRADE, AND TIPPECANOE COUNTY HISTORICAL ASSOCIATION

Some of the items the Native Americans traded for were tools, such as this ax.

Native Americans wanted metal pots because they lasted longer than clay pots and could be put directly into the fire.

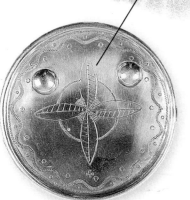

Silver collar worn to protect the neck

Analyze the Primary Source

❶ Which of these artifacts had practical uses?

❷ Why do you think the Native Americans traded for jewelry and decorations?

❸ What kinds of things do people trade for today?

This painting shows Tenskwatawa, the Prophet, wearing jewelry that was traded by the Europeans.

Silver earrings

Engraved silver ornament

ACTIVITY

Set Up a Trade Market Think of something that you can use to trade with other students in class. What items will you trade for? How will you set a value for your item? How do both parties benefit from trade? What are the benefits of trading items for items? What are the benefits of using money?

RESEARCH

Visit The Learning Site at **www.harcourtschool.com/ primarysources** to research other primary sources.

2

British Interest in Indiana

MAIN IDEA
Read to find out why the French, British, and Native American peoples in Indiana fought one another in the 1700s.

WHY IT MATTERS
Conflicts arise today between countries and between groups of people.

VOCABULARY
colonist
treaty
ally
unite
proclamation

1750–1765

The British began to settle colonies in North America at about the same time that the French founded their colony of New France. The British built their first permanent settlement in North America in 1607, at Jamestown, Virginia. In the years that followed, thousands of settlers came to live in 13 British colonies along the Atlantic coast. The people who lived in the colonies were called **colonists**.

The British had different reasons from the French for settling in North America. Most of the British were more interested in owning the land than in trading there. They wanted to live on the land and clear it for farming. In the mid-1700s English-speaking settlers started to move west across the Appalachian Mountains. By the late 1700s they had settled along the Ohio River in what is today southern Indiana.

The British Enter the Fur Trade

Looms were used to weave blankets and other goods in the British colonies.

It did not take long for traders from the British colonies to become interested in the Ohio River valley. They saw a chance to make money from the fur trade there. Soon they began taking business away from the French. The British traders offered the Native Americans better goods for fewer numbers of furs. The British could afford to do this because some of the goods they offered were made on machines in the colonies. Unlike the French, the British did not have to pay to ship their goods across the ocean.

Both the French and the British wanted to control the fur trade. Native Americans with furs to trade had to choose between them.

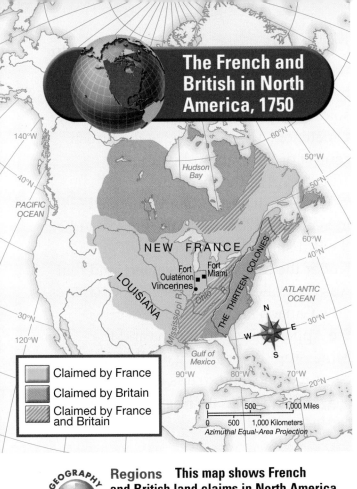

The French and British in North America, 1750

Claimed by France
Claimed by Britain
Claimed by France and Britain

GEOGRAPHY THEME

Regions This map shows French and British land claims in North America in 1750.

❓ Which country claimed more land in North America in 1750?

Most Native Americans in what is now Indiana had traded with the French for many years. By the 1740s the British had begun trading in the Wabash River valley as well. Some Native Americans there traded with both the British and the French.

Some members of the Miami tribe from the Indiana area wanted to trade with the British. They joined the leader Demoiselle (duh•mwah•ZEL) and moved east to what is now Ohio. There they could do more business with the British. In 1748 the Miami followers of Demoiselle, along with some other Native American groups, signed a treaty with the British. A **treaty** is a written agreement among

nations or groups of people. Under the treaty these Native Americans became allies of the British. An **ally** is a friend or partner, especially in times of war.

The French grew concerned when they saw many of their Native American allies trading with the British. In 1749 the French sent a military leader, Pierre-Joseph Céloron (SAY•loh•rohn), to visit Native American villages west of the Appalachians. On his trip Céloron crossed northeastern Indiana.

The main purpose of Céloron's trip was to persuade the Native Americans to trade only with the French. However, some Native American groups were not willing to stop trading with the British.

Soon the French lost more of their Native American allies. Still, they wanted to keep control of their North American fur trade. In 1752 the French and a group of Native Americans still friendly to them attacked Demoiselle's village in what is now Ohio. Demoiselle was killed. The British traders were driven back across the mountains.

REVIEW How did the British take fur-trading business away from the French?

The French and Indian War

In 1753 the French built a chain of forts from Lake Erie to what is today western Pennsylvania. They built the forts to show their claim to land in the eastern Ohio River valley and to help protect their fur trade.

Both the British and the French claimed the land in the Ohio River valley. The British believed that the French forts were being built on British soil. In 1754 conflicts between the British and the French turned into a war.

In North America the conflict was called the French and Indian War because the French and many Native Americans fought against the British colonists. In western Pennsylvania the Potawatomi helped the French. A number of Miamis also fought for the French. But other Native Americans sided with the British.

The French won most of the early battles of the war. Then, in the late 1750s, the British government sent an army to North America to help fight the war. By 1760 the British had captured the important settlements of Quebec and Montreal in New France.

Most of the fighting during the French and Indian War was in the lands west of the Appalachian Mountains and in Canada. However, as the British began to win the war, they moved onto lands left by the French. In 1760 and 1761 British soldiers captured Fort Miami and Fort Ouiatenon. These forts gave the British control of the Wabash River valley and control of the fur trade.

The French and Indian War ended in February 1763, when the French and the British signed the Treaty of Paris. Under the treaty Britain gained land that was controlled by the French in what is now Canada and the land between the Appalachian Mountains and the Mississippi River. This gave Britain control of the land that is now Indiana.

REVIEW **What was the result of the French and Indian War?**

Many Native Americans fought alongside their French allies against the British.

Pontiac united many tribes against the British.

Fighting Continues

The Treaty of Paris gave the British control of lands west of the Appalachians. However, it ignored Native Americans' claims to those lands. Most of the Native Americans west of the Appalachians did not welcome the British. Unlike the French, British settlers did not respect Native American land, and they cleared the land for farming. Also, the British did not treat the Native Americans as equal trading partners.

An Ottawa chief named Pontiac (PAHN•tee•ak) thought that Native Americans should be the ones to control these western lands. During the French and Indian War, Pontiac had taken the side of the French. Like most other Native Americans, he wanted to drive out the British. In an effort to do this, he **united**, or brought together, the Native American tribes of the Great Lakes and the valleys of the Ohio and Mississippi Rivers. Among these groups were the Miamis, the Shawnees, the Delawares, and the Potawatomi.

In May 1763 Pontiac and the warriors he united started attacking British forts. Within a few weeks they captured almost every fort between the western shores of Lake Michigan and western New York. In Indiana they forced the British to give up Fort Ouiatenon. Then they destroyed the fort. Pontiac and his army also captured Fort Miami.

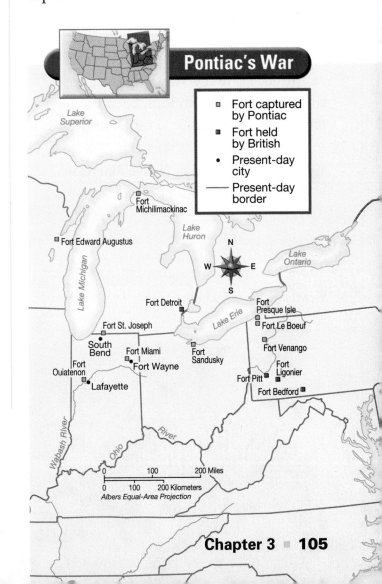

Pontiac's War

- ■ Fort captured by Pontiac
- ■ Fort held by British
- • Present-day city
- — Present-day border

Lake Superior

Lake Huron

Lake Ontario

Lake Michigan

Lake Erie

Fort Michilimackinac

Fort Edward Augustus

Fort Detroit

Fort St. Joseph

South Bend

Fort Ouiatenon

Fort Miami

Fort Wayne

Lafayette

Fort Sandusky

Fort Presque Isle

Fort Le Boeuf

Fort Venango

Fort Pitt

Fort Ligonier

Fort Bedford

Wabash River

Ohio River

N W E S

0   100   200 Miles
0   100   200 Kilometers
Albers Equal-Area Projection

Movement   **In 1763 Pontiac spent almost seven months attacking British forts.**

❖ How many British forts did Pontiac capture?

News of the Treaty of Paris and the British control of lands west of the Appalachian Mountains did not reach all of North America until the fall of 1763. By that time Pontiac and his warriors were outside Fort Detroit in what is now Michigan. They had been there for four months. The Native Americans surrounded Fort Detroit to keep supplies from reaching the British who were inside. However, the Native Americans' supplies also were low. When the Native Americans heard about the Treaty of Paris, they quickly understood why they had not received the needed supplies from their French allies. The war between the French and the British was over.

As winter came, many Native American warriors returned to their villages. Without supplies from the French, Pontiac and his men gave up control of the British forts they had captured. Pontiac's war was over, too. By winter the British took back the forts and forced most of the French in the region to leave.

REVIEW **Why did many Native Americans unite under Pontiac?**

Vincennes became a British fort after 1763.

Stopping the Move West

To avoid further conflicts, Britain's King George III issued a **proclamation**, or an order from a leader to the citizens. The Proclamation of 1763 said that no colonists could move to any lands west of the Appalachian Mountains.

· GEOGRAPHY ·

Vincennes
Understanding Human Systems

The location of Vincennes on the banks of the Wabash River was important to the British. Vincennes was a useful link between Canada and the lands west of the Appalachian Mountains. French settlers grew corn and wheat and raised cattle there. Many Native Americans in the area traded at Vincennes.

The British commander for North America did not try to break up the French community at Vincennes following the Proclamation of 1763. In 1765 almost 90 French families still lived there. Then in 1772, the British government ordered the French to leave. The settlers made a strong argument for their right to stay on their land. The British agreed but appointed a British governor for Vincennes.

ILLINOIS

Wabash River

Vincennes

GEORGE ROGERS CLARK MEMORIAL PARK, SITE OF FT. VINCENNES

INDIANA

N W E S

0   1   2 Miles
0   1   2 Kilometers

Human–Environment Interactions
The Proclamation Line of 1763 marks the place farthest west where colonists could settle.

⬥ What geography feature marks the Proclamation Line?

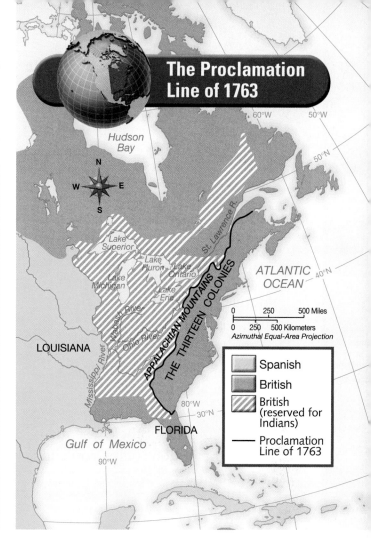

The Proclamation Line of 1763

Hudson Bay

Lake Superior
Lake Huron
Lake Michigan
Lake Ontario
Lake Erie

St. Lawrence R.

APPALACHIAN MOUNTAINS

THE THIRTEEN COLONIES

ATLANTIC OCEAN

Wabash River
Ohio River
Mississippi River

LOUISIANA

FLORIDA

Gulf of Mexico

0   250   500 Miles
0   250   500 Kilometers
Azimuthal Equal-Area Projection

Spanish
British
British (reserved for Indians)
Proclamation Line of 1763

Only Native Americans could use those lands. In addition, no one could buy land from the Native Americans. Anyone who wanted to trade with Native Americans would need special permission. By keeping colonists out of the way, the king made it easier for the British government to control the fur trade.

Native Americans were glad that the British king wanted to keep colonists off the land. However, the colonists did not like the proclamation. Many wanted to move west after the French and Indian War. Many Native Americans in the Indiana area continued to trade with the French in the Mississippi River valley.

REVIEW What was the Proclamation of 1763?

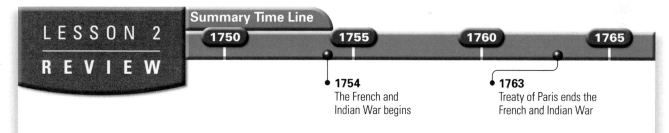

LESSON 2 REVIEW

Summary Time Line

1750   1755   1760   1765

1754
The French and Indian War begins

1763
Treaty of Paris ends the French and Indian War

❶ **MAIN IDEA** Why did the French, British, and Native Americans fight one another in the 1700s?

❷ **WHY IT MATTERS** Why do conflicts sometimes arise today between countries and between groups of people?

❸ **VOCABULARY** Use the words **colonist**, **ally**, and **treaty** in one or two sentences.

❹ **TIME LINE** How long did the French and Indian War last?

❺ **READING SKILL—Cause and Effect** What caused Pontiac to attack British forts? What happened as a result of his attacks?

❻ **ECONOMICS** Why did many Native Americans start trading with the British?

❼ **CRITICAL THINKING—Analyze** Why do you think many Native Americans sided with the French rather than with the British in the French and Indian War?

 PERFORMANCE—Write a Speech Imagine that you are a British colonist moving west to settle or that you are a Native American living on lands west of the Appalachians. Write a speech that tells how you feel about the Proclamation of 1763. Give the speech to your class.

·SKILLS·

CITIZENSHIP

Solve a Problem

VOCABULARY

consequence

➤ WHY IT MATTERS

Pontiac and many Native American groups went to war to solve a problem. That solution had serious consequences. A **consequence** is what happens as the result of an action.

Solving problems is an important skill. Thinking about the consequences of different solutions helps you choose the best solution.

➤ WHAT YOU NEED TO KNOW

Here are some steps you can use to solve a problem.

Step 1 **Identify the problem.**

Step 2 **Compare possible solutions and think about their consequences.**

Step 3 **Choose the best solution.**

Step 4 **Plan how to carry out the solution.**

Step 5 **Solve the problem and evaluate the solution.**

➤ PRACTICE THE SKILL

Imagine that you are a Native American living in the mid-1700s in what is now Indiana. Colonists are settling on the lands where you hunt.

1 What are some solutions to this problem? Start with Step 2 above.

2 What are the consequences likely to be?

3 Which solution would you choose? Tell how you would carry it out. Evaluate the solution.

➤ APPLY WHAT YOU LEARNED

Think of a problem at your school or in your community. Use the graphic organizer below to arrive at the best solution to this problem. Then plan how to carry it out. Share your solution with your classmates.

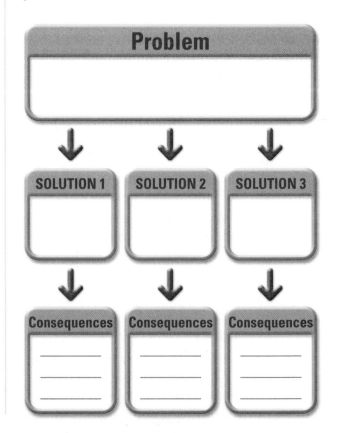

CITIZENSHIP SKILLS

Americans in Indiana

| 1500 | 1600 | 1700 | 1800 |

1775–1785

MAIN IDEA
Read to learn how American settlers helped shape Indiana.

WHY IT MATTERS
Individuals and groups can affect the course of history.

VOCABULARY
tax
representative
revolution
Declaration of Independence
pioneer
frontier
surrender
territory

Most people living in the Indiana area paid little attention to the Proclamation of 1763. However, instead of bringing peace, this new law created more conflict. Settlers still moved west, causing trouble in the region. Native Americans fought the settlers and sometimes one another.

A Fight for Freedom

People in the 13 British colonies along the Atlantic coast were angry about the king's proclamation. They also were upset over new taxes they had to pay to cover the costs of the French and Indian War. A **tax** is money that a government collects to pay for the services it provides.

"No taxation without representation!" many colonists responded. They believed that the government in Britain did not have the right to tax the colonies. Colonists living in North America did not have representatives in the British Parliament, or lawmaking body. A **representative** is someone who speaks for a group of people. Many colonists refused to pay the taxes. They joined in a decision to form their own country and make their own laws.

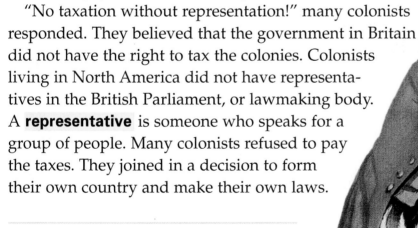

Some colonists attacked and made fun of British tax collectors (right). The British coins shown here are a shilling (below left), which was worth about a nickel, and a halfpenny (below right), which was worth half a penny.

DEMOCRATIC VALUES
Individual Rights

The colonists believed the British government did not protect their individual rights. The second paragraph of the Declaration of Independence tells what some of those rights are. First, it says that all people are created equal. Then, it says that people have certain rights that no one can take away. The most important of those rights are "Life, Liberty, and the pursuit of Happiness."

The British government did not respect those rights. For this reason, the Declaration states, the colonists had a right to form a new government.

Analyze the Value

1 Why did the Americans want to form a new government?

2 **Make It Relevant** Make an illustration of the individual rights named in the Declaration of Independence. Fold a sheet of drawing paper into three sections. Label the sections *Life, Liberty,* and *Pursuit of Happiness.* Then, in each section, draw a picture of people enjoying or using that right. Present your illustration to the class, and explain what each section shows.

Fighting broke out between the British and the colonists in 1775. The war with the British was called the American Revolution. A **revolution** is a sudden, violent change in government. Although fighting started in 1775, the colonists did not announce that they had formed a new country until July 4, 1776. They made their announcement with a document called the **Declaration of Independence**. The colonists called their new country the United States of America.

REVIEW Why did the colonists fight a war with the British?

Henry Hamilton (center) was in command of the British at Fort Detroit.

Protecting the West

At the beginning of the American Revolution, most of the fighting took place in the 13 colonies along the Atlantic coast. The war did not spread west for several years. Even so, the British supported the Native American groups by arming them. Native Americans raided American settlements in what is now Indiana and nearby states.

Colonel (KER•nuhl) Henry Hamilton now commanded the British soldiers at Fort Detroit. He knew that the British needed help from the Native Americans to win the war. The British did not have many troops in the West.

In June 1777 Hamilton called a meeting of Native American tribes, including the Miamis, the Potawatomi, and the Shawnees. He told the Native Americans that the Americans would surely force them off the land if the British lost the war. Hamilton offered the tribes knives, guns, and food in exchange for their help.

In 1777 a young settler named George Rogers Clark suggested a plan to end the attacks by the Native Americans. Clark thought that the settlers should cross the Ohio River and seize the old French forts on the Wabash and Mississippi Rivers. They might also be able to capture Fort Detroit from the British. If the British were driven out, they could no longer help the Native Americans attack colonists in the West.

Clark needed soldiers and supplies to carry out his plan. He went to the Virginia colony for help. Virginia claimed much of the land in Kentucky where Clark and other **pioneers**, or first settlers, lived. Clark was a representative from Kentucky to the Virginia government. Patrick Henry, the governor of Virginia, gave Clark money and his permission to go ahead "with as little delay and as much secrecy as possible." Clark hurried to raise an army as quickly as possible.

REVIEW Why did settlers in the land west of the Appalachians need protection?

Clark's Army

By the spring of 1778, only about 150 men had signed up with Clark. Most of the volunteers came from farms along the Virginia frontier. The **frontier** was the land beyond the settlement at the western edge of European control.

Clark's army had no uniforms. The men wore deerskin shirts and pants and brought their own hunting rifles. Clark led his small army from Virginia to Fort Pitt in western Pennsylvania. Then they traveled down the Ohio River to the Falls of the Ohio, near where the cities of Louisville in Kentucky and Jeffersonville in Indiana stand today. There, farmers from the Kentucky area joined Clark and the Virginians. The army numbered about 175 soldiers.

Clark wanted to capture a British-held fort located at Kaskaskia (kas•KAS•kee•uh) in what is today southern Illinois. Clark and his army traveled down the Ohio River to Fort Massac. They then traveled by foot. On the evening of July 4, 1778, about half of Clark's men captured the fort at Kaskaskia. The others surrounded the nearby French settlement. The French settlers supported Clark after they learned that France had become an ally of the Americans.

This statue of Clark stands 8 feet (2 m) tall in the center of the George Rogers Clark Memorial in Vincennes.

Routes of Clark and Hamilton

→	Hamilton's route, 1778
→	Clark's route, 1778–1779
—	Present-day border
▓	Northwest Territory

0   100   200 Miles
0   100   200 Kilometers
Albers Equal-Area Projection

GEOGRAPHY THEME

Movement This map shows the routes taken by Clark and Hamilton. Clark traveled west and then north while Hamilton traveled southwest.

❖ What rivers were used by Clark and Hamilton to move their armies?

Clark and the army captured other forts. They took Cahokia, about 60 miles (97 km) north on the Mississippi River, without firing a shot. Then French settlers helped Clark take control of Vincennes on the Wabash River.

By August 1778 British commander Hamilton feared that Clark's army would attack Fort Detroit next.

Hamilton decided to recapture Kaskaskia and Vincennes. He set out for Vincennes with a force of about 500 British soldiers and Native Americans.

Hamilton's soldiers canoed from Fort Detroit through Lake Erie to the Maumee River and into what is now Indiana. At Kekionga they crossed the portage to the Wabash River. Then they paddled 40 boats down the Wabash River to Vincennes. Hundreds more Native Americans joined Hamilton's army on its way down the Wabash.

On December 17, 1778, Hamilton's men attacked the fort at Vincennes. They easily defeated the small group of soldiers Clark had left there. The British changed the name *Vincennes* to *Fort Sackville* in honor of Lord Sackville, a friend of the British king. Hamilton prepared to spend a long, quiet winter at Fort Sackville.

REVIEW Why did Clark attack forts in the West?

A Long March Followed by Victory

Clark was at Kaskaskia when he learned that the British had captured Vincennes. He knew what he had to do. He wrote Virginia Governor Henry.

❝I know the case is desperate, sir . . . no time is to be lost.❞

Clark knew that he did not have enough soldiers to recapture the fort in the usual kind of battle. Clark and his small army planned a surprise attack on the British.

On February 6, 1779, Clark set out from Kaskaskia with about 170 soldiers. They had a long, hard journey ahead. Vincennes was 180 miles (290 km) away. Rain and melting snow soaked the ground. Rivers flooded their banks. Clark's soldiers marched through water and mud most of the way. At times the cold water was as high as the men's waists. After marching for more than two weeks, the soldiers finally set up camp.

• BIOGRAPHY •

George Rogers Clark   1752–1818

Character Trait: Patriotism

George Rogers Clark, born in Virginia, was one of Indiana's most patriotic leaders. He showed great patriotism, or strong feelings for his country, at an early age. He left Virginia and moved to Kentucky in search of land and adventure. At age 24 he acted as a representative of Kentucky and raised an army to fight in the West. After his victories at Vincennes, he continued to serve as a military leader until the end of the war.

MULTIMEDIA BIOGRAPHIES
Visit The Learning Site at www.harcourtschool.com/biographies to learn about other famous people.

The army was only 2 miles (3 km) from Vincennes when the soldiers prepared a surprise attack.

The British were surprised when they saw Clark's army. Clark wanted the British to believe the army was very large. Clark ordered his soldiers to march back and forth waving their battle flags. The British could see only the tops of the flags and thought a huge army was about to attack.

Clark's soldiers could shoot much better than the British. By aiming at the gaps between the posts in the fort's stockade, they hit many of the British soldiers inside. The next morning, February 25, 1779, Hamilton **surrendered**, or gave up, the fort.

When the American Revolution ended in 1783, the United States owned lands stretching from the Atlantic Ocean to the Mississippi River. The land north of the Ohio River became known as the Northwest Territory. A **territory** is land that is owned by a country but is not part of any state. Lands that Clark had protected formed a large part of this territory, and Indiana was part of it.

REVIEW How did Clark's small army recapture Fort Sackville from the British?

Clark is shown here accepting the surrender of Fort Sackville by Hamilton.

LESSON 3 REVIEW

Summary Time Line

| 1775 | 1780 | 1785 |

1775
American Revolution begins

1779
George Rogers Clark recaptures Fort Sackville from the British

1783
American Revolution ends

1. **MAIN IDEA** Why did settlers in Indiana fight in the American Revolution?

2. **WHY IT MATTERS** How did the actions of George Rogers Clark affect the Northwest Territory and Indiana?

3. **VOCABULARY** Write a sentence or two using the words **frontier** and **territory**.

4. **TIME LINE** Was Clark's victory at Fort Sackville closest to the beginning, the middle, or the end of the American Revolution?

5. **READING SKILL—Cause and Effect** What was one cause of the American Revolution?

6. **HISTORY** Who was the British commander of Fort Sackville?

7. **CIVICS AND GOVERNMENT** What was the purpose of the Declaration of Independence?

8. **CRITICAL THINKING—Hypothesize** What do you think might have happened if George Rogers Clark had not surprised the British and recaptured Fort Sackville?

 PERFORMANCE—Write an Explanatory Paragraph In a paragraph, explain how George Rogers Clark's actions affected Indiana history.

·SKILLS·

Identify Fact and Opinion

VOCABULARY

fact

opinion

CD A
Track 9

▶ WHY IT MATTERS

Every day you get information from many sources, including books, television, newspapers, the Internet, and people. How do you know if this information is true? One way is to decide whether it is a fact or an opinion. A **fact** is a statement that can be checked and proved to be true. An **opinion** is a statement that tells what the person thinks or believes.

▶ WHAT YOU NEED TO KNOW

Facts often give dates or numbers. This is an example of a fact: *George Rogers Clark recaptured Fort Sackville from the British in 1779.*

An opinion cannot be proved true. Words and phrases such as *think, believe, in my opinion,* and *doubt* as well as *most, best,* and *worst* are clues that you may be reading or hearing an opinion. This is an example of an opinion: *George Rogers Clark was the most courageous leader during the war.*

▶ PRACTICE THE SKILL

Copy the following statements on a sheet of paper. Label each as *fact* or *opinion.* Explain your choices.

1 The colonists declared that the new taxes were unfair.

2 I think the British should have allowed the colonists to send representatives to Parliament.

3 The Proclamation of 1763 was a terrible solution to the problem of American settlement in the West.

4 The governor of Virginia agreed that the western lands should be protected.

▶ APPLY WHAT YOU LEARNED

Look through newspapers or magazines to find five statements of fact and five statements of opinion. Copy the statements on a sheet of paper. Ask a classmate to identify those that are facts and those that are opinions. Then have your classmate tell how he or she can tell the difference.

Historians have different opinions about whether Clark's actions led the British to give up western lands after the war. It is a fact that the United States gained the lands Clark helped protect.

READING SKILLS

159

·CHAPTER·

3 Review and Test Preparation

USE YOUR READING SKILLS

Complete this graphic organizer to show that you understand how to identify causes and effects of some of the key events described in this chapter. A copy of this graphic organizer appears on page 34 of the Activity Book.

Claiming the Land

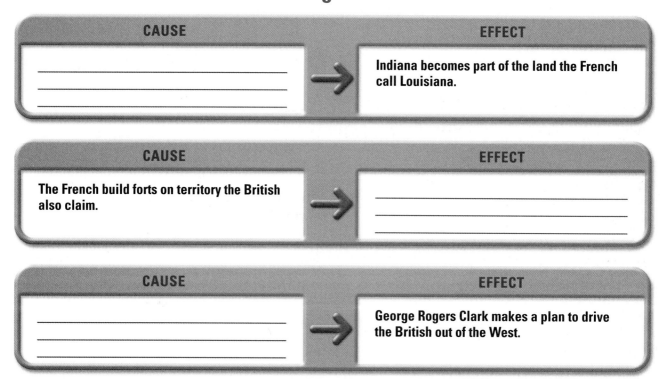

CAUSE	EFFECT
_____	Indiana becomes part of the land the French call Louisiana.

CAUSE	EFFECT
The French build forts on territory the British also claim.	_____

CAUSE	EFFECT
_____	George Rogers Clark makes a plan to drive the British out of the West.

THINK & WRITE

Compose a Conversation Write a conversation La Salle and the Native American leaders might have had at the meeting at the Council Oak. Be sure to identify the speaker of each line of conversation that you include.

Write a Journal Entry Imagine that you are a member of Clark's army. Write a journal entry about your experiences during one day of the long march to Vincennes. Describe how it feels to be one of Clark's soldiers.

1650 — **1700** — **1750** — **1800**

1679 La Salle explores the Indiana area

1754 French and Indian War begins

1763 French and Indian War ends Proclamation of 1763

1776 Declaration of Independence

1783 American Revolution ends

USE THE TIME LINE

Use the chapter summary time line to answer these questions.

1 How long was the French and Indian War?

2 What happened in 1776?

USE VOCABULARY

Identify the term that correctly matches each definition.

missionary (p. 94)

treaty (p. 103)

unite (p. 105)

tax (p. 109)

revolution (p. 110)

3 someone who teaches his or her religious beliefs to others

4 bring together

5 a written agreement among nations

6 a sudden, violent change in government

7 money a government collects to pay for the services it provides

RECALL FACTS

Answer these questions.

8 Who was the first European explorer known to have reached what is now Indiana?

9 Who controlled the lands west of the Appalachian Mountains after 1763?

Write the letter of the best choice.

10 **TEST PREP** When La Salle claimed the Mississippi River valley for the French, the land that is now Indiana became part of—
A Canada.
B Illinois.
C New France.
D Virginia.

11 **TEST PREP** The American colonists broke away from British rule because—
F they wanted to have a say in making their own laws.
G they could not settle west of the Appalachian Mountains.
H the British government was protecting their rights.
J they needed Native American allies.

THINK CRITICALLY

12 Who do you think gained more from the fur trade, the French or the Native Americans? Explain your answer.

13 What advantage, if any, do you think that Clark and his soldiers had over the British?

APPLY SKILLS

Solve a Problem

14 Think of the problems faced by American colonists who believed that the new British taxes were unfair. What solutions did the colonists consider? What were the consequences of their solutions? Do you think they chose the best solution? What solution, if any, would have been better? Why?

Identify Fact and Opinion

15 Read about a community issue in a letter to the editor in the newspaper. Underline all the facts. Circle the opinions. Then write a paragraph explaining how you identified facts and opinions in the letter.

Chapter 3 ▪ 117

GROUSELAND

Grouseland, in Vincennes, was the home of William Henry Harrison while he served as Governor of the Indiana Territory from 1800–1812. It was named after the grouse, a wild bird Harrison loved to hunt. The mansion was restored to look as it did in Harrison's time and includes furniture from the period.

LOCATE IT

INDIANA

Vincennes

CD5
Track 1

CD 5
Track 2

4

From Territory to Statehood

" The State of Indiana has . . . been received into the union. "

—from the Vincennes newspaper,
The Western Sun,
January 4, 1817

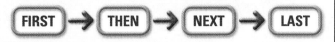

The Northwest Territory

1785	1805	1825

1785–1795

George Rogers Clark and his soldiers were among the first to settle in the new western lands of the United States. After the American Revolution the new state of Virginia rewarded soldiers by giving them land alongside the northern bank of the Ohio River, in what is now Indiana. Clark and his soldiers started farms and built homes on their new land. They named their community Clarksville. Clarksville became the first American town in what is now Indiana.

Land for Sale

Several states claimed the land in the Ohio River valley, including the land given to Clark and his soldiers. In time, these states gave up their claims to this land and turned over the property to the government of the United States.

The United States government needed a plan for settling lands in the West. Then it needed to decide how to measure the land, mark its borders, and organize the land sales.

FAST FACT By the mid-1780s more than 400 American settlers had moved to the area around Vincennes, Indiana.

The Northwest Territory, 1787

0   100   200 Miles
0   100   200 Kilometers
Albers Equal-Area Projection

Lake Superior
Lake Michigan
Lake Huron
Lake Erie
Mississippi River
Ohio River
Clarksville

N
W   E
S

Northwest Territory
Present-day border

Sections in One Township

36	30	24	18	12	6
35	29	23	17	11	5
34	28	22	16	10	4
33	27	21	15	9	3
32	26	20	14	8	2
31	25	19	13	7	1

1 mile
6 miles
6 miles

GEOGRAPHY THEME

Place Most of the land in the Northwest Territory was divided equally into townships and sections.

❖ Where might it have been difficult to divide the land into perfect squares?

In 1785 the United States government passed an **ordinance**, or law, about the sale of western lands. The Land Ordinance of 1785 provided a plan to divide the land into **townships**, or pieces of land 6 miles (about 10 km) square.

The plan divided each township into 36 numbered **sections**, or parts. Each of these sections was 1 mile (about 2 km) square. The square sections made the borders clear. Property deeds showed township names and section numbers. A **deed** is a document that describes a piece of land and tells who owns it. Deeds are still used today.

The ordinance reserved section 16 in every township for public schools. Government leaders knew that education would give all citizens in the new lands better opportunities.

REVIEW What did the Land Ordinance of 1785 do?

Governing the Territory

The Land Ordinance of 1785 organized western lands. Now these lands needed a form of government. The United States government passed the Northwest Ordinance in 1787. This new law gave the name *Northwest Territory* to the land west of the Appalachian Mountains and north of the Ohio River, including what is now Indiana. It also placed a governor in charge of the territory. On October 3, 1787, Major General Arthur St. Clair became the first governor of the Northwest Territory. The United States Congress chose the governor, a secretary, and judges for the territory. **Congress** is the part of the United States government that makes the nation's laws.

The Northwest Ordinance also described some of the ways that the territory and its government could change.

Arthur St. Clair, who was born in Scotland, came to North America in the 1760s and first lived in what is now Pennsylvania.

Gunter's Chain

Surveyors, or people who measure land, used a Gunter's chain to measure and divide land in the Northwest Territory and other parts of the early United States. An English mathematician, Edmund Gunter, invented this measuring tool in the early 1600s. A Gunter's chain was 66 feet (20 m) long. It had 100 links, each measuring about 8 inches (20 cm). Each link was made of iron or steel wire and had a ring at each end. Surveyors held the rings and laid the chain on the ground to measure land in acres. One acre measured 10 chains deep and 10 chains wide. Surveyors used a Gunter's chain until the 1900s. Then a measuring tape similar to that used today replaced the Gunter's chain.

As soon as 5,000 free adult men lived in the territory, they could set up their own territorial government and elect representatives to help make laws. One representative would go to Congress to speak for the territory. When there were 60,000 free adult men in an area of the territory, that area could become a state. Five states, including Indiana, and part of a sixth were formed from the Northwest Territory.

The people in each new state would have the same rights and freedoms as those living in the first 13 states. Unlike people in the original states, however, the settlers in the Northwest Territory and the states formed from it could not keep slaves. A **slave** is a person who is owned by another person.

The Northwest Territory was organized into counties. In 1790 Knox County became the first county in what is now Indiana and included what later would be the entire state. Other counties were created out of Knox County. Today Indiana is divided into 92 counties.

Many people in the territory were upset that they could not choose their own local leaders. For example, in 1790 the people of Knox County around Vincennes were not permitted to select their leaders. Instead, the governor, Arthur St. Clair, chose the leaders.

REVIEW **What was the Northwest Ordinance?**

Conflict in the Northwest Territory

Native Americans and the British grew unhappy about the growing number of Americans moving to the West. The Native Americans who lived on these lands saw the movement of American settlers into the Northwest Territory as a threat to their way of life. The Native Americans hunted on these lands. Their homes and villages were there, too. Soon Native Americans began attacking settlers who moved into the territory.

The British wanted to protect their fur trade with the Native Americans in the Northwest Territory. They had kept some of their forts near the Great Lakes after the American Revolution. They encouraged the Native Americans to form a confederation to fight the Americans. A **confederation** is a large group made up of smaller groups that have the same goals and want to work together. The Miamis, Delawares, Shawnees, and Potawatomi were among the tribes that joined the confederation. Their leader was Miami chief Michikinikwa (muh•chee•kee•NEE•kwah), which means "Little Turtle." Their base was the Miami village of Kekionga.

In 1790 the Americans destroyed the Miami villages on the Wabash and Maumee Rivers. Then the Americans were defeated by Little Turtle's men. The following year the American soldiers fought Little Turtle's warriors again at the Miami village of Kekionga. More than 600 of the 1,400 American soldiers were killed or badly wounded. Little Turtle lost about 150 warriors.

President George Washington chose General Anthony Wayne to lead the Americans' fight. Wayne and his troops headed west in the fall of 1793 and built Fort Greenville in Ohio.

A year later, the British built a new fort near the mouth of the Maumee River in northwestern Ohio. They called it Fort Miami.

REVIEW Why did Native Americans and settlers come into conflict in the Northwest Territory?

The Battle of Fallen Timbers

On August 20, 1794, the confederation of tribes again prepared for battle. The Shawnee chief, Blue Jacket, was in command. The warriors gathered near the Maumee River in Ohio where a tornado had uprooted trees. They thought that the fallen trees would protect them and make fighting difficult for the Americans.

The trees did not stop Wayne's soldiers or protect the Native Americans. Soon Blue Jacket and his warriors began to **retreat**, or turn away from battle.

General Anthony Wayne and his army fought the Native Americans at the Battle of Fallen Timbers. Soldiers sometimes called the general "Mad Anthony" because of his daring actions during the Revolutionary War.

Analyze
Primary Sources

The Treaty of Greenville was signed on August 3, 1795, by about 1,110 chiefs and warriors from 12 Native American tribes. Miami chief Little Turtle and Shawnee chief Blue Jacket were among the many chiefs who signed. Their names or marks—pictures representing their names—can be seen on the document shown at right.

1. The names from each tribe are grouped together. The Miami tribe is shown here.

2. The Potawatomi tribe is shown here.

3. Pictures of deer are the marks of chiefs Hee-no-sha-meek and La Malice.

◆ Why do you think many Native Americans used marks for their signatures?

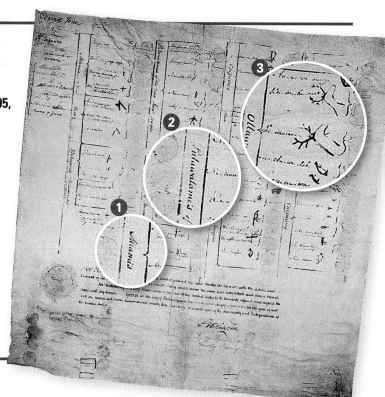

Wayne's soldiers had won the Battle of Fallen Timbers. Wayne then marched his army along the river to the Maumee-Wabash portage. The Americans built their own fort, Fort Wayne, near Kekionga.

REVIEW Why did the Native Americans choose "the place of fallen timbers" for an attack?

The Treaty of Greenville

The Battle of Fallen Timbers became a **turning point**, or event that causes an important change to take place. Losing the battle ended the Native Americans' hopes of keeping settlers out of the West. Winning the Battle of Fallen Timbers gave the Americans strong control of the Northwest Territory.

In the summer of 1795, Wayne met with Little Turtle and other chiefs at Fort Greenville in Ohio. In August the United States government and the Native American confederation signed an agreement called the Treaty of Greenville.

In the treaty the United States agreed to let Native Americans live in the western part of the Northwest Territory. It also promised to pay the Native Americans for land taken over by settlers. The Native Americans agreed to let the Americans settle in

FAST FACT

Little Turtle was given a sword by George Washington. He treasured it so much that he was buried with it.

The Native American tribes that signed the Treaty of Greenville received $20,000 in goods in exchange for the lands they turned over to the Americans.

the eastern part of the Northwest Territory, which today is much of Ohio and part of southeastern Indiana. The Native Americans also agreed to allow forts and trading posts on their land. In the area that is now Indiana, they gave up Ouiatenon, Vincennes, and the Wabash-Maumee portage.

As Little Turtle signed the treaty he said, "I have been the last to sign it and I will be the last to break it." Settlers and Native Americans in the Northwest Territory enjoyed 15 years of peace under the Treaty of Greenville.

REVIEW **What did the Americans gain from the Treaty of Greenville?**

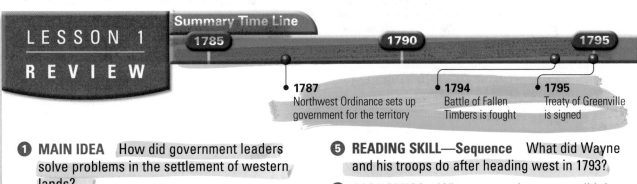

LESSON 1 REVIEW

Summary Time Line

1785 — 1790 — 1795

1787
Northwest Ordinance sets up government for the territory

1794
Battle of Fallen Timbers is fought

1795
Treaty of Greenville is signed

1. **MAIN IDEA** How did government leaders solve problems in the settlement of western lands?

2. **WHY IT MATTERS** How do government leaders today solve problems about land or other issues?

3. **VOCABULARY** In a sentence or two, use the vocabulary terms **retreat** and **turning point** to describe the Battle of Fallen Timbers.

4. **TIME LINE** Which happened first, the Battle of Fallen Timbers or the signing of the Treaty of Greenville?

5. **READING SKILL—Sequence** What did Wayne and his troops do after heading west in 1793?

6. **ECONOMICS** What economic reasons did the British have for supporting Native American attacks on American settlers?

7. **CRITICAL THINKING—Hypothesize** What might have happened if the Native Americans had won the Battle of Fallen Timbers?

PERFORMANCE—Write a Newspaper Story Imagine that you are a reporter for a newspaper in the early days of the United States. Write a news story about the Northwest Ordinance.

CD5
Track 2

2

MAIN IDEA
As you read, think about the different points of view about land ownership that led to problems between Native Americans and American settlers.

WHY IT MATTERS
Different points of view can cause conflicts between people today.

VOCABULARY
boundary
census

Some settlers traveled west by flatboat to reach Indiana.

Conflict Continues

1785   1805   1825

1795–1815

After the Treaty of Greenville, settlers in the Northwest Territory wanted to create states in the territory. They also wanted more voice in their government. William Henry Harrison, an aide to General Wayne, took the settlers' concerns to the United States Congress.

Harrison helped Congress pass the Land Act in 1800. The act divided the Northwest Territory into two parts—the Ohio Territory and the Indiana Territory. The Indiana Territory stretched west from near Indiana's present-day eastern border to the Mississippi River and north from the Ohio River to Canada. Vincennes became its capital. President John Adams chose Harrison to be the first governor of the new territory.

Changes in the Indiana Territory

The border, or **boundary**, of the Indiana Territory changed twice while Harrison led its government. In 1805 Congress created the Michigan Territory from the northern part of the Indiana Territory. Then, in 1809, the western part of the Indiana Territory became the Illinois Territory. After these changes the Indiana Territory had almost the same boundary lines that the state of Indiana has today.

Although the Indiana Territory became smaller in size, the number of people living there grew. The **census**, or official government count of people, showed only 5,641 settlers in 1800. By 1815 there were more than 60,000 settlers.

Governor Harrison was in charge of buying Native American land for settlement. Between 1803 and 1809 he bought millions of acres of land. In 1809 Harrison met with Native American leaders at Fort Wayne to buy more land for settlers. Harrison and the tribes signed the Treaty of Fort Wayne. Under its terms the United States government bought almost 3 million acres of land. The treaty set a new boundary line between Native American land and United States land. It was called the Ten O'Clock Line because it could be marked by the shadows cast by surveyor's stakes, or sticks. At ten o'clock in the morning, the sun's shadow formed a line that ran north and east of Vincennes. The Native Americans had to live north of the Ten O'Clock Line.

The United States paid about 3 cents an acre for land under the Treaty of Fort Wayne.

REVIEW What did the Treaty of Fort Wayne give the United States?

Analyze Graphs This graph shows how quickly population increased in the Indiana Territory.

❓ About how many more people lived in the Indiana Territory in 1815 compared with 1810?

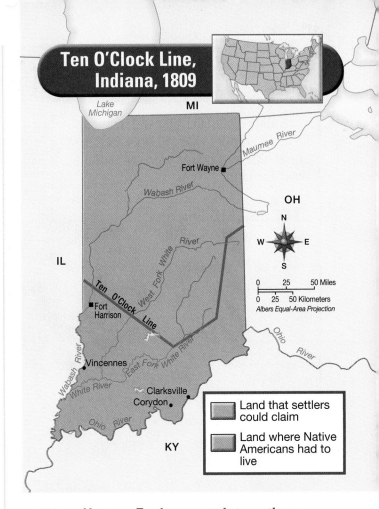

Ten O'Clock Line, Indiana, 1809

MI

Lake Michigan

Fort Wayne

Maumee River

Wabash River

OH

River

West Fork White

N
W — E
S

0   25   50 Miles
0   25   50 Kilometers
Albers Equal-Area Projection

IL

Ten O'Clock Line

■ Fort Harrison

Wabash River

Vincennes

East Fork White River

White River

Clarksville
Corydon

Ohio River

Ohio River

KY

Land that settlers could claim

Land where Native Americans had to live

GEOGRAPHY THEME

Human–Environment Interactions
The Ten O'Clock Line marked the boundary between Native American territory and United States land.

❓ Who lived near Fort Wayne—settlers or Native Americans?

Population Growth in Indiana Territory

Number of People

70,000
60,000
50,000
40,000
30,000
20,000
10,000
0

1800   1805   1810   1815
Year

POINTS OF VIEW
Disagreements over Land

Native American leader Tecumseh and Governor William Henry Harrison held different points of view about owning land.

TECUMSEH, Shawnee chief, August 15, 1810

66 [Y]ou have taken our lands from us and I do not see how we can remain at peace with you if you continue to do so. . . . You wish to prevent the Indians from doing as they wish, from uniting and considering their lands as the common property of the whole. 99

WILLIAM HENRY HARRISON, governor of the Indiana Territory, November 12, 1810

66 Is one of the fairest portions of the globe to remain in a state of nature, the haunt of a few . . . , when it seems destined . . . to give support to a large population and to be the seat of civilization? 99

Analyze the Viewpoints

1 What was Tecumseh's point of view about land? What was Harrison's point of view?

2 Why do you think each leader had the viewpoint he did?

3 **Make It Relevant** Identify an issue, or topic, that is important to your school or community. Think about different viewpoints people might have about the issue. Then find two statements in a newspaper or magazine that express two different points of view.

More Disagreements About Land

Some tribes did not sign the Treaty of Fort Wayne. They were angry that the United States government was taking over more Native American land.

Two Shawnee leaders wanted to unite the tribes against American settlers once again. They were Tenskwatawa (ten•SKWAHT•uh•wah) and his brother, Tecumseh (tuh•KUM•suh). Tenskwatawa was a religious leader. Many believed he could see into the future. For this reason, they called him the Prophet. Tecumseh, whose name means "Shooting Star," wanted to form a confederation of tribes to stop American settlement.

In 1808 the two leaders built a town called Prophetstown on the Wabash River just below the mouth of the Tippecanoe River. They wanted Prophetstown to serve as a capital for the new confederation of tribes.

In 1810 Tecumseh met with Governor Harrison in Vincennes. He told the governor that the Treaty of Fort Wayne was meaningless because land did not belong to one person or group. It belonged to all Native Americans. To show Harrison how Native Americans felt about being crowded off their lands, Tecumseh crowded Harrison off a bench on

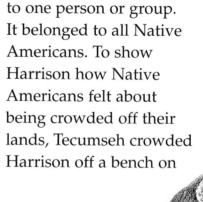

Tenskwatawa gained the name the Prophet by correctly predicting a solar eclipse.

which they were both sitting. This angered Harrison, who raised his sword. Tecumseh raised his tomahawk and warned Harrison that Native Americans would fight to save their land. The two leaders met again in 1811. Their disagreements were even stronger than before.

REVIEW Why did Tecumseh and Harrison meet?

The Battle of Tippecanoe

For some time Harrison had heard reports that Native Americans were attacking settlers in the Indiana Territory. When Tecumseh left Prophetstown to win support among tribes in the south, Harrison decided to act.

In the fall of 1811 Harrison and his army built Fort Harrison near the place the French called Terre Haute, or "high land." Harrison's troops then marched across the Ten O'Clock Line. On the

Both sides lost many fighters in the Battle of Tippecanoe.

night of November 6 they camped deep inside Native American land, about a mile from Prophetstown.

The next day the Native Americans attacked the American soldiers. The Prophet told his warriors that the Americans' bullets would not harm them. General Harrison's soldiers and the Prophet's warriors fought for two hours.

• **BIOGRAPHY** •

Frances Slocum 1773–1847
Character Trait: Courage

Frances Slocum was kidnapped by Native Americans from her home in Pennsylvania when she was five years old. She grew up among the Delawares, moved west to Kekionga, and then married a Miami chief named Shepocanah (shuh•POH•kon•ah). Known as Maconaquah (muh•KAHN•uh•kwah), she spent the rest of her life among her husband's family near Fort Wayne.

Maconaquah's family in Pennsylvania never gave up hope of finding her again. People everywhere knew about their search. In 1835 a trader met Maconaquah at her home near what is today the town of Peru, Indiana. Her brothers and sister visited two years later. Maconaquah would not return with them. She had "lived long and happy as an Indian."

MULTIMEDIA BIOGRAPHIES
Visit The Learning Site at www.harcourtschool.com/biographies to learn about other famous people.

Many Native Americans died. Then both sides retreated. This battle became known as the Battle of Tippecanoe.

The next day Harrison's troops destroyed Prophetstown. Then the army returned to Vincennes. Following the Battle of Tippecanoe, many Native Americans lost faith in the Prophet, Tecumseh, and the confederation.

Many people on both sides were killed or wounded in the battle. "Ours was a bloody victory, theirs [the Native Americans'] a bloody defeat," one of Harrison's soldiers said later. The American soldiers who died were buried at the site of the battle. Later, on the twenty-fifth anniversary of the battle, John Tipton, who owned the land where the battle took place, donated the battle-field to the state of Indiana. A monument was later built on the battle site.

The Battle of Tippecanoe did not bring peace to the Indiana Territory. In fact, the fighting helped bring about a much greater conflict.

REVIEW **What happened at the Battle of Tippecanoe and immediately afterward?**

The War of 1812

The American soldiers who entered Prophetstown after the Battle of Tippecanoe found British supplies, including guns. This meant that the British had armed the Native Americans to fight against American settlers.

At the same time, British ships attacked American trading ships on the Great Lakes and on the Atlantic Ocean. For these and other reasons, the United States declared war on Britain in June 1812. Most of the Native American tribes sided with the British. The Miamis did not support either side.

The War of 1812 lasted more than two years. Native Americans made raids into the Indiana Territory, forcing many settlers to move south of the Ohio River. The British and the Native Americans captured American forts in the region, including Fort Detroit. The fort's location near Canada was important to both the Americans and the British.

The fall of 1813 was a turning point in the war. A United States ship under the command of Oliver Hazard Perry

British and American ships fought in the War of 1812.

This scene of Tecumseh's death appears in the United States Capitol in Washington, D.C.

defeated the British on Lake Erie. The Americans now could cross Lake Erie to attack the British at Fort Detroit. The British, however, were retreating east. Harrison and his troops caught up with the British on the banks of the Thames (TEMZ) River, near the present-day Canadian city of London, Ontario.

The Battle of the Thames was brief. Harrison's soldiers defeated the British and the Native Americans. Among those who died in the battle was Tecumseh. After Tecumseh's death the Native American confederation fell apart. Conflicts soon ended between settlers and Native Americans in the areas that once formed part of the Northwest Territory. When the war ended in 1814, settlers in the Indiana Territory were ready to form a new state.

REVIEW How did the Battle of the Thames affect the Indiana Territory?

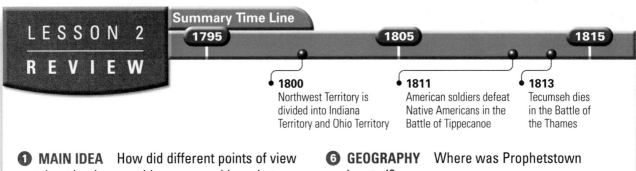

LESSON 2
REVIEW

Summary Time Line

1795   1805   1815

1800 Northwest Territory is divided into Indiana Territory and Ohio Territory

1811 American soldiers defeat Native Americans in the Battle of Tippecanoe

1813 Tecumseh dies in the Battle of the Thames

1 **MAIN IDEA** How did different points of view about land ownership cause problems between Native Americans and American settlers?

2 **WHY IT MATTERS** What are two different points of view held by leaders that cause conflicts today?

3 **VOCABULARY** How are the words **boundary** and **census** related?

4 **TIME LINE** How long after the Battle of Tippecanoe was the death of Tecumseh?

5 **READING SKILL—Sequence** What event occurred before the Battle of the Thames?

6 **GEOGRAPHY** Where was Prophetstown located?

7 **CRITICAL THINKING—Analyze** Why did the British help the Native Americans in the early 1800s? Why did the Native Americans help the British?

PERFORMANCE—Role-Play a Conversation With a partner, role-play a conversation between Tecumseh and William Henry Harrison. Each of you should discuss your point of view about land. Share your conversation with the class.

·SKILLS·

MAP AND GLOBE

Compare Historical Maps

VOCABULARY

historical map

▶ WHY IT MATTERS

One way to learn about history is to use historical maps. **Historical maps** give information about places at certain times in the past. Some historical maps show where events in the past took place. Others show how places looked at a certain time in the past. Knowing how to compare maps of the same place at different times can help you in several ways. You can discover how a place was and how it changed over time.

▶ WHAT YOU NEED TO KNOW

In 1800 Congress divided the Northwest Territory into the Ohio Territory and the Indiana Territory. Between 1800 and 1809 the Indiana Territory became smaller. The historical maps on page 133 show how the Indiana Territory changed. Look at the dates in the map titles. The map on the left shows the borders of Indiana and Ohio in 1800. The map on the right shows the borders in 1809.

Mapmakers have always used special instruments for measuring land and drawing maps.

Indiana Territory in 1800

Indiana Territory in 1809

PRACTICE THE SKILL

Study the maps, and look at the map keys to learn what the lines and colors on the maps stand for. Then use the maps to answer these questions.

1. What does the red line on both maps show?

2. What color is used to show the Indiana Territory on both maps? How did the size of the Indiana Territory change from 1800 to 1809?

3. By 1809 what territories had been formed out of parts of the Indiana Territory and Northwest Territory?

APPLY WHAT YOU LEARNED

List three things you learned about the history of the Indiana Territory from these maps. Be prepared to share your list with your class.

Practice your map and globe skills with the **GeoSkills CD-ROM.**

The Nineteenth State

1785　　　　　1805　　　　　1825

1810–1825

By the end of the War of 1812, Indiana's leaders had taken steps to make the territory a state. The 1815 census showed that more than 63,000 free adults lived in the Indiana Territory at that time. According to the Northwest Ordinance, this meant that Indiana's leaders could ask Congress to make the territory a state.

The Road to Statehood

A young man named Jonathan Jennings was eager to lead Indiana into statehood. Although he grew up in Pennsylvania, Jennings lived most of his adult life in the Indiana Territory. He worked as a lawyer in Vincennes and then moved to Charlestown in 1808.

In 1809 the voters of the Indiana Territory chose Jennings to **represent** them, or speak for them, in the United States Congress. Jennings had won votes by traveling across the territory. He gave speeches in town halls and churches and visited voters in their homes. The people learned that he worked hard. They believed that he had their best interests at heart. They again elected him to represent them in Congress in 1811, 1813, and 1815.

In January 1816 Jennings asked Congress to pass an enabling act for statehood. An **enabling act** was a special law that let a territory become a state. Congress passed an enabling act for Indiana on April 19, 1816. President James Madison then signed it into law. The law set Indiana's state borders. It also called for voters in Indiana to elect **delegates**, or representatives who would write Indiana's constitution.

The Harrison County Courthouse, in Corydon, was used as Indiana's state capitol from 1816–1825.

At a special meeting, or **convention**, Indiana's elected delegates voted to form a state. Then they wrote a constitution for the future state. A **constitution** is a written plan of government that describes basic laws and explains how the government should work.

The convention took place in the summer of 1816 in Corydon (KAWR•ih•duhn). Corydon had been the Indiana Territory's capital since 1813, when Indiana's leaders moved it there from Vincennes. They had wanted their place of government to be closer to the part of the territory along the Ohio River that was more settled.

Indiana voters sent 43 delegates to the convention. First, the delegates chose Jennings to lead the meeting. Next, they took a vote "to proceed to form a Constitution and State Government." Thirty-four of the forty-three delegates voted yes. The delegates who voted no thought Indiana should wait to become a state. These delegates believed that Indiana needed more money, more people, and stronger leaders. Because a majority, or most, of the delegates voted yes, the plan went forward.

The delegates then met in Corydon at the Harrison County Courthouse to write Indiana's new constitution.

These rooms are inside the capitol at Corydon. Today the building is a museum.

This painting of the Constitutional Elm is by Indiana artist William Forsyth. At right is Indiana's first constitution.

It was hot and humid that summer, so the 43 delegates worked outside in the shade of a huge elm tree. Because of the important work that took place beneath its branches, the tree came to be known as the Constitutional Elm.

REVIEW How did Jonathan Jennings help Indiana become a state?

A Plan for Government

In the first part of the constitution, the delegates wrote that "all power is inherent in [belongs to] the people." This means that the people of Indiana would control their own government and choose their leaders.

The 1816 Indiana Constitution provided for the rights and freedoms of its citizens. It said that "all men are born equally free and independent, and have certain natural, inherent, and unalienable [permanent] rights." Among these rights were life, liberty, property, and safety. The Indiana Constitution did not give everyone the right to vote. Under this first constitution, women, African Americans, and Native Americans could not vote. Only white men who had lived in Indiana for at least one year had this right. Indiana citizens also would enjoy freedom of religion, freedom of speech, and other rights guaranteed by the United States Constitution.

The constitution of Indiana, like the United States Constitution, set up a government with three parts, each with separate jobs to do. The General Assembly would be made up of representatives who would make the laws. A governor would carry out the laws. The state supreme court would decide whether the laws were fair.

The delegates also made sure that no one part of the government had more author-ity, or power, than the others. Each part of the government was given ways to check, or stop, the others' actions if needed.

The delegates did not always agree on what Indiana's constitution should say. For example, they argued over whether slavery should be allowed. Some dele-gates wanted to allow it. Jennings and other delegates believed that it was wrong for one person to take away the freedom of another. Finally the delegates voted to make slavery illegal, or against the law, in Indiana. This decision set Indiana apart from many other states.

Another section of Indiana's constitu-tion made the new state different from all other states. This section promised a state public school system. It would support schools from the elementary level through college. The constitution granted land in one township for a public univer-sity. Indiana University, in Bloomington, was later built in this township.

The delegates finished writing the con-stitution in less than one month. They signed it on June 29, 1816. Then they sent it to Washington, D.C. On December 11, 1816, President James Madison signed the act that made Indiana the nineteenth state of the United States. Indiana was now "on an equal footing with the original States in all respects whatever," as stated in the Northwest Ordinance of 1787.

REVIEW **When did Indiana become a state?**

A Capital for the New State

Indiana's constitution took effect as soon as the delegates signed it. In August 1816, voters made their choices for the new government in elections. They elected Jonathan Jennings to be Indiana's first governor. They also chose representatives to work in the General Assembly. The General Assembly first gathered in November 1816 at Corydon. The first Indiana Supreme Court also met at Corydon.

Indiana's constitution named Corydon as the state capital. It remained the center of state government until 1825.

• HERITAGE •

Statehood Day

Statehood Day, or Indiana Day, is celebrated each year on December 11. On that day in 1816, Indiana became the nineteenth state in the United States. The governor marks the day with a special proclamation, or official announce-ment, that tells why the date is important. Statehood Day reminds the people of Indiana that they have many reasons to be proud of their state.

Indiana was the nineteenth state—symbolized by the nineteen stars in its state flag.

Meanwhile, in 1818 the state bought land from the Miamis, Delawares, and other Native American tribes in the central part of Indiana. Settlers quickly spread out throughout this area. Many people now thought Corydon was too far south to be the capital. Indiana's leaders agreed that a location in the center of the state would make it easier for all citizens to reach the capital. They also thought that a location in central Indiana would encourage more people to settle there and to the north.

In 1820 the General Assembly sent a group of people to the center of the state to look for a good location for a new capital. The group found a wooded site in the area where Fall Creek flows into the White River. They decided on a square mile there for the new capital. The General Assembly approved the site in 1821 and chose a name for the future capital. It would be called Indianapolis. *Indianapolis* includes the name of the new state—*Indiana* and the Greek word for city—*polis*. The name means just what Indianapolis is— Indiana's city or its capital.

The General Assembly hired Alexander Ralston to develop a plan for the city. Ralston had worked with Pierre L'Enfant (lahn•FAHNT) in mapping Washington, D.C. He designed the plan for the square mile that would form the center of Indianapolis. Most of the government buildings would stand

Plan for Indianapolis, 1821

Analyze Primary Sources

This map shows the plan Ralston made for Indianapolis in 1821. The state government moved there in 1825. Two years later 1,000 people called Indianapolis home.

❶ The governor never moved into the house at Governor's Circle because the builders forgot to include a kitchen.

❷ Squares 12, 19, and 90 were set aside for religious purposes.

❸ The State House was square 53.

◈ What is similar about most of the street names of Indianapolis?

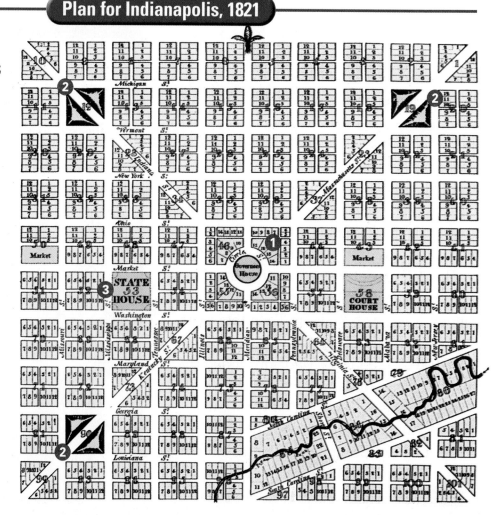

around a circle at the center of the city. Four wide streets, or avenues, would run from the circle to the four corners of the square mile. Other streets formed a grid within the square.

Lots, or pieces of land, in the new capital city went on sale in fall 1821. The county courthouse was built first. A governor's mansion and state capitol, where the General Assembly would meet, were built near the center circle. In 1824, wagons carried all the state's records over rough roads from Corydon to the new capital. By 1825, state lawmakers were doing government business in Indianapolis.

REVIEW Why was the new capital located in the center of the state?

Indiana's second state capitol, in Indianapolis

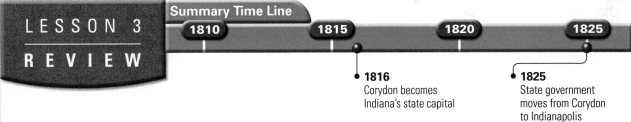

LESSON 3

REVIEW

Summary Time Line

1810 | 1815 | 1820 | 1825

1816
Corydon becomes Indiana's state capital

1825
State government moves from Corydon to Indianapolis

1 **MAIN IDEA** How did the people of Indiana work to set up their new state?

2 **WHY IT MATTERS** How are state governments in the United States today organized in similar ways?

3 **VOCABULARY** Where might you find a **delegate**? Explain.

4 **TIME LINE** For how many years was the Indiana capital located in Corydon?

5 **READING SKILL—Sequence** What had to happen before delegates could meet at a convention to write a constitution for Indiana?

6 **HISTORY** What happened in 1815 that enabled the Indiana Territory to become a state in 1816?

7 **CRITICAL THINKING—Hypothesize** What would have happened if most of the delegates to the convention had voted against forming a state government?

PERFORMANCE—Research Government Documents Skim a copy of Indiana's first constitution. Choose a small section to study more closely. In your own words, explain to your classmates what the section says. Explain why the section is important or interesting.

·SKILLS·

CHART AND GRAPH

Read a Line Graph

VOCABULARY

population
line graph

CD 5
Track 6

▶ WHY IT MATTERS

Information comes in many different forms. Graphs can make information that includes numbers easy to understand. You have read about how the **population**, or number of people, of Indiana changed as more settlers moved west. This increase in population can be shown on a line graph. A **line graph** shows how

numbers change over a period of time. Learning to read a line graph can help you understand how quickly or slowly numbers change.

▶ WHAT YOU NEED TO KNOW

Look at the line graph on the next page. To understand the information it shows, first read the title. The title tells

Urban populations grew quickly in early Indiana. The image below is of Washington Street in Indianapolis.

140

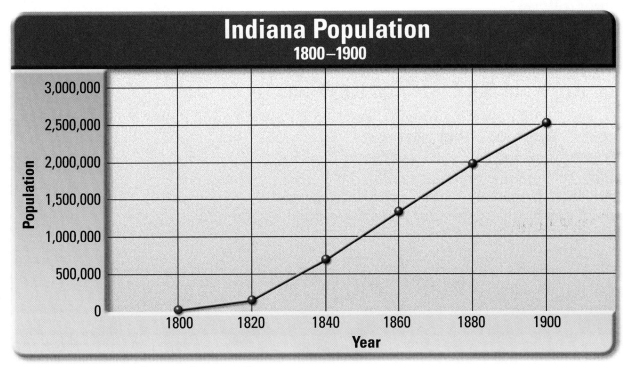

Indiana Population
1800–1900

SOURCE: United States Census Bureau

you that this is a graph of the population of Indiana between 1800 and 1900.

Now read the information on the bottom and left side of the graph. The dates along the bottom tell you the years in which Indiana's population was counted. The numbers on the left side of the graph give the number of people living in the state each year.

The dot on each line shows the population for that year. The red line connecting the dots clearly shows how the population changed over the years.

▶ PRACTICE THE SKILL

Find the year 1840 at the bottom of the graph. With your finger, trace the line upward until you reach the dot. Then move your finger to the left to find the population number. Because the numbers on the left are rounded

off, this number is not the exact number of people in 1840. It is a rough figure for the population in 1840. There were about 700,000 people in Indiana then.

1 Find the year 1860. Repeat the process. What was the population in that year?

2 Look at the red line on the graph. What happened to Indiana's population between 1840 and 1860?

3 In what 20-year period did the population grow the most?

▶ APPLY WHAT YOU LEARNED

Create a line graph to show the change in the population of Indianapolis between 1850 and 2000. Use this information: 1850 (8,091), 1900 (169,164), 1950 (427,173), 2000 (781,870).

4 Review and Test Preparation

Summary Time Line

1785   1790

1785
Land that would become
Indiana is part of the
Northwest Territory

CD5 Track 7

USE YOUR READING SKILLS

Complete this graphic organizer to show that you understand
the sequence of key events that led to Indiana's statehood.
A copy of this graphic organizer appears on page 43 of the
Activity Book.

From Territory to Statehood

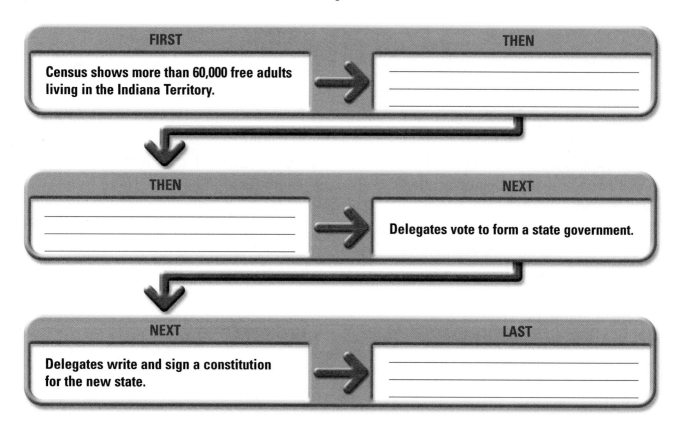

FIRST
Census shows more than 60,000 free adults living in the Indiana Territory.

THEN
_____

THEN
_____

NEXT
Delegates vote to form a state government.

NEXT
Delegates write and sign a constitution for the new state.

LAST
_____

THINK & WRITE

Write a Poem   Think about how Native
Americans in what is now Indiana may have
felt about settlers moving onto their lands.
Write a poem about their possible feelings.
Be sure to use descriptive words in your
poem. Read your poem aloud to the class.

Write a Persuasive Letter   Imagine that
you are a delegate to the state convention in
1816. You think it is too soon for Indiana to
become a state. Write a letter to Jonathan
Jennings to persuade him to agree with your
point of view.

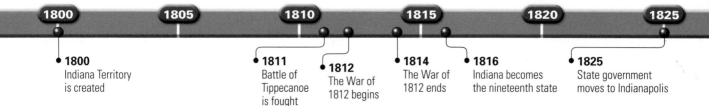

| 1800 | 1805 | 1810 | 1815 | 1820 | 1825 |

1800
Indiana Territory is created

1811
Battle of Tippecanoe is fought

1812
The War of 1812 begins

1814
The War of 1812 ends

1816
Indiana becomes the nineteenth state

1825
State government moves to Indianapolis

USE THE TIME LINE

Use the chapter summary time line to answer these questions.

1 Which came first, the Battle of Tippecanoe or the War of 1812?

2 How soon after the end of the War of 1812 did Indiana become a state?

USE VOCABULARY

Fill in the blanks with the correct terms.

ordinance (p. 121)

confederation (p. 123)

retreat (p. 123)

census (p. 127)

enabling act (p. 134)

3 The 1815 _____ showed the territory had more than 63,000 free adults.

4 Harrison's army forced the Native Americans to _____ at the Battle of Tippecanoe.

5 The Native American _____ broke up after Tecumseh died in the Battle of the Thames.

6 An _____ allowed the Indiana Territory to become a state.

7 The _____ passed in 1785 told how land was to be divided and sold.

RECALL FACTS

Answer the questions.

8 What was the first American town in Indiana and the Northwest Territory?

9 What was the Ten O'Clock Line?

10 Who was Indiana's first governor?

Write the letter of the best choice.

11 **TEST PREP** The Land Ordinance of 1785 set aside land in every township for—
  A settlers.
  B public schools.
  C a new capital.
  D Native Americans.

12 **TEST PREP** Tecumseh met with Governor Harrison to discuss—
  F the borders of the Ten O'Clock Line.
  G Harrison's visit to Prophetstown.
  H settlement on Native American land.
  J the British fur trade.

THINK CRITICALLY

13 Why do you think some Native American leaders signed the Treaty of Fort Wayne and others did not?

14 Why was it important to many people that Indiana become a state?

APPLY SKILLS

Compare Historical Maps

15 Use the maps on page 133 to name the territories or states formed from the Northwest Territory between 1800 and 1809.

Read a Line Graph

16 Find a line graph in a newspaper or magazine. Copy the graph, or cut it out. Write at least two sentences about the changes shown on the graph. Explain the graph to a classmate.

CD5 Track 8

The GEORGE ROGERS CLARK
National Historical Park

GET READY

The George Rogers Clark National Historical Park honors a military hero of the American Revolution. In 1779 Clark successfully captured Fort Sackville, a British outpost near Vincennes. To get there, he and his troops traveled more than 180 miles (290 km). Clark's victory contributed to the decision by the British to surrender a large land area. This area included present-day Ohio, Indiana, Illinois, Michigan, Wisconsin, and Minnesota and was the largest land capture of the Revolutionary War. A granite memorial to Clark's victory was created to mark the 150th anniversary of the American Revolution. The memorial, which overlooks the Wabash River, was dedicated in 1936 at a ceremony led by President Franklin D. Roosevelt.

The walls of the memorial are two feet (almost 1 m) thick.

LOCATE IT

INDIANA

Vincennes

People dressed as British soldiers reenact the surrender at Fort Sackville. Others, dressed as frontiersmen, get ready to re-create the charge led by George Rogers Clark.

Inside the memorial, seven murals line the walls surrounding the central statue of Clark. The 28-foot-tall (9-m) murals show the events leading up to and immediately following the capture of Fort Sackville.

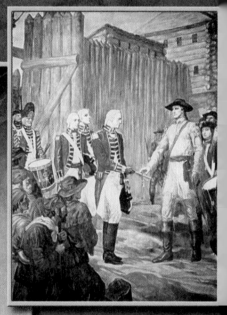

One of the murals at the memorial, *Fort Sackville: British Yield Possession*, shows the British colonel giving up his sword to Clark.

TAKE A FIELD TRIP

A VIRTUAL TOUR
Visit The Learning Site at
www.harcourtschool.com/tours
to take virtual tours of other parks and scenic areas.

CD5
Track 9

2 Review and Test Preparation

USE VOCABULARY

Write a paragraph about how the Indiana Territory became a state. Use the following terms.

census (p. 127)   **convention** (p. 135)

Congress (p. 121)   **delegate** (p. 134)

constitution (p. 135)   **enabling act** (p. 134)

RECALL FACTS

Answer these questions.

1. What was the first permanent French settlement in the Indiana area?

2. What law organized western lands and gave the name *Northwest Territory* to the land west of the Appalachian Mountains and north of the Ohio River?

3. Who was the first governor of the state of Indiana?

Write the letter of the best choice.

4. **TEST PREP** Anthony Wayne and his army defeated the Native Americans at the—
   A Battle of Fallen Timbers.
   B Battle of the Thames.
   C Battle of Tippecanoe.
   D War of 1812.

5. **TEST PREP** Tenskwatawa and his brother Tecumseh's main goal was to—
   F unite the Native Americans against settlers.
   G make treaties with the United States.
   H fight as allies of the French.
   J attack British forts.

6. **TEST PREP** To become a state, an area in the Northwest Territory needed at least—
   A 3 million acres of open land.
   B 60,000 free adult men living there.
   C 43 delegates at the convention.
   D 5,000 settlers farming there.

7. **TEST PREP** The first Indiana constitution provided for—
   F the governor to be William Henry Harrison.
   G women to be given voting rights.
   H a public school system to be created.
   J the state capital to be Indianapolis.

THINK CRITICALLY

8. How did the arrival of Europeans change life for Native Americans?

9. How did George Rogers Clark show his patriotism?

10. As a pioneer settler in Indiana, how might you have felt about the Proclamation of 1763? How would you have felt toward the Native Americans living in Indiana?

11. Why was Clark's victory at Fort Sackville important to American history?

12. Under which treaty did the United States government buy almost 3 million acres of land?

146

APPLY SKILLS

Compare Historical Maps
Use the historical maps below to answer the following questions.

13 What part of Indiana was not claimed by Native Americans in 1816?

14 About how much of Indiana did Native Americans claim in 1816?

15 How did land claims in Indiana change from 1816 to 1825?

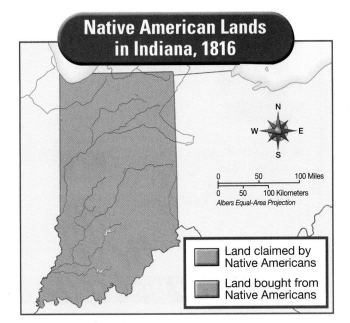

Native American Lands in Indiana, 1816

0   50   100 Miles
0   50   100 Kilometers
Albers Equal-Area Projection

Land claimed by Native Americans

Land bought from Native Americans

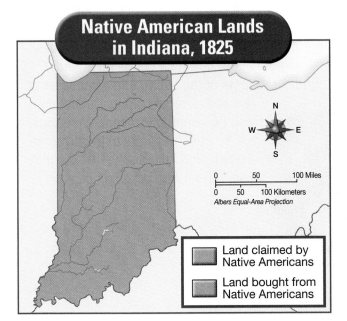

Native American Lands in Indiana, 1825

0   50   100 Miles
0   50   100 Kilometers
Albers Equal-Area Projection

Land claimed by Native Americans

Land bought from Native Americans

1675

1725

1775

1825

Visual Summary

1679 La Salle explores the Indiana area p. 95

1763 French and Indian War ends p. 104

1779 George Rogers Clark captures Fort Sackville pp. 113–114

1810 Tecumseh meets with William Henry Harrison at Vincennes p. 128

1816 Indiana becomes the nineteenth state p. 137

147

Unit Activities

 Visit The Learning Site at
www.harcourtschool.com/
socialstudies/activities
for additional activities.

Perform an Interview

Choose a person from early Indiana history. Find out more about that person's life and what he or she did for Indiana. Then prepare a script containing at least ten questions and answers. Ask a classmate to be your interviewer. Have the interviewer ask you the questions in the script. Then imagine you are that person from history as you answer the questions.

Write an Eyewitness Account

Imagine that you fought in the Battle of Fallen Timbers or in the Battle of Tippecanoe. Research the battle you chose. Then write a report about it as if you were there as it happened. Use the information you have gathered to make your account as detailed as possible. Describe the scene, using descriptive language and images. Be sure to use first-person pronouns such as *I*, *me*, and *my*. Read your account of the battle to the class.

VISIT YOUR LIBRARY

■ *These Lands Are Ours: Tecumseh's Fight for the Old Northwest (Stories of America)* by Kate Connell. Raintree/Steck-Vaughn.

■ *William Henry Harrison, Young Tippecanoe* by Howard Peckham. Patria.

■ *George Rogers Clark: American General* by Michael Burgan. Chelsea House Publishing.

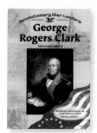

COMPLETE THE UNIT PROJECT

Historical Medal Work with three or four classmates to complete the unit project—a medal marking a key event in Indiana history before 1816. Choose an event that can be easily illustrated in the form of a scene on a medal. Check the facts of the event, and discuss what the scene should show. Decide on a short title for your medal. Then draw the scene on a piece of posterboard, color it, and include the title. Display your medal with others in the classroom.

Progress as a State

Canal Boat Lantern,
middle 1800s

Whitewater Canal in Metamora, Indiana

CD 6
Track 1

3

Progress as a State

" The Crossroads of America "

—Indiana's state motto, chosen in 1937

Preview the Content

Read the title and the Main Idea statement for each lesson
in the unit. Then use what you have read to make a web for
each chapter. Write down words or phrases that will help you
identify the main topics to be covered in the unit.

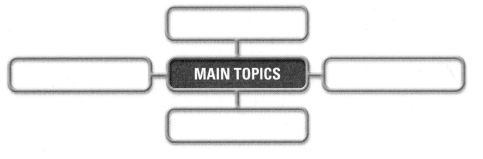

MAIN TOPICS

Preview the Vocabulary

Context Clues   Context clues are words that can help you
figure out the meaning of an unfamiliar word. Scan the unit
and find the terms **navigable**, **surplus**, and **suburbs**. For each
term, write a sentence that defines it.

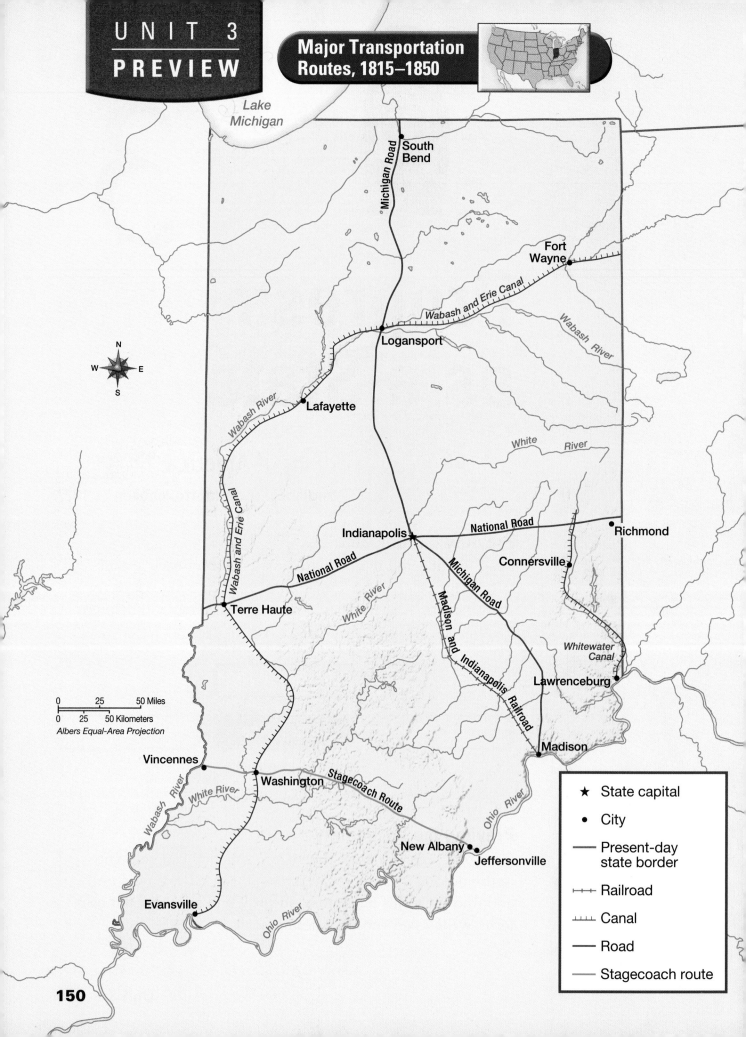

Lake Michigan

South Bend

Michigan Road

Fort Wayne

Wabash and Erie Canal

Wabash River

Logansport

Wabash River

Lafayette

White River

Wabash and Erie Canal

National Road

Richmond

Indianapolis

National Road

Connersville

Michigan Road

Madison and Indianapolis Railroad

Whitewater Canal

Terre Haute

White River

Lawrenceburg

Madison

Vincennes

Wabash River

White River

Washington

Stagecoach Route

Ohio River

New Albany

Jeffersonville

Evansville

Ohio River

N
W E
S

0 25 50 Miles
0 25 50 Kilometers
Albers Equal-Area Projection

★ State capital
• City
— Present-day state border
┼┼┼ Railroad
⊔⊔⊔ Canal
— Road
— Stagecoach route

Indiana's Ten Largest Cities

1860	1950
Indianapolis	Indianapolis
New Albany	Gary
Evansville	Fort Wayne
Lafayette	Evansville
Fort Wayne	South Bend
Terre Haute	Hammond
Richmond	Terre Haute
La Porte	Muncie
Vincennes	Anderson

Rural and Urban Population
in Indiana, 1850–1990

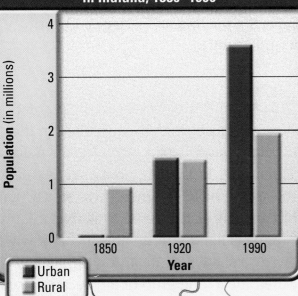

Population (in millions)

Year

- Urban
- Rural

Key Events

1816   The Lincoln family moves to Indiana   pp. 158–159

1829   Steamboats start traveling on the Wabash River   p. 165

1921   Indiana women vote in state elections for the first time   p. 203

1945   World War II ends   p. 210

1961   Gus Grissom becomes the second American in space   p. 212

1800

1850

1900

1950

2000

151

A Place Called Freedom

by Scott Russell Sanders
illustrated by Thomas B. Allen

A Place Called Freedom tells the story of Joshua Starman, his wife, and their two children. They worked as slaves on a Tennessee plantation until their master freed them in 1832. The family makes the journey to Indiana, where they begin a new life. Joshua returns to the South many times, bringing relatives and friends back to Indiana with him each time.

As the community grows into a village, the people must decide what to call their new home. The story is based on the founding of Lyles Station, one of Indiana's historic African American communities.

Down in Tennessee, on the plantation where I was born, Mama worked in the big house and Papa worked in the fields. The master of that big house set us free in the spring of 1832, when I was seven years old and my sister, Lettie, was five.

Papa called Lettie a short drink of water, because she was little and wriggly, and he called me a long gulp of air, because I was tall and full of talk.

As soon as we could pack some food and clothes, we left the plantation, heading north for Indiana. Our aunts and uncles and cousins who were still slaves hugged us hard and waved until we were out of sight.

Papa said it would be safer to travel at night.

"How're we going to find our way in the dark?" I asked him.

"We'll follow the drinking gourd," Papa answered. He pointed to the glittery sky, and I saw he meant the Big Dipper. He showed me how to find the North Star by drawing an arrow from the dipper's lip. Papa loved stars. That's why, when he gave up his old slave's name and chose a new one, he called himself Joshua Starman. And that's why my name is James Starman.

It was a weary, long way. Night after night as we traveled, the buttery bowl of the moon filled up, then emptied again. When Lettie got tired, she rode on Papa's shoulders for a while, or on Mama's hip. But I walked the whole way on my own feet.

At last one morning, just after sunrise, we came to the Ohio River. A fisherman with a face as wrinkled as an old boot carried us over the water in his boat. On the far shore we set our feet on the free soil of Indiana. White flowers covered the hills that day like feathers on a goose.

By and by we met a Quaker family who took us into their house, gave us seed, and loaned us a mule and a plow, all because they believed that slavery was a sin. We helped on their farm, working shoulder to shoulder, and we planted our own crops.

That first year Papa raised enough corn and wheat for us to buy some land beside the Wabash River, where the dirt was as black as my skin. Papa could grow anything, he could handle horses, and he could build a barn or a bed.

Before winter, Papa and Mama built us a sturdy cabin. Every night we sat by the fire and Papa told stories that made the shadows dance. Every morning Mama held school for Lettie and me. Mama knew how to read and write from helping with lessons for the master's children. She could sew clothes that fit you like the wind, and her cooking made your tongue glad.

Quaker   a religious group that opposed slavery

While the ground was still frozen, Papa rode south through the cold nights, down to the plantation in Tennessee. We fretted until he showed up again at our door, leading two of my aunts, two uncles, and five cousins. They stayed with us until they could buy land near ours and build their own cabins.

Again and again Papa went back to Tennessee, and each time he came home with more of the folks we loved.

Hearing about our settlement, black people arrived from all over the South, some of them freed like us, some of them runaways. There were carpenters and blacksmiths, basket weavers and barrel makers.

Soon we had a church, then a store, then a stable, then a mill to grind our grain. For the first time in our lives, we had money, just enough to get by, and we watched every penny.

After a few years, the railroad decided to run tracks through our village, because so many people had gathered here. If our place was going to be on the map, it needed a name. At a meeting, folks said we should call it Starman, in honor of Mama and Papa. But Mama and Papa said, "No, let's name it Freedom."

And that's how we came to live in a place called Freedom.

We all celebrated the new name by building a school, where Mama could teach everyone, young and old, to read and write and do sums. She made me want to learn everything there was to know.

When Mama first told me about the alphabet, I wondered how I could ever remember twenty-six different letters. But I learned them all in a flash. It was like magic to me, the way those letters joined up to make words.

Papa's farming was also like magic. He would put seeds in the ground, and before you knew it, here came melon vines or cornstalks. He planted trees, and here came apples or nuts or shade.

fretted worried
blacksmiths craftspeople who made goods out of iron

For a long while, I couldn't decide whether I wanted to grow up and become a farmer like Papa or a teacher like Mama.

"I don't see why a teacher can't farm," Mama said.

"I don't see why a farmer can't teach," said Papa.

They were right, you know, because I raised the beans and potatoes for supper, and I wrote these words with my own hand.

Analyze the Literature

1 Why do you think Joshua Starman told his son that it would be safer for their family to travel during the night?

2 Why did Joshua Starman and his wife want to name their village "Freedom"?

READ A BOOK

START THE UNIT PROJECT

Create a Visual Time Line
Work with a partner to create a visual time line of how life in Indiana has changed since 1850. Find or draw pictures to illustrate those changes. As you read the unit, take notes on how the lives of people in Indiana changed throughout the nineteenth and twentieth centuries.

USE TECHNOLOGY

GO ONLINE

Visit The Learning Site at **www.harcourtschool.com/socialstudies** for additional activities, primary sources, and other resources to use in this unit.

ROUND BARN IN HANCOCK COUNTY

Round barns can be found throughout the Middle West. The largest round barn in Indiana is located in Hancock County, but Fulton County has more round barns than any other county. Each year, Fulton County holds a Round Barn Festival to celebrate the unique style of barns built in the late nineteenth and early twentieth centuries.

LOCATE IT

INDIANA

Hancock County

CD 6 3
Track 3

CD 6
Track 4

5

A New State

" Doubtless future generations may see this a flourishing place. "

—Lydia Bacon, pioneer, 1811

CHAPTER READING SKILL

Compare and Contrast

To **compare** people, places, events, or ideas, you find the ways in which they are alike. To **contrast** people, places, events, or ideas, you find the ways in which they are different.

As you read this chapter, compare and contrast the people, places, events, and ideas that you find.

COMPARE ←→ CONTRAST

MAIN IDEA
Read to find out how and why settlers in Indiana created communities in the early 1800s.

WHY IT MATTERS
Community life is still important in Indiana today.

VOCABULARY
self-sufficient
isolated
communal
gristmill
industry

Pioneers in Indiana

1815   1865   1915

1815–1850

In 1816 Indiana became a state. That year the whole country seemed to be on the move. Morris Birkbeck, a British traveler, wrote in 1817 that the United States was "breaking up and moving westward." To thousands of people in the 1800s, the territory west of the Appalachian Mountains promised more land and the chance to build a better life.

The Lincoln Family

Thomas Lincoln, the father of Abraham Lincoln, was typical of Indiana's pioneers. In 1816 he decided to move from Kentucky to southern Indiana with his wife and their children. Lincoln wanted land of his own to farm as well as new opportunities. In addition, the Lincoln family was growing uncomfortable with slavery in Kentucky. Tom Lincoln knew that Indiana was offering land to settlers for a good price. He also knew that Indiana's constitution did not allow slavery.

FAST FACT Abraham Lincoln attended school for less than one year, yet he was always a student. He was known to walk miles to borrow a book.

Pioneer families lived in small, one-room log cabins.

While his family stayed behind in Kentucky, Tom Lincoln crossed the Ohio River. Then he set off on foot into what is now Spencer County. There he chose a site for his family's new home on the thickly forested banks of Little Pigeon Creek.

Pioneer settlers like Lincoln had to make sure that the land they were buying would support their families. Most of these settlers wanted land to farm. They looked for land that had rich soil and water nearby. Lincoln cleared all the brush from his land. He piled it up to form a fence and used an ax to mark the trees that bordered his future fields. In this way Lincoln made his claim to the land. Later, he went to the land office in Vincennes and paid for his 160 acres.

Tom Lincoln returned to Kentucky for his wife, Nancy, and their two children. Sally was nine years old, and Abraham was seven. The family headed to Little Pigeon Creek with a cow and four horses. They pulled a cart loaded with tools for farming and carpentry, a spinning wheel for making cloth, and all their household goods. The Lincoln family made Indiana their home for 14 years.

REVIEW What two reasons did Tom Lincoln have for moving his family from Kentucky to Indiana?

Starting from Scratch

There was no new house waiting for the Lincoln family in Indiana. Like most pioneer families, the Lincolns had to start from scratch to build their new life.

Their first home in Indiana was a simple shelter called a half-faced camp. It had three walls and a slanted roof made with poles and woven branches.

The Lincoln Family's Migration

Movement Many families moved from Kentucky to Indiana in the early 1800s.

In what directions might pioneers have traveled from Kentucky to Indiana?

The fourth side of the shelter was left open. A half-faced camp was certainly not meant to be a permanent home. After the Lincolns cleared the fields of trees and planted the first crops, they began work on a log cabin. Everyone worked together to raise the log walls. The pioneers fitted the walls together without any nails. They filled in the cracks between the logs with moss, clay, or mud.

Pioneer cabins usually had just one room, with a floor of dirt pounded flat. At night the children climbed to a loft to sleep. The loft was part of the cabin between the ceiling and the roof. The adults slept downstairs on beds made from dry leaves covered with blankets.

A CLOSER LOOK
A Log Cabin

Log cabins were usually no more than 20 feet (6 m) long and 10 to 15 feet (3–5 m) wide.

1 Logs were fitted together without nails. Spaces were filled with moss, clay, or mud.

2 Children often slept in an overhead loft.

3 Fireplaces were used for cooking and heat.

4 Pioneers used spinning wheels to make yarn or thread for cloth.

In what ways are log cabins the same as homes today?

Over time, the Lincoln family made their home more comfortable. Tom and Abe made furniture and utensils. Nancy and Sally sewed clothing and blankets and made colorful quilts.

As the Lincolns learned, pioneer life was not easy. People had to supply their own food. Mostly they ate corn, which they pounded into a mush. The meat they ate came from hogs they raised or wild animals they hunted. Pioneers had to be **self-sufficient**, or able to produce everything they needed to live. They faced snowy winters, rainy summers, and lots of hard work. Even though life was hard, most of Indiana's early settlers did well.

By 1830 Tom Lincoln thought that southern Indiana had become too crowded. He decided to move on again. This time he took his family to the Illinois frontier. Thousands of other pioneer families stayed in Indiana to help build the new state.

REVIEW How was a half-faced camp different from a log cabin?

Building a Community

During the early 1800s most Indiana families lived far from their neighbors. Pioneer homes and farms were **isolated**, or separated from one another. There were few roads, and travel was difficult. Even though families were mostly self-sufficient, they knew the importance of cooperation. It took every member of

MAIN IDEA
Read to find out how transportation contributed to Indiana's growth in the nineteenth century.

WHY IT MATTERS
The movement of people, goods, and ideas continues to be important today.

VOCABULARY

flatboat
steamboat
navigable
trace
stagecoach
canal
locomotive
hub

New Ways to Travel

CD6
Track 5

1815 — 1865 — 1915

1815–1860

One of the greatest challenges for Indiana pioneers in the early nineteenth century was transportation. Travel between Indiana's settlements was difficult and took a long time. As Indiana's population increased and towns became larger, new ways of travel helped the state grow and change.

Travel by Water

Long before Indiana's first roads were built, most people traveled by water. Rivers were one of Indiana's first ways of transportation. Eastern Woodlands Indians and French and British fur traders traveled Indiana's rivers in canoes. Later, pioneers arrived in Indiana by boat on the Ohio River.

Early pioneers used flatboats to carry passengers and take goods to market. A **flatboat** looks like a large raft. Farmers taking goods to market could use a flatboat for one-way trips only. Flatboats can float only downstream, or in the direction of the current. At the end of the trip, farmers would break up their flatboats and sell the wood. Then they would either walk back or pay to travel back upstream on a keelboat.

Keelboats were similar to flatboats, except that they could be pushed upriver with long poles.

FAST FACT There were more than 400 covered bridges in Indiana in 1836. By 2002 only 93 remained.

LOCATE IT

INDIANA

Bridgeton

Gristmills were among Indiana's earliest **industries**, or businesses that make one kind of product. Most towns also had a general store that sold everything from nails to laces for boots. General stores were also good places for farmers to hear news from inside and outside their town.

As settlements grew, Native Americans were forced to leave the area. In 1838 more than 800 Potawatomi were forced to march from northern Indiana to what is now Kansas. This forced march was called the Trail of Death because more than 150 Native Americans died along the way.

Indiana's towns continued to grow. By 1850 Indiana had eight towns with populations of more than 2,500.

REVIEW What kinds of communal activities did early Indiana pioneers participate in?

General stores sold all sorts of goods.

LESSON 1 REVIEW

Summary Time Line

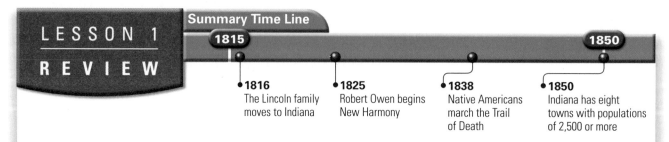

1815 — 1850

- **1816** The Lincoln family moves to Indiana
- **1825** Robert Owen begins New Harmony
- **1838** Native Americans march the Trail of Death
- **1850** Indiana has eight towns with populations of 2,500 or more

1 MAIN IDEA How did Indiana's settlers establish communities in the early 1800s?

2 WHY IT MATTERS How are communities important to Hoosiers today?

3 VOCABULARY Sort the following vocabulary words into two groups on the basis of their meanings. Then give each word's meaning. **self-sufficient, gristmill, isolated, industry**

4 TIME LINE How many years after the Lincoln family moved to Indiana did the state have eight towns with populations of 2,500 or more?

5 READING SKILL—Compare and Contrast How were early pioneer farms different from the first communities in Indiana? How were they similar?

6 GEOGRAPHY From which regions of the United States did most Indiana pioneers come? How did they travel?

7 ECONOMICS How did Indiana pioneers in the early 1800s get the goods and services they needed?

8 CRITICAL THINKING—Synthesize Why did so many people choose the hard life of a pioneer?

 PERFORMANCE—Write a Letter Imagine what it must have been like to move to Indiana in the early 1800s. Write a letter to a friend describing life on a pioneer farm. Include three things you like about life on your farm and three things you miss about your old home.

Steamboats traveled up and down the Wabash and Ohio Rivers.

A better solution for going up and down rivers came when Robert Fulton invented a steam-powered boat in the early 1800s. By 1829 steamboats were traveling the Mississippi River, the Ohio River, and the lower part of the Wabash River. A **steamboat** has a large paddle wheel, powered by steam, that pushes it through the water. The paddle wheel allowed the steamboat to travel downstream twice as fast as a flatboat. Steamboats traveled upstream almost as quickly, allowing goods to move in both directions.

Steamboats could be used only on navigable rivers. Any river wide and deep enough for ships to travel is considered to be **navigable** (NA•vih•guh•buhl). Of Indiana's rivers only the Ohio River and the lower part of the Wabash River were navigable by steamboats. Steamboats also traveled on the Great Lakes. Michigan City, on Lake Michigan, became an important port for steamboat traffic.

REVIEW What was the biggest drawback to flatboat travel?

Linking Indiana's Towns

When the first pioneers arrived in Indiana, there were no roads. There were only trails made by animals looking for water. These trails, or **traces**, crossed through wooded areas and between rivers and creeks. Traces were narrow, with room for no more than one person or one animal at a time. Pioneers began clearing the brush so the trails would be wide enough for wagons.

To make travel easier, pioneers laid logs across the trails. People called the log trails "corduroy roads" because they looked like bumpy corduroy cloth. The corduroy roads were drier but so bumpy that they made the ride uncomfortable. The settlers tried splitting the round logs into flat planks. These "plank roads" were smoother, but rainy weather made them slippery.

• HERITAGE •

The Crossroads of America

Indiana's state motto is Crossroads of America. A crossroads is a place where transportation routes come together. Although the state motto was not officially adopted until 1937, the name Crossroads of America has its roots in the nineteenth century. The roads, ports, canals, and railroads Hoosiers built helped connect Indiana communities and other places in the United States. Today, Indiana has more interstate highways than any other state. Its central location makes Indiana perfect for business, industry, and tourism.

Road markers helped travelers on the National Road in Indiana.

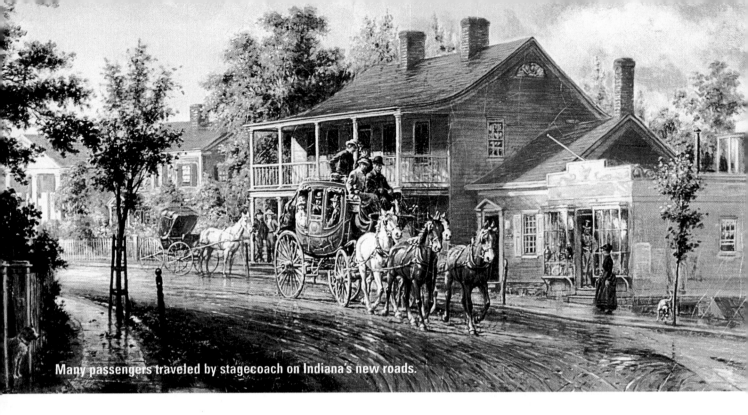

Many passengers traveled by stagecoach on Indiana's new roads.

Hoosier leaders understood the importance of connecting Indiana's towns with one another and with places outside the state. In the 1820s Indiana built the Michigan Road. This road connected Madison, Indiana, on the Ohio River, to Lake Michigan in the north. The Michigan Road passed through Indiana's new capital, Indianapolis.

In 1829 the National Road, which was built by the United States government, stretched from Maryland to Indiana. The National Road passed through Richmond, Indianapolis, and Terre Haute and continued into Illinois.

Within a few years a steady stream of wagons and stagecoaches traveled the National Road. A **stagecoach** was a wagon with a closed carriage, pulled by horses. Stagecoaches carried people as well as goods on these roads, linking Indiana with other parts of the United States.

REVIEW What road in Indiana connected the Ohio River with Lake Michigan?

Indiana Canals

Many farmers lived far from Indiana's two navigable rivers and the Great Lakes. This made it hard for them to ship their goods to market.

To help farmers and townspeople, Indiana's leaders decided to build a network of canals. A **canal** is a narrow, human-made waterway. It can connect lakes to rivers or one river to another. The canals would make it possible for farmers all over the state to transport goods by water. Canal boats could carry passengers, too.

The Wabash and Erie Canal was the longest canal built in Indiana. Digging began in 1832 and ended in 1853. The canal allowed passengers and goods to travel by water from the Great Lakes to the Ohio River. From Lake Erie the route of the canal followed the Maumee River southwest to Fort Wayne. It crossed the state to follow the Wabash River south to Terre Haute and then continued south to Evansville, on the Ohio River.

Indiana's canals contributed to the growth of the state's economy by offering farmers better ways to move their crops and livestock to market. The canals helped Indiana grow in other ways, too. Many workers who came to build the canals settled in Indiana after the canals were completed. As traffic increased on the canals, towns along the canals grew. Soon more people moved to Indiana to open shops and build homes along the canals.

Indiana state lawmakers passed the Internal Improvements Act of 1836 to pay for eight different transportation projects, including canals. In 1837 Indiana and the rest of the nation had an economic slowdown. During this time, trade nearly stopped. Businesses closed. Many workers lost their jobs. Construction on Indiana's canals stopped. Some canals were never completed because of a lack of money.

REVIEW Why did the state of Indiana build canals?

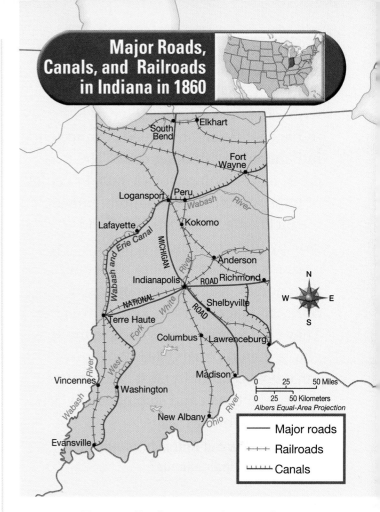

Major Roads, Canals, and Railroads in Indiana in 1860

Human–Environment Interactions
Major roads, canals, and railroads helped people travel throughout Indiana.

GEOGRAPHY THEME

❷ What two major waterways did the Wabash and Erie Canal connect?

Early Railroads

By the 1850s a new form of transportation was becoming popular. Railroads were being built across the United States. They brought great changes to Indiana and to the whole country.

Judge J. W. Peasley built Indiana's first railroad near Shelbyville in 1834. The entire track stretched about one mile (2 km). Indiana's first railroad line, a single railroad car pulled by horses, connected Madison and Indianapolis.

Canal boats carried goods and passengers up and down Indiana waterways.

When the first **locomotive**, or train engine, arrived in Indianapolis on October 1, 1847, the people celebrated with a fireworks display. Five of Indiana's first eight railroads connected Indianapolis with other cities. The railroads made Indianapolis a **hub**, or center, of transportation. Indianapolis gained the nickname "Railroad City" and quickly grew into Indiana's largest city.

Trains could carry more passengers than horses, wagons, or stagecoaches could, in just about any kind of weather. They could carry more goods to more places than flatboats, steamboats, or canal boats could. In most cases it was cheaper to travel and ship goods by rail than by any other means.

REVIEW How did railroads contribute to the growth of Indianapolis?

Rail lines linked Indiana to the rest of the United States.

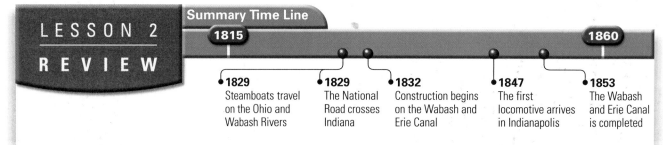

LESSON 2 REVIEW

Summary Time Line

1815				1860

1829
Steamboats travel on the Ohio and Wabash Rivers

1829
The National Road crosses Indiana

1832
Construction begins on the Wabash and Erie Canal

1847
The first locomotive arrives in Indianapolis

1853
The Wabash and Erie Canal is completed

1 MAIN IDEA What new developments in transportation helped Indiana grow during the nineteenth century?

2 WHY IT MATTERS Which kinds of transportation from this period are still important to Indiana today?

3 VOCABULARY Write a short description of river travel in nineteenth-century Indiana. Use the terms **flatboat**, **steamboat**, and **navigable** in your writing.

4 TIME LINE How long did it take to build the Wabash and Erie Canal?

5 READING SKILL—Compare and Contrast How were plank roads better than earlier kinds of roads? What was a disadvantage of plank roads?

6 GEOGRAPHY Where did the Wabash and Erie Canal begin and end?

7 CRITICAL THINKING—Hypothesize What might have happened if railroads had not become so widespread in Indiana?

8 CRITICAL THINKING—Apply Imagine that you are in charge of Indiana state spending on transportation in 1850. How will you divide the money among roads, canals, and railroads? Explain your choices.

PERFORMANCE—Make an Advertisement Choose one kind of transportation you learned about in this lesson. With a partner, make an advertisement for this kind of transportation. Use your advertisement to tell Hoosiers how it would benefit them.

Changes on Farms

1815 — 1865 — 1915

1815–1900

MAIN IDEA
Read to find out how changes in farming affected growth in Indiana.

WHY IT MATTERS
Farming continues to be an important part of life in Indiana.

VOCABULARY
subsistence farming
surplus
productivity
reaper
sod
thresher

When canal boats, steamboats, and railroad cars moved Indiana goods to market, it was often farm produce that they carried. Throughout the nineteenth century many Hoosiers continued to make their living by farming, as their pioneer parents and grandparents had done. However, improvements in farming changed the way Hoosiers worked their land.

Pioneer Farms

Farming was the most important activity for Indiana pioneers. Before building a log cabin, a pioneer farmer planted the seeds for the family's first food crops. At first Indiana's pioneers practiced **subsistence farming**. Every crop they grew and every animal they raised was needed to feed their own families. Over time, some farmers managed to grow a little extra, or **surplus**, corn or wheat. They took their surplus grain to the mills to be ground into cornmeal or flour. They kept what they needed and sold or traded the rest.

In the early 1800s all farm chores were done by hand with simple tools. For example, to harvest wheat, a pioneer farmer had to cut the stalks by hand with sharp-bladed tools called sickles and scythes (SYTHS). Even with every family member pitching in, a small wheat field might take days to harvest.

One of Indiana's most successful pioneer farmers was William Conner. He built a house, farmed many acres at Conner Prairie on the banks of the White River, and operated a gristmill and a sawmill. He also turned his trading post into a general store.

REVIEW In addition to farming, how did William Conner earn money?

Conner Prairie, a historical site near Indianapolis, lets visitors see how people lived on nineteenth-century farms. The young man in the photo (right) wears the clothes of a farmer of long ago.

169

Young men (above) at present-day Conner Prairie show how people farmed in the nineteenth century. Conner Prairie was the home of William and Elizabeth Conner (left) in the early 1800s.

Machines Change Farming

New developments in farming helped farmers increase their productivity. **Productivity** is the amount of goods or services produced in a period of time using certain resources. New machines helped make farmers' work easier and allowed them to produce more.

In 1831 Cyrus McCormick of Virginia invented a machine for cutting wheat. McCormick's horse-drawn **reaper** was a machine that could cut the wheat faster and with less work. This new machine cut and bundled the wheat. With a reaper a farmer working alone could harvest a whole field in just a few hours.

One problem pioneer farmers faced was how to keep cattle and hogs from straying. Farm animals easily toppled log fences. Also, log fences did little to protect farm herds from wild animals. Farmers planted thorny Osage (oh•SAYJ) orange bushes to act as a natural fence. The sharp thorns kept wild animals out of the crop fields. By the mid-1800s new barbed-wire fences replaced these bushes on many Indiana farms.

Farmers also needed a better way to plant crops. Pioneer farmers made their own hand or horse-drawn plows out of wood and iron. Plow blades were not very sharp and broke easily when a farmer tried to cut the Indiana sod.

The Oliver Chilled-Iron Plow

James Oliver worked on a farm in Indiana. He knew how difficult it was to plow the thick prairie soil with simple iron plows. The iron blades were too soft to hold a sharp edge, and they broke easily. Oliver experimented to make a stronger, sharper plow. He built a special mold for cooling the molten, or liquid, iron as it came out of a furnace. Oliver's chilled mold quickly hardened the outer surface of the plowshare, or blade, and allowed the interior to cool more slowly. This process created a plow blade that kept its sharp edge and was hard enough to resist breaking. It was advertised as "the plow that broke the prairie." By the late 1800s James Oliver's South Bend company was one of Indiana's most successful businesses.

Posters advertised the chilled-iron plow to farmers.

Sod is soil held together by grass and its roots. James Oliver's chilled-iron plow in 1855 allowed farmers to prepare land for planting in less time. More plowed land meant more seeds could be planted and more crops harvested.

In the mid-1800s farm machinery began to be powered by steam engines. The first steam-powered farm machine was a **thresher**, used for separating wheat grains from the dry stalks after harvest. Steam-powered threshers saved enormous amounts of time and labor by farmers and horses. These new threshers finally ended the isolation of many Indiana farmers. Because few individual farmers could afford to purchase them, farmers formed cooperative groups. They put their money together to buy one steam thresher to share among several farms.

Threshing days became times of communal work and celebration. Every family in the group gathered at the farm that had the thresher that day. Adults fed bundles of wheat into the machine and carried heavy sacks of grain to the storage bins. Children carried water to thirsty workers. At the end of the day, everyone shared a picnic meal.

REVIEW How did Cyrus McCormick and James Oliver help farmers?

Creating a Stronger Community for Farmers

With improvements in farm machinery and methods, Hoosier farmers began to increase productivity. This helped farmers make more money. It also helped people trade, which strengthened the economy, and allowed people to save money.

Growth of Indiana's Farms, 1850 to 1900

Analyze Graphs The number of farms in Indiana grew as new farming machines were invented.

◆ Which ten-year period between 1850 and 1900 had the smallest increase in the number of farms?

In 1851 Indiana's state government created a State Board of Agriculture. The board's main goal was to create a state fair. One year later, the first Indiana State Fair was held in Indianapolis. The fair celebrated the importance of farming in Indiana. Over the years the fair was held in other Indiana cities, including Lafayette (1853), Madison (1854), New Albany (1859), Fort Wayne (1865), and Terre Haute (1867). The Indiana State Fair began as a yearly show of farm products and machinery.

Farmers gathered at the fair to try out the latest inventions and share new ideas. Visitors to the 1876 state fair saw one of the first steam-powered engines. In 1877, two years after the telephone was invented by Alexander Graham Bell, the new invention was displayed at the Indiana State Fair. Over time, businesses began advertising their products and services at the fair, too. Today the Indiana State Fair continues to bring people together to share new ideas about farming.

The organization called the Grange grew out of the needs of nineteenth-century farmers. *Grange* is an old word for "farm." The purpose of the Grange was to bring farmers together, often in homes or schools, to help build a stronger community. Farming was the focus of the organization, but members of the Grange also gathered together for social reasons.

· HERITAGE ·

Indiana's State Fair and Farm Journals

Farmers built stronger communities and reduced their sense of isolation by attending the yearly state fair, which was first held in the 1850s. Farmers showed off their best livestock and produce. They also gathered at these fairs to learn new ideas about farming and to see new inventions. Another way Hoosier farmers learned about new ideas was through the publication of farm journals. The most widely read farm journal in Indiana during the 1800s was called *Indiana Farmer*. The journal introduced farmers to new ideas that would make their farms more profitable. Articles encouraged farmers to use fertilizers, to rotate crops annually, and to keep records, or logs, of their daily farm operations.

An 1885 Indiana State Fair poster.

They met to share in the good times and to solve problems. A song that became popular among Grange members follows:

> **The Farmer's the chief of the nation,**
> **The oldest of nobles is he,**
> **How blest beyond the others his station,**
> **From want and from envy how free. . . .**
> **Oh the farmer, the farmer forever,**
> **Three cheers for the plow, spade and hoe!**

Grange members suggested laws to limit fees that railroads charged farmers. They also worked to provide rural mail delivery and improve education.

REVIEW How did the Indiana State Fair and the Grange bring farmers together?

The Grange helped strengthen farm communities.

LESSON 3 REVIEW

Summary Time Line

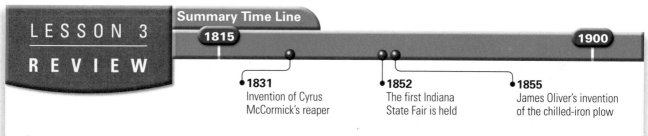

1815			1900

1831
Invention of Cyrus McCormick's reaper

1852
The first Indiana State Fair is held

1855
James Oliver's invention of the chilled-iron plow

1. **MAIN IDEA** What developments helped Indiana farms become more successful in the second half of the 1800s?

2. **WHY IT MATTERS** What developments from the 1800s still help Indiana farmers today?

3. **VOCABULARY** Write one or two sentences explaining the difference between **subsistence farming** and raising **surplus** crops.

4. **TIME LINE** Which event occurred first, the invention of the McCormick reaper or the invention of Oliver's chilled-iron plow?

5. **READING SKILL—Compare and Contrast** How were pioneer ways of reaping wheat different from the process as it was done with the McCormick reaper?

6. **ECONOMICS** How did improved ways of farming benefit Indiana's economy in the late 1800s?

7. **CULTURE** What new farm machinery ended the isolation of Indiana farmers?

8. **CRITICAL THINKING—Hypothesize** What might have happened to Indiana farmers if James Oliver had not invented the chilled-iron plow?

PERFORMANCE—Give an Oral Report In small groups, use the Internet or other resources to research 4-H clubs or other clubs in your community. Find out how the 4-H helps get Indiana's young people interested in farming. Give a report to your class.

Read a Double-Bar Graph

VOCABULARY

double-bar graph

➡ WHY IT MATTERS

A good way to compare statistics, or facts shown with numbers, is to make a graph. A bar graph is a good way to compare statistics for several different time periods. If you want to compare and contrast two statistics during the same time period, you can use a double-bar graph. A **double-bar graph** makes it possible to compare and contrast information not only for different time periods but also within the same time period.

➡ WHAT YOU NEED TO KNOW

The double-bar graph on page 175 shows how much corn and wheat Indiana farmers grew between 1850 and 1900. The years covered by the graph are shown horizontally. The scale on the left of the graph shows the number of bushels of corn and wheat grown in each of the six years. The vertical bars show the two different crops grown for each year on the graph. The blue bars show the amount of wheat grown. The orange bars show the amount of corn grown.

Some wheat is still raised on Indiana farms.

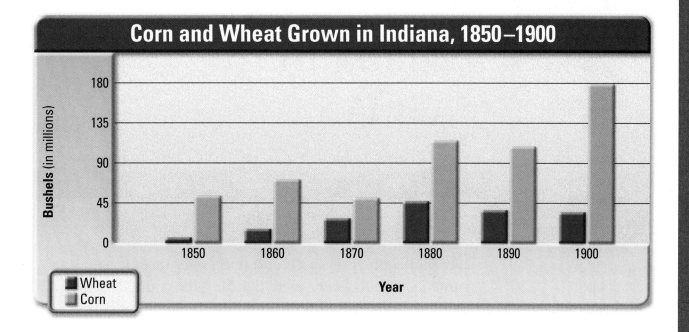

Corn and Wheat Grown in Indiana, 1850–1900

Bushels (in millions)

180
135
90
45
0

1850   1860   1870   1880   1890   1900

Year

Wheat
Corn

To find out how much corn was grown during a year shown on the graph, locate the year at the bottom of the graph. Then, with your eyes or your finger, follow the orange bar from the bottom up. Notice where the bar ends. The number on the left scale closest to the end of the bar is the number of bushels (in millions) of corn harvested that year. Follow the same process with the blue bar to find out how much wheat was grown by Indiana farmers. Compare and contrast the information shown to learn more about Indiana's changes in farming in the nineteenth century.

▶ PRACTICE THE SKILL

Study the double-bar graph on this page. Then use the information in the graph to answer these questions.

❶ Which crop decreased in the number of bushels grown between the years of 1880 and 1900?

❷ What crop increased the most in the number of bushels between 1850 and 1900?

❸ Were farmers growing more wheat in 1880 or in 1900?

❹ In what year did wheat production come closest to corn production?

▶ APPLY WHAT YOU LEARNED

For the next seven days, keep track of how much time you spend playing or exercising and how much time you spend watching television. Make a double-bar graph to show your findings. Be sure to title and label your graph and supply a legend. Display your completed double-bar graph in the classroom.

MAIN IDEA
Read to find out reasons
behind the Civil War.

WHY IT MATTERS
The outcome of the Civil
War kept the United
States one nation.

VOCABULARY

slave state
abolitionist
free state
Underground
    Railroad
secede
civil war
infantry
cavalry

Indiana in the Civil War

1815	1865	1915

1850–1865

By mid-century a dark cloud hung over the nation. Arguments about slavery were dividing the country. The debate over slavery and the war that followed divided Hoosiers as well as other Americans.

Slavery in the United States

By the 1850s more than four million Africans had been forced to work as slaves in the United States. Enslaved people lived mainly in the South, where slavery was legal. The Southern states that allowed slavery were known as **slave states**. Most enslaved people worked on large farms called plantations. They planted, cared for, and harvested cotton and other crops. A few slaves worked as house servants. They cooked, cleaned, and sewed and took care of the children of the plantation owners. Whether they were men, women, or children, slaves worked long and hard. Often they worked from sunrise to sunset.

Some people living in the North wanted the United States government to pass laws to make it against the law to buy, sell, or own slaves. People who wanted to abolish, or end, slavery were known as **abolitionists** (a•buh•LIH•shuhn•ists). Most abolitionists lived in **free states**, where slavery was against the law. Some religious groups, such as the Quakers, opposed slavery. Other people did not want to end slavery but did not want it to expand into new territories or states.

On large plantations the small cabins where slaves lived were separated from the large houses of the owners.

Even though Indiana was a free state, not all Hoosiers were abolitionists. Some felt slavery should be allowed to continue. Even those who opposed slavery were not always in favor of letting the United States government tell individual states what to do. In 1851 a new state constitution was written to try to avoid the slavery problem. It included an article to prevent any more African Americans from settling in Indiana even though thousands of African Americans already lived there.

REVIEW What did abolitionists want the United States government to do?

North to Freedom

Some enslaved people in the South tried to escape. One by one or in small groups, they fled to the North. Runaway slaves headed north to the Ohio River, the boundary line between most slave states and most free states. Evansville was one place where many enslaved people crossed the river into Indiana.

Thousands of runaway slaves stopped at Levi Coffin's house (below), in present-day Fountain City.

LOCATE IT

INDIANA

Fountain City

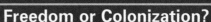

POINTS OF VIEW
Freedom or Colonization?

In the years before the Civil War, Hoosiers held very different views about African Americans and slavery. Some Hoosiers believed that free African Americans should leave their homes in Indiana to resettle in the Republic of Liberia in West Africa. The following views are statements by African Americans.

W. M. FINDLAY, of Covington, Indiana, April 6, 1842

"I have concluded, that to be truly independent, we must enjoy rights and privileges . . . [like] those enjoyed by white citizens of the United States. But such independence we cannot obtain in the United States, therefore I seek it outside the United States . . . in the Republic of Liberia. . . ."

AFRICAN REPOSITORY AND COLONIAL JOURNAL, October 1849

"Though denied in some things the full enjoyment of liberty and pursuit of happiness at present . . . we are determined to use all lawful means and to continue in so doing, until we shall be allowed the full privileges of American citizens. . . . we feel bound . . . to prevent our people from colonizing in Liberia. . . ."

Analyze the Viewpoints

❶ Why do you think some African American Hoosiers wanted to move to Liberia?

❷ **Make It Relevant** Think of a topic or issue that interests you. Read letters to the editor in your community's newspaper. Choose letters that state different positions, or arguments, and then write a letter expressing your point of view on the issue.

There they received help from a community of free African Americans. Many of these people had once been slaves.

The journey did not end at the Ohio River. After 1850 most runaway slaves kept traveling north to Canada, where they could not be captured. Along the way they were given shelter by people who thought slavery should be ended.

• BIOGRAPHY •

Levi Coffin   1798–1877
Character Trait: Heroic Deeds

Levi Coffin was a Quaker who had lived in North Carolina, where slavery was allowed. When Coffin and his wife, Catharine, moved to Indiana, they started a store in Newport, now called Fountain City. The Coffins opened their home to more than 2,000 runaway slaves traveling to Canada. Coffin's courage inspired others to join in or to support his efforts.

MULTIMEDIA BIOGRAPHIES
Visit The Learning Site at
www.harcourtschool.com/biographies
to learn about other famous people.

GO ONLINE

The routes taken by escaping slaves became known as the **Underground Railroad**. The Underground Railroad was not a real railroad, and it was not underground. It was a system of routes along which runaway slaves could find help in getting to freedom. The homes where runaway slaves hid were called stations. The people who helped move runaways from one station to the next were known as conductors. As conductor Levi Coffin stated:

> 66 The roads were always in running order, the connections good, the conductors active and zealous, and there was no lack of passengers. 99

REVIEW What was the Underground Railroad?

Abolitionists helped runaway slaves on their journey toward freedom.

A CLOSER LOOK
Underground Railroad

Many homes on the Underground Railroad had special places for hiding escaped slaves.

1 Heavy curtains blocked the windows so that neighbors could not see lantern lights.

2 Slaves were hidden in attics, cellars, haylofts, or special windowless rooms.

3 Slaves also hid in wagons with false bottoms.

❖ Why do you think many runaway slaves traveled during nighttime hours?

A Nation Divided

The debate over slavery continued for many years. In 1861 Abraham Lincoln became President of the United States. Many people in the South believed that President Lincoln might outlaw slavery. In February 1861 seven southern states decided to **secede** (suh•SEED), or separate from, the United States. These states formed a new country called the Confederate States of America, or the Confederacy. Four other states joined the Confederacy in April and May.

In April 1861 Confederate soldiers fired cannons at Fort Sumter, a fort in South Carolina held by soldiers of the United States, or the Union. This was the opening attack in what became a four-year war between the Union and the Confederacy.

The conflict became known as the Civil War. A **civil war** is a fight between groups of citizens of the same country.

REVIEW How did some Southern states react to the election of Abraham Lincoln as President?

Hoosiers Fight for the Union

President Lincoln called upon the governors of Northern states, such as Indiana's Oliver P. Morton, to send soldiers to fight in the Union army. About 200,000 people from Indiana served in the Union army.

People who fought for the Union ranged from boys as young as eight to grandfathers. Some served as **infantry**, or foot soldiers. Others served as **cavalry**, or soldiers on horses.

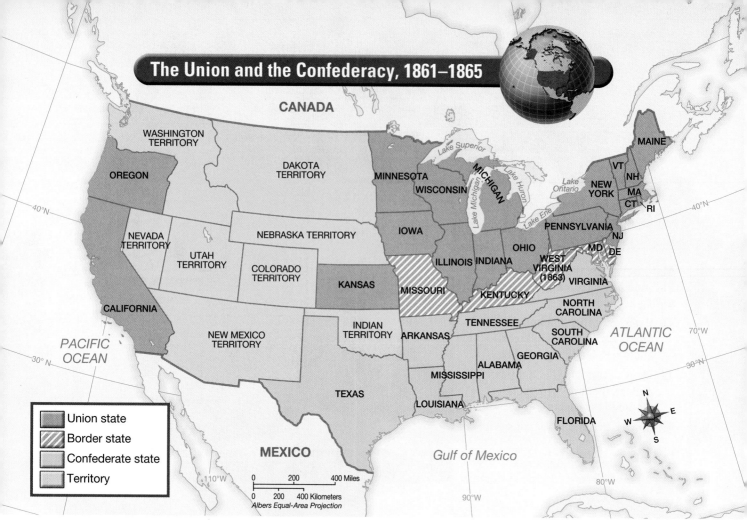

The Union and the Confederacy, 1861–1865

CANADA

WASHINGTON TERRITORY

OREGON

DAKOTA TERRITORY

MINNESOTA

WISCONSIN

MICHIGAN

Lake Superior

Lake Huron

Lake Michigan

Lake Ontario

Lake Erie

MAINE

VT

NH

NEW YORK

MA

CT

RI

NEVADA TERRITORY

UTAH TERRITORY

NEBRASKA TERRITORY

IOWA

PENNSYLVANIA

NJ

COLORADO TERRITORY

KANSAS

ILLINOIS

INDIANA

OHIO

WEST VIRGINIA (1863)

MD

DE

VIRGINIA

CALIFORNIA

MISSOURI

KENTUCKY

NORTH CAROLINA

PACIFIC OCEAN

NEW MEXICO TERRITORY

INDIAN TERRITORY

ARKANSAS

TENNESSEE

SOUTH CAROLINA

ATLANTIC OCEAN

GEORGIA

ALABAMA

MISSISSIPPI

TEXAS

LOUISIANA

FLORIDA

MEXICO

Gulf of Mexico

40°N

30°N

40°N

30°N

70°W

80°W

90°W

110°W

N

E

W

S

Union state

Border state

Confederate state

Territory

0   200   400 Miles

0   200   400 Kilometers

Albers Equal-Area Projection

GEOGRAPHY THEME

Regions **This is the way the United States was divided at the beginning of the Civil War.**

◆ **How many Southern states joined the Confederate States of America?**

More than a thousand Hoosiers took part as sailors and marines. In 1863 some Hoosiers enlisted in the 28th Indiana Regiment, an all–African American unit.

The Civil War cost many lives. One out of every eight Hoosiers who fought in the war died. In 1863 more than 3,000 Indiana soldiers lost their lives in one battle alone, at Chickamauga in Georgia.

Even those who did not fight were affected by the Civil War. Many women took over farms and businesses while men were away fighting. Other women volunteered as nurses in hospitals.

Not all people in Indiana supported the Union. Some wanted the Confederacy to win the war. Hoosiers who supported the Union called these people copperheads, from the name of a poisonous snake.

REVIEW **On which side did most Hoosiers fight during the Civil War?**

Morgan's Raid

During the war only one conflict between Northern and Southern soldiers took place in Indiana. A Confederate officer named John Hunt Morgan led 2,500 cavalry soldiers into Indiana in July 1863. Morgan's Raiders crossed the Ohio River from Kentucky, landing south of Corydon, where they stole horses.

Governor Morton asked General Lewis Wallace of Brookville to organize troops to protect Indianapolis. When Morgan heard this, his raiders moved into Ohio. A few weeks later, Union forces captured Morgan and his men.

REVIEW Where did the only conflict between Northern and Southern soldiers in Indiana take place?

Abraham Lincoln issued the Emancipation Proclamation in January 1863.

Proclamation was only the beginning of a long struggle to guarantee the rights of African Americans living in the United States.

After the war ended in 1865, hard feelings between the North and the South did not end easily. In Indiana, people who had lost family members fighting for the Union tried to pass a law called the "bloody shirt law." This law would have forced people who wanted to vote in elections to tell which side they had supported in the Civil War.

REVIEW When did the Civil War end?

An End to Slavery

On January 1, 1863, President Abraham Lincoln issued the Emancipation Proclamation. This statement gave freedom to enslaved people living in the Confederate states. The Emancipation

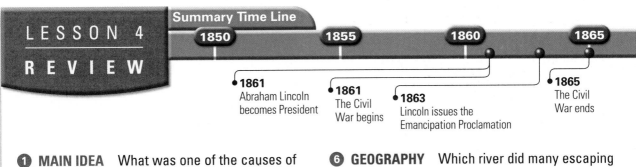

LESSON 4 REVIEW

Summary Time Line

1850   1855   1860   1865

- **1861** Abraham Lincoln becomes President
- **1861** The Civil War begins
- **1863** Lincoln issues the Emancipation Proclamation
- **1865** The Civil War ends

1 **MAIN IDEA** What was one of the causes of the Civil War?

2 **WHY IT MATTERS** Why was the outcome of the Civil War important?

3 **VOCABULARY** Write a sentence about when Abraham Lincoln became President, using the terms **slave state**, **free state**, and **secede**.

4 **TIME LINE** How long after the Civil War began did Lincoln issue the Emancipation Proclamation?

5 **READING SKILL—Compare and Contrast** Contrast the positions of abolitionists in free states and plantation owners in slave states on the issue of slavery.

6 **GEOGRAPHY** Which river did many escaping slaves cross to become free in the North?

7 **HISTORY** Why was it important for runaway slaves who reached Indiana to continue their journey to Canada?

8 **CRITICAL THINKING—Analyze** Why do you think so many Hoosiers volunteered to serve in the Union army?

PERFORMANCE—Compose a Narrative Imagine that you are a conductor on the Underground Railroad. Write a description of your experiences helping runaway slaves. Read your description aloud to your classmates or record it on a tape.

Compare Maps with Different Scales

▶ **WHY IT MATTERS**

Many battles in the Civil War were fought in the eastern United States in states such as Pennsylvania, Maryland, and Virginia. One such battle, the Battle of Gettysburg, fought in Pennsylvania in 1863, was a major turning point in the war.

If you wanted to learn more about the battles of the Civil War, you could use maps with different scales. *Scale* refers to the size of the area shown on a map. Most maps have a scale bar, a line with numbers showing a unit of measurement (usually inches or centimeters) and the number of miles or kilometers this unit represents.

Map scales differ in size depending on how much area is shown on a map. This means that different maps are drawn to different scales. Maps that show a large area must use a small scale because places must be drawn small enough for all the information to fit. On the other hand, maps that show only small areas can use a large scale. Using a large scale allows mapmakers to show more detailed information.

▶ **WHAT YOU NEED TO KNOW**

The maps on page 183 are maps with different scales. The scale used for a map depends on the kind of information to be shown. Map A is a small-scale map. It shows the locations of Civil War battles in the East. Map B is a large-scale map. It is drawn to a larger scale, so it shows many more details about Gettysburg than Map A can. The map scale on each map compares the distance on the map to the distance in the real world.

Use a ruler to measure the length of the map scale on Map A. You can see that 1 inch (2.5 cm) stands for 100 miles (161 km). Next measure the map scale on Map B. You can see that on this map 1 inch (2.5 cm) equals 1 mile (1.6 km). By using your ruler and the map scale you can measure distances on the maps and figure out the distances in the real world. You also can use a piece of paper to measure distances on a map. Place the paper below the map scale. With a pencil, mark the distances either in miles or kilometers. Then use the piece of paper as you would a ruler and convert your measurements using the map scale.

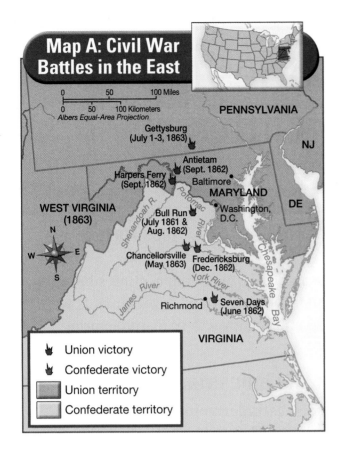

Map A: Civil War Battles in the East

0   50   100 Miles
0   50   100 Kilometers
Albers Equal-Area Projection

PENNSYLVANIA

Gettysburg
(July 1-3, 1863)

NJ

Antietam
(Sept. 1862)

Harpers Ferry
(Sept. 1862)

Baltimore

MARYLAND

DE

WEST VIRGINIA
(1863)

Bull Run
(July 1861 &
Aug. 1862)

Washington,
D.C.

Shenandoah R.

Potomac River

Chancellorsville
(May 1863)

Fredericksburg
(Dec. 1862)

York River

Chesapeake Bay

James River

Richmond

Seven Days
(June 1862)

VIRGINIA

Union victory

Confederate victory

Union territory

Confederate territory

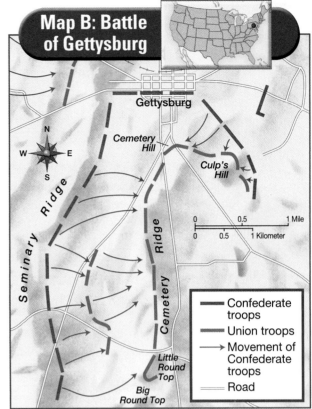

Map B: Battle of Gettysburg

Gettysburg

Cemetery
Hill

Culp's
Hill

Seminary Ridge

Cemetery Ridge

0   0.5   1 Mile
0   0.5   1 Kilometer

Little
Round
Top

Big
Round Top

Confederate troops

Union troops

Movement of Confederate troops

Road

► PRACTICE THE SKILL

Use the maps on this page to answer the following questions.

❶ Find Gettysburg on both maps. Which map shows detailed information about the Battle of Gettysburg? Which map shows other battlefields in the eastern United States?

❷ Suppose you wanted to find the distance between Gettysburg and Fredericksburg. Which map would you use?

❸ Use the map scale on Map B to find the distance between Cemetery Hill and Big Round Top.

❹ Use the map scale on Map A to find the distance between Gettysburg and Bull Run.

► APPLY WHAT YOU LEARNED

Think about maps you use when you and your family travel. Use a road atlas or the Internet to find two maps with different scales. One map could be of Indiana. A second map could be of your community or a large city within the state. Write a sentence explaining when it would be more useful to use the state map, with the smaller scale. Write another sentence stating when it would be more useful to use a city or community map, with a larger scale.

Practice your map and globe skills with the **GeoSkills CD-ROM.**

Big Factories and Big Cities

1815   1865   1915

1865–1915

The late nineteenth and early twentieth centuries brought rapid changes to Indiana. Two important developments were the rise of Indiana cities and the growth of manufacturing.

New Industries

The Civil War created new opportunities for the growth of manufacturing in Indiana. **Manufacturing** is the making of finished products out of raw materials. Most manufacturing takes place in factories. After the war, manufacturing continued to grow. More and more people moved to cities to work in factories. Their jobs included packing meat, milling grain, and making household products. Indianapolis, South Bend, Terre Haute, Madison, and Evansville were among the Indiana cities that grew rapidly after the Civil War.

The discovery of new natural resources also drew industries to Indiana. Natural gas, an important source of fuel for factories, was discovered in northern Indiana, near Portland, in 1886. Several cities also used natural gas for street lamps.

Government leaders offered free natural gas to businesses from other states that would build factories in Indiana. The

The Standard Oil Company built a refinery in Whiting, Indiana, in 1889. It was one of the largest refineries in the Middle West.

The Ball brothers' factory stored manufactured jars in a field (above) next to the factory. The Ball brothers manufactured more glass jars (right) than any other company in the United States.

Ball brothers—Edmund, William, Lucius, George, and Frank—took advantage of an offer from the city of Muncie. The Ball brothers received free land and free natural gas from Indiana leaders for moving their glass factory from New York. The Ball brothers' factory became the largest producer of glass jars in the United States. Kitchens and cellars all over the country contained shelves of Ball jars full of preserved fruits and vegetables.

Indiana's supply of natural gas lasted only 15 years. Yet many industries remained in the state, switching to coal for energy. Some manufacturers moved into the Calumet region of Indiana, near Lake Michigan, where there were supplies of oil. In 1889 the Standard Oil Company of Ohio built one of the world's largest oil refineries in this region, near the Illinois border. A **refinery** is a factory where resources such as oil are made into products people can use. Soon many other factories and refineries were built in the area. Oil would become one of the most important sources of energy during the twentieth century.

REVIEW How did government leaders persuade industries to move to Indiana from other states?

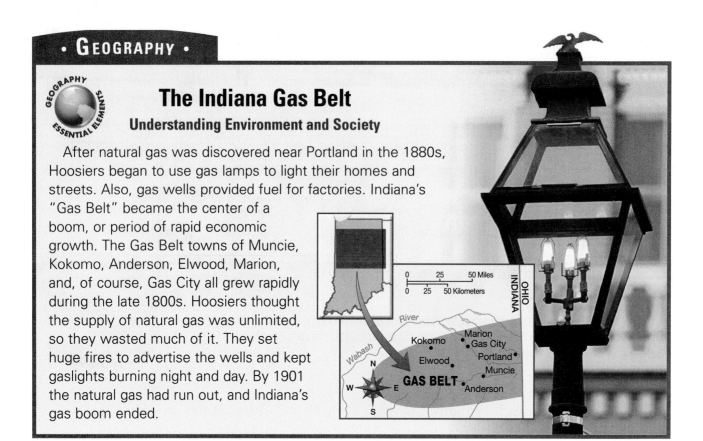

The Indiana Gas Belt
Understanding Environment and Society

After natural gas was discovered near Portland in the 1880s, Hoosiers began to use gas lamps to light their homes and streets. Also, gas wells provided fuel for factories. Indiana's "Gas Belt" became the center of a boom, or period of rapid economic growth. The Gas Belt towns of Muncie, Kokomo, Anderson, Elwood, Marion, and, of course, Gas City all grew rapidly during the late 1800s. Hoosiers thought the supply of natural gas was unlimited, so they wasted much of it. They set huge fires to advertise the wells and kept gaslights burning night and day. By 1901 the natural gas had run out, and Indiana's gas boom ended.

A New City

One of Indiana's largest industrial cities did not exist before the early 1900s. The city of Gary came into being because of the steel industry. Steel is a strong blend of iron and other metals. It was used to build railroad tracks, bridges, buildings, and many kinds of machines. In the early 1900s the United States Steel Company developed a new process for making steel. The company wanted to build a steel mill in the Middle West. It needed a place close to large supplies of the coal, iron, and limestone used in making steel. The mill also would have to be located on good transportation routes. That way, resources could be moved in and the steel shipped out to markets.

Indiana's Calumet area seemed to be the perfect place. There, railroads could easily bring limestone from southern Indiana and coal from Pennsylvania.

Ships on the Great Lakes could bring iron ore from Minnesota and transport the finished steel. The mill that United States Steel built on the shore of Lake Michigan in 1909 was one of the largest steel mills in the world.

Workers busy manufacturing steel in Gary, Indiana

To house the many workers the new steel mill would need, United States Steel built a town in 1906. The company chose a site south of the mill, on the Grand Calumet River. The town was named after Elbert H. Gary, the chairman of the board of United States Steel at the time.

Life in Gary was different from life in other Indiana towns and cities. Gary was a "company town," with most goods and services controlled by United States Steel. The rush to provide housing meant that many buildings were poorly built. Because of this, Gary had to deal with the challenges that other big cities would not face until much later.

REVIEW **Why was the city of Gary founded?**

Newcomers from Near and Far

In the early 1900s newcomers came to Indiana from other parts of the United States and from countries around the world. Many African Americans moved to Indiana from the southern states.

After the Civil War many former slaves had tried to make a living in the South as sharecroppers. A **sharecropper** is someone who rents land to farm. Sharecroppers are given cabins, tools, and seeds. They farm the land and pay the landowner a share of the crops at harvest time. For African American sharecroppers at the turn of the century, the crops were small and the owner's share was large. There was little or nothing left for a sharecropper's family.

Thousands of African American sharecroppers left the South when they heard about jobs in northern factories. They moved north to such cities as New York, Chicago, Detroit, Pittsburgh, Cleveland, and Indianapolis.

Another group of newcomers to Indiana was made up of immigrants from Europe. An **immigrant** is a person who moves to one country from another country. In the early 1900s many immigrants came to Indiana from such European countries as Germany and Ireland.

These immigrants from Eastern Europe arrived in the United States in the early 1900s.

Madam C. J. Walker 1867–1919

Character Trait: Perseverance

Sarah Breedlove was born in Louisiana, the daughter of former slaves. She once said, "I got my start by giving myself a start."

She married Charles J. Walker and became known as Madam C. J. Walker. In 1905 she developed a system of hair-care products and cosmetics for African American women. Madam C. J. Walker's Manufacturing Company, located in Indianapolis, hired more than 3,000 workers. Women known as Walker Agents sold the products door to door. Madam Walker was the first African American woman to become a millionaire. She shared her wealth with others by supporting charities and organizations that helped women and African Americans.

Walker explained her life this way: "I am a woman who came from the cotton fields of the South. . . . I promoted myself into the business of manufacturing. . . . I have built my own factory on my own ground."

Madam Walker (driving) became one of Indiana's most successful entrepreneurs.

MULTIMEDIA BIOGRAPHIES

Visit The Learning Site at **www.harcourtschool.com/biographies** to learn about other famous people.

GO ONLINE

They found their way to Indiana's new factories and growing cities. Immigrants were looking for a better life for themselves and their families. All of these newcomers added to Indiana's economy and the cultural mix.

REVIEW **What two groups of people moved to Indiana in the early 1900s?**

Freedom of Opportunity

Many industries in Indiana grew because of free enterprise. **Free enterprise** means that people are free to start and run their own businesses.

People who start and run new businesses are sometimes called **entrepreneurs** (ahn•truh•pruh•NERZ). Two of the best-known Indiana

entrepreneurs of this time were Eli Lilly and Madam C. J. Walker. Like many other southerners, Walker decided to migrate to the North in search of new opportunities. She became very successful. She ran a business that sold hair care products to African American women.

Eli Lilly returned to Indiana after serving as a colonel in the Union Army during the Civil War. In 1876 Colonel Lilly founded a business in Indianapolis that made medicines. He became known for treating workers with respect. He made use of new ideas from scientists to improve his products.

To start and run a new business, entrepreneurs need three kinds of resources. They need natural resources such as land, water, fuel, and raw materials. They also need human resources, or workers. Entrepreneurs also need capital resources—money, buildings, machines, and tools to run the new business.

If the new business does well, the entrepreneur makes a profit. **Profit** is the amount of money that businesses have left over after they have paid for the costs of producing the items. The chance of making a profit is the main reason an entrepreneur goes into business.

Profitable businesses usually help the communities in which they are located. Many companies used their profits to help people in the community. For example, the Ball brothers purchased a private teacher's college in Muncie and gave it to the state in the early 1900s. This new state university was later named Ball State University.

REVIEW What is the main reason an entrepreneur goes into business?

In Indianapolis Eli Lilly ran a successful company that made medicines.

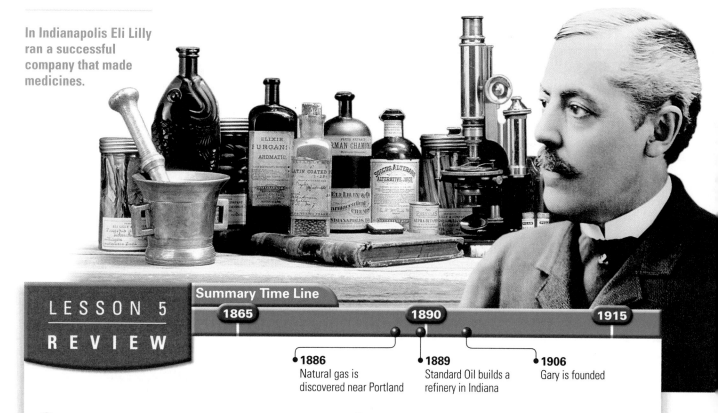

LESSON 5
REVIEW

Summary Time Line

1865 — 1890 — 1915

● **1886** Natural gas is discovered near Portland

● **1889** Standard Oil builds a refinery in Indiana

● **1906** Gary is founded

1. **MAIN IDEA** How did the growth of manufacturing change Indiana?

2. **WHY IT MATTERS** How do changes in the economy affect people in Indiana today?

3. **VOCABULARY** Describe two groups of newcomers who came to Indiana in the early 1900s. Use the terms **sharecropper** and **immigrant** in your writing.

4. **TIME LINE** In what year was natural gas discovered in Portland?

5. **READING SKILL—Compare and Contrast** How was the founding of Gary different from the founding of other Indiana cities?

6. **GEOGRAPHY** What made the Calumet region so favorable to new industries?

7. **ECONOMICS** What role does profit play in the development of new businesses?

8. **CRITICAL THINKING—Evaluate** Besides the Civil War, what factors caused manufacturing to change in the late 1800s?

PERFORMANCE—Design a Business Card Imagine that you and a partner are entrepreneurs. Make a business card that tells what you do and where in Indiana your business is located. Share your business card with the class.

· CHAPTER ·

5 Review and Test Preparation

Summary Time Line
1815

• 1829
National Road
reaches Indianapolis

USE YOUR READING SKILLS

Complete this graphic organizer to show that you understand how to compare and contrast people, places, events and ideas. A copy of this graphic organizer appears on page 53 of the Activity Book.

Oliver's chilled-iron plow and McCormick's reaper

SIMILARITIES	DIFFERENCES

Battle of Chickamauga and Morgan's Raid

SIMILARITIES	DIFFERENCES

Sharecroppers and Immigrants

SIMILARITIES	DIFFERENCES

THINK & WRITE

Write to Persuade   Imagine that you are an Indiana farmer in the late 1800s. You want to form a cooperative, or group, so that you and your neighbors can purchase a steam thresher. Write a short speech that you would give to your neighbors at a meeting. Give at least three reasons to join the cooperative.

Write a Journal Entry   Imagine that you are a newcomer to Indianapolis in the early 1900s. You might be either an African American who has migrated from the South or a European immigrant. Write a journal entry about your family, your job, or your community, and share it with classmates.

1852
First Indiana
State Fair
is held

1853
Wabash and
Erie Canal is
completed

1861
Civil War
begins

1863
Emancipation Proclamation
grants freedom to enslaved
people in Confederate states

1865
Civil War ends

1886
Natural gas is
discovered near
Portland

1909
United States Steel
opens mill in Gary

USE THE TIME LINE

Use the chapter time line to answer these questions.

1 How long after the National Road reached Indiana was the Wabash and Erie Canal completed?

2 How many years did the Civil War last?

3 When was natural gas discovered in Portland?

USE VOCABULARY

Match the vocabulary terms in Column A with related terms in Column B. Then use each pair of terms correctly in a sentence.

Column A

4 navigable (p. 165)

5 free enterprise (p. 188)

6 abolitionist (p. 176)

Column B

A. entrepreneur (p. 188)

B. canal (p. 166)

C. Underground Railroad (p. 178)

RECALL FACTS

Answer these questions.

7 What was the name of the planned community founded by Robert Owen?

8 What kind of improvement did James Oliver introduce to farmers in the 1830s?

9 Where did the only Civil War conflict in Indiana take place?

10 Which Indiana entrepreneur developed hair care products especially for African American women?

Write the letter of the best choice.

11 **TEST PREP** The first industry in a pioneer community was usually a —
   A factory.
   B railroad.
   C gristmill.
   D toll road.

12 **TEST PREP** The city of Gary was founded by —
   F abolitionists.
   G United States Steel.
   H Standard Oil.
   J the Ball brothers.

THINK CRITICALLY

13 How did nineteenth-century improvements in farming, transportation, and industry work together to help Indiana grow?

14 How do you think African American Hoosiers reacted to the Emancipation Proclamation?

APPLY SKILLS

Read a Double-Bar Graph

15 Study the double-bar graph on page 175. Use the information presented on that graph to write a paragraph about the changes in farming that occurred in Indiana from 1850 to 1900.

Compare Maps with Different Scales

16 Draw a map of your school. Then, draw a second map of your school that includes the neighborhood around your school. Which is small-scale? Which is large-scale?

GRISSOM AIR MUSEUM STATE HISTORIC SITE

The Grissom Air Museum State Historic Site is named for Indiana's famous astronaut Gus Grissom. The air museum is located in Peru, Indiana, in the north-central region of the state. Visitors can see a variety of military airplanes, some of which date from World War II.

LOCATE IT

Grissom Air Museum

Peru

INDIANA

CD 8 Track 1

Indiana in the Twentieth Century

> 66 I think when you have gone
> from horse and buggy to
> outer space travel, you have
> covered a good many miles. 99
>
> —Elizabeth McCullough,
> *Buggies and Bad Times*, 1985

CHAPTER READING SKILL

Draw Conclusions

A conclusion is a decision or idea reached by using evidence from what you read plus what you already know. To **draw a conclusion**, combine new facts with the facts you already know.

As you read this chapter, use evidence and what you already know to draw conclusions about Indiana in the twentieth century.

EVIDENCE	
KNOWLEDGE	→ CONCLUSION

Into a New Century

1900   1950   2000

1900–1920

MAIN IDEA
Read to find out how the automobile industry and other industries changed life in Indiana.

WHY IT MATTERS
Improvements in transportation still affect where people live and work, how they travel, and how they spend their money.

VOCABULARY
automobile
labor union
centennial
interurban rail

As the twentieth century began, Indiana was no longer a land of pioneers. By 1900 more than 2½ million people lived in Indiana. One-third of these people lived in towns and cities. As in the past, improvements in transportation were important to the growth of Indiana in the twentieth century. One new kind of transportation changed Indiana and the rest of the country forever.

A New Industry

On Independence Day in 1894, Kokomo inventor Elwood Haynes took a short ride down a twisting country road called Pumpkinvine Pike. Haynes was testing his gasoline-powered **automobile**. The word *automobile* means "self-moving." Haynes's invention did indeed move under its own power. Haynes drove 1½ miles (more than 2 km) at a speed of 7 miles (11 km) an hour, surprising a group of children on bicycles. The Kokomo police had asked Haynes to test his automobile outside of town. They were afraid his "horseless carriage" might blow up.

After Haynes's success many automobile factories opened for business. The largest of these belonged to the Studebaker Company of South Bend. The Studebaker brothers had once made wagons and horse-drawn carriages. In 1904 they rebuilt their plant so that they could make automobiles there.

Elwood Haynes test-drives his new invention.

FAST FACT
By the late 1890s Indiana had automobile factories in 88 cities and towns.

Race cars have changed since Ray Harroun won the first Indianapolis 500 in 1911.

Like automobile companies today, Indiana's early carmakers used advertising to interest people in buying their products. Races were the most popular ways to advertise automobiles in the early years. On May 30, 1911, a 500-mile (805-km) automobile race was held at the Indianapolis Motor Speedway, a new racetrack. Ray Harroun won the first Indianapolis 500 race in his Indiana-made Marmon Wasp. Harroun's average speed was 76 miles (122 km) an hour.

REVIEW What was Indiana's largest automobile company in the early twentieth century?

Automobiles Bring Changes

At first, automobiles cost a lot to build and to buy. Each one was built by hand. It took a long time to produce just a few automobiles. Only the richest people could afford automobiles, which were seen as status symbols.

In time, car companies found ways to make many automobiles quickly. By producing more automobiles, carmakers could sell cars at lower prices. Soon the average person could afford to buy an automobile.

Life changed in Indiana as more people began buying and using automobiles. Farm families could get to towns and cities more easily. City people used cars to explore the countryside and see the natural wonders of their state.

Analyze Primary Sources

This 1894 political cartoon shows Eugene V. Debs, the founder and first president of the American Railway Union. Debs is pictured as "king of the railways." He led the union's workers in successful strikes, or protests, against the railway companies to improve working conditions.

❶ Debs is sitting on top of an open bridge labeled "Highway of Trade."

❷ The trains, labeled with the names of goods, cannot cross the waterway because the bridge is open.

❸ Although the United States never has had kings, the crown Debs is wearing makes him appear to be one.

◆ What do you think the artist is trying to say about Debs's role as the "king of the railways"?

When companies started the mass production of automobiles, or producing many of them at one time, workers formed labor unions. A **labor union** is an organization of workers who do the same kinds of jobs. These unions wanted to improve working conditions at factories and to raise workers' pay. One Hoosier who wanted to improve conditions for workers was Eugene V. Debs of Terre Haute. Debs became an important leader of the organized labor movement in the late 1800s and early 1900s.

The Automobile Age, as that time came to be called, brought changes to Indiana. Many dirt roads in Indiana were paved. In time, new gas stations, garages, motels, and parking lots changed the country.

REVIEW What changes made it possible for the average person to own an automobile?

An early speed limit sign in Indiana

Transportation and Indiana Cities

The automobile industry brought growth to Indiana's cities and towns. It brought many workers to factories in Indianapolis, South Bend, Kokomo, Evansville, Columbus, Logansport, and Mishawaka (mish•uh•WAHK•uh). At one time more than 60 different automobile companies had factories in Indiana.

Interurban trains connected several Indiana cities.

Indiana's Centennial, 1916

In 1916 Hoosiers celebrated 100 years of Indiana statehood. Across the state they held parades and fireworks displays and put on plays about Indiana history.

The President of the United States, Woodrow Wilson, visited Indiana to help celebrate the state's centennial, or 100-year anniversary. Hoosiers made efforts to preserve, or save, the state's natural environment and historic sites. In the centennial year, Indiana's first two state parks—McCormick's Creek, near Spencer, and Turkey Run, near Marshall—were established.

President Woodrow Wilson (far left) visits Indianapolis during the state's centennial.

As Indiana celebrated its **centennial**, or 100 years, of being a state, Hoosiers took advantage of a new kind of transportation. This new **interurban rail** system ran on electricity. A network of rail lines connected rural areas with nearby cities and towns. Low cost and ease of travel made these trains popular. The Indianapolis Traction Terminal was the largest station in the state interurban rail network. In 1918 trains made more than 128,000 trips to carry 7½ million passengers into and out of this terminal.

REVIEW What was the interurban rail system?

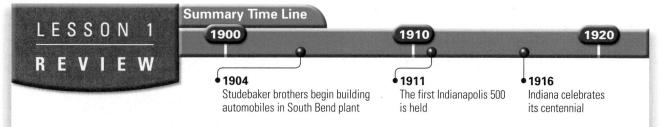

LESSON 1 REVIEW

Summary Time Line

| 1900 | 1910 | 1920 |

1904 Studebaker brothers begin building automobiles in South Bend plant

1911 The first Indianapolis 500 is held

1916 Indiana celebrates its centennial

1. **MAIN IDEA** How did the invention of the automobile affect the growth of Indiana cities?

2. **WHY IT MATTERS** How did improvements in transportation change the way people lived in Indiana?

3. **VOCABULARY** Describe a few events that took place in celebration of Indiana's 100 years of statehood. Use the term **centennial**.

4. **TIME LINE** Could people have driven Studebaker cars to the first Indianapolis 500?

5. **READING SKILL—Draw Conclusions** What types of challenges did the invention of the automobile bring to Indiana?

6. **ECONOMICS** What caused some of Indiana's factory workers to form labor unions in the late nineteenth century?

7. **CRITICAL THINKING—Synthesize** How was the development of the automobile similar to developments in other transportation in the 1800s?

PERFORMANCE—Write a Description It is the early 1900s. You and your family have just gotten your first automobile. Write a description of how your life has changed. Describe a day in your life now that you have a car.

CD 8
Track 3

Automobile Advertisements

The Auburn Cord Duesenberg Museum in Auburn, Indiana, displays automobiles from the former Auburn Automobile Company, which manufactured its products from 1900 to 1937. These elegant luxury cars were advertised to wealthy Americans in the 1920s and 1930s. The museum was originally the company's office building and was built in 1930. It is an example of art deco architecture. There are several automobiles on display as well as advertisements that appeared in magazines.

E. L. Cord was president of the Auburn Automobile Company in 1925.

FROM THE AUBURN CORD
DUESENBERG MUSEUM

Hood ornaments were a symbol of the automobile's elegance.

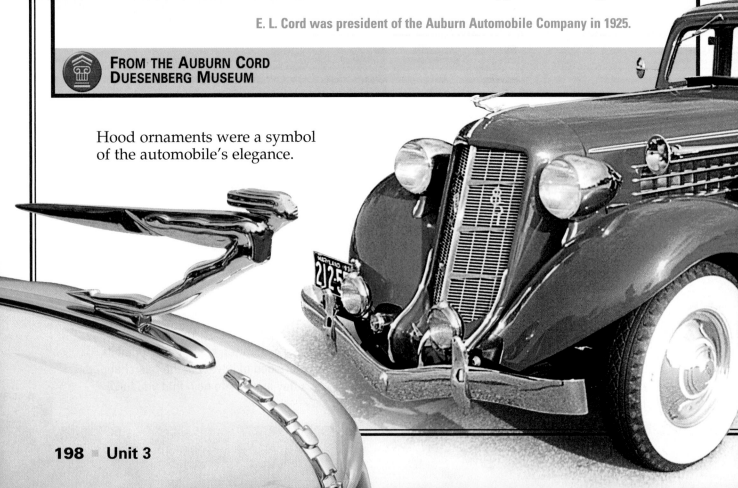

1. How much did the automobile cost?

2. Who do you think would buy this car?

3. Compare the making and advertising of automobiles in the past and today. How are they the same? How are they different?

The world's Smartest low priced car— 119-inch wheelbase Six, low as

$695

*Car illustrated above is the 126-inch Wheelbase, Straight Eight, 115 Horse Power, 5 passenger Custom Salon $1145

Not only does the new Auburn introduce a new high standard of quick acceleration, combined with quiet, smooth, flexible power—not only does it "hold the road" in a manner that makes it easier to drive and safer to ride in—not only does it run in an even, straight line with a minimized tendency to side-sway or roll—But climaxing all these performance-advan-

tages are the many ways in which the new Auburn takes the "work" out of driving. Auburn for 1934 makes automobile driving remarkably easy; more restful; more comfortable; requires less exertion and leaves you refreshed even after long drives. We invite you to ride in and drive the new Auburn models. If the car does not sell itself you will not be asked to buy.

6 CYLINDER MODELS $695 TO $945; 8 CYLINDER MODELS $945 TO $1225; SALON 12 MODELS $1395 TO $1545
All prices at the factory, subject to change without notice. Equipment other than standard, extra
AUBURN AUTOMOBILE COMPANY, AUBURN, INDIANA, Division of Cord Corporation

AUBURN

This advertisement for the 1934 Auburn (above) appeared in magazines. Factory workers assemble automobiles by hand (above left).

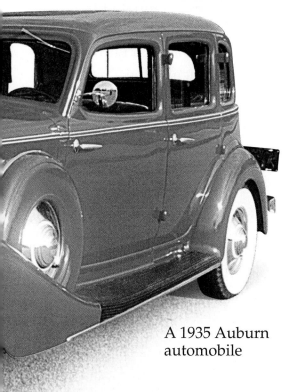

A 1935 Auburn automobile

ACTIVITY

Write an Advertisement Imagine that you have designed a new automobile. Make an advertisement for your product. Who do you want to buy it? What symbols will you put in your ad?

RESEARCH

Visit The Learning Site at **www.harcourtschool.com/ primarysources** to research other primary sources.

2

MAIN IDEA
Read to find out how Hoosiers took part in national and world events in the early 1900s.

WHY IT MATTERS
Life in Indiana today continues to be affected by events happening outside the state.

VOCABULARY
bonds
shortage
temperance
amendment
suffrage
consumer goods
aviation
depression
unemployment

Changing Times

1900		1950		2000

1910–1940

As Hoosiers celebrated Indiana's centennial, events happening thousands of miles away were about to change their lives. War had broken out in Europe in 1914, with Britain, France, and Russia fighting Germany and Austria-Hungary. At first, the United States sent supplies, but no soldiers, to support Britain and France. Then, in 1917, German submarines attacked United States ships in the Atlantic Ocean. These attacks led President Woodrow Wilson to ask the United States Congress to declare war on Germany. The United States began sending soldiers to fight in Europe.

World War I

Before 1917, Hoosiers were divided about whether the United States should enter World War I. Many Hoosiers thought that the United States should help France and Britain. Others believed that the nation should not get involved in a European war. Members of certain religious groups, such as the Quakers, refused to take part in any war. When United States ships were attacked by German submarines, most Hoosiers set aside their

During World War I troops used tanks for the first time.

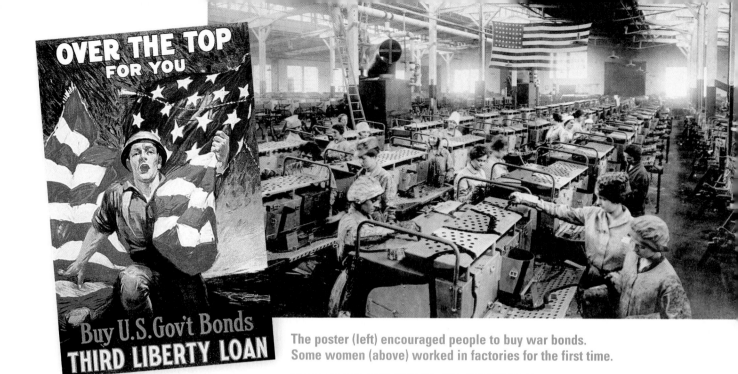

The poster (left) encouraged people to buy war bonds.
Some women (above) worked in factories for the first time.

differences and worked together in support of the war. More than 130,000 Hoosiers served in military forces during the war. More than 3,000 Hoosiers died in World War I. Fifteen of those killed were women serving as nurses.

At home people of all ages helped the war effort by buying war bonds. The **bonds** allowed the government to use people's money for a certain amount of time and pay it back later. Some students paid a dime a week to buy war bonds.

When men went off to fight in the war, women often took their places in the factories. The steel, cars, trucks, and foods they helped produce made Indiana important to the war effort. Producing goods for the war was good for the state's economy, too.

Hoosiers at home faced many hardships. The war caused shortages of food and other goods. A **shortage** of something means that there is not enough of it to go around. Many Hoosiers gave up meat on Mondays and wheat on Tuesdays so that there would be

enough of these foods to be shipped to soldiers overseas.

In addition to dealing with shortages, Hoosiers also faced disease. An outbreak of influenza, or the flu, in late 1918 and early 1919 killed thousands in Indiana and in other parts of the United States.

World War I ended when the Germans surrendered on November 11, 1918. Like people around the world, Hoosiers hoped that the end of the war would bring lasting peace. They wanted World War I to be "the war to end all wars."

REVIEW How did Hoosiers at home support the war effort during World War I?

French citizens and American soldiers in Europe celebrated the end of World War I.

African American Population in Indiana, 1910 to 1940

Population

160,000
120,000
80,000
40,000
0

1910 1920 1930 1940

Year

Analyze Graphs African Americans came to Indiana cities looking for jobs.

◈ Between which years did the African American population in Indiana increase the most?

Change and Social Movements

Following World War I, Indiana faced new challenges. Its population continued to change. After 1920 the number of people moving to Indiana from Europe slowed. At the same time, the movement of African Americans from the South to the Middle West increased. Many African Americans moved to Indiana. They came looking for jobs in cities such as Gary, Indianapolis, Fort Wayne, Muncie, Terre Haute, and Evansville. This movement became known as the Great Migration.

Another important change related to the war years was the temperance movement. **Temperance** means drinking little or no alcohol. Many Hoosiers supported temperance for religious

reasons. Some people also believed that temperance might help reduce crime.

For many years some people in Indiana and elsewhere in the United States tried to pass laws that limited or did not allow the use of alcohol. To save grain for use in World War I, Indiana had passed a law in 1917 that made the making of alcohol illegal. Two years later Indiana joined with other states to approve the Eighteenth Amendment to the United States Constitution. This **amendment**, or change, outlawed the making, sale, and use of alcohol. The years that followed, the 1920s, were known as the years of Prohibition (pro•uh•BIH•shun). During this time alcohol was prohibited, or not allowed.

REVIEW After World War I, where were most of Indiana's newcomers from?

The Role for Women Expands

The years after World War I brought changes for women. Before 1920, women could run a business and own property, but they were not allowed to vote.

Posters and buttons for temperance (near right) and suffrage (far right) identify two issues in Indiana and the United States in the early 1900s that were important to women.

Since the founding of New Harmony, Hoosiers such as May Wright Sewall of Indianapolis had worked for **suffrage** (SUH•frij), or the right to vote. Many of these same women were also active in the temperance movement.

In 1920 Indiana joined with other states to add the Nineteenth Amendment to the United States Constitution. This amendment gave women across the country the right to vote in national elections. A year later Indiana allowed women to vote in state elections. However, even without the votes of women, in 1920 Julia D. Nelson became the first woman elected to serve in Indiana's state government. Eighty years later, twenty-four women were elected to serve in the state's government.

 **REVIEW** In what year did Indiana women gain the right to vote in state elections?

Indiana Industries in the 1920s

By 1920 more Hoosiers lived in towns and cities than on farms. Improvements in farming, such as the corn-picking machine, allowed farms to produce more with fewer workers.

The two leading industries in the 1920s were steelmaking and automobile manufacturing. These and other Indiana industries, such as glass production at the Ball brothers' factory in Muncie, continued to offer jobs and help the state's economy.

Many new industries also came about during the postwar period. Peace and a good economy increased the market for **consumer goods**—products meant for personal use. Indiana factories began making vacuum cleaners, radios, washing machines, and other household products.

DEMOCRATIC VALUES
The Right to Vote

CITIZENSHIP

Some citizens of the United States take the right to vote for granted. Our founding fathers believed that it was the right of citizens in a democracy to choose their own representatives in government. In the twenty-first century any United States citizen over the age of 18 may register to vote. It was not until the Fifteenth Amendment to the Constitution was passed in 1870 that suffrage was given to all male citizens "regardless of race, color, or previous condition of servitude [slavery]." Fifty more years passed before the Nineteenth Amendment gave women suffrage.

Analyze the Value

1 Why is the right to vote important?

2 Why do you think it took so long to extend suffrage to all American citizens?

3 **Make It Relevant** Interview an adult family member. Ask him or her to tell you what it was like to vote for the first time. Share your findings with your classmates. Work as a class to make a mural celebrating suffrage.

Women and girls parade for suffrage.

The market for these products grew even more as rural areas began receiving electric power.

Wilbur Wright, an inventor born near Millville, worked with his brother Orville to create another new industry. In 1903 the Wright brothers made the first successful airplane flight at Kitty Hawk, North Carolina. By the 1920s **aviation**, the making and flying of airplanes, brought new economic opportunities to Indiana. Indianapolis became an important center for air travel.

REVIEW What developments increased the market for consumer goods during the 1920s?

Hard Times

The 1920s were good times for Hoosiers who had jobs and money to spend. However, these times did not last long. In 1929 the United States entered an economic depression. A **depression** is a time when there are few jobs and people have little money. The depression of the 1930s was so bad that it came to be known as the Great Depression.

The Great Depression had many causes. Some banks had lent too much money to new businesses. When people could not repay the loans, the banks had to close. Many families lost their savings when the banks suddenly closed. Because these people had less money, they bought fewer goods. This caused many businesses to fail. Workers in these failed businesses lost their jobs.

Many Hoosiers who lost their jobs during the Great Depression relied on soup kitchens for their meals.

Unemployment, or the number of people without jobs, was high across the United States in the 1930s. About one in four workers lost his or her job. Others could find jobs that lasted only a few months.

Indiana's government did its best to help its citizens. Governor Paul V. McNutt started a plan to make sure older people with little money would be cared for.

Most Hoosiers looked to the national government for help. Under the leadership of President Franklin D. Roosevelt, new government programs such as the Civilian Conservation Corps were created. The CCC put young adult men to work building state parks and bridges.

REVIEW What is a depression?

Civilian Conservation Corps Camps in Indiana

Analyze Graphs Many unemployed Hoosiers worked in Civilian Conservation Corps camps during the Great Depression. They lived in different camps as they moved from job to job.

◆ In which year were there the most CCC camps in Indiana?

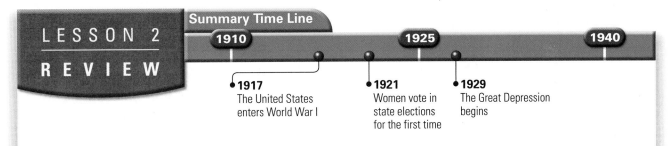

LESSON 2 REVIEW

Summary Time Line

1910 — 1925 — 1940

1917
The United States enters World War I

1921
Women vote in state elections for the first time

1929
The Great Depression begins

1. **MAIN IDEA** What world and national events affected life in Indiana in the years between 1910 and 1940?

2. **WHY IT MATTERS** What world and national events affect life in Indiana today?

3. **VOCABULARY** Use the headings below to group the following terms: **amendment, aviation, consumer goods, depression, shortage, temperance, unemployment, bonds**.

   World War I
   Change and Social Movements
   New Industries
   Hard Times

4. **TIME LINE** When did the United States enter World War I?

5. **READING SKILL—Draw Conclusions** How did women contribute to the growth of Indiana's economy in the early twentieth century?

6. **ECONOMICS** What were some of the causes of the Great Depression?

7. **CIVICS/GOVERNMENT** Why was the Nineteenth Amendment important?

8. **CRITICAL THINKING—Hypothesize** What might have happened if the United States had not entered World War I?

PERFORMANCE—Write to Persuade Imagine that you support political and social movements of the early twentieth century. Write a speech persuading others to work for prohibition or for suffrage for women. You may want to deliver your speech to your classmates.

· SKILLS · Resolve a Conflict

VOCABULARY

resolve
compromise

➡ WHY IT MATTERS

Most people work well together when they agree. Sometimes, however, people have different ideas about how things should be done. That can lead to conflict. It is important to learn how to handle conflict with civility, or politeness. Knowing how to **resolve**, or settle, conflicts with other people is an important life skill.

There are many ways to resolve conflict. You can explain your ideas and try to get others to change their minds and agree with you. Sometimes resolving conflict involves talking about and listening to different points of view. It may mean making a compromise. In a **compromise** both sides in a conflict give up something they want so they can reach an agreement.

➡ WHAT YOU NEED TO KNOW

To resolve a conflict, you can use these steps.

Step 1 Before you begin talking to the person with whom you disagree, understand that you may have to give up some of the things you want.

Step 2 Tell the other person clearly what you want.

Step 3 Listen carefully to what the other person wants.

Step 4 Decide which part is most important to you and what you are willing to give up. Present a plan for a compromise.

Step 5 Let the other person present his or her plan.

Step 6 Talk about the differences. Keep talking until you can agree on a compromise. You may need to change your plans several times before you reach an agreement.

Step 7 If you begin to feel angry or frustrated, take a break to calm down before you go on talking.

President Franklin D. Roosevelt addresses people on the radio during the Great Depression.

During the early 1930s many Hoosiers lost their jobs and were unable to repay money they had borrowed from banks. Some banks in Indiana and in other states were forced out of business. When banks began to close, many depositors, or people who had saved money in banks, wanted to get their money back. They had placed, or deposited, money in a bank account. They no longer trusted the banks with their money. These depositors grew angry when bank owners refused to return their money.

President Franklin D. Roosevelt came up with a compromise to resolve this conflict between depositors and bank owners. During a 1933 radio address, Roosevelt declared a "bank holiday." Any bank that was still open for business was now closed.

During the brief "holiday" that followed, Roosevelt made most banks stronger. He made more money available to banks. As a result, most banks reopened after a few days or weeks, and depositors were able to get their money if they wanted it. President Roosevelt encouraged depositors to keep what money they did not need in banks. Roosevelt said, "I can assure you that it is safer to keep your money in a reopened bank than under the mattress."

Hoosiers would face more hard times and economic challenges during the 1930s. Still, Roosevelt's ability to reopen banks quickly gave many people a reason to believe that things would get better.

▶ PRACTICE THE SKILL

Read the passage on this page. Then use what you have learned about resolving conflicts to answer these questions.

1. How did economic hard times in the 1930s create a conflict between bank owners and their depositors?

2. What kind of compromise did President Roosevelt suggest to resolve the conflict?

▶ APPLY WHAT YOU LEARNED

With your classmates, choose an issue that you do not all agree on. You might select an issue that affects your neighborhood, your school, or your community. Or you might choose an issue that has an impact on all people in the United States. After you have selected an issue, form two groups to discuss it. Both groups should follow the steps outlined on page 206 to resolve the conflict.

CP8 Track 6

3

World War II and After

1900   1950   2000

1940–2000

MAIN IDEA
Read to find out how World War II and postwar events changed the lives of the people of Indiana and the rest of the United States.

WHY IT MATTERS
People today are still facing some of the challenges that came about during the period following World War II.

VOCABULARY
defense plant
suburb
commute
interstate highway
leisure time
discrimination
segregation
civil rights
orbit
space shuttle

By 1940 the economy of the United States had begun to improve. Businesses reopened, and many people were able to find jobs. By this time, however, countries in Europe and Asia were at war again. Hoosiers and other Americans were about to be drawn into a new conflict. The war and the events that followed it changed life in Indiana once again.

Hoosiers and World War II

In the early morning hours of December 7, 1941, Japanese war planes dropped bombs on United States Navy ships at Pearl Harbor, Hawaii. Many people were killed, and most of the ships were destroyed. Thelma Robeson, of Fayette County, Indiana, later remembered hearing on the radio the news of the attack at Pearl Harbor.

> **The next day we heard President Roosevelt had declared war, which really set everyone to thinking, when it got to something like that. We just did all the things that we could do to help out.**

Japan attacked airfields as well as ships in Hawaii on the morning of December 7, 1941. The United States entered World War II after Japan's attack.

Ernie Pyle 1900–1945

Character Trait: Compassion

Ernest Taylor Pyle lived on a farm near Dana, Indiana. He joined the Naval Reserve during World War I, but the war ended before he was called to serve. Pyle then went to Indiana University to study journalism. During World War II Pyle found a new way to serve Indiana and his country—as a journalist covering the war. Millions of people at home learned about World War II from Pyle's articles. The articles appeared in 700 newspapers around the world. Pyle traveled with the troops and told their personal stories in a simple, moving way. He helped persuade the government to pay soldiers higher salaries for combat duty. Ernie Pyle shared the dangers of military life, too. In 1945 he was killed on the Pacific island of Ie Shima, near Okinawa, Japan.

War reporter Ernie Pyle (center) talks with American soldiers.

GO ONLINE

MULTIMEDIA BIOGRAPHIES
Visit The Learning Site at **www.harcourtschool.com/biographies** to learn about other famous people.

Hoosiers did help during the conflict that came to be known as World War II. The United States joined the Allied Powers. Along with Britain, France, and the Soviet Union, the United States fought against Germany, Italy, and Japan. More than 300,000 men and women from Indiana served in the United States armed forces. By the time the war ended with an Allied victory in 1945, more than 10,000 Hoosiers had been killed.

During the war Indiana's factories once again made supplies for soldiers. Automobile factories began making army trucks and jeeps. Metal for ships and tanks came from Gary's steel mills. Evansville factories made airplanes and ships. These factories were called **defense plants** because they made things needed to defend the country.

Women worked in defense plants as they had during World War I. LaVerda Shearer worked in General Electric's Fort Wayne plant. "I learned to run a lathe like the men run," she recalled. "When the . . . men were coming back from the war . . . they switched me to a girl's job. I had to take quite a cut in pay."

Women took over men's factory jobs during World War II.

Children supported the war by collecting scrap metal to be reused.

Life in Postwar Indiana

On September 2, 1945, Indiana stores and city offices closed as Hoosiers celebrated the end of World War II. Cheering crowds filled the streets. Some people in Indianapolis jumped into the Monument Circle pool.

For many people in the United States life was good after the war. Returning soldiers quickly settled down and began to raise families. This began a population increase in the United States known as the baby boom. The number of businesses also increased, providing more jobs and more money than ever before.

Among the first things many Hoosiers bought with their increased incomes were cars and houses. New houses were built in **suburbs**, or smaller towns and cities on the edges of large cities. As more people moved to the suburbs, new shopping centers were built near those areas. People who lived in the suburbs **commuted**, or traveled, to jobs in the cities. During the 1950s and 1960s, the United States government built an **interstate highway** system, which linked major cities and suburbs across the country.

Shortages were a fact of life for Hoosiers during World War II. Young people collected scrap metal, old tires, and paper to be recycled, or used again, in defense plants. Supplies of goods such as meat, gasoline, and rubber were controlled, or rationed, by the government because their quantities were limited. As a result, people could buy only small amounts of these items.

REVIEW **What were defense plants?**

After World War II ended, many new highways were built to link Indiana's major cities.

In 1955 the Crispus Attucks Tigers became the first all African American high school sports team to win the state basketball championship in Indiana.

Higher salaries meant that people could work fewer hours. They had more time away from work, or **leisure time**, to enjoy new kinds of entertainment such as television. People also played and watched many kinds of sports.

The sport preferred by most Hoosiers was basketball. Their love of basketball has been called "Hoosier Hysteria." Throughout the twentieth century, high school, college, and professional basketball games drew huge crowds.

REVIEW How did the development of suburbs change life in Indiana after World War II?

Hoosiers Struggle for Civil Rights

Not all people in Indiana shared equally in the good times that followed World War II. African Americans in Indiana and other states continued to face **discrimination**, or unfair treatment. Many African Americans were unemployed or earned low wages. They did not have the same opportunities that other citizens of the United States had.

In Indiana, as in other parts of the United States, state and local laws still allowed segregation. **Segregation** means keeping people in separate groups because of their race or culture. African Americans in Indiana could not get some kinds of jobs, go to certain restaurants, or visit some parks or other public places.

Some Hoosiers took action to gain full civil rights for African Americans. **Civil rights** are the rights and freedoms given by the Constitution to all citizens. In 1949 Henry J. Richardson, Jr., an African American lawyer, led a successful fight against segregation in Indiana public schools.

These efforts were part of a larger civil rights movement. Dr. Martin Luther King, Jr., a minister from Georgia, worked to protect the civil rights of African Americans. Millions of people in the United States of many backgrounds supported Dr. King and his work.

Dr. Martin Luther King, Jr., makes a speech at a civil rights event in Washington, D.C.

Richard Hatcher, Indiana's first African American mayor, served the citizens of Gary for 20 years.

By the mid-1960s the federal government had outlawed segregation. African Americans began voting in large numbers and electing leaders at all levels of government. In 1967 the citizens of Gary elected Richard Hatcher as their mayor. Hatcher was one of the first African Americans to head a large city. He served as Gary's mayor for 20 years, winning election four times.

At the same time that Indiana and the rest of the United States were struggling over civil rights, the nation also fought another war. From the early 1960s until 1973, United States soldiers, including many Hoosiers, fought in Vietnam, in Southeast Asia. More than 58,000 people died in this war. Unlike World War II, the Vietnam War was an unpopular war, especially among young people.

REVIEW Who was one African American leader who worked for civil rights on the state level?

Hoosiers Explore Space

During the 1950s and 1960s, the United States space program made many advances in science and technology. Hoosiers took part in the exploration of space as scientists, engineers, and astronauts. Many of those who work for NASA, the agency that runs the United States space program, studied, taught, or did research at Purdue University in West Lafayette.

In July 1961 astronaut Virgil "Gus" Grissom, who grew up in Mitchell, Indiana, became the second American in space. Alan B. Shepard, Jr., had become the first American in space just two months earlier.

Frank Borman, of Gary, made history in 1968 when he and two other astronauts became the first to **orbit**, or circle, the moon. They took photographs of the moon's surface. Their work helped make possible the first moon landing, in 1969.

Today's astronauts fly in vehicles called **space shuttles**, carrying out experiments and working on an international space station. Hoosiers continue to remain active in the space program.

Hoosier astronaut Gus Grissom became the second American to go into space.

In 1997 David Wolf, of Indianapolis, spent 128 days in space. For most of that mission (119 days), he was aboard the Russian space station *Mir*. Astronaut Janice Voss, of South Bend, flew five missions in space between 1993 and 2000.

REVIEW Who was the first astronaut from Indiana?

Like many other astronauts, Janice Voss attended Purdue University.

• SCIENCE AND TECHNOLOGY •

Stellite

Automobile inventor Elwood Haynes helped make space travel possible. Haynes began his career as a metalworker. He continued to look for new uses for metals throughout his life. In 1907 Haynes patented an alloy, or mixture of metals, called stellite. Stellite is an extremely hard mix of cobalt, chromium, and tungsten. Layers of stellite are added to steel to make the steel stronger and more able to stand high temperatures. Stellite is used in jet engines, dental instruments, and nuclear power equipment. Haynes's invention also helped scientists develop superalloys, even stronger mixes of metals, for use in spacecraft.

LESSON 3
REVIEW

Summary Time Line

1940 — 1970 — 2000

1941
United States enters World War II

1945
World War II ends

1949
Segregation is outlawed in Indiana schools

1961
Gus Grissom becomes the second American to go into space

1. **MAIN IDEA** How did life change for many Hoosiers after World War II?

2. **WHY IT MATTERS** How does your community reflect the changes that took place after World War II?

3. **VOCABULARY** Write a short description of the challenges African Americans faced after World War II. Use the terms **discrimination** and **segregation** in your writing.

4. **TIME LINE** When did World War II end?

5. **READING SKILL—Draw Conclusions** What challenges might the growth of suburbs have presented for Indiana cities during the postwar years?

6. **CULTURE** What leisure activities enjoyed by Hoosiers in the 1950s are still popular today?

7. **CULTURE** In what ways have Hoosiers contributed to the space program?

8. **CRITICAL THINKING—Synthesize** Why was it important for African Americans to have the right to vote?

PERFORMANCE—Write a Diary Entry
Imagine that you are a woman working in a defense plant during World War II, an African American teenager attending a segregated high school, or a shuttle astronaut in training. Write a diary entry describing a day in your life. Share your work with a family member.

·SKILLS· MAP AND GLOBE

Following Routes on a Map

VOCABULARY

route

➡ WHY IT MATTERS

Every time you go for a walk, a bike ride, or a car ride, you follow a route. A **route** is a path that a person takes to get from one place to another. You follow a route in your neighborhood to go to school. You and your family can follow a route from your community to another state. Learning to follow a route on a map can help you find the best ways to travel. Following routes on a historical map can show you how people traveled in earlier times.

➡ WHAT YOU NEED TO KNOW

Use these steps to follow a route on a map.

Step 1 Study the map. Become familiar with the places shown on the map.

Step 2 Look at the map features. The map key may show symbols that stand for cities, towns, and other places. It may also identify different kinds of roads and routes.

Step 3 The compass rose shows you directions for north, south, east, and west. It also helps you see the direction in which different routes go. The scale helps you figure out the distance between two places on the map.

Step 4 Trace some of the routes with your finger.

➡ PRACTICE THE SKILL

Trace the routes shown on the road map on page 215. Then answer these questions.

1 In which directions does United States Highway 40 go?

2 Which route links the industrial city of Gary with the Port of Indiana at Portage?

3 Which three communities on the map are linked by United States Highway 31?

4 What United States Highway links the cities of Evansville and Terre Haute?

5 Which highway links the cities of Lafayette and Indianapolis?

▶ APPLY WHAT YOU LEARNED

Look at a road map of Indiana. Choose a major road or highway that runs through or near your community. Using tracing paper and a pen or pencil, trace the route on the map. What other Indiana communities are linked by this road or highway with your community?

Label the communities on your tracing. Add a title. Compare your completed map with those of other students in your class. Display your map in your classroom or school library.

Practice your map and globe skills with the **GeoSkills CD-ROM.**

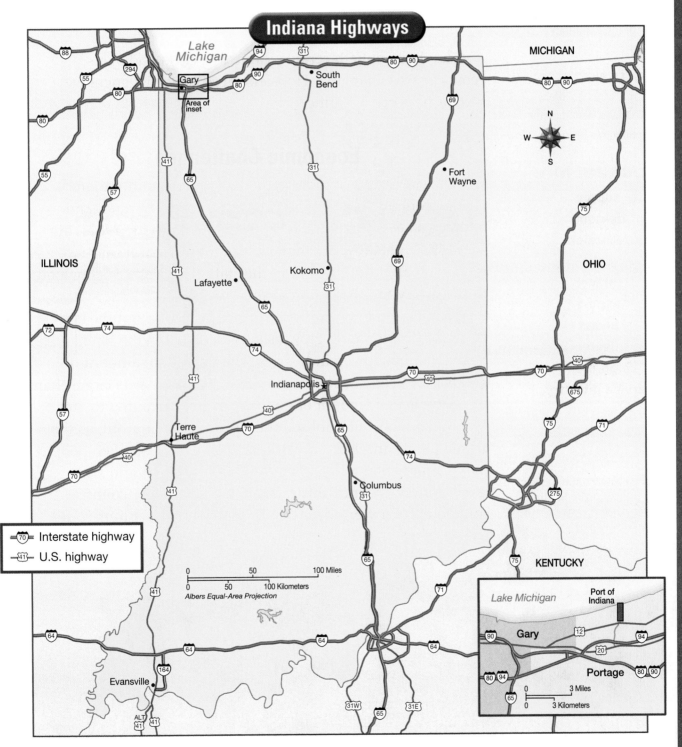

Indiana Highways

Lake Michigan

MICHIGAN

Gary
Area of inset

South Bend

Fort Wayne

ILLINOIS

Kokomo

Lafayette

OHIO

Indianapolis

Terre Haute

Columbus

🔘70 Interstate highway
🔘41 U.S. highway

| 0   50   100 Miles |
| 0   50   100 Kilometers |
Albers Equal-Area Projection

KENTUCKY

Evansville

Lake Michigan   Port of Indiana

Gary

Portage

| 0   3 Miles |
| 0   3 Kilometers |

4

The Twentieth Century Ends

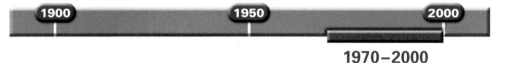

1900   1950   2000

1970–2000

As the twentieth century came to a close, Indiana's economy was changing. Hoosiers faced new challenges as well as new opportunities.

Economic Challenges

The last decades of the twentieth century found Indiana facing economic challenges. The state's roads, bridges, and highways needed repairs. In 1973 and again in the 1980s, the state government raised the sales tax in Indiana. A sales tax is a tax on all products sold in the state. This higher tax helped the state pay for needed programs.

Indiana's economy suffered during the 1980s and the early 1990s. Unemployment grew as jobs were lost in the steel and heavy manufacturing industries. The **supply**, or amount of goods producers had to sell, in these industries was larger than the **demand**, or amount of goods consumers wanted to buy. Manufacturers could not sell their products at a profit, so they closed plants and laid off workers. Jobs were lost when people in the United States began buying steel products and automobiles from other countries. Companies in other countries sold goods at lower prices than Indiana manufacturers could.

The last International Scout rolls off the assembly line in 1980.

In the 1980s Hoosier John Mellencamp helped organize Farm Aid concerts to help farm families. They are held every year.

FARM AID
Keep America Growing!

Indiana's economy suffered a recession in the 1980s. A **recession** is an economic slowdown that is slightly less damaging than a depression. Indiana's recession was costly to the state. High unemployment caused many Hoosiers to move to other states in search of jobs. For the first time, Indiana's population decreased. With fewer people living and working in the state, Indiana's government had less tax money to use to help those in need.

Indiana farmers faced hard times in the 1980s, too. Like farmers in other states, Hoosiers paid high costs for fuel, fertilizer, and other supplies. To buy what they needed, many farmers went into **debt** (DET) by borrowing money from banks. Prices for farm products dropped, and the amount of money that farmers received from sales of their goods to other countries decreased. As a result, many farmers could not pay back money they had borrowed. They were forced to sell their farms to get out of debt. In the 1980s and 1990s in Indiana and other parts of the United States, it became harder for a family to own and operate a farm. Today, careful management is required to keep a family farm going.

REVIEW What economic challenges did Hoosiers face in the 1980s?

Analyze Graphs The number of Indiana farms decreased in the late twentieth century.

How many fewer farms were there in Indiana in 1997 than in 1982?

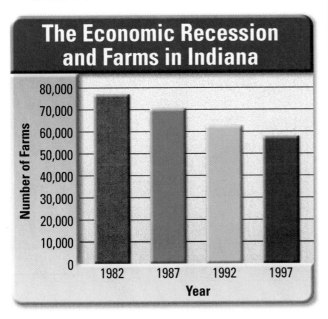

The Economic Recession and Farms in Indiana

Number of Farms (y-axis: 0 to 80,000 in increments of 10,000)
Year (x-axis): 1982, 1987, 1992, 1997

Interdependence

In spite of its economic challenges, Indiana also found new economic opportunities in the last years of the twentieth century. These opportunities came from the state's economic interdependence. This means that Indiana's economy—what it made and traded—had become linked with the economies of other states in the United States and also with the economies of other countries.

Changes in transportation brought opportunities for trade with other countries. In 1970 the Port of Indiana opened at Burns Harbor on Lake Michigan. The Port of Indiana is on the Great Lakes transportation route called the St. Lawrence Seaway. Ships heading inland from the Atlantic Ocean travel along this seaway to Burns Harbor. They are used by businesses that **import**, or bring products from other countries into the state, and **export**, or send Indiana products to be sold in other countries.

In addition to the new Great Lakes port, Indiana opened two new Ohio River ports. From the Southwind Maritime Center, at Mount Vernon, barges carry grain and other products to ports around the world. Southwind is part of a free-trade zone. That means that companies from other countries do not have to pay duties, or taxes, for doing business there. The port at Mount Vernon, which opened in 1979, is Indiana's busiest port. It is also the second-largest port on the Ohio River. Another Indiana port opened at Jeffersonville in 1984.

Indiana became interdependent in another way. Some companies based in other countries began to **invest** in Indiana companies. Investing means putting money and other business

---

• GEOGRAPHY •

St. Lawrence Seaway
Understanding Places and Regions

What gives an inland state like Indiana an ocean port? The answer is the St. Lawrence Seaway, a system of natural and human-made waterways. During the 1950s Canada and the United States worked together to build the seaway. Its canals link the St. Lawrence River, Lake Ontario, and Lake Erie. Oceangoing ships can enter the St. Lawrence River from the Atlantic Ocean, and travel through the St. Lawrence Seaway and all the Great Lakes. The Port of Indiana at Burns Harbor, shown here, is on Lake Michigan. Because of the St. Lawrence Seaway, ships can travel even farther inland than Indiana—to ports such as Chicago, Illinois, and Duluth, Minnesota.

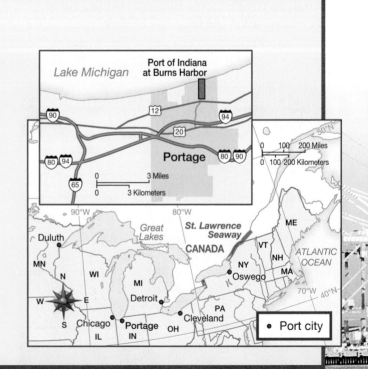

resources into companies in order to make money. The international companies received a share of any profits the Indiana companies made. International companies also purchased Indiana companies or opened branches of their own businesses in Indiana. In turn, some Indiana-owned businesses began expanding into countries in other parts of the world.

REVIEW During the 1970s and 1980s, what developments in transportation helped Indiana?

Indiana's Changing Economy

In the 1990s Indiana's economy began to improve. Part of this improvement was because of global interdependence. Each year Indiana exports goods worth billions of dollars. Most exports are machinery and agricultural products. Indiana also imports many goods and raw materials. Indiana trades not only with other states but also with countries around the world. Canada, Europe, Mexico, and Japan are Indiana's most important international trading partners. During the year 2000

Indiana's Global Trade, 2000

Dollars (in millions)

Canada, Mexico, Japan, United Kindom, Germany

Analyze Graphs Indiana trades with countries throughout the world.

❖ Which country is Indiana's largest trade partner?

Indiana exported more than one billion dollars' worth of machinery to other countries. Another way trade occurs with other countries is when international companies locate businesses in Indiana. For example, Japan's Toyota Corporation makes trucks in Princeton.

The Port of Indiana links the state's economy to a global market.

Indiana Exports, 2000

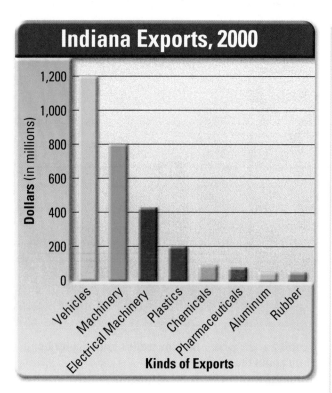

Kinds of Exports

Dollars (in millions): 0, 200, 400, 600, 800, 1,000, 1,200

Vehicles, Machinery, Electrical Machinery, Plastics, Chemicals, Pharmaceuticals, Aluminum, Rubber

Analyze Graphs Indiana manufactures goods that are exported to other countries.

❖ What is the approximate total value of Indiana's top three exports?

Vehicles, like these Toyota trucks, are Indiana's leading export.

Indiana's economy had suffered during the 1980s because it was too closely tied to only a few industries. Steel, heavy equipment manufacturing, and farming did not make money during those years. To make up for those losses, Indiana tried to find new kinds of industries to make the economy more diverse. A **diverse**, or mixed, economy has a wide variety of industries. Diverse economies are usually stronger than economies that rely on only a few kinds of industries. In a diverse economy, if one industry fails, others can make up the difference.

During the 1990s Indiana's state government passed laws to encourage new industries to come into the state. Two new industries—high-tech businesses and service industries—took advantage of these laws. They helped make Indiana's economy stronger and more diverse.

High-technology, or **high-tech**, businesses are those that invent, build, and use computers or other new technologies. They also may conduct scientific research. The Sony Corporation of America opened a factory in Terre Haute. This factory makes digital video discs, or DVDs. The Eli Lilly Company, in Indianapolis, hires scientists to work on new pharmaceuticals (fahr•muh•SOO•tih•kuhlz), or medicines, to help people who are sick.

Scientific research is a big part of Indiana's high-tech businesses.

The demand for high-tech products grew rapidly during the 1990s. Meeting that demand helped high-tech companies offer many new jobs to Hoosiers.

Service industries also have helped Indiana's economy. **Service industries** do not make goods. They provide services that people need or want. Examples of service industries are car dealerships, shopping malls, and restaurants. In the 1990s the Circle Centre Mall and entertainment center was built in downtown Indianapolis. This is an example of how service industries brought new jobs and new economic opportunities to Indiana's cities. Indiana also attracted other kinds of service industries, such as hotels, law offices, insurance companies, and health care centers.

Both high-tech businesses and service industries contributed to the growth and renewal of Indiana cities during

Service industries, such as this shopping mall, are an important part of Indiana's economy.

the 1990s. Indianapolis, Fort Wayne, Evansville, and South Bend all began or carried out major rebuilding projects to close out the twentieth century.

REVIEW What kinds of new industries did Indiana attract during the 1990s?

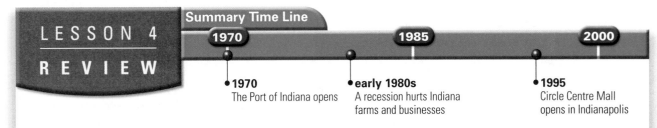

LESSON 4 REVIEW

Summary Time Line

1970	1985	2000
•1970 The Port of Indiana opens	•early 1980s A recession hurts Indiana farms and businesses	•1995 Circle Centre Mall opens in Indianapolis

❶ **MAIN IDEA** How did Indiana's economy change during the last decades of the twentieth century?

❷ **WHY IT MATTERS** How did the economic changes affect Hoosiers' lives?

❸ **VOCABULARY** Write an explanation of the rise in unemployment in the Indiana steel industry during the 1980s. Use the terms **supply** and **demand** in your writing.

❹ **TIME LINE** During what years did a recession hurt Indiana's economy?

❺ **READING SKILL—Draw Conclusions** How did Indiana's efforts to make its economy more diverse help the state's cities?

❻ **ECONOMICS** Why did Indiana raise sales taxes in the 1970s and 1980s?

❼ **GEOGRAPHY** How do ships reach the inland Great Lakes Port of Indiana from the ocean?

❽ **CRITICAL THINKING—Hypothesize** What might have been the result if Indiana's economy had not become more diverse in the 1990s?

PERFORMANCE—Create an Advertisement Imagine that you are the advertising director of a new Indiana company involved in a high-tech business or a service industry. Create a magazine advertisement for one of your company's products or services. Display your ad in class.

CD8
Track 9

6 Review and Test Preparation

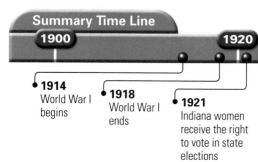

Summary Time Line

1900 — 1920

1914 World War I begins

1918 World War I ends

1921 Indiana women receive the right to vote in state elections

USE YOUR READING SKILLS

Complete this graphic organizer to draw conclusions about Indiana's economy. A copy of this graphic organizer appears on page 64 of the Activity Book.

Indiana's Economy

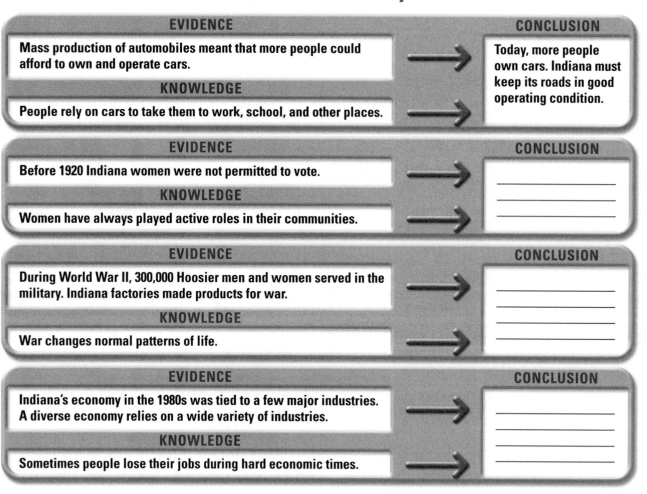

EVIDENCE
Mass production of automobiles meant that more people could afford to own and operate cars.

KNOWLEDGE
People rely on cars to take them to work, school, and other places.

CONCLUSION
Today, more people own cars. Indiana must keep its roads in good operating condition.

EVIDENCE
Before 1920 Indiana women were not permitted to vote.

KNOWLEDGE
Women have always played active roles in their communities.

CONCLUSION
_____

EVIDENCE
During World War II, 300,000 Hoosier men and women served in the military. Indiana factories made products for war.

KNOWLEDGE
War changes normal patterns of life.

CONCLUSION
_____

EVIDENCE
Indiana's economy in the 1980s was tied to a few major industries. A diverse economy relies on a wide variety of industries.

KNOWLEDGE
Sometimes people lose their jobs during hard economic times.

CONCLUSION
_____

THINK & WRITE

Creative Writing Think about the civil rights that Hoosiers now have. Choose one of these rights. Write a poem or the words to a song about why this right is important to you. Share your writing with classmates.

Write a Diary Entry Imagine that you are a factory worker or a farmer in Indiana in the 1930s. Write a diary entry about the economic challenges you face. Display your diary entry in your school library.

1945
World War II ends

1949
Segregation outlawed
in Indiana schools

1970
Port of Indiana opens on Lake Michigan

USE THE TIME LINE

Use the chapter summary time line to answer these questions.

1 When did Indiana women receive the right to vote in state elections?

2 How many years were there between the end of World War I and the end of World War II?

3 When was segregation outlawed in Indiana schools?

USE VOCABULARY

For each pair of terms below, write a sentence that uses the terms correctly.

4 **discrimination** (p. 211), **segregation** (p. 211)

5 **supply** (p. 216), **demand** (p. 216)

6 **recession** (p. 217), **unemployment** (p. 205)

7 **orbit** (p. 212), **space shuttle** (p. 212)

RECALL FACTS

Answer these questions.

8 Who invented Indiana's first gasoline-powered automobile?

9 What cause did Indiana's May Wright Sewall work for?

10 On what body of water is the Port of Indiana located?

Write the letter of the best choice.

11 **TEST PREP** During the 1980s Indiana's steel industry experienced a _____
   A debt.
   B recession.
   C depression.
   D diverse economy.

12 **TEST PREP** _____ became one of the first African American mayors of a major city in 1970.
   F Henry J. Richardson, Jr.
   G Dr. Martin Luther King, Jr.
   H Richard Hatcher
   J Oscar Robertson

THINK CRITICALLY

13 How did transportation changes in the early 1900s affect the lives of rural Hoosiers?

14 Why did Hoosiers have more leisure time after World War II than they did in pioneer days?

APPLY SKILLS

Resolve a Conflict
Find a current issue that has caused a conflict in your community. Look for information on the editorial page of your local newspaper, or watch TV news. Use this information to answer the following questions:

15 What is the issue?

16 What are the positions in this conflict?

17 What kind of compromise would you suggest?

Follow Routes on a Map

18 Look at a road map of Indiana. Tell which roads are the most direct routes from the community where you live to the following places: Port of Indiana on Lake Michigan, the Indiana State Capitol in Indianapolis, the Ohio River port at Jeffersonville.

VISIT

New Harmony
STATE HISTORIC SITE

GET READY

The New Harmony State Historic Site preserves the history of two nineteenth-century communities. Each in turn tried to create utopian, or perfect, living conditions. The first community was started in 1814 by a religious group from Pennsylvania led by George Rapp. The colonists named their community Harmonie and constructed several buildings around a town plan. In 1825 Rapp sold the community to Robert Owen, a British scholar, who renamed it New Harmony. Owen's community believed in educational equality without social class or personal wealth. New Harmony attracted scientists, scholars, and educators from all over the world.

LOCATE IT

INDIANA

New Harmony

WHAT TO SEE

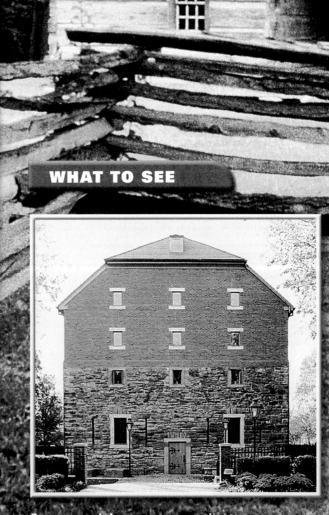

Owen turned the granary, or grain storage building, into a laboratory for scientific research. The studies done there provided some of the earliest natural science collections for the Smithsonian Institution.

The confusing paths of the labyrinth, or maze, represented the struggle of the Harmonie colonists to achieve perfection in their lives. After the 1825 sale of Harmonie, the labyrinth was no longer kept up and became completely overgrown. The present labyrinth was built next to the site of the original one.

Visitors to New Harmony can see demonstrations of crafts that were daily activities in the colonial period.

This single-family home is like many from the 1820s. It is filled with original artifacts and copies of colonial items. The tabletop is a large slab sliced from a tree trunk!

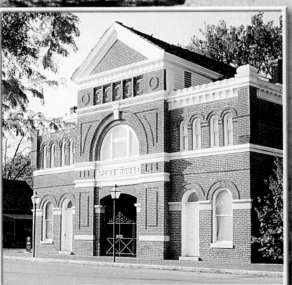

When Owen purchased the property, this former dormitory, or sleeping center, was turned into a community meeting hall for social activities. Renamed Thrall's Opera House in the late 1800s, it is now used as a theater.

TAKE A FIELD TRIP

GO ONLINE

A VIRTUAL TOUR
Visit The Learning Site at
www.harcourtschool.com/tours
to take virtual tours of other
historic sites.

3 Review and Test Preparation

USE VOCABULARY

For each pair of terms, write a sentence or two to explain how the terms are related.

1 **reaper** (p. 170), **thresher** (p. 171)

2 **slave state** (p. 176), **abolitionist** (p. 176)

3 **depression** (p. 204), **recession** (p. 217)

RECALL FACTS

Answer these questions.

4 Why were gristmills important?

5 Which roads were built in Indiana during the 1820s?

6 How did automobiles change Hoosiers' lives?

Write the letter of the best choice.

7 **TEST PREP** Indiana had eight towns with populations of more than 2,500 by—
  A 1800.
  B 1810.
  C 1820.
  D 1850.

8 **TEST PREP** A boat that carried passengers only one way was called a—
  F steamboat.
  G keelboat.
  H canoe.
  J flatboat.

9 **TEST PREP** When seven Southern states seceded from the United States in 1861, what did they call their new country?
  A the Confederate States of America
  B the Union
  C the Southern States
  D the Seceded States

10 **TEST PREP** What were the factories called that made supplies for soldiers during World War II?
  F defense plants
  G steel mills
  H scrap plants
  J navy plants

THINK CRITICALLY

11 Why do you think pioneers chose to settle in Indiana even though life was often difficult?

12 What might have happened to the farm industry if there had not been improvements in farm machinery?

13 Why might some Hoosiers in the 1980s have felt that buying an American-made car would help the economy?

APPLY SKILLS

Compare Maps with Different Scales
Use the two maps on page 227 to answer the following questions.

14 How many miles are represented by 1 inch on the scale of Map A?

15 How many miles are represented by 1 inch on Map B?

16 Is Map A a small-scale map or a large-scale map?

17 Many Civil War recruits for Indiana regiments trained at Camp Morton, in Indianapolis. Use Map B to determine the distances between Indianapolis and the nearby towns of Lawrence and Bridgeport.

18 Some Hoosiers volunteered to defend military supplies in Indianapolis when they heard about Morgan's raid at Corydon. What is the distance between Indianapolis and Corydon?

Map A: Small Scale

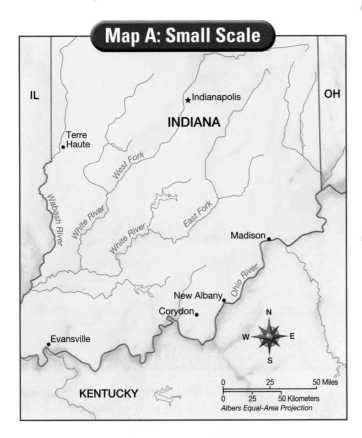

IL

INDIANA

OH

★Indianapolis

Terre Haute

West Fork

Wabash River

White River

White River

East Fork

Madison

Ohio River

New Albany

Corydon

Evansville

N
W   E
S

KENTUCKY

0   25   50 Miles
0   25   50 Kilometers
Albers Equal-Area Projection

Map B: Large Scale

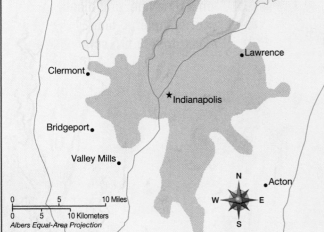

Clermont

Lawrence

★Indianapolis

Bridgeport

Valley Mills

N
W   E
S

Acton

0   5   10 Miles
0   5   10 Kilometers
Albers Equal-Area Projection

Visual Summary

1816   The Lincoln family moves to Indiana pp. 158–159

1829   Steamboats start traveling on the Wabash River p. 165

1921   Indiana women vote in state elections for the first time p. 203

1945   World War II ends p. 210

1961   Gus Grissom becomes the second American in space p. 212

Unit Activities

 GO ONLINE Visit The Learning Site at www.harcourtschool.com/socialstudies/activities for additional activities.

Write a Diary

Use resources such as the library or the Internet to learn about a specific Underground Railroad route. Imagine that you are helping people on that part of the Underground Railroad. Write diary entries telling about the things you do and see during seven days. When you have finished writing, add a cover made of construction paper. Then fold or staple the pages together to form a booklet. Display your completed diary in the school library.

Build a Log Cabin

Work in a group to build a miniature log cabin. Collect materials such as sticks, rocks, clay, leaves, toothpicks, small pieces of cloth, and colored paper to use in your construction. Refer to the illustration on page 160, or use other resources to help guide you in building your log cabin. When you are finished, present the log cabin to the class, and describe each part.

VISIT YOUR LIBRARY

■ *Train to Somewhere* by Eve Bunting. Houghton Mifflin.

■ *Freedom River* by Doreen Rappaport. Hyperion Books for Children.

■ *Vision of Beauty: The Story of Sarah Breedlove Walker* by Kathryn Lasky. Candlewick Press.

COMPLETE THE UNIT PROJECT

Create a Visual Time Line Work with a partner. Select the images that best illustrate important changes in life in Indiana during the 1800s and 1900s. Assemble the images on a time line, and display your completed time line in your classroom or the school library.

1861 Many Hoosiers Fight in the Civil War

1910 Many people in Indiana work in factories

1961 Gus Grissom goes to space

1850

1900

Important Changes in Indiana History

1990

Into the Twenty-First Century

United States
Quarter, 2002

Indianapolis Motor Speedway

4

Into the Twenty-First Century

**" With kindly word and friendly hand
She welcomes sons of every land. "**
—Sarah Knowles Bolton, "Indiana," 1915

Preview the Content

Scan the pictures in the unit. Make a web, listing famous Hoosiers. Use the categories of artists, sports figures, government officials, and other famous Hoosiers. Then list any questions you have about these famous Hoosiers.

Preview the Vocabulary

Antonyms   An antonym is a word that means the opposite of another word. For each word in the chart below, write its antonym. Then write a sentence using both the vocabulary word and its antonym.

VOCABULARY WORD	ANTONYM	SENTENCE
conserve		
assemble		
majority		

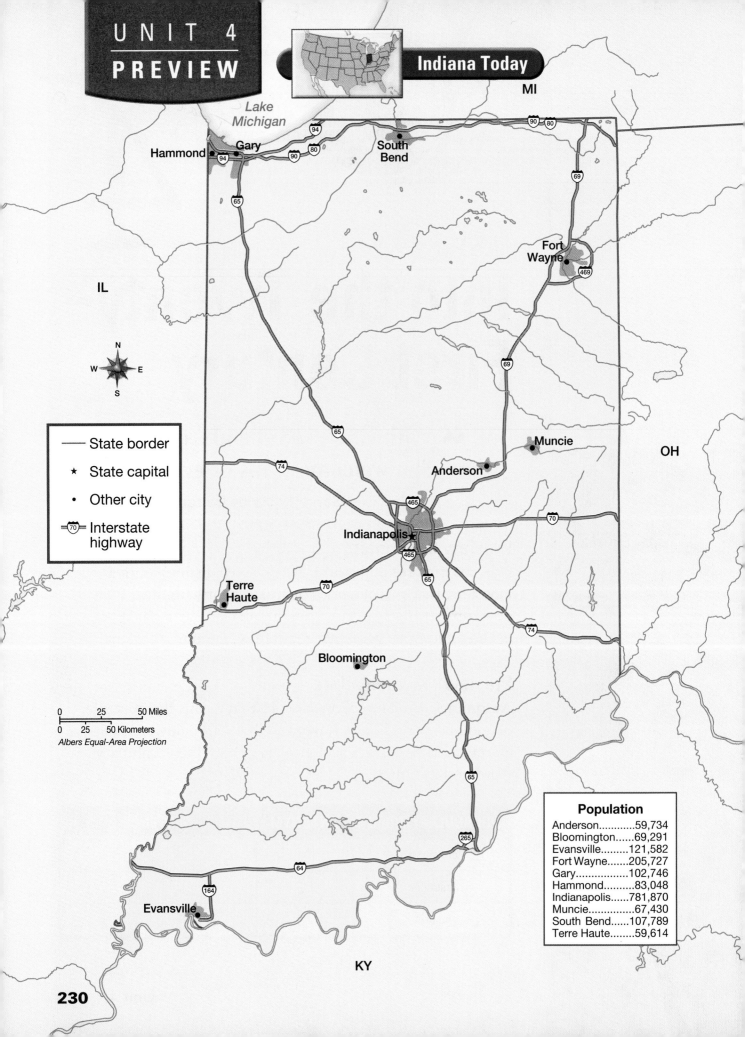

MI

Lake
Michigan

Hammond   Gary

South
Bend

IL

Fort
Wayne

OH

Muncie

Anderson

Indianapolis

Terre
Haute

Bloomington

— State border

★ State capital

• Other city

🛡70 Interstate
highway

0   25   50 Miles
0   25   50 Kilometers
Albers Equal-Area Projection

Population
Anderson............59,734
Bloomington......69,291
Evansville.........121,582
Fort Wayne.......205,727
Gary.................102,746
Hammond..........83,048
Indianapolis......781,870
Muncie..............67,430
South Bend......107,789
Terre Haute........59,614

Evansville

KY

Indiana's Most Populated Counties

COUNTY	NUMBER OF PEOPLE
Allen	🧍🧍🧍🧍🧍🧍
Elkhart	🧍🧍🧍🧍
Hamilton	🧍🧍🧍🧍
Lake	🧍🧍🧍🧍🧍🧍🧍🧍🧍🧍
Madison	🧍🧍🧍
Marion	🧍🧍🧍🧍🧍🧍🧍🧍🧍🧍🧍🧍🧍🧍🧍🧍🧍🧍
Porter	🧍🧍🧍
St. Joseph	🧍🧍🧍🧍🧍🧍
Tippecanoe	🧍🧍🧍
Vanderburgh	🧍🧍🧍

🧍 = 50,000 persons

Indiana Employment by Industry

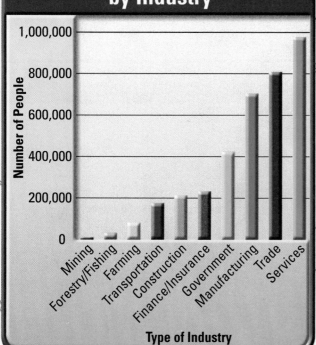

Number of People (y-axis): 0, 200,000, 400,000, 600,000, 800,000, 1,000,000

Type of Industry (x-axis): Mining, Forestry/Fishing, Farming, Transportation, Construction, Finance/Insurance, Government, Manufacturing, Trade, Services

**START
with a
POEM**

Indiana

by Arthur Franklin Mapes

"Indiana" became the Hoosier state's official state poem when it was approved by Indiana's General Assembly in 1963. Written by Kendallville native Arthur Franklin Mapes, the poem describes Indiana's natural beauty.

God crowned her hills with beauty,
Gave her lakes and winding streams,
Then He edged them all with woodlands
As the settings for our dreams.
Lovely are her moonlit rivers,
Shadowed by the sycamores,
Where the fragrant winds of Summer
Play along the willowed shores.
I must roam those wooded hillsides,
I must heed the native call,
For a Pagan voice within me
Seems to answer to it all.
I must walk where squirrels scamper
Down a rustic old rail fence,
Where a choir of birds is singing
In the woodland . . . green and dense.
I must learn more of my homeland
For it's paradise to me,
There's no haven quite as peaceful,
There's no place I'd rather be.
Indiana . . . is a garden
Where the seeds of peace have grown,
Where each tree, and vine, and flower
Has a beauty . . . all its own.
Lovely are the fields and meadows,
That reach out to hills that rise
Where the dreamy Wabash River
Wanders on . . . through paradise.

| Pagan | loving nature in a deep, almost religious way |
| haven | safe, secure place |

Analyze the Literature

1 What words or phrases does the author use to describe Indiana as a "paradise"?

2 How does the poem "Indiana" make you feel about your state? Do you agree with the author's descriptions? Write a poem about Indiana.

READ A BOOK

START THE UNIT PROJECT

Perform a Skit   With several classmates, plan a skit showing how Indiana's government works. As you read this unit, take notes about the key positions in Indiana's government. Your notes will help you decide which government positions to include in your skit.

USE TECHNOLOGY

Visit The Learning Site at **www.harcourtschool.com/ socialstudies** for additional activities, primary sources, and other resources to use in this unit.

OLDENBURG, INDIANA

Oldenburg, in Franklin County, is a small town of fewer than 750 residents. It is known as the "Village of Spires" because of its tall church steeples. Oldenburg is an example of German heritage in Indiana.

LOCATE IT

INDIANA

Oldenburg

7

Indiana in the Twenty-First Century

❝ Well, I was born in a
small town
And I can breathe in a
small town. ❞

—John Mellencamp,
from "Small Town," 1985

CHAPTER READING SKILL

Generalize

When you **generalize**, you summarize a group of facts and show the relationship between them.

As you read this chapter, identify important facts. Then use those facts to make several generalizations for each lesson.

FACTS → GENERALIZATION

A Mix of People

MAIN IDEA
Read to find out about the various people who live in Indiana today.

WHY IT MATTERS
Indiana's various cultures add to the richness of life in the state.

VOCABULARY
urban
rural
Hispanic
exile
fable

Every ten years the United States government takes a count of its people, or a census. The 2000 census showed that Indiana's population is growing and is diverse, or made up of various groups of people. The census counted more than 6 million Hoosiers. Officials predict that the state's population will reach 6½ million by the year 2020. As Indiana moves into the future, its success will depend on its people.

Where Hoosiers Live

Indiana's population is spread unevenly throughout the state. In Indiana most people live in **urban** areas, or cities or towns. Urban areas of Indiana have higher populations than **rural** areas, or farmlands, forests, and other parts of the countryside.

Urban areas can be found throughout the state. In the north are Gary, South Bend, Hammond and Fort Wayne. In the center are Indianapolis and Bloomington. South are Evansville and Jeffersonville.

Some of the fastest-growing areas in Indiana are the suburbs. During the ten years between 1990 and 2000, three Indiana communities—Fishers, Carmel, and Noblesville—had the state's highest rates of increase in population. All three of these Hamilton County cities are suburbs of Indianapolis. In contrast, Indiana communities that had a decrease in population in the 1990s were all large industrial cities. These cities include East Chicago, Evansville, Gary, and Muncie. This pattern of people leaving cities and moving to suburbs is common throughout the United States.

REVIEW In what county are Indiana's fastest-growing communities located?

A diverse population lives in the capital city of Indianapolis. Shown here is a sign in Spanish for a butcher shop and supermarket.

Indiana's People

The census shows that Indiana's population is becoming more diverse. Even so, almost nine out of ten Hoosiers are of a European background. However, the Hispanic population is the fastest-growing cultural group in Indiana. **Hispanics** are people whose families come from Spanish-speaking countries in North America and South America. The state's Hispanic population more than doubled between 1990 and 2000, with 215,000 people now identifying themselves as Hispanic.

Hispanics are not the largest minority group in Indiana. More than 500,000 Hoosiers are African Americans. Most African Americans live in the state's largest cities, such as Indianapolis, Gary, and East Chicago.

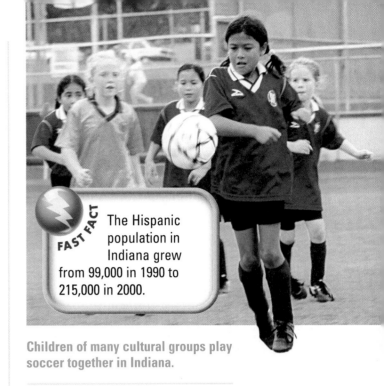

FAST FACT The Hispanic population in Indiana grew from 99,000 in 1990 to 215,000 in 2000.

Children of many cultural groups play soccer together in Indiana.

People from many different countries live in Indiana. More than 59,000 Hoosiers have Asian backgrounds. Native Americans make up only a small part of Indiana's population. In the 2000 census more than 75,000 Hoosiers declared that they were of mixed heritage.

Today more of Indiana's newcomers come from outside the United States. Indianapolis has a large Mexican American community. Bloomington has the third-largest community of Tibetans (tuh•BEH•tuhnz) outside Asia. Tibetans came to Indiana as exiles. **Exiles** are people who decide to or are forced to leave their countries.

People celebrate and share their cultures with others. In Indianapolis alone, people of all cultures celebrate the German Oktoberfest, Hispanic fiestas, and other festivals. The city's annual Indiana Black Expo is the largest and longest-running exhibition of African American culture in the nation.

Analyze Graphs This graph shows the six Indiana counties with the largest Hispanic populations.

❖ Which county had the largest increase in the number of Hispanics from 1990 to 2000?

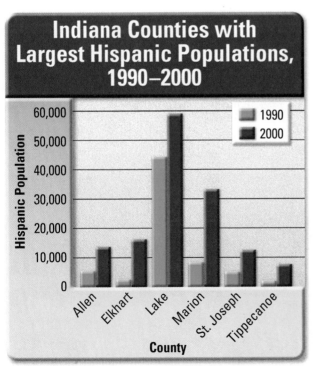

Indiana Counties with Largest Hispanic Populations, 1990–2000

- 1990
- 2000

Hispanic Population: 0, 10,000, 20,000, 30,000, 40,000, 50,000, 60,000

County: Allen, Elkhart, Lake, Marion, St. Joseph, Tippecanoe

Bean Blossom Bluegrass Festival

Many people in Indiana have cultural ties to the southern states of Kentucky and Tennessee. Many of them enjoy bluegrass music, a kind of music first played in the Appalachian Mountains. Bluegrass musicians sing and play instruments such as fiddles, guitars, and banjos. Every year Hoosiers gather in the small community of Bean Blossom, just north of Nashville, Indiana. There they enjoy bluegrass music and other parts of southern culture.

Elsewhere, Indiana's Native Americans and early European settlers are honored with celebrations. The Feast of the Hunters' Moon, held at Fort Ouiatenon on the Wabash River, is one of Indiana's largest festivals.

For the most part Indiana's cultural diversity can best be seen in urban areas. Jobs have drawn many immigrants to the cities. Few African Americans, Hispanics, or Asians make their homes in Indiana's rural communities.

REVIEW What is Indiana's fastest-growing cultural group?

Religions in Indiana

Part of the heritage of many Hoosiers is their religion. Most Hoosiers practice Christianity. However, they belong to a wide variety of churches, including Methodist, Roman Catholic, Baptist, Presbyterian, Lutheran, Episcopal, and Mormon.

Indiana's religious diversity can be seen by looking at its houses of worship. Mosques (below), synagogues (right), and churches (far right) can be found.

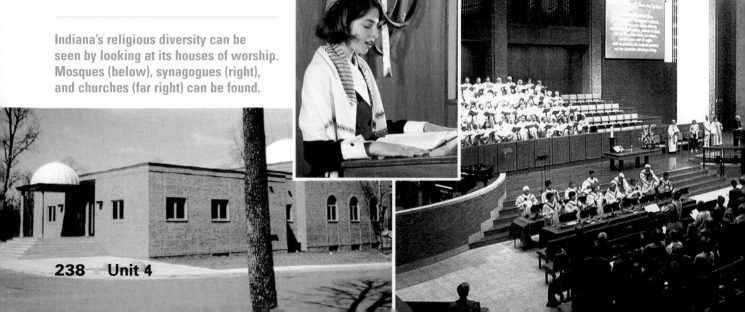

Other Hoosiers are Muslims, Jews, Buddhists, or Hindus. The Amish (AH•mish) are another of Indiana's religious groups. The Amish faith, a form of Christianity, began in the European country of Switzerland. Amish people do not wear clothes that have bright colors or decorations, and they live simply. Because of this, the Amish are sometimes known as Plain People.

Most of Indiana's Amish families live on farms. They usually do not have electricity in their homes or on their farms. Amish people use hand tools and machines pulled by animals to do their farmwork. Instead of automobiles, the Amish drive closed wagons called buggies, which are pulled by horses.

REVIEW **What religious groups can be found in Indiana?**

Amish farmers use mule- or horse-drawn plows to prepare their fields for planting.

Some Famous Hoosiers

In the twenty-first century Hoosiers look with pride at the many well-known people from Indiana. Some of our country's best-loved writers and poets have been Hoosiers. Sarah Bolton is one of Indiana's most popular poets. James Whitcomb Riley, of Greenfield, wrote poems about everyday life in Indiana. Booth Tarkington, Riley's neighbor, wrote novels about life in Indianapolis. Another early twentieth-century Hoosier, George Ade, became famous for writing humorous fables. A **fable** is a story that teaches a lesson. Other Indiana writers include novelists Gene Stratton-Porter, Kurt Vonnegut (VON•ih•guht), Jr., and Theodore Dreiser (DRY•ser). Lewis Wallace was a Hoosier author as well as a Civil War general.

Hoosiers have also made important contributions to music. Paul Dresser, brother of Theodore Dreiser, became famous for writing songs, including Indiana's state song, "On the Banks of the Wabash, Far Away."

Oscar Robertson ("The Big O") 1938–
Character Trait: Perseverance

Oscar Robertson is considered to be one of the greatest all-around players in the history of basketball. Robertson moved with his family to Indianapolis when he was four. In 1955 and 1956 Robertson led the Crispus Attucks High School team of Indianapolis to two state championships.

In the late 1950s Robertson thought about quitting college and joining the world-famous Harlem Globetrotters. He was frustrated by racial segregation at the university. He said, "There's a café and a movie house just a few steps off campus where I'm not welcome." Fortunately, Robertson did not let this keep him from graduating.

In 1960 Robertson served as co-captain of the United States Olympic basketball team, which won a gold medal. He was a star player for the Cincinnati Royals and for the Milwaukee Bucks in the National Basketball Association from 1960 to 1974. In 1997 Robertson donated one of his kidneys to his daughter, who suffered from a life-threatening disease.

MULTIMEDIA BIOGRAPHIES
Visit The Learning Site at www.harcourtschool.com/biographies to learn about other famous people.

GO ONLINE

During the mid-1900s people were entertained by the popular songs and Broadway musicals of Hoosier musicians Hoagy Carmichael and Cole Porter. More recently pop music stars John Mellencamp, of Seymour, and Michael Jackson and Janet Jackson, of Gary, have entertained millions of people around the world.

Indiana artists T. C. Steele and William Forsyth are known for their paintings of nature. They were members of the Hoosier Group. A modern sculptor named Robert Clark showed his Hoosier pride by changing his name to Robert Indiana. Janet Scudder of Terre Haute created garden sculptures and fountains, and Marion County's Marie Webster was a famous quilter. Jim Davis, creator of the

Robert Indiana's "LOVE" design was used on a postage stamp in the mid-1970s.

Garfield cartoon strip, is another native Indiana artist.

Indiana also has given the sports world some of its greatest stars, including Jeff Gordon of NASCAR, NBA players Oscar Robertson

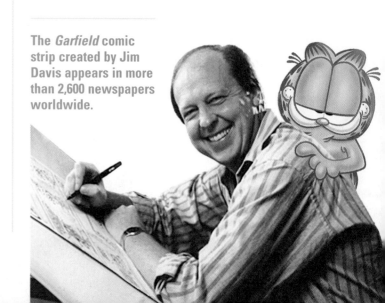

The *Garfield* comic strip created by Jim Davis appears in more than 2,600 newspapers worldwide.

and Larry Bird, and NCAA coach John Wooden. Other well-known Hoosier sports figures include former Notre Dame football coach Knute Rockne (NOOT RAHK•nee) and baseball greats Carl Erskine, Don Larsen, and Don Mattingly. Olympic swimmer Mark Spitz and track-and-field star Wilma Rudolph are both from Indiana.

Television and movies have also benefited from the talents of Hoosiers. These Hoosiers include film directors Robert Wise and Howard Hawks and actors James Dean, Shelley Long, and Brendan Fraser. Hoosiers who have become known for their work in television include comedians Red Skelton and David Letterman, singer and actor Florence Henderson, journalist Jane Pauley, and dancer Twyla Tharp.

REVIEW What was the Hoosier Group known for?

FAST FACT The Major Taylor Velodrome in Indianapolis is a center for international bicycle races. The track was named for Hoosier Marshall ("Major") Taylor, a world champion bicycle racer at the turn of the twentieth century.

Marshall "Major" Taylor

LESSON 1 REVIEW

1 MAIN IDEA To which cultural group do most Hoosiers trace their backgrounds?

2 WHY IT MATTERS How do Hoosiers celebrate their cultural diversity?

3 VOCABULARY Use the terms **urban** and **rural** to write one or two sentences describing where most Hoosiers live today.

4 READING SKILL—Generalize From what you have learned about the religious beliefs of Hoosiers, how would you describe religion in Indiana?

5 CULTURE What is the nation's longest-running exhibition of African American culture? Where is this celebration held?

6 HISTORY Who wrote Indiana's state song?

7 CRITICAL THINKING—Synthesize Why do you think more Hoosiers live in urban areas than in rural areas?

PERFORMANCE—Write a Biography Choose one of the famous Hoosiers mentioned in this lesson or another well-known person from Indiana. Use reference resources to find out more about the person. Write a brief biography to share with your classmates. Tell when and where this person was born and what he or she did to become famous.

· SKILLS ·

MAP AND GLOBE

Read a Population Map

VOCABULARY

population density

▶ WHY IT MATTERS

Maps display many different kinds of information. Population maps show information about where people live. A **population density** map, for example, shows how many people live in an area of a certain size. The size is usually one square mile or one square kilometer. A square mile is a square piece of land with each of its four sides one mile long. A square kilometer is a square piece of land with sides that are each one kilometer long. Knowing how to read a population density map can help you find out which places have few people and which places have many.

▶ WHAT YOU NEED TO KNOW

Population density maps use colors to stand for different population densities. To read a population density map, follow these steps.

Step 1 Look at the map key to find out which colors are used for the different population densities. The key also tells you which unit of measure (square miles or square kilometers) is being used.

Step 2 On the map, find the place you are interested in knowing about.

Rural areas and small towns (right) have fewer people and lower population densities than cities (below).

Step 3 Look at the color of the area in which that place is located.

Step 4 Check the map key for that color to learn the population density of a square mile or square kilometer of the place you are interested in.

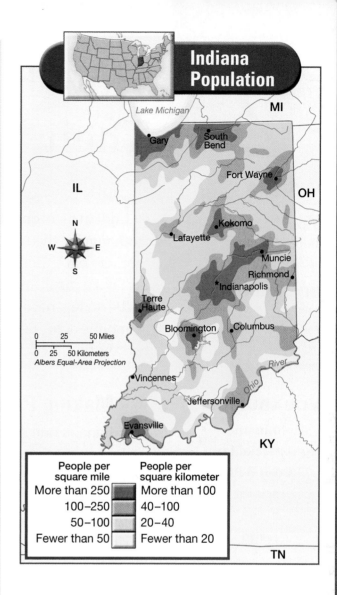

Indiana Population

People per square mile		People per square kilometer
More than 250		More than 100
100–250		40–100
50–100		20–40
Fewer than 50		Fewer than 20

0   25   50 Miles
0   25   50 Kilometers
Albers Equal-Area Projection

▶ **PRACTICE THE SKILL**

Study the population density map of Indiana on this page. Then use what you have learned about reading a population density map to answer the following questions.

❶ On the map, which color shows the areas of highest population density (the most people per square mile or square kilometer)? Which color shows the areas of lowest population density?

❷ For each of the following pairs of Indiana cities, tell which city has more people: Fort Wayne or Columbus? Vincennes or Terre Haute? Lafayette or Kokomo?

❸ Is Indiana's population density higher near Lake Michigan or along the Ohio River? How can you tell?

❹ What is the population density of the northeast corner of the state? What is the population density of Bloomington? What is the population density of Richmond?

▶ **APPLY WHAT YOU LEARNED**

Use an atlas to locate five Indiana cities not shown on the above population density map. Then look at the map above to find the population density of the cities selected. On a sheet of paper, list the name of each city and give its population density in square miles and in square kilometers.

Practice your map and globe skills with the **GeoSkills CD-ROM.**

2

How Hoosiers Earn Their Living

MAIN IDEA

Read to find out about the variety of economic activities that take place in Indiana.

WHY IT MATTERS

Indiana's industries and natural resources affect the day-to-day lives of people in the state.

VOCABULARY

tourism
commercial farm
Corn Belt
reclaim
barge
cargo

Indiana's economy has changed over time and will continue to change in the future. In the twenty-first century, Hoosier workers earn their livings in many different ways. Some of Indiana's most important economic activities have grown out of the state's natural resources and its past industries. Other economic activities have developed to meet the needs of the twenty-first century.

Making Products and Providing Services

Indiana is one of the most important manufacturing centers in the United States. Since the early 1900s, making steel and other metal products has been the state's top industry. Indiana ranks sixth in the world in steel production. Hoosiers use steel from Indiana's Calumet region to make trucks in Indianapolis, refrigerators in Evansville, and diesel engines in Columbus. Hoosier factories make vehicles and parts for automakers from nearby Detroit, Michigan, to Tokyo, Japan, in Asia. Factories in Indiana's Wayne County lead the world in the production of recreational vehicles, or RVs, and mobile homes.

Other Indiana factories, such as the Eli Lilly Company of Indianapolis and the Miles Laboratories of Elkhart, make pharmaceuticals, or medicines. Still other factories make furniture, motors, televisions, and computers. Indiana also makes high-tech products such as CDs and DVD players.

FAST FACT

More than half of all band instruments used in the United States today are manufactured in Elkhart, Indiana.

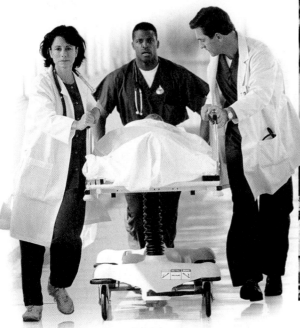

Health-care workers (above left), restaurant employees (above right), and automotive technicians (right) are examples of people employed in service industries.

Although manufacturing remains strong in Indiana, a growing number of Hoosiers earn their livings in service industries. Indiana's service industries employ more people than the manufacturing and farming industries put together. Some of Indiana's more than 975,000 service workers are plumbers, mechanics, lawyers, teachers, or health-care workers. Others have jobs in government. Some hotel workers, restaurant chefs, and museum guides also work in the tourism industry. **Tourism** is the industry that offers services to people who travel.

REVIEW What is the top manufacturing industry in Indiana?

Indiana's most important crops are corn and soybeans.

Farming

Indiana has about 59,000 farms. On some of these farms, families raise crops for their own use and sell any extra crops. Most of the state's largest farms are **commercial farms**, or farms where all the crops raised are sold to make money.

Farm incomes vary across Indiana. About two-thirds of the state's farm income is from crops. About one-third comes from the sale of livestock and dairy products.

As you have learned, corn and soybeans are the state's most important crops. Indiana ranks fifth among all states in growing corn, second in popcorn, and third in soybeans. Much of the success of Indiana's farms comes from the rich soil. Indiana lies in the **Corn Belt**, a region in the Middle West where more corn is grown than anywhere else in the world.

In addition to Indiana, the states of Ohio, Illinois, and Iowa and parts of Missouri and Nebraska make up the Corn Belt.

Indiana is fifth in the nation in raising hogs and fourth in raising poultry. Poultry includes turkeys, chickens, and ducks that are raised for food.

In the early twentieth century, most Hoosiers lived and worked on farms. Today, only about 1 in 40 Hoosiers lives and works on a farm. As in the rest of the United States, Indiana now has larger but fewer farms. Few of Indiana's small farms are full-time businesses.

REVIEW Indiana is part of what important agricultural region?

A CLOSER LOOK
Quarrying Limestone

More than half of the limestone used in the United States comes from Indiana quarries. The process of mining limestone is described below.

1 Quarry workers first remove a large section of stone called the key block. This clears a space to work.

2 Workers cut the limestone into square blocks. Then they pry each block out of the surrounding stone.

3 Workers use cranes to lift the blocks onto trucks or trains that carry them away.

4 Workers cut a new key block and begin the same process on the next level.

❓ Why do you think limestone is quarried in large blocks?

Mining

About 9,000 people work in Indiana's mining industry. Most of these workers mine limestone in the quarries near Bedford and Bloomington. They cut blocks of stone from the quarries or crush the stone to be used in making steel and cement. Sand, gravel, gypsum, and clay are also mined in Indiana.

Coal mines can be found in southwestern Indiana. The coal lies close to Earth's surface and can be removed by strip mining. Large machines clear, or strip, the soil from above the coal. Then other machines scoop up the coal and load it into trucks to be hauled away.

Strip mining leaves the land bare of soil and plants. Laws require companies to reclaim the land after the coal has been removed. To **reclaim** the land is to make it usable again by people and wildlife. Companies do this by replacing soil and planting new grasses and trees.

REVIEW What effect does strip mining have on Indiana's land?

Indiana's official motto is The Crossroads of America, stressing the importance of transportation.

Moving Goods and People

Transportation is important in Indiana's economy. Hoosiers today continue to rely on various kinds of transportation to move goods and people in and out of the state. Many barges travel on the Ohio River and the Great Lakes. **Barges** are ships with flat beds that carry items such as coal, iron, and grain in large containers. The containers protect the **cargo**, or goods being shipped.

Railroads move goods over long distances across land. Trains also carry cargo containers to and from Indiana's ports. Trucks use Indiana's seven interstate highways—the most in any state—to transport goods to other cities around the United States. Indiana's airports also are used to transport people and cargo.

REVIEW **Which kinds of transportation are important to Indiana's economy?**

LESSON 2
REVIEW

1 **MAIN IDEA** What are Indiana's main industries?

2 **WHY IT MATTERS** Which industries employ the most people in Indiana?

3 **VOCABULARY** Describe in a few sentences how the terms **commercial farm** and **Corn Belt** are related.

4 **READING SKILL—Generalize** How is Indiana's economy today different from the state's economy in the early 1900s?

5 **SCIENCE AND TECHNOLOGY** How do mining companies reclaim land after strip mining?

6 **ECONOMICS** Why is transportation important to Indiana's economy?

7 **CRITICAL THINKING—Analyze** Why do you think so many Indiana farms are commercial farms?

PERFORMANCE—Have a Hoosier Job Fair Think of a job you might like to have when you are older. Write a paragraph that tells how this job contributes to Indiana's economy. Use drawings to illustrate your paragraph. Then display your illustrated paragraph at a class job fair.

·SKILLS· MAP AND GLOBE

Read a Land Use and Resources Map

➡ WHY IT MATTERS

Have you ever wondered where some of the products you use every day come from? Where are the natural resources found that were used to make those goods? To find the answers to these questions, you can read a land use and resources map. This kind of map shows how land is used and where certain resources are located within that land. These maps do not show every resource found in a certain place or tell every way the land is used. Instead, they show the most important resources and the most common uses of land in a given area.

Indiana's natural resources include (below from left to right) gypsum, coal, and limestone.

➡ WHAT YOU NEED TO KNOW

Land use and resources maps show two kinds of information. Mapmakers use a different way to display each kind of information.

Land use is shown by color. In the map key, each color stands for one kind of land use. To find out the most common way land is used in a given area, look on the map at the color for that area. Then check the map key to see which land use this color stands for.

Natural resources are shown by symbols. In the map key, each symbol stands for one kind of resource. To identify the main natural resources of an area, look on the map at the symbols for that area. Then check the map key to see which resource each symbol stands for.

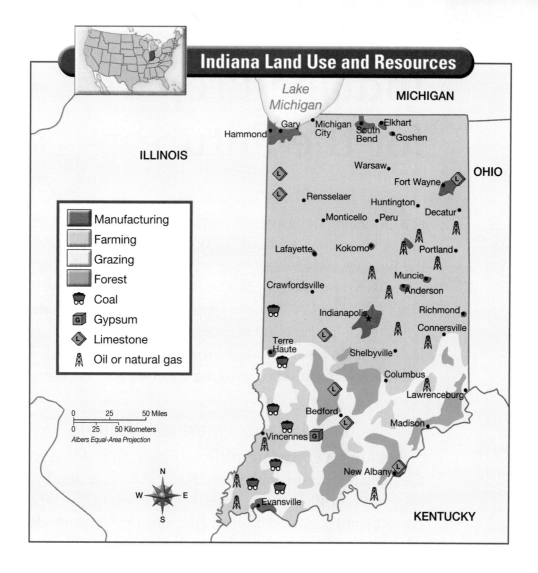

Indiana Land Use and Resources

Key:
- Manufacturing
- Farming
- Grazing
- Forest
- Coal
- Gypsum
- Limestone
- Oil or natural gas

0 25 50 Miles
0 25 50 Kilometers
Albers Equal-Area Projection

N W E S

➡ PRACTICE THE SKILL

Study the land use and resources map of Indiana above. Then answer the following questions.

1 Overall, what is the main land use in Indiana?

2 What is the main land use of the area in which Gary is located?

3 Where are most of Indiana's forests found?

4 In what part of the state is most of Indiana's coal located?

5 Which resource is found near Bloomington?

➡ APPLY WHAT YOU LEARNED

Use reference sources to find out more about the land use and resources of your county. Work with your classmates to make a county land use and resources map. Choose colors to show different ways of using land. Draw symbols for the county's main resources. Be sure to draw a key that shows what each color and symbol stands for.

Practice your map and globe skills with the **GeoSkills CD-ROM.**

MAP AND GLOBE SKILLS

3

Indiana Prepares for the Future

Hoosiers have always worked together to meet challenges and solve problems. George Rogers Clark led Hoosiers in the fight for independence from British rule. Little Turtle, Tecumseh, and the Prophet worked to protect the rights of Native Americans. William Henry Harrison and Jonathan Jennings helped the Indiana Territory prepare for statehood. Indiana faces new challenges today, but Hoosiers still follow the Indiana tradition of working together to meet them.

Educating Indiana's People

Providing a good education for Indiana's children is one of the most important challenges the state faces today. Indiana's constitution called for free public education before other states passed similar laws. The state continues to support education. Almost a million students attend Indiana's public schools, from kindergarten through high school. Indiana requires students to pass special tests at several grade levels to assess, or judge, their learning. The state government also encourages teachers to get advanced training.

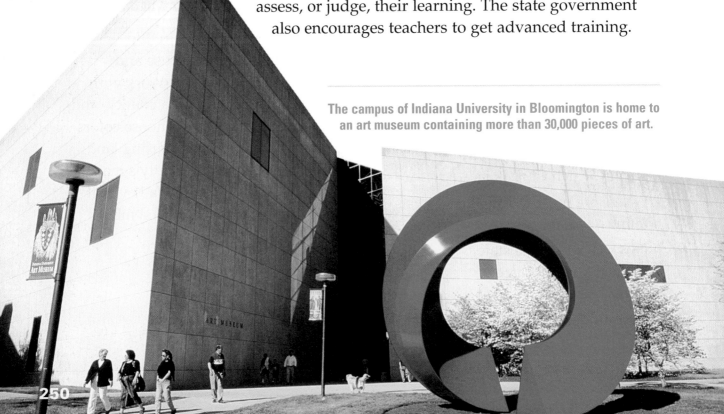

The campus of Indiana University in Bloomington is home to an art museum containing more than 30,000 pieces of art.

Continuing Education in Indiana

WHERE GRADS GO	NUMBER
Four-year college or university	👤👤👤👤👤👤👤👤👤👤👤👤 👤👤👤👤👤👤👤👤👤👤👤👤 👤👤👤👤👤👤
Two-year community college	👤👤👤👤👤👤
Job-training or high-tech program	👤👤👤👤👤

👤 = 1,000 graduates

Analyze Graphs This graph shows how Hoosier high school graduates continue their education.

About how many more high school graduates continue their education at a four-year college or university than at a two-year community college?

Indiana's attention to education benefits the state's public high school graduates. Nearly seven out of every ten graduates in Indiana go on to higher education in colleges, universities, and technical institutions.

Indiana's colleges and universities provide ways for students to advance their education. Public universities such as Indiana University, Purdue University, and the Ivy Tech State Colleges prepare Hoosiers for careers in many fields. The five Ball brothers of the Ball glass jar company donated land for the site of what is today Ball State University. This shows the close link between Indiana's industry and education.

Voters in Indiana elect local, state, and national government officials.

Religious groups founded some of Indiana's private schools, colleges, and universities. These schools include the University of Notre Dame, Earlham College, and the University of Evansville. Today people of all backgrounds study at these centers of higher learning.

Educated people are important to the economy as human resources. A **human resource** is a worker and all the knowledge and skill he or she brings to the job. Educated, well-informed citizens are also important to the democratic governments of Indiana and of the United States as a whole. Informed citizens understand why things happen in the community, the state, the country, and the world. They are more likely to understand other people's points of view, to vote, and to take part in their government.

REVIEW Why is education important?

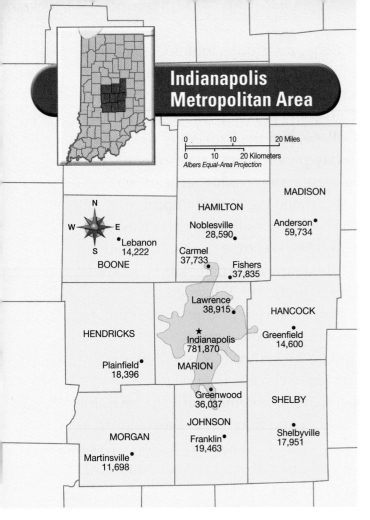

Indianapolis Metropolitan Area

0   10   20 Miles
0   10   20 Kilometers
Albers Equal-Area Projection

MADISON

HAMILTON

Noblesville
28,590

Anderson
59,734

Lebanon
14,222

Carmel
37,733

Fishers
37,835

BOONE

Lawrence
38,915

HANCOCK

HENDRICKS

Indianapolis
781,870

Greenfield
14,600

Plainfield
18,396

MARION

Greenwood
36,037

SHELBY

JOHNSON

MORGAN

Franklin
19,463

Shelbyville
17,951

Martinsville
11,698

Keeping Cities Safe and Clean

One of every four Hoosiers lives in or near Indianapolis, the state's largest metropolitan area. A **metropolitan area** is a large city plus all the suburbs, towns, and small cities around it. In 2000 the census listed the population of Indianapolis at 781,870. However, the metropolitan area of Indianapolis has more than 1½ million people.

Indiana's population grew from more than 5½ million in 1990 to more than 6 million in 2000. The Indiana counties of Hamilton, Hendricks, Johnson, Owen, Noble, Hancock, Steuben, Boone, and Jasper had the largest increases in population from 1990 to 2000. Hamilton County's population increased by 80,000 during that time.

Location This map shows the nine Indiana counties that make up the Indianapolis metropolitan area.

❷ Which five cities in the Indianapolis metropolitan area have the largest populations?

Police patrols (below left) and fire protection (below) are ways to keep cities safe.

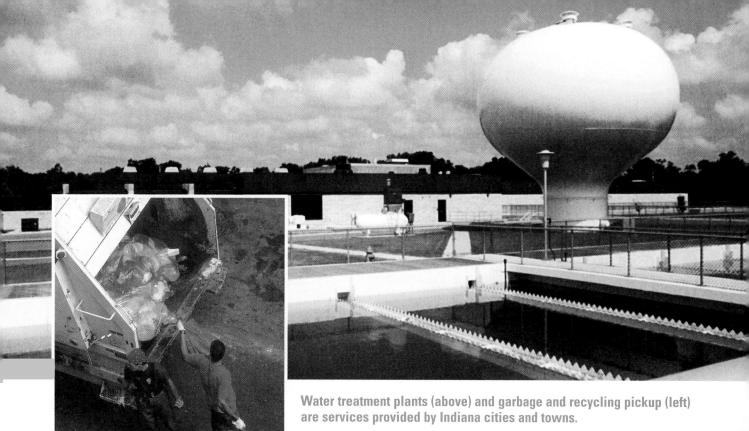

Water treatment plants (above) and garbage and recycling pickup (left) are services provided by Indiana cities and towns.

As Indianapolis and Indiana's other large cities grow, they are faced with the challenge of providing city services for more people. These services, including water supply, garbage pickup, and police and fire protection, help keep the cities clean and safe. Some city governments have begun to share services among the many communities that make up a metropolitan area. In this way the cost of providing city services is lessened by dividing it equally among communities.

Meeting transportation needs is another important challenge facing Indiana's cities today. More people mean an increase in traffic. Growth also means increased air pollution from the additional cars and trucks. New roads, highways, and bridges must be built, or old ones must be repaired.

Public transportation, such as buses and trains, helps reduce traffic problems.

Like most urban areas in the United States, Indiana's cities must find ways to deal with high crime rates. Hoosiers are working together to address some of the problems that lead to crime. Providing jobs and encouraging students to stay in school are just two ways Hoosiers help lower crime rates.

REVIEW **What kinds of services do cities provide?**

Many Indiana cities provide public transportation, such as this electric trolley, for their citizens.

Pioneer Mothers Memorial Forest

Understanding Environment and Society

Just south of Paoli (PAY•oh•lee), Indiana, you can see what Indiana's forests looked like when the area's first European settlers arrived. The 88-acre Pioneer Mothers Memorial Forest contains ancient oaks and towering walnut trees. They have been there since Hoosier pioneer Joseph Cox claimed the land in 1816. In 1940 the land, then called Cox's Forest, was going to be sold to a lumber company. The United States Forest Service agreed to save the forest if volunteers would buy it, which they did. One of the largest donations came from Indiana's Pioneer Mothers Club, for which the forest was named in 1951. The forest has been protected ever since.

Protecting the Environment

Today most people understand that natural resources must be protected for the future. Careless treatment of natural resources causes land, air, and water to be polluted, or harmed. Indiana's waterways can become polluted from chemicals or other wastes dumped by industries. They can also be harmed by soils and fertilizers (FER•tuhl•eye•zerz) that run off farm lands.

Hoosiers are working together to protect the environment in various ways. National and state laws set limits on where harmful wastes may be dumped. Laws have been passed to clean up polluted land and water sites. Clean-air standards limit the amount of chemicals that can be released into the air from car engines and factories.

One of the biggest challenges Indiana faces is how to handle the trash produced by the state's growing population. Wastes such as paper and garbage quickly fill dump sites. Hoosiers can help control the buildup of trash by not littering and by recycling. Aluminum (uh•LOO•muh•nuhm) cans, glass bottles,

People in Indiana recycle, which reduces the amount of waste in landfills and helps the environment.

plastic containers, and newspapers all can be recycled, or broken down for use in new products. Recycling helps protect the environment by reducing the amount of waste sent to landfills. In addition, resources are saved when new products are made from old materials. The businesses that recycle help Indiana's economy and environment.

Another way Hoosiers protect the environment is by conserving natural resources. To **conserve** a resource is to save it. Many farmers work to conserve their soil. They may plant trees to keep the heavy rains from washing the soil away. Others plant crops without plowing, or plant only part of their farmland. These actions help keep the fertile soil from being used up or washed away.

Forests, dunes, and wetlands all need to be conserved and protected. Over time, to make room for their farms and towns, Hoosiers have cut down many forests that once covered the state. Today there are few large forests left in Indiana.

Farmers plant rows of grass and trees to keep soil from running off into streams when heavy rains come.

Since 1952 an organization called Save the Dunes has been working to protect Indiana's dunes. This group was helpful in getting laws passed that created the Indiana Dunes National Lakeshore. More than two million people a year visit this one-of-a-kind park in northwestern Indiana.

REVIEW How does recycling help Indiana's environment and economy?

LESSON 3 REVIEW

1 MAIN IDEA What are three important challenges that Hoosiers face in the twenty-first century?

2 WHY IT MATTERS Why should people living in Indiana today work together to find solutions to problems that the state faces?

3 VOCABULARY What are some of the **metropolitan areas** near where you live?

4 READING SKILL—Generalize What might happen if there were no laws to protect Indiana's environment?

5 HISTORY What is an example of a Hoosier industry's ties to education?

6 CIVICS AND GOVERNMENT Why are informed citizens important in a democratic government?

7 CRITICAL THINKING—Evaluate Which of the challenges facing Indiana in the twenty-first century do you think deserves the most attention? Explain your choice.

PERFORMANCE—Be an Informed Citizen In small groups, brainstorm ways that people your age can become involved in improving education, keeping cities clean, or protecting the environment. Share your ideas with the class in the form of a speech.

·SKILLS· # Predict a Likely Outcome

READING

VOCABULARY

conclusion

prediction

➡ WHY IT MATTERS

Sometimes you might like to know what will happen next in a story you are reading or in a situation you face. You can use the details you have read and your own experiences to form a conclusion and predict a likely outcome. A **conclusion** is a decision or an idea reached by thoughtful study. To form a conclusion, you combine new facts with facts you already know.

After you have formed a conclusion about something, you may also make a prediction. A **prediction** is an educated guess about the outcome. The likely outcome is what is most likely to happen next or to be the result of an action.

➡ WHAT YOU NEED TO KNOW

When you are reading, pay attention to details that can serve as clues to what may happen next. If you imagine several possible outcomes, choose the one that is most likely to happen, based on what you know.

Follow steps such as these to predict a likely outcome.

Step 1 Think about the information you already have about the topic.

Step 2 Gather new information.

Step 3 Form a conclusion by deciding what the information means.

Step 4 Make a prediction based on your conclusion.

Most Hoosiers believe that Indiana's wetlands must be preserved.

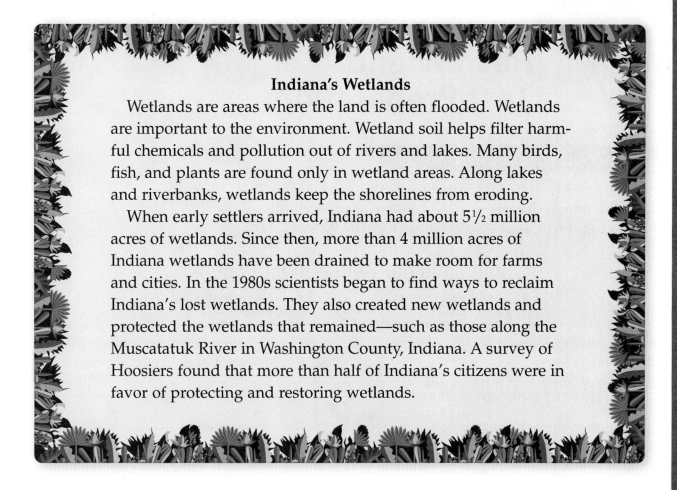

Indiana's Wetlands

Wetlands are areas where the land is often flooded. Wetlands are important to the environment. Wetland soil helps filter harmful chemicals and pollution out of rivers and lakes. Many birds, fish, and plants are found only in wetland areas. Along lakes and riverbanks, wetlands keep the shorelines from eroding.

When early settlers arrived, Indiana had about 5½ million acres of wetlands. Since then, more than 4 million acres of Indiana wetlands have been drained to make room for farms and cities. In the 1980s scientists began to find ways to reclaim Indiana's lost wetlands. They also created new wetlands and protected the wetlands that remained—such as those along the Muscatatuk River in Washington County, Indiana. A survey of Hoosiers found that more than half of Indiana's citizens were in favor of protecting and restoring wetlands.

When you are reading, continue to find out whether your prediction was accurate. In a real-life situation, pay attention to what really does happen.

▶ PRACTICE THE SKILL

Read the passage about Indiana's wetlands at the top of this page. Then use what you have learned about predicting a likely outcome to answer these questions.

❶ What happens when Indiana's wetlands are drained?

❷ What clues in the passage led you to this likely outcome?

Great blue herons can be found in Indiana's wetland areas.

❸ What do you think will happen to Indiana's wetlands in the future?

❹ On what facts did you base this prediction?

▶ APPLY WHAT YOU LEARNED

Write a description of an experience you have had, such as a soccer game that you played or watched or an interesting conversation you had. Do not include the outcome of the experience. Exchange papers with a partner. Try to predict the most likely outcome of your partner's experience. Have him or her try to predict the outcome of yours. If the predictions are not accurate, review the clues with each other.

CD9 Track 10

Review and Test Preparation

Complete this graphic organizer to make generalizations about Indiana in the twenty-first century. A copy of this graphic organizer appears on page 75 of the Activity Book.

Indiana in the Twenty-First Century

| FACTS | → | GENERALIZATIONS |

LESSON 1
- Indiana's cities and suburbs are growing.
- Many people from other countries are moving to Indiana.
- Jobs have drawn many immigrants to the cities.

1. In the twenty-first century more Hoosiers will live in cities than in the countryside.
2. _____
3. _____

LESSON 2
-
-
-

1. _____
2. _____
3. _____

LESSON 3
-
-
-

1. _____
2. _____
3. _____

THINK & WRITE

Write an E-Mail Message   Imagine that your class is exchanging e-mail with a class in another state. Write a message that describes the people of Indiana today. Tell how Hoosiers make their living.

Write a Letter to Your Newspaper
Write a letter to your local newspaper about an environmental problem or concern in your community. Call attention to the problem, and suggest ways for solving it.

USE VOCABULARY

Use a term from the list to complete each of the sentences that follow.

A. Hispanic (p. 237)

B. fables (p. 239)

C. Corn Belt (p. 245)

D. cargo (p. 247)

E. conserve (p. 255)

1 Indiana lies in the _____, a rich agricultural region.

2 A barge traveling on a river carries _____ in containers.

3 People who are _____ make up the fastest-growing part of Indiana's population.

4 Hoosier George Ade wrote humorous _____, or stories that teach a lesson.

5 Hoosiers _____ natural resources so the resources will be available in the future.

RECALL FACTS

Answer these questions.

6 Which industry employs more Hoosiers than manufacturing and agriculture put together?

7 In what part of the state does one out of every four Hoosiers live?

Write the letter of the best choice.

8 **TEST PREP**   The Amish are also known as—
A exiles.
B Plain People.
C Methodists.
D Tibetans.

9 **TEST PREP**   T. C. Steele and William Forsyth were members of the—
F Indiana writers' group.
G United States Olympic team.
H Indiana Pacers.
J Hoosier Group.

THINK CRITICALLY

10 How do cultural festivals improve cooperation among Indiana's diverse peoples?

11 Why is improving education good for Indiana?

12 How can conservation of natural resources help Indiana's environment?

APPLY SKILLS

Read a Population Map

13 Locate your community on the map on page 243. What is the population density of your community? What is the nearest city or town with a population density greater than that of your community?

14 What is the nearest city or town with a population density less than that of your community?

Read a Land Use and Resources Map

15 Locate your community on the map on page 249. What is the main land use in your part of Indiana?

16 What are the main resources in your part of Indiana?

Predict a Likely Outcome

17 What might happen if people in Indiana stopped recycling?

18 What might happen if people in Indiana stopped driving automobiles three days a week?

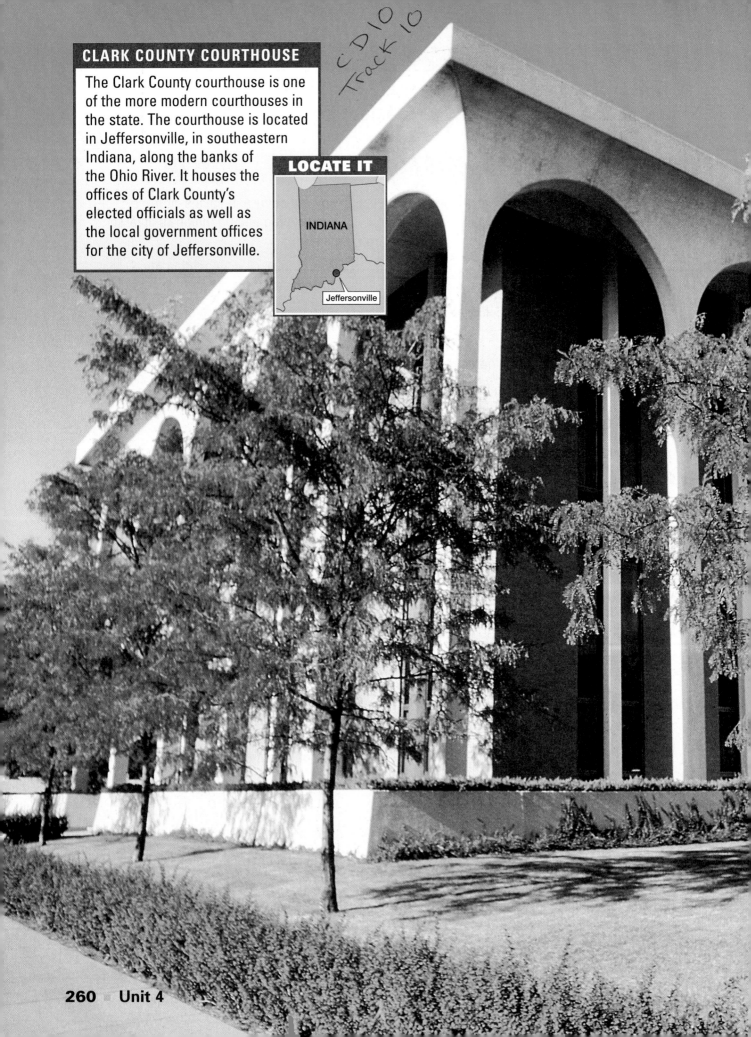

CLARK COUNTY COURTHOUSE

The Clark County courthouse is one of the more modern courthouses in the state. The courthouse is located in Jeffersonville, in southeastern Indiana, along the banks of the Ohio River. It houses the offices of Clark County's elected officials as well as the local government offices for the city of Jeffersonville.

LOCATE IT

INDIANA

Jeffersonville

8

Government in Indiana

❝ Hoosiers take great pride in bettering their communities for future generations. **❞**
—Patrick J. Kiely, former state senator, in a speech, 2000

Identify Fact and Opinion

A **fact** is a statement that can be checked and proved. An **opinion** tells what a person thinks or believes to be true but cannot prove.

As you read this chapter, separate facts from opinions about the government in Indiana.

MAIN TOPIC

FACT ➔ OPINION

CD10
Track 2

1

Indiana State Government

MAIN IDEA

Read to find out how the work of government in Indiana is shared among three different branches.

WHY IT MATTERS

Understanding the organization of state government helps Hoosiers be informed and responsible citizens.

VOCABULARY

Bill of Rights
assemble
legislative branch
budget
executive branch
bill
veto
majority
agency
judicial branch
jury trial

Government has always been important to the people of Indiana. Early laws helped organize the sale of land and establish schools. The government built roads, canals, and railroads in Indiana. Today the government protects the rights of the citizens of Indiana just as it has in the past.

The Indiana Constitution

The United States Constitution, which set up the government of our country, became law in 1788. It was a model for the Indiana Constitution of 1816. About 35 years later, the 1816 constitution was replaced by the Indiana Constitution of 1851. The 1851 constitution set up the state government that Hoosiers have today.

The first ten amendments to the United States Constitution make up the **Bill of Rights**, which lists the many freedoms of citizens. The Indiana Constitution begins with a state Bill of Rights. It lists many of the same freedoms found in the national Bill of Rights. Among these are freedom of speech, freedom of the press, freedom of religion, and freedom to **assemble**, or gather in groups.

FAST FACT

Governor Frank O'Bannon invited all fourth-grade students in Indiana to the ceremony to swear him in as governor of Indiana on January 8, 2001. More than 25,000 students and other visitors attended.

Preamble of the Indiana State Constitution

The United States Constitution and the Indiana Constitution each begin with a preamble. Each preamble helps explain the ideas that are found in the rest of the constitution. In 1851 lawmakers revised Indiana's constitution. They also wrote a new preamble, which states:

TO THE END, that justice be established, public order maintained, and liberty perpetuated [upheld]; WE the people of the State of Indiana, grateful to ALMIGHTY GOD for the free exercise of the right to choose our own form of government, do ordain this Constitution.

Over the years lawmakers have made several changes to the amendments listed in the state constitution. Yet the text of the preamble has remained the same since 1851.

Like the United States Constitution, the Indiana Constitution sets up a government with three branches. Each branch has its own work to do. One branch makes the laws of the state. A second branch sees that the laws are carried out. A third branch decides whether a law has been broken or whether a law goes against the constitution. The idea of dividing the government into different branches is known as separation of powers.

REVIEW What freedoms are in both the United States Constitution and Indiana's constitution?

Making Laws for Indiana

The **legislative** (LEH•juhs•lay•tiv) **branch** of government makes, or passes, laws. The state legislative branch is called the General Assembly. It has two houses, or groups of lawmakers—the House of Representatives and the Senate. The House of Representatives is made up of 100 lawmakers. Each is elected for a two-year term. The Indiana Senate is made up of 50 senators, each elected to a four-year term. Both houses work in the capitol building in Indianapolis.

A major responsibility of the General Assembly is to pass state tax laws. The taxes help pay the cost of running the state government. Lawmakers must decide how to spend Indiana's tax money.

Analyze Diagrams The Indiana state government, like the United States government, is divided into three branches.

❖ Which branch enforces the laws of the state?

Branches of State Government

LEGISLATIVE BRANCH

Makes the laws of the state.

EXECUTIVE BRANCH

Enforces the laws of the state, or sees that they are carried out.

JUDICIAL BRANCH

Decides whether laws have been broken or whether they go against the Constitution.

They must develop a written plan for spending money, known as a **budget**.

REVIEW What two houses make up the Indiana General Assembly?

Enforcing Indiana's Laws

The government is responsible for seeing that laws are enforced, or put into use and obeyed. The branch of government responsible for enforcing the laws is called the **executive branch**. Indiana's governor is the leader of the state's executive branch. The governor is elected for a four-year term.

After the General Assembly approves a **bill**, or a written plan for a new law, the bill is sent to the governor. If he or she agrees to the bill and signs it, it becomes a law. The governor also has the power to **veto**, or stop, a bill by refusing to sign it. A bill vetoed by the governor can still be made a law if a **majority**, or more than half, of the House and the Senate vote to make it a law.

The governor shares the work of the executive branch with other state leaders. One of those leaders is the lieutenant governor. The governor and

Lieutenant Governor Joseph Kernan (left) assists the governor in performing official duties for the state.

the lieutenant governor always run for office as a team. Many different agencies also help the executive branch run smoothly. People who head executive state **agencies**, or departments, such as the Department of Natural Resources, are appointed, or chosen, by the governor.

REVIEW Who has the power to veto a bill?

State Seal

Analyze Primary Sources

The Indiana General Assembly approved the design for the current state seal in 1963.

❶ Near the center of the seal, a pioneer stands in a field with an ax. The scene is a reminder of how hard early settlers worked to clear the land.

❷ At the bottom of the seal is the date 1816. Indiana became a state in that year.

❸ To the right and the left of the date are tulip tree leaves. The tulip tree is the state tree of Indiana.

◈ A buffalo is also pictured in the Indiana state seal. Why do you think this is so?

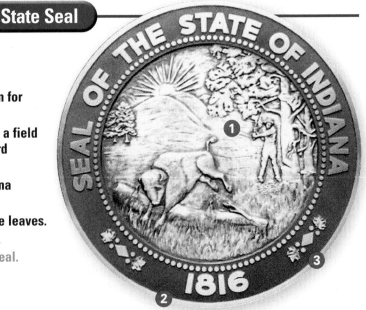

Judging Indiana's Laws

The branch of government that decides whether a law has been broken and makes sure that laws agree with the state constitution is the **judicial** (joo•DISH•uhl) **branch**. The judicial branch is made up of courts and judges that hear and decide law cases.

The highest court in Indiana is the state supreme court. Five judges serve on Indiana's supreme court. One of these judges is chosen to be chief justice, or head judge. Supreme court judges decide cases about the Indiana Constitution and the rights and freedoms of Indiana citizens. It is the governor's responsibility to appoint new judges to serve on the state supreme court. Every ten years the citizens of Indiana vote whether to keep the justices in office.

The next highest court is the court of appeals. These judges hear cases asking for changes in decisions made in Indiana's lower courts.

The state's lower courts are the county circuit courts and the superior courts.

Justices on the Indiana state supreme court serve terms lasting ten years.

Many of the cases heard by these courts are jury trials. In a **jury trial** a group of citizens decides whether a person accused of a crime is guilty or not guilty on the basis of facts of the case.

REVIEW What is the highest court in Indiana?

LESSON 1 REVIEW

1 MAIN IDEA What are the three branches of government in Indiana and in the United States?

2 WHY IT MATTERS Why is it important to learn about Indiana's state government?

3 VOCABULARY Link a branch of Indiana's state government to each of the following terms: **veto, jury trial, budget**.

4 READING SKILL—Identify Fact and Opinion Why is it important for officials in state government to distinguish fact from opinion?

5 HISTORY When did the state constitution used in Indiana today become law?

6 CIVICS AND GOVERNMENT What is the purpose of a bill of rights?

7 CRITICAL THINKING—Analyze What might happen if the executive branch both made the laws and made sure that they were obeyed?

 PERFORMANCE—Make a Brochure Imagine that you work at the Indiana state capitol. Write and illustrate a brochure that tells visitors about the responsibilities of Indiana's legislative branch. Be sure to include illustrations in your brochure.

·SKILLS· Read a Flow Chart

VOCABULARY

flow chart

▶ WHY IT MATTERS

Some information is easier to understand when it is explained in the form of a drawing. To understand a process, or a series of steps, you may find it helpful to look at a flow chart. A **flow chart** is a drawing that shows the order in which things happen. The arrows on the flow chart help you read the steps in their correct order.

▶ WHAT YOU NEED TO KNOW

Here is how to read a flow chart. First, start with the step of the flow chart that does not have an arrow leading into it. This step tells what happens first. It often appears at the top of the chart. Sometimes it is on the left side of the chart or is marked with the number *1* or the letter *A*. Study the flow chart on page 267, and read the words that describe the first step.

Follow the arrow that leads from the first step to the second step, and read the information. Continue following the arrows until you reach the last step, which has no arrow leading out of it.

Sometimes more than one arrow will lead from the same step. This means that the next step involves a choice between two or more possibilities. If the steps branch in more than one direction, follow each set of arrows separately. The separate paths may come together at the last step. That means that all choices result in the same outcome.

If you lose your place, follow the path of the arrows backward to the beginning and start again.

▶ PRACTICE THE SKILL

The flow chart on page 267 shows the process by which laws are made in the Indiana General Assembly. The process begins when a member of the legislature writes a bill. Usually the process ends when the bill becomes a law.

Look at the flow chart. Use the information in it to answer these questions.

1 After a bill is written, what happens next?

2 What has to happen for the bill to be sent to the governor?

3 What possibilities does the flow chart show with a branched arrow?

4 What happens if the governor signs a bill? How can a bill become a law after the governor vetoes it?

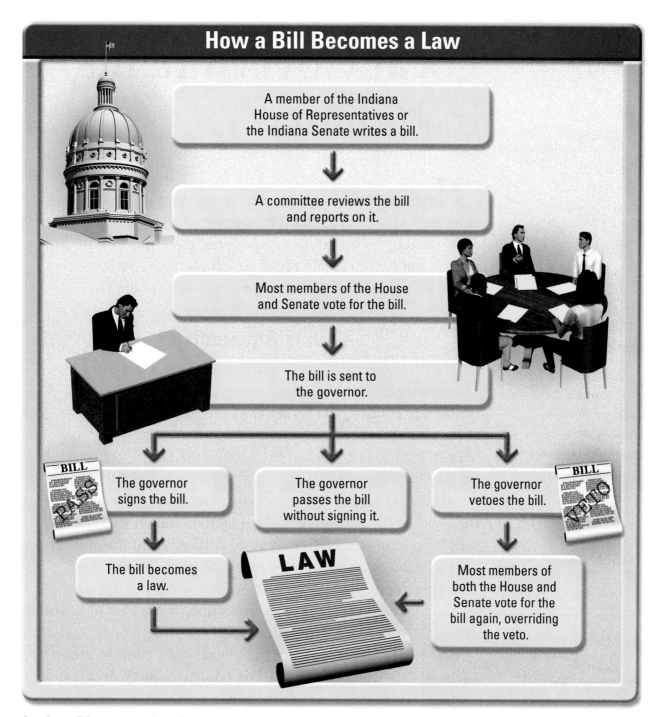

How a Bill Becomes a Law

A member of the Indiana House of Representatives or the Indiana Senate writes a bill.

A committee reviews the bill and reports on it.

Most members of the House and Senate vote for the bill.

The bill is sent to the governor.

BILL PASS

The governor signs the bill.

The governor passes the bill without signing it.

The governor vetoes the bill.

BILL VETO

The bill becomes a law.

LAW

Most members of both the House and Senate vote for the bill again, overriding the veto.

Analyze Diagrams In Indiana, as in other states, a bill must follow a certain process before it becomes a law.

♦ What happens after a bill is sent to the governor?

APPLY WHAT YOU LEARNED

Work with a partner to make a flow chart that will explain to younger students how something works or how to do something. Write each step on a strip of paper. Illustrate each step with a drawing. Glue the steps in order onto a sheet of posterboard. Connect the steps with arrows. Give your flow chart a title. If possible, share your flow chart with younger students.

2

CD 10
Track 4

Local Governments in Indiana

MAIN IDEA
Read to find out how Hoosiers take part in local government.

WHY IT MATTERS
Local governments shape everyday life in Indiana communities.

VOCABULARY

county seat
county commissioner
county council
township trustee
township board
common council
town board
special district
school board

Hoosiers look to local governments to serve the needs of cities, towns, and counties. Local governments perform many of the same jobs that state and national governments do. In each Indiana community, local governments make laws, see that laws are obeyed, and decide whether laws are fair.

County Governments

One town or city in each county serves as the county seat. The **county seat** is the center of government for a county. Leaders of county governments meet to carry out business at the county seat's courthouse.

Each county is governed by a board made up of three **county commissioners**. Voters in the county elect their commissioners to serve four-year terms. The board does much of the work of the executive and legislative branches. It makes ordinances, or laws, for the county and sees that the laws are obeyed. Commissioners have many responsibilities. They help run county-owned buildings such as hospitals, libraries, and courthouses. Commissioners are also responsible for seeing that county roads are maintained.

Voters also elect the members of another group, the county council. The **county council** decides how the county's money is spent. The county council also checks on the county commissioners to make sure that they do not become too powerful.

In addition, counties have judges and courts to carry out the work of the judicial branch. Some counties share a court system made up of circuit and superior courts.

REVIEW What is the job of the county commissioners?

County courthouses keep records on the births, deaths, and marriages of people living in that county.

268

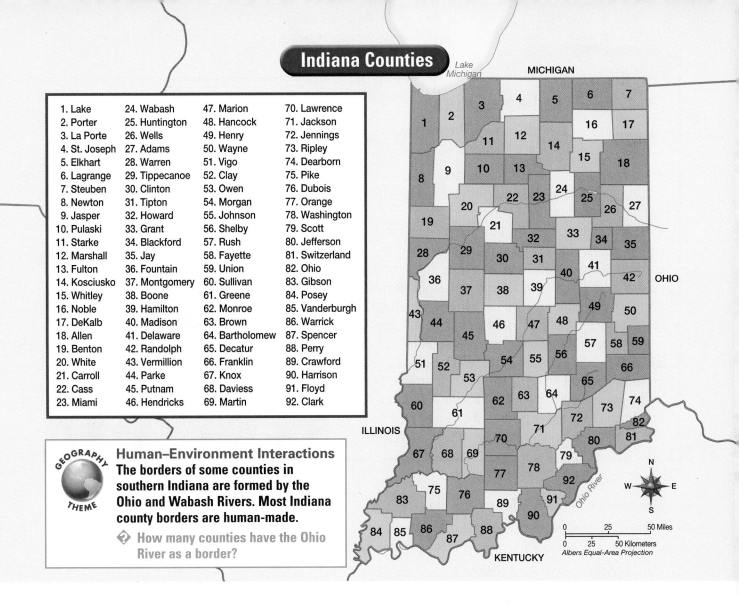

Indiana Counties

Lake Michigan   MICHIGAN

1. Lake	24. Wabash	47. Marion	70. Lawrence
2. Porter	25. Huntington	48. Hancock	71. Jackson
3. La Porte	26. Wells	49. Henry	72. Jennings
4. St. Joseph	27. Adams	50. Wayne	73. Ripley
5. Elkhart	28. Warren	51. Vigo	74. Dearborn
6. Lagrange	29. Tippecanoe	52. Clay	75. Pike
7. Steuben	30. Clinton	53. Owen	76. Dubois
8. Newton	31. Tipton	54. Morgan	77. Orange
9. Jasper	32. Howard	55. Johnson	78. Washington
10. Pulaski	33. Grant	56. Shelby	79. Scott
11. Starke	34. Blackford	57. Rush	80. Jefferson
12. Marshall	35. Jay	58. Fayette	81. Switzerland
13. Fulton	36. Fountain	59. Union	82. Ohio
14. Kosciusko	37. Montgomery	60. Sullivan	83. Gibson
15. Whitley	38. Boone	61. Greene	84. Posey
16. Noble	39. Hamilton	62. Monroe	85. Vanderburgh
17. DeKalb	40. Madison	63. Brown	86. Warrick
18. Allen	41. Delaware	64. Bartholomew	87. Spencer
19. Benton	42. Randolph	65. Decatur	88. Perry
20. White	43. Vermillion	66. Franklin	89. Crawford
21. Carroll	44. Parke	67. Knox	90. Harrison
22. Cass	45. Putnam	68. Daviess	91. Floyd
23. Miami	46. Hendricks	69. Martin	92. Clark

OHIO

ILLINOIS

Human–Environment Interactions
The borders of some counties in southern Indiana are formed by the Ohio and Wabash Rivers. Most Indiana county borders are human-made.

❓ How many counties have the Ohio River as a border?

Ohio River

N W E S

0   25   50 Miles
0   25   50 Kilometers
Albers Equal-Area Projection

KENTUCKY

Township Governments

Within each of Indiana's counties are smaller government units called townships. A **township trustee** is the head of each township government. He or she serves as the executive branch. The legislative branch is the **township board**. Board members make laws for the township.

The township governments have two main duties. They help people who do not have enough money for food or shelter. They can also run the township's public schools.

REVIEW What branch of township government is handled by the trustee?

City and Town Governments

All cities and towns in Indiana have governments that make laws, see that laws are obeyed, and decide law cases. People living in cities and towns depend on their local governments to provide important services such as fire and police protection, waste removal, libraries, and parks for their communities.

In Indiana cities, the **common council** is the legislative branch of city government. Another name for the common council is the city council. In towns, the legislative branch is called the **town board**. Voters elect members to serve on the city councils and town boards.

Indiana Cities
Understanding Places and Regions

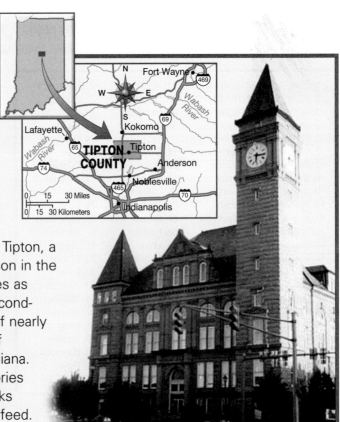

Indianapolis, Gary, Evansville, and other Indiana cities have increased in size during the twentieth century. Even so, many Hoosiers continue to live in small cities such as Tipton. Tipton is typical of many small communities in Indiana. It is named for John Tipton, a soldier who fought with William Henry Harrison in the Battle of Tippecanoe. The city of Tipton serves as the county seat of Tipton County. It is the second-largest city in the county, with a population of nearly 5,000. Tipton is located between the cities of Indianapolis and Kokomo, in north-central Indiana. Many people who live in Tipton work in factories that build parts for airplanes, make metal racks for stores, or produce plant seed and animal feed.

The mayor is the leader of the executive branch of government in a city or town. It is the mayor's job to see that the city's or town's laws are obeyed.

REVIEW What branch of government does the common council or town board represent?

Unified Governments

In 1970 the city government of Indianapolis joined with the government of Marion County. Most of the responsibilities of the county and city officials were combined. This new kind of government became known as Unigov, which is short for "unified government." In Indiana this special system of local government can be found only in the Indianapolis and Marion County area.

A 29-member city-county council took the place of the common

City governments hire firefighters to protect city residents, or those people living in the city.

Structure of Unigov

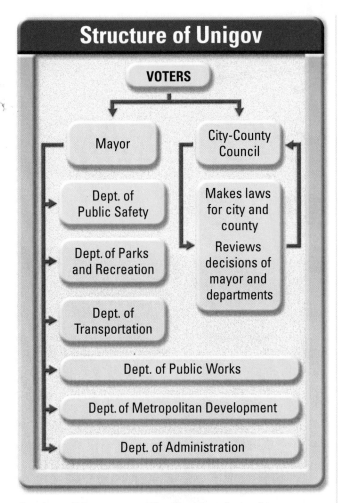

VOTERS

Mayor

City-County Council

Dept. of Public Safety

Makes laws for city and county

Dept. of Parks and Recreation

Reviews decisions of mayor and departments

Dept. of Transportation

Dept. of Public Works

Dept. of Metropolitan Development

Dept. of Administration

Analyze Diagrams The diagram shows how government in Indianapolis and Marion County works.

◈ How does Unigov differ from other forms of local government in Indiana?

council of Indianapolis. It makes laws for both the city and the county. The mayor heads the executive branch, which is made up of six departments. The departments work together to provide police and fire services, keep up parks, streets, and sewers, and run the day-to-day business of government. Within Unigov, however, each township in Marion County has its own police, fire, and park services and its own schools.

REVIEW Which two kinds of local government were combined to form Unigov?

District Governments

Indiana has other units of local government called special district governments. A **special district** is an area in which a specific problem, such as flooding, needs to be solved. In townships that do not supply educational services, voters in a school district elect a **school board**. The school board is responsible for meeting the district's educational needs.

REVIEW What is the job of a school board?

LESSON 2 REVIEW

❶ **MAIN IDEA** What are three kinds of local governments in Indiana?

❷ **WHY IT MATTERS** Why do Hoosiers need local governments?

❸ **VOCABULARY** Write a sentence for each of the following terms: **township board, county seat, common council, special district**.

❹ **READING SKILL—Identify Fact and Opinion** Write two sentences about a county official, one stating an opinion and one stating a fact.

❺ **ECONOMICS** How does a township government use the money it gets by collecting taxes?

❻ **HISTORY** When was Unigov created?

❼ **CRITICAL THINKING—Hypothesize** What might happen to county government if there were no county council?

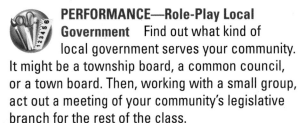
PERFORMANCE—Role-Play Local Government Find out what kind of local government serves your community. It might be a township board, a common council, or a town board. Then, working with a small group, act out a meeting of your community's legislative branch for the rest of the class.

CD 10
Track 5

Tippecanoe County Courthouse

The Tippecanoe County Courthouse stands today in downtown Lafayette. The courthouse was built in the 1880s to show the pride citizens felt for their county. Completed in 1885, it was built in the shape of a 150-foot (46-m) cross. The 226-foot-high (69-m) building is made of Indiana limestone and brick. It has 100 columns and 5 floors. When Mark Twain saw the courthouse in 1885, he said, "A striking courthouse, very striking indeed."

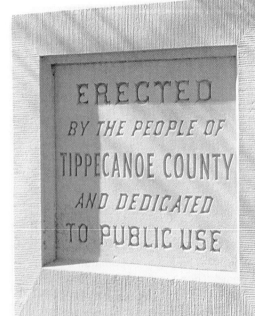

ERECTED BY THE PEOPLE OF TIPPECANOE COUNTY AND DEDICATED TO PUBLIC USE

COMMENCED A.D. 1881; COMPLETED A.D. 1885 MAY TRUTH AND JUSTICE EVER PREVAIL.

The cornerstone of the building is limestone from Bedford, Indiana. A copper box containing several items was placed inside the stone. The cornerstone ceremony, on October 26, 1882, was celebrated with bands playing and schoolchildren singing.

The dome has 4 large clock faces and a bell. It is topped by a 14-foot (4-m) statue called the Goddess of Liberty. Since the figure is holding scales, many people think it represents justice.

Analyze the Primary Source

❶ How long did it take to build the courthouse? How old is it today?

❷ Why do you think the figures were chosen for the pediment? Why do you think the statue of Lafayette was added?

Relief carvings on the pediment are of George Rogers Clark, George Washington, and Tecumseh.

In 1887 a statue of the Marquis de Lafayette was added to the square. Today it stands in the northeast corner on top of the fountain.

ACTIVITY

Draw a Building Plan A building plan shows where all the features of the building are located. Draw a plan of your classroom or of a room in your home. Show furniture as well as doors and windows. Share your plan with the class.

RESEARCH

Visit The Learning Site at **www.harcourtschool.com/ primarysources** to research other primary sources.

Making Economic Choices

CD 10 Track 6

VOCABULARY

savings plan

▶ WHY IT MATTERS

Imagine that you earned $15 doing jobs around the house. You could use the money to buy something, or you might decide to save it. Such possible decisions are called economic choices.

You could develop a savings plan with the help of an adult family member. A **savings plan** is a long-term plan, or goal, for how you will use your money in the future. If you are saving for an item such as a new bike, you and a family member might decide to open a savings account at a bank.

▶ WHAT YOU NEED TO KNOW

Like individuals, local governments have to make economic choices. Governments sometimes must develop savings plans to pay for services in their communities.

▶ PRACTICE THE SKILL

Imagine that leaders in your community have decided to build a recreation center. They already have $250,000, but they need $25,000 more to complete the project. Picture yourself as the mayor of this community. Here are some steps you can follow to reach your goal.

Step 1 State your goal. Why does your community need to save money?

Step 2 Develop a savings plan. If your town could save $5,000 of the money it collects in taxes each month, how long would it take to meet your goal?

Step 3 Take action. When you have saved enough money, you can complete the building of the recreation center.

▶ APPLY WHAT YOU LEARNED

You want to buy something that costs $120. Develop a savings plan to help you reach your goal within one year. How much money will you have to save each month? Share your plan with your classmates.

Opening a savings account is an important part of developing a savings plan.

Hoosiers and the National Government

Over the years many Hoosiers have served in the United States government. The national government, located in Washington, D.C., is also called the **federal** government. Those who work in government at the federal level help Hoosiers at home, too. Many decisions affecting life in Indiana are made at the national level.

Hoosier Presidents

Three United States Presidents have connections to Indiana. The first person from Indiana to serve as President was William Henry Harrison, who led Indiana through its earliest growth. Known as "the Hero of Tippecanoe," Harrison served as a military leader and as the governor of the Indiana Territory from 1800 to 1812. In 1840 Harrison won election as the ninth President of the United States. He took office on March 4, 1841, a cold, rainy day. Harrison became ill and died after serving only 30 days as President.

MAIN IDEA
Read to find out how Hoosiers have served as national government leaders.

WHY IT MATTERS
National leaders from Indiana demonstrate qualities of responsible citizenship.

VOCABULARY
federal
veteran
nominate

The White House (below) in Washington, D.C., is the official residence, or home, of the President of the United States. At right is a campaign poster for Hoosier candidate Benjamin Harrison, who was elected President in 1888.

Abraham Lincoln is the best-known President with a connection to Indiana. Although born in Kentucky, he spent his boyhood years in Indiana and then moved to Illinois. In 1861 he became the sixteenth President. Lincoln led the United States during the Civil War, one of the most difficult times the country ever faced.

Benjamin Harrison, the grandson of William Henry Harrison, became the twenty-third President in 1889. The younger Harrison had risen to the rank of general during the Civil War. During his term as President, he helped soldiers who had been wounded in the Civil War and could not work. He persuaded the federal government to give the former soldiers, or **veterans**, enough money on which to live.

In 1940, the year before the United States entered World War II, Hoosier Wendell L. Willkie was **nominated**, or named, as a candidate for President. President Franklin D. Roosevelt won the election by many votes.

REVIEW Which three United States Presidents had connections to Indiana?

Indiana: Mother of Vice Presidents

Indiana has been given the nickname Mother of Vice Presidents. Five Hoosiers have served as Vice President of the United States.

Analyze Diagrams Three of the five Hoosiers who became Vice President made Indianapolis their home.

◈ Which Vice President came from northern Indiana?

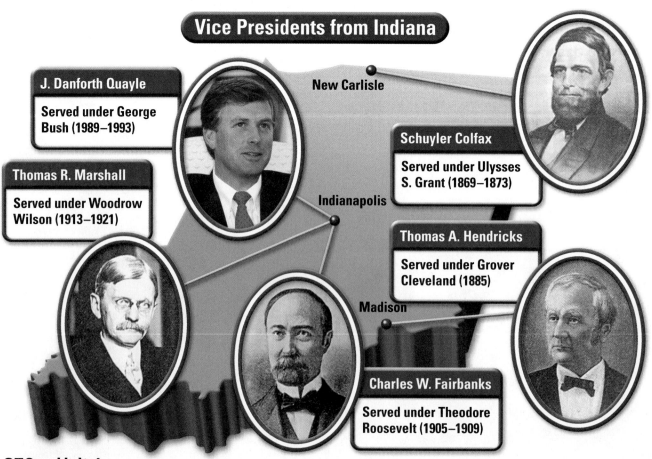

Vice Presidents from Indiana

J. Danforth Quayle
Served under George Bush (1989–1993)

Thomas R. Marshall
Served under Woodrow Wilson (1913–1921)

New Carlisle

Schuyler Colfax
Served under Ulysses S. Grant (1869–1873)

Indianapolis

Thomas A. Hendricks
Served under Grover Cleveland (1885)

Madison

Charles W. Fairbanks
Served under Theodore Roosevelt (1905–1909)

The Technology of Voting

The outcome of the 2000 presidential election was unknown for 36 days because some ballots from the state of Florida were hard to read. The hard-to-read ballots were punch-card ballots. On a punch-card ballot, the voter pushes a pin through the card next to the name of the person for whom he or she wants to vote. Some of the punch-card ballots could not be read correctly. Beginning in 2005, punch-card ballots will no longer be used.

Indiana is encouraging its county governments to begin using direct recording electronic voting machines, also known as DREs.

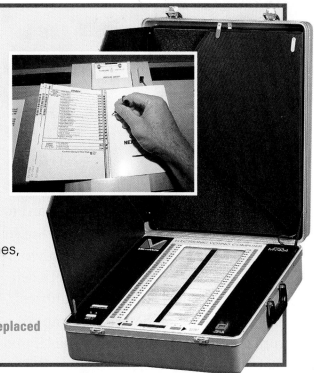

Within a few years punch-card ballots (top right) will be replaced by newer methods of voting, such as DREs (bottom right).

The first Hoosier Vice President was Schuyler (SKY•luhr) Colfax, who served as Ulysses S. Grant's Vice President from 1869 to 1873. Then Thomas Hendricks served as Vice President under Grover Cleveland in 1885. Charles W. Fairbanks served as Theodore Roosevelt's Vice President from 1905 to 1909. Between 1913 and 1921, Thomas Marshall was Woodrow Wilson's Vice President.

In the 1988 presidential election, George Bush chose J. Danforth Quayle as his running mate. Dan Quayle served as George Bush's Vice President from 1989 to 1993.

REVIEW Why is Indiana called Mother of Vice Presidents?

Other Leaders from Indiana

Hoosiers have been leaders in the United States Congress, too. Indiana, and every other state, sends two representatives to the Senate. The number of people a state sends to the House of Representatives is based on the population of the state according to the most recent census. On the basis of the 2000 census, Indiana is entitled to send nine members to the House of Representatives.

One of the state's best-known senators was Birch Bayh (BY). He was elected to three six-year terms, beginning in 1962. Birch Bayh's son Evan served two terms as governor of Indiana from 1989 to 1997. The youngest governor in the country when he was elected, Evan Bayh went on to become one of Indiana's most popular leaders. He was elected to the United States Senate in 1998.

Richard Lugar is the only Hoosier to have been elected to four terms in the United States Senate. He has held the office of senator since he was first elected in 1976. Before his election to the Senate, Lugar was the mayor of Indianapolis.

Evan Bayh

Richard Lugar

Virginia Jenckes

Jill Long

As a senator, Lugar has worked hard to help farmers as well as people living in cities. Lugar is also very active in working to develop good relations between the United States and other countries.

Indiana women have made important contributions as members of the United States Congress. In 1932 Virginia Ellis Jenckes became the first Hoosier woman elected to the House of Representatives. Having run her family's farm, Jenckes was familiar with the challenges farmers faced. In Congress she worked to pass laws that would help them get through the hard times of the Great Depression.

Hoosier women continue to make important contributions as elected

officials. More recently, Jill Long served two terms as a member of the House of Representatives, from 1991 to 1995. She drew on her previous experience and knowledge to help businesses in Indiana. After serving in Congress, Long held other positions in the federal government.

In 1996, Julia Carson was elected to Congress to represent the people of Indiana. She has introduced a number of important bills to help Hoosiers. In 2000 Carson was elected to a third term as a member of the House of Representatives.

The United States Capitol building, in Washington, D.C., is where the legislative branch of the federal government does its work.

Julia Carson 1938–

Character Trait: Compassion

In 1996 Julia Carson was elected by the people of Indianapolis to serve in the United States House of Representatives. Carson had worked in the state and county governments in Indiana. She had served in the General Assembly and had been a township trustee for Center Township, in Marion County.

As a member of Congress, Carson has shown compassion in the hundreds of bills she has helped enact as laws. She has worked hard to keep children safe, improve health care and transportation, and help veterans. In 1999 she helped introduce a bill to honor civil rights leader Rosa Parks.

MULTIMEDIA BIOGRAPHIES
Visit The Learning Site at www.harcourtschool.com/biographies
to learn about other famous people.

GO ONLINE

In addition to serving in Congress, people from Indiana serve the federal government in many other ways. Many Hoosiers perform a wide variety of jobs for agencies within the executive branch of the federal government in Washington, D.C., and other locations. Postal carriers are among the most familiar federal employees of the agencies.

REVIEW Who are some Hoosiers who have served Indiana in the United States Senate and House of Representatives?

LESSON 3
REVIEW

1 MAIN IDEA How have Hoosiers provided national leadership?

2 WHY IT MATTERS How does the national government affect Hoosiers today?

3 VOCABULARY What does it mean when someone is **nominated** for a government office?

4 READING SKILL—Identify Fact and Opinion Read each statement. Tell whether it expresses a fact or an opinion.

"Virginia Jenckes was the first woman elected to represent Indiana in Congress."

"Hoosiers should stick to local issues and stay out of government at the national level."

5 CIVICS AND GOVERNMENT How many senators does Indiana send to Washington, D.C.?

6 CRITICAL THINKING—Evaluate Which Hoosier do you think has made the greatest contribution to American life by serving in the federal government? Give a reason for your choice.

PERFORMANCE—Present a Campaign Speech Imagine that you have decided to run for election to the United States House of Representatives. Write a short speech telling voters why they should elect you. Explain what you hope to contribute. Present your speech to your classmates.

Indiana Citizenship

Indiana became a state in 1816. Since that time Hoosiers have been citizens of both Indiana and the United States. The word *citizen* means "a member of a state or a country." As a citizen a person has both rights and responsibilities. A **responsibility** is a duty.

Becoming a Citizen

Most Americans are citizens of the United States because they were born in this country. Not all United States citizens were born here, however. Some people immigrated to this country from other countries and have become naturalized citizens. A **naturalized citizen** is an immigrant who has become a citizen of the United States. The United States Constitution says that "all persons born or naturalized in the United States . . . are citizens of the United States and of the State wherein they reside [live]."

After an immigrant has lived in the United States for at least five years, he or she can become a naturalized citizen. First, the person must ask a judge, in writing, for permission to become a citizen. Second, the person must pass a test about the history and government of the United States. Third, the person takes part in a ceremony in which he or she promises to be loyal to the United States. When adults become naturalized citizens, any of their children under the age of 18 become citizens as well.

REVIEW In what three ways do people become citizens of the United States?

Students display patriotism at a flag raising ceremony.

Citizenship Day

Many immigrants become naturalized citizens of the United States and of Indiana on Citizenship Day, September 17. In 1952 President Harry S. Truman established September 17 as Citizenship Day because this date is the anniversary of the signing of the United States Constitution. Hoosiers, like citizens in other states, celebrate Citizenship Day with parades, speeches, picnics, and other celebrations. The high point of the day in many communities is the ceremony in which immigrants become naturalized citizens.

At the 2001 International Festival, held at the Indiana State Fairgrounds, immigrants took the oath of allegiance and became United States citizens.

Citizens Have Rights

Citizens of Indiana have the rights outlined in both the United States and Indiana Constitutions. Citizens have many freedoms, including freedom of speech, freedom of the press, freedom of religion, and freedom to assemble in groups. They have the right to travel throughout their home state and all of the United States. They also have the right to be treated fairly by their government.

Among the most important rights of citizenship are the right to vote and the right to hold public office. Citizens can participate in their government in many ways. They can choose the leaders who will represent them in local, state, and national government. By voting, citizens play a role in who is elected and what kinds of laws are passed. Citizens also have a voice in how tax money is spent.

Governments cannot take away a citizen's constitutional rights. However, some rights have certain limits. For example, the United States government limits the right to vote to citizens who are at least 18 years old. Most state governments require citizens to **register**, or sign up in writing, to vote.

People who are not citizens have many of the same rights that citizens enjoy.

Indiana citizens show their patriotism at a rally for firefighters from Indiana who helped people after terrorist attacks in New York City on September 11, 2001.

However, they cannot vote, hold public office, or carry out certain jobs, such as serving on a trial jury. Throughout Indiana's history Hoosiers have worked to protect and extend the rights of citizens and noncitizens alike.

REVIEW In which documents are the rights of Indiana citizens outlined?

Citizens Have Responsibilities

With the right to vote comes the responsibility to use that right by voting. With freedom of the press and freedom of speech comes the responsibility to be an informed citizen. With the right to be treated fairly comes the responsibility to treat others fairly.

Some responsibilities of citizenship are stated in laws. United States laws and Indiana laws say that it is a citizen's responsibility to pay taxes, obey laws, and be loyal. Some of these responsibilities, such as paying taxes and obeying laws, also apply to people who are not citizens. They apply to anyone who lives or works in this country.

Many citizens of Indiana and the United States take on additional responsibilities that help make their communities better places in which to live. **Volunteers**, or people who choose to work without receiving payment, help out in places such as schools, libraries, and parks. In the 1950s and 1960s, for example, Dorothy Buell worked to protect the natural beauty of thousands of acres of dunes on Indiana's shoreline.

Other responsibilities may not be spelled out in laws but are understood

---

• BIOGRAPHY •

Dorothy Buell   1886–1977

Character Trait: Civic Virtue

Early efforts to preserve the dunes on Indiana's shoreline along Lake Michigan led the state's General Assembly to create Indiana Dunes State Park in 1926. The newly created park protected only three miles of shoreline. Thousands of acres of dunes and wetlands remained unprotected from industrial development.

In 1952 Dorothy Buell, a concerned Indiana citizen, helped organize a citizens' group called Save the Dunes Council. This group made a film about the importance of saving the dunes. They also collected more than 250,000 signatures of people who were in favor of saving the dunes. In 1966 the United States Congress passed a law that protected more than 8,000 acres of dunes. The new area was called Indiana Dunes National Lakeshore. In 1992 Congress named the park's visitor center after Dorothy Buell to honor her "vision, dedication, and work in saving the Indiana dunes."

MULTIMEDIA BIOGRAPHIES
Visit The Learning Site at www.harcourtschool.com/biographies to learn about other famous people.

to be part of citizenship. Practicing **civic virtues**, or good habits of citizenship, is a responsibility of all citizens. Some examples of civic virtues are self-discipline, honesty, and respect for the rights of others.

In the twenty-first century, Hoosiers displayed their civic virtues during a time of tragedy. On September 11, 2001, several terrorists from other countries took control of four airplanes in the United States. A terrorist is someone who uses force or violence to promote a cause. The terrorists crashed two of those airplanes into tall office buildings in New York City. Terrorists crashed another airplane into a government building near Washington, D.C. A fourth airplane crashed in a field in western Pennsylvania. Thousands of people died as a result of those crashes. A few days later, Indiana sent a crew of 62 emergency rescue workers to New York City to help search for people

After the terrorist attack in September 2001, Indiana sent rescue workers to New York City.

in the ruins of the buildings. This concern for fellow citizens shows how people from Indiana and elsewhere act as responsible citizens.

REVIEW What are some responsibilities that citizens have?

LESSON 4
REVIEW

1 MAIN IDEA What is one right and one responsibility of a citizen?

2 WHY IT MATTERS Why is voting an especially important right and responsibility?

3 VOCABULARY Write a paragraph about the duties that come with the rights of citizens. Use the terms **responsibility**, **civic virtue**, and **volunteer** in your writing.

4 READING SKILL—Identify Fact and Opinion What does it mean to be a citizen of Indiana and of the United States? Write one fact and one opinion.

5 HISTORY During the 1960s who worked to protect the sand dunes on Indiana's northern shoreline?

6 CIVICS AND GOVERNMENT What three steps must an immigrant follow to become a naturalized citizen?

7 CRITICAL THINKING—Synthesize Why do people volunteer to carry out responsibilities that are not required by law?

 PERFORMANCE—Make a Poster With a small group, choose one civic virtue or quality of informed citizenship. Make a poster that illustrates this civic virtue or quality. Draw pictures or use photographs of people who are practicing the virtue or demonstrating the quality. Display your poster in the classroom.

Act as a Responsible Citizen

CD10 Track 9

➡ WHY IT MATTERS

Imagine that you are walking through a new park with a few of your friends. You see a person drop an empty lunch sack on the ground. You pick it up and throw it into a trash can. Your friend says, "People get paid to pick up trash. You do not have to do it!"

By picking up the trash and throwing it away, you acted as a responsible citizen. Although government workers do many jobs, cities and states depend on their citizens to act responsibly. When a responsible citizen sees a problem, he or she takes action to help solve it. Acting responsibly is an important part of being a citizen.

As you have read, volunteers work to make their communities better places in which to live. In the 1950s and 1960s, Dorothy Buell acted responsibly to save Indiana's dunes. Today, concerned Hoosiers continue to act responsibly by raising money and helping care for the Indiana Dunes National Lakeshore.

➡ WHAT YOU NEED TO KNOW

There are many ways for citizens to act responsibly. They can learn about their community and state. They can take part in government and help choose good leaders. They can do their jobs well and work cooperatively with other citizens to solve community problems.

Helping keep your community clean is one way you can be a good citizen.

Sometimes, acting as a responsible citizen requires special thought and action. By reading and following the steps below, you can learn to act as a responsible citizen.

Step 1 **Identify an issue or a problem in your school or community, and learn more about it.**

Step 2 **Think about ways to solve the problem. Try to think of solutions that would be good for other people as well as for yourself.**

Step 3 **Decide what you can do to help, acting either alone or with other people. Then work to bring about change.**

Step 4 **Remember to be careful. Never try to solve a problem by risking your safety or the safety of someone else. If you cannot solve the problem yourself, get help from others, such as an adult family member, a police officer, or a community official.**

▶ **APPLY WHAT YOU LEARNED**

Find an issue or problem that your community is facing. Use books, newspapers, magazines, television, news programs, and the Internet to find more information about the issue. Share with your classmates what you have learned about acting as a responsible citizen.

Students join in a parade to show their support for maintaining a drug-free school and community.

CD 10
Track 10

8 Review and Test Preparation

USE YOUR READING SKILLS

Complete this graphic organizer to show how you can identify facts and opinions about government in Indiana. A copy of this graphic organizer appears on page 85 of the Activity Book.

Government in Indiana

STATEMENT	FACT	OPINION
The executive branch makes sure that laws are enforced.		
The executive branch is the most important part of state government.		
Indianapolis and Marion County joined their city and county governments in the 1970s in a plan called Unigov.		
Other counties and cities should join their governments the way Unigov did.		
Richard Lugar has served longer in the United States Senate than any other Hoosier.		
Indiana should be allowed to send more than nine members to the House of Representatives.		

THINK & WRITE

Write a Letter to the Editor   Think of a problem in your community that government could solve. Write a letter to the editor of your local newspaper that includes the following information: (1) what the problem is, (2) which level of government would be able to solve the problem, (3) what you think government should do.

Write a Journal Entry   Imagine that you have just become a naturalized citizen. In a journal entry, describe what it was like to prepare for the citizenship test and how it feels to be a United States citizen. Use the Internet or your public library to research this assignment. Share your journal entry with students in your class.

USE VOCABULARY

Identify the term that best completes the following sentences.

legislative (p. 263)

judicial (p. 265)

county commissioners (p. 268)

township board (p. 269)

common council (p. 269)

1. A _____ does the work of the legislative branch in Indiana's townships.

2. The Indiana supreme court is part of the state's _____ branch.

3. A board of _____ does the work of the executive branch for the county.

4. The _____ branch of Indiana's state government is called the General Assembly.

5. A _____ does the work of the legislative branch for cities.

RECALL FACTS

Answer these questions.

6. What are the duties of the legislative branch of a government?

7. Under which United States President did Hoosier J. Danforth Quayle serve as Vice President?

8. What is a naturalized citizen?

Write the letter of the best choice.

9. **TEST PREP** If the state government needs to take care of a specific problem, such as flooding, it might create a—
   A township.
   B common council.
   C special district.
   D county seat.

10. **TEST PREP** The first Hoosier to serve as President of the United States was—
    F Wendell L. Willkie.
    G Benjamin Harrison.
    H Abraham Lincoln.
    J William Henry Harrison.

11. **TEST PREP** Who was the first Hoosier woman to be elected to the United States Congress?
    A Jill Long
    B Julia Carson
    C Virginia Jenckes
    D Dorothy Buell

THINK CRITICALLY

12. Why do the United States and Indiana Constitutions both outline the rights of citizens in a bill of rights?

13. How would life in your community be different if there were no volunteers?

APPLY SKILLS

Making Economic Choices

14. Suppose that you need to choose between buying a DVD or going to a movie with friends. How would you go about making this economic choice? Use the steps you read about on page 274 to help you make a choice.

Act as a Responsible Citizen

15. Identify a person you think is a responsible citizen. Write a paragraph explaining why you think this person is a responsible citizen.

VISIT

The Indiana State Capitol

GET READY

Indianapolis is the second city in Indiana to serve as the state capital. The capital was moved there from Corydon, Indiana, in 1825. The present capitol building, designed in 1878 by Edwin May, was completed in 1886. Whenever possible, materials native to Indiana were used in its construction both inside and outside. The cornerstone, set in 1880, contains a time capsule holding more than forty items! In 1988 the capitol building underwent renovations that cost more than $10 million.

WHAT TO SEE

The Victorian stained glass in the rotunda dome is more than 100 feet (30 m) above the main floor.

LOCATE IT

INDIANA

Indianapolis

All of the furnishings in the Supreme Court chamber are original. Only the carpet has been replaced, but with an exact copy of the original.

The 100 lights in the chandelier in the House of Representatives represent the House's 100 members. The chandelier weighs almost 1,200 pounds (544 kg)!

Governor Frank O'Bannon delivers a speech at the capitol.

TAKE A FIELD TRIP

GO ONLINE

A VIRTUAL TOUR
Visit The Learning Site at **www.harcourtschool.com/tours** to take virtual tours of other capitols and government buildings.

4 Review and Test Preparation

CD 10
Track 12

Write a Poem Choose one of the photographs from those on the next page. Write a poem that describes what is shown in the photograph.

USE VOCABULARY

Identify the term that best completes each of the following sentences.

rural (p. 236)   **reclaim** (p. 246)

urban (p. 236)   **federal** (p. 275)

1 _____ areas of Indiana have a low population density.

2 _____ areas of Indiana have a high population density.

3 Companies are required by law to _____ the land after coal is removed.

4 Some people who have jobs in the _____ government have jobs at the national level.

RECALL FACTS

Answer these questions.

5 About how many people live in Indiana?

6 What cultural groups are found in Indiana?

7 Why are educated citizens important to Indiana and the United States?

8 What is a major responsibility of Indiana's General Assembly?

Write the letter of the best choice.

9 **TEST PREP**   Indiana ranks sixth in the world in the production of—
A corn.
B steel.
C coal.
D pharmaceuticals.

10 **TEST PREP**   Recycling helps Hoosiers protect the—
F population density.
G quality of education.
H service industry.
J environment.

11 **TEST PREP**   The branch of government that makes Indiana laws is the—
A supreme court.
B executive branch.
C legislative branch.
D governor's office.

12 **TEST PREP**   How many counties are in Indiana?
F 22
G 62
H 92
J 152

THINK CRITICALLY

13 Why do you think the right to a public education is important?

14 How might communities in Indiana be different if their citizens had no say in the election of local government officials?

15 How might practicing civic virtues help improve your community?

APPLY SKILLS

Read a Population Map

Use the map on this page to answer the following questions.

MAP AND GLOBE SKILLS

16 How many counties in Indiana have populations of more than 100,000?

17 How many counties have populations of less than 10,000?

18 How many Indiana counties have populations between 50,000 and 99,999?

19 Is more of Indiana's population in the southern part of the state or in the northern part of the state?

20 Why do you think Marion County and counties close to it have large populations?

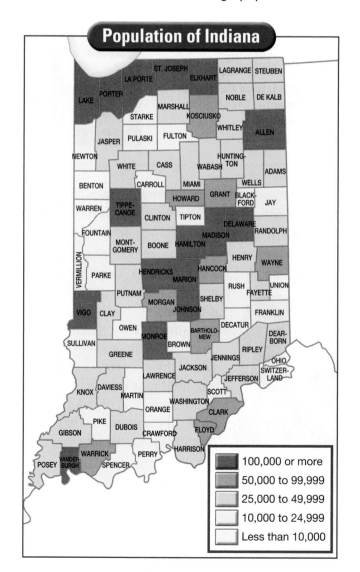

Population of Indiana

⬛	100,000 or more
⬛	50,000 to 99,999
⬜	25,000 to 49,999
⬜	10,000 to 24,999
⬜	Less than 10,000

Modern industry thrives in Indiana p. 244

Indiana's cities are safe and clean p. 252

Indianapolis is the center of Indiana state government p. 262

Local governments make decisions that affect communities p. 268

Young Hoosiers display their civic virtue p. 283

Unit Activities

GO ONLINE

Visit The Learning Site at
**www.harcourtschool.com/
socialstudies/activities**
for additional activities.

Make a Population Map

Work in a group to find out the number of people in your school. Count how many students are in each class and how many teachers and other workers are in the school. Use the information you gather to make a population map of your school. Display your map, and compare it with those of others.

Write a Letter to a Government Official

Write a letter to an official in the local, state, or federal government. In your letter, discuss a concern that you have about your community, state, or country. Use the library, an almanac, or the Internet to find out who should get your letter and where it should be sent. Share your letter with the class.

VISIT YOUR LIBRARY

■ *H Is for Hoosier: An Indiana Alphabet* by Cynthia Furlong Reynolds. Sleeping Bear Press.

■ *How the U.S. Government Works* by Syl Sobel. Barron's Educational Series, Inc.

■ *Sir Johnny's Recycling Adventure* by Rachael Peterpaul Paulson. Crestmont Publishing.

COMPLETE THE UNIT PROJECT

Perform a Skit Working with several other students, prepare a skit. The characters should be officials of Indiana state government (senators, justices, the governor) or officials of your local government (the mayor, city council, trustees). Write a scene in which the characters act out their jobs by discussing a problem in all of Indiana or just in your community. Perform your skit for the class.

For Your Reference

Almanac

Biographical Dictionary

Gazetteer

Glossary

Index

Almanac
Facts About Indiana

Indiana

LAND	SIZE	CLIMATE	POPULATION*	LEADING PRODUCTS
Highest Point: Hoosier Hill (Wayne County) in eastern Indiana 1,257 feet (383 m) **Lowest Point:** Near the Ohio and Wabash Rivers (Posey County) in southwestern Indiana 320 feet (98 m)	**Area:** 36,185 square miles (93,712 sq km) **Distance North/South:** 270 miles (435 km) **Distance East/West:** 140 miles (225 km)	**Highest Recorded Temperature:** 116° F (47° C) at Collegeville on July 14, 1936 **Lowest Recorded Temperature:** -36° F (-38° C) at New Whiteland on January 19, 1994 **Average Temperature:** 75° F (24° C) in July, 28° F (-2° C) in January **Average Yearly Rainfall:** 40 inches (102 cm) Climate varies widely	6,080,485 * 2000 Census population figures	**Crops:** corn, wheat, soybeans, hay, mint **Fishing:** bass, crappies, catfish **Livestock:** cattle, hogs, poultry **Manufacturing:** steel, food products, furniture, pharmaceuticals, trucks, musical instruments, electronics **Natural Resources:** limestone, coal, natural gas, gypsum

Indianapolis is the largest city in the state of Indiana. It was founded in 1821 and four years later became the state's new capital. Indianapolis was selected to become the new capital because of its central location.

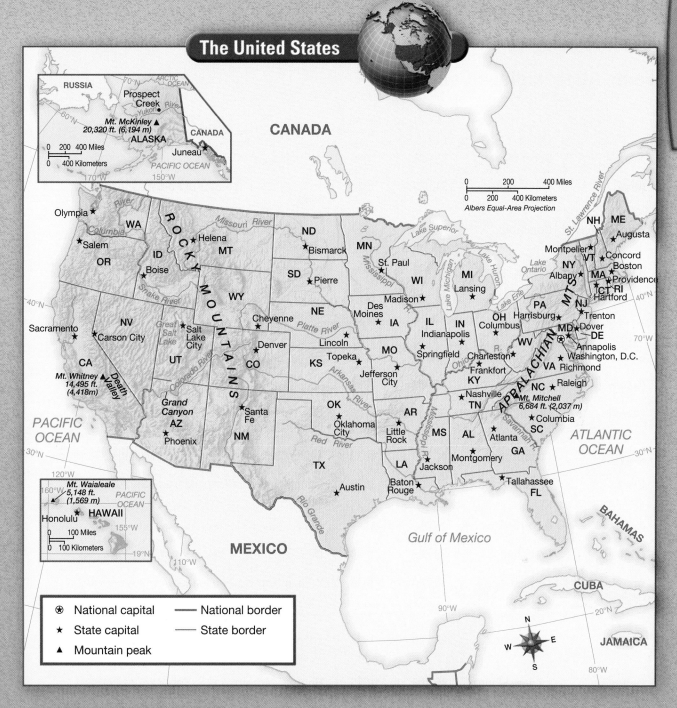

The United States

RUSSIA

CANADA

ARCTIC OCEAN

Prospect
Creek •
70°N
Yukon River

Mt. McKinley ▲
20,320 ft. (6,194 m)

ALASKA
Juneau ★

CANADA

| 0 | 200 | 400 Miles |
| 0 | 400 Kilometers |

PACIFIC OCEAN

170°W   150°W   60°N

CANADA

| 0 | 200 | 400 Miles |
| 0 | 200 | 400 Kilometers |

Albers Equal-Area Projection

St. Lawrence River

Olympia ★

Columbia River

WA

★ Salem

OR

ID
★ Boise

Helena ★

MT

Missouri River

ND
★ Bismarck

Lake Superior

MN

★ St. Paul

Lake Michigan

Lake Huron

Lake Ontario

Lake Erie

NH **ME**
★ Augusta

Montpelier ★
VT ★ Concord
Boston

NY
Albany ★
MA
★ Providence
CT **RI**
Hartford

R
O
C
K
Y

M
O
U
N
T
A
I
N
S

Snake River

WY

SD
★ Pierre

NE

WI

Madison ★

Lansing ★

MI

Des
Moines
★

IA

IL

IN

Columbus ★

OH

Harrisburg ★

PA

Trenton ★
NJ

MD ★ Dover
DE

40°N

Sacramento ★

NV
Carson City ★

Great
Salt
Lake

★ Salt
Lake
City

Cheyenne ★

Denver ★

CO

Lincoln ★

Topeka ★

KS

MO
Jefferson
City ★

Springfield ★

Indianapolis ★

Charleston ★
WV
Frankfort ★
KY

VA
Richmond ★

⊛ Annapolis
Washington, D.C.

70°W

Mt. Whitney ▲
14,495 ft.
(4,418m)

CA

Death Valley

Colorado River

UT

Grand
Canyon

AZ

Santa
Fe ★

NM

OK
Oklahoma
City ★

Arkansas River

Platte River

Ohio R.

Nashville ★

TN

A
P
P
A
L
A
C
H
I
A
N

M
T
S

Mt. Mitchell
6,684 ft. (2,037 m)

NC
★ Raleigh

★ Columbia

SC

**ATLANTIC
OCEAN**

**PACIFIC
OCEAN**

Phoenix ★

AR
Little
Rock ★

Red River

Mississippi R.

MS

AL

Atlanta ★

GA

Savannah R.

30°N

TX

Austin ★

Baton
Rouge ★

LA

Jackson ★

Montgomery ★

Tallahassee ★

FL

120°W

Mt. Waialeale
5,148 ft.
▲ (1,569 m)

PACIFIC
OCEAN

160°W

Honolulu ★ **HAWAII**

155°W

| 0 | 100 Miles |
| 0 | 100 Kilometers |

19°N

110°W

MEXICO

Rio Grande

Gulf of Mexico

90°W

BAHAMAS

CUBA

JAMAICA

20°N

80°W

30°N

N
W E
S

⊛ National capital	—— National border
★ State capital	—— State border
▲ Mountain peak	

Census 2000 revealed that the
state of Indiana had 6,080,485
people of many diverse
heritages and ages.

The design of the Indiana State
Capitol, built in 1888, was
modeled after the United States
Capitol in Washington, D.C.

Almanac

Facts About Indiana Counties

County Name	County Seat	Population*	Year Organized	Named For
Adams	Decatur	33,625	1836	John Quincy Adams, a President of the United States
Allen	Fort Wayne	331,849	1824	John Allen, a liberator of Fort Wayne in the War of 1812
Bartholomew	Columbus	71,435	1821	Joseph Bartholomew, a hero of the Battle of Tippecanoe
Benton	Fowler	9,421	1840	Thomas H. Benton, a U.S. Senator from Missouri
Blackford	Hartford City	14,048	1839	Isaac Newton Blackford, the first Speaker of Indiana's House of Representatives and, later, a justice of the state supreme court
Boone	Lebanon	46,107	1831	Daniel Boone, an American pioneer
Brown	Nashville	14,957	1836	Jacob Brown, a hero of the War of 1812
Carroll	Delphi	20,165	1828	Charles Carroll of Maryland, a signer of the Declaration of Independence
Cass	Logansport	40,930	1829	Lewis Cass, a governor of the Michigan Territory
Clark	Jeffersonville	96,472	1801	George Rogers Clark, a hero of the American Revolution
Clay	Brazil	26,556	1825	Henry Clay, a U.S. Senator from Kentucky
Clinton	Frankfort	33,866	1830	DeWitt Clinton, a governor of New York
Crawford	English	10,743	1818	William Crawford, a leader in the American Revolution; or William H. Crawford, a U.S. Secretary of the Treasury
Daviess	Washington	29,820	1817	Joseph Hamilton Daviess, a soldier in the Battle of Tippecanoe
Dearborn	Lawrenceburg	46,109	1803	Henry Dearborn, a U.S. Secretary of War
Decatur	Greensburg	24,555	1822	Stephen Decatur, a hero of the War of 1812
De Kalb	Auburn	40,285	1837	Johann De Kalb, an officer in the American Revolution
Delaware	Muncie	118,769	1830	Delaware Indians
Dubois	Jasper	39,674	1818	Toussaint Dubois, an officer in the Battle of Tippecanoe
Elkhart	Goshen	182,791	1830	Elkhart Indians
Fayette	Connersville	25,588	1819	Marquis de Lafayette, a French officer in the American Revolution
Floyd	New Albany	70,823	1819	John Floyd, a governor of Virginia; or Davis Floyd, the county's first circuit court judge

*2000 U.S. Census figures

County Name	County Seat	Population*	Year Organized	Named For
Fountain	Covington	17,954	1826	James Fountain, an officer at the Battle of Maumee
Franklin	Brookville	22,151	1811	Benjamin Franklin, an inventor and a leader in the American Revolution
Fulton	Rochester	20,511	1836	Robert Fulton, an American engineer and inventor who built the first moneymaking steamboat
Gibson	Princeton	32,500	1813	John Gibson, a governor of the Indiana Territory
Grant	Marion	73,403	1832	Samuel and Moses Grant of Kentucky
Greene	Bloomfield	33,157	1821	Nathanael Greene, an officer in the American Revolution
Hamilton	Noblesville	182,740	1823	Alexander Hamilton, a leader in the American Revolution and the first U.S. Secretary of the Treasury
Hancock	Greenfield	55,391	1828	John Hancock, the first signer of the Declaration of Independence
Harrison	Corydon	34,325	1808	William Henry Harrison, the first governor of the Indiana Territory and, later, a President of the United States
Hendricks	Danville	104,093	1824	William Hendricks, a governor of Indiana
Henry	New Castle	48,508	1822	Patrick Henry, a leader in the American Revolution
Howard	Kokomo	84,964	1844	Tilghman Howard, an Indiana congressional representative
Huntington	Huntington	38,075	1834	Samuel Huntington, a Connecticut delegate to the Continental Congress and a signer of the Declaration of Independence
Jackson	Brownstown	41,335	1816	Andrew Jackson, a hero of the War of 1812 and, later, a President of the United States
Jasper	Rensselaer	30,043	1838	William Jasper, a soldier in the American Revolution
Jay	Portland	21,806	1836	John Jay, the first chief justice of the United States Supreme Court
Jefferson	Madison	31,705	1811	Thomas Jefferson, author of the Declaration of Independence and later, a President of the United States
Jennings	Vernon	27,554	1817	Jonathan Jennings, the first governor of Indiana
Johnson	Franklin	115,209	1823	John Johnson, an Indiana supreme court justice
Knox	Vincennes	39,256	1790	Henry Knox, an officer in the American Revolution and the first U.S. Secretary of War
Kosciusko	Warsaw	74,057	1837	Thaddeus Kosciusko, a Polish patriot and an officer in the American Revolution
Lagrange	Lagrange	34,909	1832	The Marquis de Lafayette's country home near Paris, France

County Name	County Seat	Population*	Year Organized	Named For
Lake	Crown Point	484,564	1837	Lake Michigan
La Porte	La Porte	110,106	1832	French for "the door"
Lawrence	Bedford	45,922	1818	James Lawrence, a hero of the War of 1812
Madison	Anderson	133,358	1823	James Madison, a President of the United States
Marion	Indianapolis	860,454	1822	Francis Marion, a hero of the American Revolution
Marshall	Plymouth	45,128	1836	John Marshall, a chief justice of the United States Supreme Court
Martin	Shoals	10,369	1820	Major John T. Martin of Kentucky; or Major Thomas Martin of Kentucky
Miami	Peru	36,082	1834	Miami Indians
Monroe	Bloomington	120,563	1813	James Monroe, a President of the United States
Montgomery	Crawfordsville	37,629	1823	Richard Montgomery, an officer in the American Revolution
Morgan	Martinsville	66,689	1822	Daniel Morgan, a soldier in the American Revolution
Newton	Kentland	14,566	1859	John Newton, a soldier in the American Revolution
Noble	Albion	46,275	1836	James Noble, a U.S. Senator from Indiana
Ohio	Rising Sun	5,623	1844	Ohio River
Orange	Paoli	19,306	1816	Prince William IV of Orange; or Orange County, North Carolina
Owen	Spencer	21,786	1819	Abraham Owen, a hero of the Battle of Tippecanoe
Parke	Rockville	17,241	1821	Benjamin Parke, an Indiana Territory delegate to Congress
Perry	Tell City	18,889	1814	Oliver Hazard Perry, a hero of the War of 1812
Pike	Petersburg	12,837	1817	Zebulon M. Pike, an officer in the War of 1812 and an American explorer
Porter	Valparaiso	146,798	1836	David Porter, an officer in the War of 1812
Posey	Mount Vernon	27,061	1814	Thomas Posey, a governor of the Indiana Territory
Pulaski	Winamac	13,755	1822	Casimir Pulaski, a Polish patriot and an officer in the American Revolution
Putnam	Greencastle	36,019	1822	Israel and Rufus Putnam, officers in the American Revolution
Randolph	Winchester	27,401	1818	Thomas Randolph, an Indiana politician and soldier killed in the Battle of Tippecanoe; or Randolph County, North Carolina
Ripley	Versailles	26,523	1818	Eleazar Wheelock Ripley, an officer in the War of 1812

*2000 U.S. Census figures

County Name	County Seat	Population*	Year Organized	Named For
Rush	Rushville	18,261	1822	Benjamin Rush, a physician and a signer of the Declaration of Independence
St. Joseph	South Bend	265,559	1830	Joseph, the patron saint of New France; or St. Joseph River
Scott	Scottsburg	22,960	1820	Charles Scott, an officer in the American Revolution and a governor of Kentucky
Shelby	Shelbyville	43,445	1822	Isaac Shelby, a governor of Kentucky
Spencer	Rockport	20,391	1818	Spier Spencer, a hero of the Battle of Tippecanoe
Starke	Knox	23,556	1850	John Stark, an officer in the French and Indian War and in the American Revolution
Steuben	Angola	33,214	1837	Friedrich von Steuben, a German patriot and a trainer of soldiers in the American Revolution
Sullivan	Sullivan	21,751	1817	Daniel Sullivan, a soldier in the American Revolution
Switzerland	Vevay	9,065	1814	Country of Switzerland
Tippecanoe	Lafayette	148,955	1826	Battle of Tippecanoe; or Tippecanoe River
Tipton	Tipton	16,577	1844	John Tipton, a soldier in the Battle of Tippecanoe and a U.S. Senator from Indiana
Union	Liberty	7,349	1821	The union of parts of Wayne, Franklin, and Fayette counties to form the county; or Union, an early town in the area
Vanderburgh	Evansville	171,922	1818	Henry Vanderburgh, a Revolutionary War soldier and Indiana Territory judge
Vermillion	Newport	16,788	1824	Big Vermillion River
Vigo	Terre Haute	105,848	1818	Francis Vigo, a supplier of money and goods for the American Revolution
Wabash	Wabash	34,960	1835	Wabash River
Warren	Williamsport	8,419	1827	Joseph Warren, an officer in the American Revolution
Warrick	Boonville	52,383	1813	Jacob Warrick, a hero of the Battle of Tippecanoe
Washington	Salem	27,223	1814	George Washington, Revolutionary War leader and the first President of the United States
Wayne	Richmond	71,097	1811	Anthony Wayne, an officer in the American Revolution and at the Battle of Fallen Timbers, and a signer of the Treaty of Greenville
Wells	Bluffton	27,600	1837	William A. Wells, a scout for Anthony Wayne
White	Monticello	25,267	1834	Isaac White, an officer at the Battle of Tippecanoe
Whitley	Columbia City	30,707	1839	William Whitley of Kentucky

Almanac

Facts About Indiana Governors

Governors of the Indiana Territory

Governor	(birth/death)	Place of Birth	Political Party	Term
William Henry Harrison	(1773–1841)	Berkeley, Virginia		1800–1812
John Gibson	(1740–1822)	Lancaster, Pennsylvania	Democratic-Republican	1812–1813
Thomas Posey	(1750–1818)	Alexandria, Virginia	Democratic-Republican	1813–1816

Governors of the State of Indiana

Governor	(birth/death)	Place of Birth	Political Party	Term
Jonathan Jennings	(1787–1834)	Hunterdon County, New Jersey	Democratic-Republican	1816–1822
Ratliff Boon	(1781–1844)	Franklin County, North Carolina	Democratic-Republican	1822
William Hendricks	(1782–1850)	Ligonier, Pennsylvania	Democratic-Republican	1822–1825
James Brown Ray	(1794–1848)	Jefferson County, Kentucky	Independent	1825–1831
Noah Noble	(1794–1844)	Clarke County, Virginia	Whig	1831–1837
David Wallace	(1799–1859)	Mifflin County, Pennsylvania	Whig	1837–1840
Samuel Bigger	(1802–1846)	Warren County, Ohio	Whig	1840–1843
James Whitcomb	(1795–1852)	Windsor, Vermont	Democratic	1843–1848
Paris C. Dunning	(1806–1884)	Greensboro, North Carolina	Democratic	1848–1849
Joseph A. Wright	(1810–1867)	Washington, Pennsylvania	Democratic	1849–1857
Ashbel P. Willard	(1820–1860)	Oneida County, New York	Democratic	1857–1860
Abram A. Hammond	(1814–1874)	Brattleboro, Vermont	Democratic	1860–1861
Henry S. Lane	(1811–1881)	Bath County, Kentucky	Republican	1861
Oliver P. Morton	(1823–1877)	Salisbury, Indiana	Republican	1861–1867
Conrad Baker	(1817–1885)	Franklin County, Pennsylvania	Republican	1867–1873
Thomas A. Hendricks	(1819–1885)	Zanesville, Ohio	Democratic	1873–1877
James D. Williams	(1808–1880)	Pickaway County, Ohio	Democratic	1877–1880
Isaac P. Gray	(1828–1895)	Chester County, Pennsylvania	Democratic	1880–1881
Albert G. Porter	(1824–1897)	Lawrenceburg, Indiana	Republican	1881–1885

Governor	(birth/death)	Place of Birth	Political Party	Term
Isaac P. Gray	(1828–1895)	Chester County, Pennsylvania	Democratic	1885–1889
Alvin P. Hovey	(1821–1891)	Mount Vernon, Indiana	Republican	1889–1891
Ira J. Chase	(1834–1895)	Clarkson, New York	Republican	1891–1893
Claude Matthews	(1845–1898)	Bath County, Kentucky	Democratic	1893–1897
James A. Mount	(1843–1901)	Montgomery County, Indiana	Republican	1897–1901
Winfield T. Durbin	(1847–1928)	Lawrenceburg, Indiana	Republican	1901–1905
J. Frank Hanly	(1863–1920)	St. Joseph, Illinois	Republican	1905–1909
Thomas R. Marshall	(1854–1925)	North Manchester, Indiana	Democratic	1909–1913
Samuel M. Ralston	(1857–1925)	Tuscarawas County, Ohio	Democratic	1913–1917
James P. Goodrich	(1864–1940)	Winchester, Indiana	Republican	1917–1921
Warren T. McCray	(1865–1938)	Kentland, Indiana	Republican	1921–1924
Emmett Forrest Branch	(1874–1932)	Martinsville, Indiana	Republican	1924–1925
Edward L. Jackson	(1873–1954)	Howard County, Indiana	Republican	1925–1929
Harry G. Leslie	(1878–1937)	West Lafayette, Indiana	Republican	1929–1933
Paul V. McNutt	(1891–1955)	Franklin, Indiana	Democratic	1933–1937
M. Clifford Townsend	(1884–1954)	Blackford County, Indiana	Democratic	1937–1941
Henry F. Schricker	(1883–1966)	North Judson, Indiana	Democratic	1941–1945
Ralph F. Gates	(1893–1978)	Columbia City, Indiana	Republican	1945–1949
Henry F. Schricker	(1883–1966)	North Judson, Indiana	Democratic	1949–1953
George N. Craig	(1909–1992)	Brazil, Indiana	Republican	1953–1957
Harold W. Handley	(1909–1972)	La Porte, Indiana	Republican	1957–1961
Matthew E. Welsh	(1912–1995)	Detroit, Michigan	Democratic	1961–1965
Roger D. Branigin	(1902–1975)	Franklin, Indiana	Democratic	1965–1969
Edgar D. Whitcomb	(1917–)	Hayden, Indiana	Republican	1969–1973
Otis R. Bowen	(1918–)	Rochester, Indiana	Republican	1973–1981
Robert D. Orr	(1917–)	Evansville, Indiana	Republican	1981–1989
Evan Bayh	(1955–)	Terre Haute, Indiana	Democratic	1989–1997
Frank O'Bannon	(1930–)	Louisville, Kentucky	Democratic	1997–

Biographical Dictionary

The Biographical Dictionary lists many of the important people introduced in this book. The page number tells where the main discussion of each person starts. Also listed are some other famous Hoosiers you might like to know about. See the Index for other page references.

A

Ade, George *1866–1944* Newspaper writer and essayist born in Kentland. He worked for the *Chicago Record*. p. 239

Alford, Steve *1964–* Basketball player and coach from Franklin. He played for Indiana University from 1984 to 1987 and now coaches basketball at the University of Iowa.

B

Ball brothers Edmund, William, Lucius, George, and Frank Ball owned one of the nation's largest glassmaking factories, in Muncie. They gave money to start Ball State University. p. 185

Baxter, Anne *1923–1985* Academy Award-winning motion picture actor from Michigan City.

Bayh, Birch *1928–* U.S. Senator from Indiana who served in Congress from 1963 to 1981. p. 277

Bayh, Evan *1955–* Indiana governor from 1989 to 1997 and U.S. Senator since 1999. He is the son of Birch Bayh. p. 277

Bird, Larry *1956–* Professional basketball player from French Lick. He was the National Basketball Association's Most Valuable Player three years in a row, from 1984 to 1986. p. 241

Blass, Bill *1922–* Fashion designer from Fort Wayne.

Blue Jacket *mid-1700s–1810* Shawnee leader defeated at the Battle of Fallen Timbers. p. 123

Bolton, Sarah *1814–1893* Indianapolis poet who became well known for her popular poem "Paddle Your Own Canoe." p. 239

Borman, Frank *1928–* Astronaut from Gary. He orbited the moon in *Apollo 8* in 1968. p. 212

Buell, Dorothy *1886–1977* Environmental activist who campaigned for the creation of the Indiana Dunes National Lakeshore. p. 282

C

Carmichael, Hoagy (KAR•my•kuhl, HOH•gee) *1899–1981* Songwriter from Bloomington. p. 240

Carson, Julia *1938–* U.S. Representative who became the first woman and African American to be elected to Congress from Indianapolis, in 1996. p. 279

Chapman, John *1774–1845* Pioneer who traveled through the Middle West planting apple seeds and tending apple orchards. He is known to most as Johnny Appleseed.

Clark, George Rogers *1752–1818* Leader of the American forces that defeated the British at Fort Sackville (Vincennes) during the American Revolution. This victory helped the Americans gain control of the Northwest Territory. p. 111

Coffin, Catharine *1803–1881* One of Indiana's best-known stationmasters on the Underground Railroad and wife of Levi Coffin. p. 178

Coffin, Levi *1798–1877* One of Indiana's best-known stationmasters on the Underground Railroad and husband of Catharine Coffin. p. 178

Colfax, Schuyler *1823–1885* Vice President from South Bend. He served under President Ulysses S. Grant from 1869 to 1873. p. 277

Conner, William *1777–1855* Pioneer in central Indiana. Today his settlement, Conner Prairie, is a living history museum. p. 169

D

Davis, Jim *1945–* Artist from Marion. He created the comic strip "Garfield." p. 240

Dean, James *1931–1955* Motion picture actor born in Marion. p. 241

Debs, Eugene V. *1855–1926* Railroad union leader from Terre Haute. He ran for President in 1900, 1904, 1908, 1912, and 1920. p. 196

Dreiser, Theodore *1871–1945* Author from Terre Haute and brother of Paul Dresser. Paul Americanized the family name. p. 239

Dresser, Paul *1859–1906* Songwriter from Terre Haute. He wrote "On the Banks of the Wabash, Far Away," Indiana's state song. p. 239

E

Erskine, Carl *1926–* Professional baseball player from Anderson. p. 241

F

Fairbanks, Charles W. *1852–1918* Vice President from Indianapolis. He served under President Theodore Roosevelt from 1905 to 1909. p. 277

Forsyth, William *1854–1935* Artist from Indianapolis. He helped start the Herron School of Art in Indianapolis, Indiana's oldest and largest art school. p. 240

Fox, Vivica A. *1964–* Television and motion picture actor from Indianapolis.

Fraser, Brendan *1968–* Motion picture actor from Indianapolis. p. 241

Gary, Elbert H. *1846–1927* Head of the United States Steel Corporation when the company built a mill and town in the Calumet region. The city of Gary is named for him. p. 187

Gordon, Jeff *1971–* Race car driver from Pittsboro. p. 240

Griese, Bob *1945–* Professional football player and television sports analyst from Evansville.

Grissom, Virgil ("Gus") *1926–1967* Astronaut from Mitchell. He was the second American in space. p. 212

Hall, Katie Beatrice *1938–* First African American woman from Indiana elected to the U.S. Congress. She was one of several members of Congress who introduced the bill that made the birthday of Dr. Martin Luther King, Jr., a federal holiday.

Hamilton, Henry *1734?–1796* British general who was defeated at Fort Sackville by George Rogers Clark in the American Revolution. p. 111

Harrison, Benjamin *1833–1901* Twenty-third President of the United States. He fought in the Civil War. Later, as President, he helped Civil War veterans get payments from the government. p. 276

Harrison, William Henry *1773–1841* Ninth President of the United States. Earlier he led American soldiers at the Battle of Tippecanoe. He was also a commander in the War of 1812 and the first governor of the Indiana Territory. p. 126

Harroun, Ray *1879–1968* Winner of the first Indianapolis 500 automobile race, in 1911. p. 195

Hatcher, Richard *1933–* Mayor of Gary from 1968 to 1988. He was one of the first African Americans elected as mayor of a large United States city. p. 212

Hawks, Howard *1896–1977* Motion picture director from Goshen. p. 241

Haynes, Elwood *1857–1925* Inventor from Kokomo. He test-drove one of the first automobiles. p. 194

Henderson, Florence *1934–* Singer and television actor from Dale. p. 241

Hendricks, Thomas *1819–1885* Vice President from Indianapolis. He served under President Grover Cleveland in 1885. p. 277

Indiana, Robert *1928–* Artist from New Castle. p. 240

J

Jackson, Janet *1966–* Musician from Gary. p. 240

Jackson, Michael *1958–* Musician from Gary. p. 240

Jenckes, Virginia Ellis *1877–1975* First Indiana woman in the U.S. House of Representatives, elected in 1932. She was from Terre Haute. p. 278

Jennings, Jonathan *1784–1834* First governor of the state of Indiana. He was one of the main writers of the state constitution in 1816. p. 134

K

Kelley, Oliver H. *1826–1913* Founder of the Grange organization for farmers.

Kernan, Joseph E. *1946–* Lieutenant Governor of Indiana since 1997. p. 264

Kinnear, Greg *1963–* Motion picture actor from Logansport.

L

La Salle, René-Robert Cavelier, Sieur de (luh•SAL) *1643–1687* First European to reach what is now Indiana. He also explored the Mississippi River valley and claimed the land for France. p. 95

Larsen, Don *1929–* Professional baseball player from Michigan City. He threw the only perfect game in World Series history, for the New York Yankees in 1956. p. 241

Letterman, David *1947–* Television host and comedian from Indianapolis. p. 241

Lilly, Eli *1838–1898* Business leader in Indianapolis. The pharmaceutical company he started in 1876 became one of the world's largest. p. 188

Lincoln, Abraham *1809–1865* Sixteenth President of the United States. He grew up in Indiana. p. 158

Little Turtle *1752–1812* Chief of the Miamis who defeated American soldiers at Kekionga in 1791. p. 123

Lombard, Carole *1908–1942* Motion picture actor from Fort Wayne.

Long, Shelley *1949–* Television and motion picture actor from Fort Wayne. p. 241

Lugar, Richard *1932–* U.S. Senator from Indiana and former mayor of Indianapolis. p. 277

M

Malden, Karl *1912–* Academy Award-winning motion picture actor from Gary.

Marshall, Thomas *1854–1925* Vice President from North Manchester. He served under President Woodrow Wilson from 1913 to 1921. p. 277

Mattingly, Don *1961–* Professional baseball player from Evansville. p. 241

McCormick, Cyrus *1809–1884* Inventor of a reaping machine for harvesting wheat. p. 170

McNutt, Paul V. *1891–1955* Governor of Indiana during the Great Depression. p. 205

Mellencamp, John *1951–* Musician from Seymour. p. 240

Morgan, John Hunt *1825–1864* Confederate general who led soldiers into southern Indiana during the Civil War. p. 180

Morton, Oliver P. *1823–1877* Governor of Indiana during the Civil War. p. 179

N

Nelson, Julia D. *1863–1936* Politician from Mooresville. In 1920 she became the first woman to be elected to the Indiana state legislature. p. 203

O

O'Bannon, Frank *1930–* Governor of Indiana since 1997. p. 262

Oliver, James *1823–1908* Inventor of the chilled-iron plow. He owned the largest plow factory in Indiana. p. 171

Owen, Robert *1771–1858* Wealthy entrepreneur. He bought the community of Harmonie from George Rapp in 1824 and renamed it New Harmony. p. 162

P

Pauley, Jane *1950–* Television newscaster from Indianapolis. p. 241

Perry, Oliver Hazard *1785–1819* Commander of the U.S. naval fleet that defeated British forces in the Battle of Lake Erie during the War of 1812.

Pontiac *1720–1769* Ottawa chief who led Indian attacks on British forts in 1763. p. 105

Porter, Cole *1891–1964* Songwriter from Peru, Indiana. Many of his songs were written for musical shows. p. 240

Pyle, Ernest Taylor *1900–1945* Newspaper reporter from Dana. He wrote about the experiences of soldiers in World War II. p. 209

Q

Quayle, J. Danforth *1947–* Vice President from Huntington. He served under President George Bush from 1989 to 1993. p. 277

R

Ralston, Alexander *1771–1827* Surveyor of the site selected for Indiana's capital, Indianapolis, in 1821. p. 138

Rapp, George *1757–1847* Minister who, with his followers, started the community of Harmonie in 1814. p. 161

Redenbacher, Orville (RED•uhn•bah•ker) *1907–1995* Entrepreneur born in Brazil, Indiana. He began one of the most successful popcorn businesses in the United States.

Richardson, Jr., Henry J. *1902–1983* African American lawyer who worked to end segregation in Indiana's schools. p. 211

Riley, James Whitcomb *1849–1916* Known as the Hoosier Poet. He wrote more than 1,000 poems about the state he loved, Indiana. He was born in Greenfield and lived in Indianapolis. p. 239

Robertson, Oscar *1938–* Basketball player from Indianapolis. He was co-captain of the 1960 Olympic basketball team and was a star in the National Basketball Association. p. 240

Rockne, Knute (RAHK•nee, NOOT) *1888–1931* Coach of the University of Notre Dame football team in the early 1900s. p. 241

Rudolph, Wilma *1940–1994* Olympic track and field champion. She won three gold medals at the 1960 Olympics. p. 241

S

St. Clair, Arthur *1736–1818* First governor of the Northwest Territory. p. 121

Sanders, "Colonel" Harland *1890–1980* Entrepreneur born in Henryville. He started the famous Kentucky Fried Chicken fast-food restaurants.

Scudder, Janet *1869–1940* Sculptor from Terre Haute. p. 240

Sewall, May Wright *1844–1920* Leader from Indianapolis who worked to help women gain the right to vote. p. 203

Skelton, Red *1913–1997* Comedian and actor from Vincennes. p. 241

Slocum, Frances *1773–1847* Pioneer who lived most of her life with the Delawares. p. 129

Spitz, Mark *1950–* Swimming champion at Indiana University. He won seven gold medals at the 1972 Olympic Games in Munich. p. 241

Steele, Theodore C. *1847–1926* Artist from Owen County. He painted nine of the portraits in the Governors' Portraits Collection. p. 240

Stratton-Porter, Geneva *1863–1924* Author whose books show her love of nature and geography. She is known to most as Gene Stratton-Porter. p. 44

Studebaker brothers Clement and Henry Studebaker were wagonmakers from South Bend. They later became leading manufacturers of automobiles. p. 194

T

Tarkington, Booth *1869–1946* Author who described life in Indianapolis. Some of his books were written for young people. p. 239

Taylor, "Major" Marshall *1878–1932* Bicyclist from Indianapolis. He was one of the best-known African American athletes at the beginning of the 1900s. p. 241

Tecumseh (tuh•KUM•suh) *1768–1813* Shawnee leader of Native Americans in the Northwest Territory. He wanted to form a strong Indian confederation. p. 128

Tenskwatawa (ten•SKWAHT•uh•wah) *1768–1834* Shawnee leader known as the Prophet. He worked with his brother Tecumseh. p. 128

Tharp, Twyla *1941–* Dancer and choreographer from Portland. p. 241

Tipton, John *1786–1839* Soldier and legislator. He fought in the Battle of Tippecanoe and later served in the U.S. Senate. Tipton County, Indiana, is named for him. p. 130

Urey, Harold C. *1893–1981* Scientist from Walkerton. He was awarded the Nobel Prize for Chemistry in 1934.

Vonnegut, Jr., Kurt *1922–* Author from Indianapolis. p. 239

Voss, Janice E. *1956–* Astronaut from South Bend. p. 213

Walker, Madam C. J. *1867–1919* African American entrepreneur from Louisiana. She started her own business in Indianapolis making hair care products for women. She became one of the country's wealthiest women. p. 188

Wallace, Lewis *1827–1905* Author from Brookville. He was also a Civil War general. p. 181

Wariner, Steve *1954–* Musician and songwriter from Noblesville.

Wayne, Anthony *1745–1796* General of the U.S. Army. He led the victory over the Miamis at the Battle of Fallen Timbers in 1794. He was known to his soldiers as "Mad Anthony." p. 123

Webster, Marie *1859–1956* Quilter from Wabash. p. 240

White, Ryan *1971–1990* High school student who died of AIDS. Before his death in Cicero, he worked to educate people about the disease.

Willkie, Wendell L. *1892–1944* Candidate for President in 1940. The Elwood citizen lost the election to Franklin D. Roosevelt. p. 276

Wise, Robert *1914–* Academy Award-winning motion picture director and editor from Winchester. p. 241

Wolf, David *1956–* Astronaut from Indianapolis. p. 213

Wooden, John *1910–* Former basketball player and coach from Martinsville. He played at Purdue University and became the basketball coach at the University of California, Los Angeles. p. 241

Wright brothers Orville and Wilbur Wright flew the first powered aircraft at Kitty Hawk, North Carolina, in 1903. Wilbur was born on a farm near Millville. p. 204

BIOGRAPHICAL DICTIONARY

Gazetteer

The Gazetteer is a geographical dictionary that will help you locate places discussed in this book. The page number tells where each place appears on a map.

A

Anderson The county seat of Madison County, in eastern Indiana. (40°N, 86°W) p. 186

Angel Mounds A historic site in southwestern Indiana, near Evansville, with earthworks constructed by Mound Builders about 1,000 years ago. (38°N, 87°W) p. 56

Angola (an•GOH•luh) The county seat of Steuben County, in northeastern Indiana. (42°N, 85°W) p. 14

Appalachian Mountains Mountains in eastern North America that served as the boundary for the Proclamation Line of 1763, west of which the settlers were not supposed to go. p. 107

B

Bedford A city in southern Indiana, near Bluespring Caverns; the county seat of Lawrence County. (39°N, 86°W) p. 31

Big Blue River A tributary of the East Fork of the White River. p. 14

Bloomington The county seat of Monroe County, in south-central Indiana; home of Indiana University. (39°N, 87°W) p. 27

Blue River A river in southern Indiana and a tributary of the Ohio River. p. 35

Bluespring Caverns A cavern in southern Indiana; one of the longest underground rivers in the United States flows through this cavern. (39°N, 86°W) p. 31

Bridgeton A town in Parke County, in western Indiana. (39°N, 87°W) p. 164

Brookville The county seat of Franklin County, in southeastern Indiana. (39°N, 85°W) p. A16

Brookville Lake A large lake in southeastern Indiana. p. 14

Brownsburg A town in Hendricks County, in central Indiana. (40°N, 86°W) p. A16

C

Cagles Mill Lake A large lake in south-central Indiana. p. 14

Carmel A town in Hamilton County, in central Indiana. (40°N, 86°W) p. 252

Central Till Plain A natural region of flat, fertile land in the central part of Indiana. p. 27

Charlestown A city in Clark County, in southern Indiana. (38°N, 86°W) p. 14

Clarksville A town in Clark County, in southern Indiana. (38°N, 86°W) p. 127

Clifty Falls State Park A state park in southeastern Indiana, near Madison. p. 37

Columbia City The county seat of Whitley County, in northeastern Indiana. (41°N, 85°W) p. 14

Columbus The county seat of Bartholomew County, in south-central Indiana. (39°N, 86°W) p. 41

Connersville The county seat of Fayette County, in eastern Indiana. (40°N, 85°W) p. 41

Corydon The county seat of Harrison County, in southern Indiana; capital of Indiana Territory, 1813–1816; capital of Indiana until 1825. (38°N, 86°W) p. 127

Crawfordsville The county seat of Montgomery County, in west-central Indiana. (40°N, 87°W) p. 249

D

Decatur (dih•KAY•tuhr) The county seat of Adams County, in eastern Indiana. (41°N, 85°W) p. 41

E

East Fork of the White River A tributary of the White River. p. 35

Eel River A tributary of the White River. p. 35

Elkhart A city in Elkhart County, in northern Indiana. (42°N, 86°W) p. 14

Elwood A city in Madison County, in central Indiana. (40°N, 86°W) p. 186

Evansville The county seat of Vanderburgh County, in southwestern Indiana; located on the Ohio River. (38°N, 88°W) p. 25

F

Falls of the Ohio An area of rapids on the Ohio River near where Louisville, Kentucky, and Jeffersonville, Indiana, are now located. (38°N, 86°W) p. 112

Fishers A city in Hamilton County, in central Indiana. (40°N, 86°W) p. 252

Flatrock River A tributary of the East Fork of the White River. p. 14

Fontanet A town in Vigo County, in western Indiana. (40°N, 87°W) p. 14

Fort Detroit A British fort in present-day Michigan, captured by the Americans in the Revolutionary War. (42°N, 83°W) p. 112

Fort Greenville American fort in present-day Ohio; built by General Anthony Wayne in 1793. (40°N, 84°W) p. 133

Fort Harrison A fort built on the Wabash River, near what is now Terre Haute. (39°N, 87°W) p. 127

Fort Miami An early trading post and fort built by the French in 1721, near present-day Fort Wayne. (41°N, 85°W) p. 103

Fort Ouiatenon (wee•AHT•uh•nohn) The first French trading post in Indiana; it was built in 1717 near present-day Lafayette. (40°N, 87°W) p. 105

Fort Sackville The name given to the fort at Vincennes after it was captured by the British during the American Revolution. (39°N, 88°W) p. 112

Fort St. Joseph An early fort built near present-day South Bend. (42°N, 86°W) p. 105

Fort Wayne The county seat of Allen County, in northeastern Indiana; site of the early Miami Indian settlement called Kekionga. (41°N, 85°W) p. 25

Fountain City A town in Wayne County, in eastern Indiana; the site of the Levi Coffin home, which was part of the Underground Railroad. (40°N, 85°W) p. 177

Frankfort The county seat of Clinton County, in central Indiana. (40°N, 87°W) p. 14

Franklin The county seat of Johnson County, in central Indiana. (39°N, 86°W) p. 252

French Lick A town in Orange County, in southern Indiana. (39°N, 87°W) p. 31

Gary A city in Lake County, in northwestern Indiana; located on Lake Michigan. (42°N, 87°W) p. 25

Gas City A city in Grant County, in central Indiana. (40°N, 86°W) p. 186

Goshen The county seat of Elkhart County, in northern Indiana. (42°N, 86°W) p. 41

Great Lakes Plain A broad, lowland plain covering the northern one-third of Indiana. p. 27

Greencastle The county seat of Putnam County, in west-central Indiana. (40°N, 87°W) p. A16

Greenwood A city in Johnson County, in central Indiana. (40°N, 86°W) p. 252

Hammond A city in Lake County, in northwestern Indiana. (42°N, 87°W) p. 41

Hardy Lake A lake in southeast Indiana. p. 33

Hoosier National Forest A national forest in southern Indiana; the state's largest forest. p. 43

Huntington The county seat of Huntington County, in northeast Indiana. (41°N, 85°W) p. 41

Huntington Lake A large lake in northern Indiana, formed by a dam built across the Wabash River. p. 14

Illinois The state to the west of Indiana. p. 159

Indiana Dunes National Lakeshore A national park in northwestern Indiana on the shore of Lake Michigan. p. 28

Indianapolis The state capital of Indiana since 1825, and the state's largest city; the county seat of Marion County, in central Indiana. (40°N, 86°W) p. 25

Indianapolis Museum of Art Ravine Garden A part of the 26-acre estate located on the grounds of the Museum of Art. (40°N, 86°W) p. 19

Indiana Territory Part of the Northwest Territory that was divided in 1800, originally including the present-day states of Indiana, Illinois, parts of Michigan and Wisconsin. p. 133

Iroquois River (IR•uh•kwoy) A river that begins in northwestern Indiana and flows into the Kankakee River, in Illinois. p. 35

Jasper The county seat of Dubois County, in southwestern Indiana. (38°N, 87°W) p. 14

Jeffersonville The county seat of Clark County, in southeastern Indiana, across the Ohio River from Louisville, Kentucky. (38°N, 86°W) p. 243

Kankakee River (kahng•kuh•KEE) A large river that begins in northern Indiana and flows southwest into Illinois. p. 33

Kekionga (kee•kee•ohn•GUH) A settlement built by the Miamis at the headwaters of the Maumee River, where the city of Fort Wayne is today. (41°N, 85°W) p. 67

Kendallville A city in Noble County, in northeastern Indiana. (41°N, 85°W) p. 14

Kentucky The state to the south of Indiana. p. 159

Kokomo (KOH•kuh•moh) The county seat of Howard County, in north-central Indiana. (40°N, 86°W) p. 186

La Crosse A town in La Porte County, in northern Indiana. (41°N, 87°W) p. 14

La Porte The county seat of La Porte County, in northern Indiana. (42°N, 87°W) p. 14

Lafayette (lah•fee•ET) The county seat of Tippecanoe County, in west-central Indiana; home of Purdue University. (40°N, 87°W) p. 25

Lake Erie One of the five Great Lakes. p. 95

Lake Freeman A lake in northern Indiana, formed by a dam built across the Tippecanoe River. p. 14

Lake Huron One of the five Great Lakes. p. 95

Lake Manitou (MAN•uh•too) A lake in Fulton County, in northern Indiana. p. A17

Lake Michigan One of the five Great Lakes; forms part of Indiana's northern border. p. 25

Lake Ontario One of the five Great Lakes. p. 95

Lake Shafer A lake in White County, in northwestern Indiana; formed by a dam built across the Tippecanoe River. p. 14

Lake Superior One of the five Great Lakes. p. 95

Lake Wawasee (wah•wuh•SEE) A large lake in Kosciusko County, in northern Indiana. p. 33

GAZETTEER

Lawrence A city in Marion County, in central Indiana. (40°N, 86°W) p. 252

Lawrenceburg The county seat of Dearborn County, in southeastern Indiana; located on the Ohio River. (39°N, 85°W) p. 41

Lebanon The county seat of Boone County, in central Indiana. (40°N, 86°W). p. 252

Little Pigeon Creek A tributary of the Ohio River; Abraham Lincoln's family settled there. p. 159

Logansport The county seat of Cass County, in north-central Indiana. (41°N, 86°W) p. 167

Lost River A tributary of the East Fork of the White River; it flows underground for several miles. p. 31

Louisiana Territory Name given to land claimed by the French in 1682, including the entire Mississippi River valley and lands drained by its tributaries. p. 103

Lyons A town in Greene County, in southwestern Indiana. (39°N, 87°W) p. 25

M

Madison The county seat of Jefferson County, in southeastern Indiana; located on the Ohio River. (39°N, 85°W) p. 167

Marengo Cave A cave in south-central Indiana. p. 14

Marion The county seat of Grant County, in north-central Indiana. (41°N, 86°W) p. 186

Martinsville The county seat of Morgan County, in central Indiana. (39°N, 86°W) p. 252

Maumee River (maw•MEE) A river that begins in northeastern Indiana and flows into the state of Ohio. p. 33

Metamora A town in Franklin County, in southeastern Indiana. (39°N, 85°W) p. 162

Michigan The state to the north of Indiana. p. 95

Michigan City A city in La Porte County, in northern Indiana; located on Lake Michigan. (42°N, 87°W) p. 41

Midland A city in Greene County, in southwestern Indiana. (39°N, 87°W) p. 25

Mississinewa Lake (mih•sih•SIH•nuh•weh) A lake in northern Indiana; formed by a dam built across the Mississinewa River. p. 14

Mississinewa River (mih•sih•SIH•nuh•weh) A tributary of the Wabash River. p. 14

Mississippi River A large river flowing north to south in the central United States. p. 95

Mitchell A city in Lawrence County, in southern Indiana. (39°N, 87°W) p. 14

Monroe Lake A large lake in southern Indiana, formed by a dam built across a tributary of the East Fork of the White River. p. 14

Monticello (mahnt•uh•SEL•oh) The county seat of White County, in northwestern Indiana; located on the Tippecanoe River. (41°N, 87°W) p. 27

Morse Reservoir A large reservoir in central Indiana; formed by a dam built across a tributary of the East Fork of the White River. p. 33

Moscow A town in Rush County, in east-central Indiana. (39°N, 86°W) p. 25

Mt. Vernon The county seat of Posey County, in southwestern Indiana; located on the Ohio River where the Wabash River empties into it. (38°N, 88°W) p. 36

Muncie The county seat of Delaware County, in east-central Indiana; home of Ball State University. (40°N, 85°W) p. 27

Muscatatuck River (muhs•kuh•TAH•tuck) A tributary of the East Fork of the White River. p. 14

N

Napoleon (nuh•POH•lee•uhn) A town in Ripley County, in southeastern Indiana. (39°N, 85°W) p. 14

New Albany The county seat of Floyd County, in southern Indiana; located on the Ohio River, across from Louisville, Kentucky. (38°N, 86°W) p. 41

New Harmony A town in Posey County, in southwestern Indiana. (38°N, 88°W) p. 14

Noblesville The county seat of Hamilton County, in central Indiana. (40°N, 86°W) p. 252

North America Continent in the Northern and Western Hemispheres. p. 22

Northwest Territory Name given to lands west of the Appalachians and north of the Ohio River. p. 121

O

Ohio The state to the east of Indiana. p. 95

Ohio River A large river that forms Indiana's southern border. p. 35

Ohio Territory Part of the Northwest Territory that was divided in 1800, originally including the present-day state of Ohio and part of Michigan. p. 133

Oldenburg A town in Franklin County, in eastern Indiana. (39°N, 85°W) p. 234

Orleans A town in Orange County, in southern Indiana. (39°N, 86°W) p. 31

P

Paoli (pay•OH•lee) The county seat of Orange County, in southern Indiana. (39°N, 86°W) p. 254

Patoka Lake (puh•TOH•kuh) A lake on the Patoka River in southern Indiana. p. 33

Patoka River (puh•TOH•kuh) A tributary of the Wabash River. p. 35

Peru The county seat of Miami County, in north-central Indiana; the location of the Grissom Air Museum. (41°N, 86°W) p. 192

Pigeon River A river in northeastern Indiana that flows into the more-northern of the St. Joseph Rivers. p. 33

Pioneer Mothers Memorial Forest A forest of old-growth trees in Orange County, in southern Indiana. p. 254

Plainfield A town in Hendricks County, in central Indiana. (40°N, 86°W) p. 252

Plymouth The county seat of Marshall County, in northern Indiana. (41°N, 86°W) p. 14

Portage A city in Porter County, in northern Indiana, on the shore of Lake Michigan. (42°N, 87°W) p. 218

Portland The county seat of Jay County, in eastern Indiana. (40°N, 85°W) p. 25

Proclamation Line of 1763 Boundary line in North America (Appalachian Mountains) set by King George III of Britain, west of which the settlers were not supposed to go. p. 107

Rensselaer (REN•suh•luhr) The county seat of Jasper County, in northwestern Indiana. (41°N, 87°W) p. 41

Richmond The county seat of Wayne County, in eastern Indiana. (40°N, 85°W) p. 25

Rochester The county seat of Fulton County, in northern Indiana. (41°N, 86°W) p. 14

Rushville The county seat of Rush County, in east-central Indiana. (40°N, 85°W) p. A16

St. Bernice A town in Vermillion County, in western Indiana. (40°N, 88°W) p. 14

St. Joseph River A river that flows across northern Indiana; one of two St. Joseph Rivers in Indiana. p. 35

St. Joseph River A river in eastern Indiana; a tributary of the Maumee River; one of two St. Joseph Rivers in Indiana. p. 35

St. Marys River A tributary of the Maumee River. p. 35

Salamonie Lake (SA•luh•moh•nee) A lake in northern Indiana, formed by a dam built across the Salamonie River. p. 33

Salamonie River (SA•luh•moh•nee) A tributary of the Wabash River. p. 35

Salem The county seat of Washington County, in southern Indiana. (39°N, 86°W) p. 14

Scottsburg The county seat of Scott County, in southeastern Indiana. (39°N, 86°W) p. 14

Shelbyville The county seat of Shelby County, in central Indiana. (40°N, 86°W) p. 167

Shoals (SHOHLZ) The county seat of Martin County, in southwestern Indiana. (39°N, 87°W) p. 14

South Bend The county seat of St. Joseph County, in northern Indiana; home of the University of Notre Dame. (42°N, 86°W) p. 25

Southern Hills and Lowlands A natural region that covers much of the southern part of Indiana. p. 27

Ten O'Clock Line A boundary line set by the Treaty of Fort Wayne in 1809 that separated United States lands from Native American lands. p. 127

Terre Haute (TER•uh HOHT) The county seat of Vigo County, in western Indiana; home of Indiana State University. (39°N, 87°W) p. 25

Tippecanoe River (tih•pee•kuh•NOO) A tributary of the Wabash River. p. 35

Tipton The county seat of Tipton County, in central Indiana. (40°N, 86°W) p. 270

Turtle Creek Lake A lake in west-central Indiana. p. 14.

United States Country in North America. p. 22

Versailles (vuhr•SAYLZ) The county seat of Ripley County, in southeastern Indiana. (39°N, 85°W) p. 25

Versailles State Park A state park in southeastern Indiana. p. 38

Vincennes (vin•SENZ) The county seat of Knox County, in southwestern Indiana; site of an early French fort and the first permanent European settlement in Indiana; capital of Indiana Territory until 1813. (39°N, 88°W) p. 106

Wabash (WAW•bash) The county seat of Wabash County, in northern Indiana. (41°N, 86°W) p. 27

Wabash River (WAW•bash) The longest river in Indiana; it flows west across the state from Ohio before turning south and forming part of the Indiana-Illinois border. p. 34

Warsaw The county seat of Kosciusko County, in northern Indiana. (41°N, 86°W) p. 41

Washington The county seat of Daviess County, in southwestern Indiana. (39°N, 87°W) p. 167

West Fork of the White River A branch of the White River that flows through the central part of Indiana. p. 112

White River A large river with two forks, the East Fork and the West Fork, that flows across south-central Indiana and is a tributary of the Wabash River. p. 35

Whitewater River A river in southeastern Indiana that flows into Ohio. p. 35

Wildcat Creek A tributary of the Wabash River. p. 33

Wyandotte Cave A cave in southern Indiana. p. 14

Glossary

The Glossary contains important social studies words and their definitions. Each word is respelled as it would be in a dictionary. When you see this mark ´ after a syllable, pronounce that syllable with more force than the other syllables. The page number at the end of the definition tells where to find the word in your book.

add, āce, câre, pälm; end, ēqual; it, īce; odd, ōpen, ôrder; tŏŏk, pōōl; up, bûrn; yōō as *u* in *fuse*; oil; pout; ə as *a* in *above*, *e* in *sicken*, *i* in *possible*, *o* in *melon*, *u* in *circus*; check; ring; thin; this; zh as in *vision*

A

abolitionist (ab•ə•li´shən•ist) A person who wanted to abolish, or end, slavery. p. 176

absolute location (ab´sə•lōōt lō•kā´shən) The exact position of a place on Earth. p. 24

agency (ā´jən•sē) A group of state officials who make sure that laws are obeyed. p. 264

ally (a´lī) A friend, especially in time of war. p. 103

amendment (ə•mend´mənt) An addition or change to the Constitution. p. 202

analyze (a´nəl•īz) To examine each part of something. p. 3

ancestor (an´ses•tər) An early family member; a person from whom another person has descended. p. 74

assemble (ə•sem´bəl) To gather in a group. p. 262

automobile (ô•tə•mə•bēl´) A vehicle that can move by itself, powered by its own engine; a car. p. 194

aviation (ā•vē•ā´shən) The making and flying of airplanes. p. 204

B

band (band) A small group of families who lived and worked together. p. 59

barge (bärj) A ship with a flat bed that carries items such as coal or grain in large containers. p. 247

bill (bil) A written plan for a new law. p. 264

Bill of Rights (bil uv rīts) The first ten amendments to the United States Constitution. p. 262

biosphere (bī´ō•sfir) All the plants and animals in the environment. p. 44

bonds (bonds) Documents that allow the government to use people's money for a certain amount of time and pay it back later. p. 201

boundary (boun´drē) An imaginary line forming the border of an area of land. p. 126

budget (buj´it) A plan for spending money. p. 264

C

canal (kə•nal´) A narrow human-made waterway. p. 166

cargo (kär´gō) Goods being shipped. p. 247

cause (kôz) An action that makes something else happen. p. 63

cavalry (ka´vəl•rē) A group of soldiers on horses. p. 179

census (sen´səs) An official government count of people. p. 127

centennial (sen•ten´ē•əl) The one-hundredth anniversary of a special event. p. 197

century (sen´chər•ē) A period of time lasting 100 years. p. 77

chronology (krə•näl´ə•jē) The order in which events take place. p. 2

citizen (sit´ə•zən) A member of a country, state, city, or town. p. 9

civic virtue (siv´ik vər´chōō) A good habit of citizenship. p. 283

civics (siv´iks) The study of citizenship. p. 9

civil rights (siv´əl rīts) The rights and freedoms given by the Constitution to all citizens. p. 211

civil war (siv´əl wôr) A fight between groups of citizens of the same country. p. 179

clan (klan) A group of closely related people. p. 69

classify (klas´ə•fī) To group information according to a pattern. p. 53

climate (klī´mit) The kind of weather a place has over a long period of time. p. 46

colonist (kol´ə•nist) Person living in a colony. p. 102

colony (kol´ə•nē) A settlement set up and ruled by another country. p. 94

commercial farm (kə•mûr´shəl färm) A farm where all the crops are sold to make money. p. 245

common council (kom´ən koun´səl) The legislative branch of a city government; a city council. p. 269

communal (kə•myōōn´əl) Relating to a group. p. 161

commute (kə•myōōt´) To travel back and forth. p. 210

compromise (kom´prə•mīz) An agreement in which each side in a conflict gives up some of what it wants. p. 206

conclusion (kən•klōō´zhən) A decision or idea reached by thoughtful study. p. 256

confederation (kən•fed•ə•rā´shən) A large group made up of smaller groups that have the same goals and want to work together. p. 123

Congress (kong´gris) The part of the United States government that makes the nation's laws. p. 121

consequence (kon´sə•kwens) Something that happens because of an action. p. 108

conserve (kən•sûrv´) To save something, such as a resource. p. 255

constitution (kon•stə•tōō´shən) A written plan of government that describes basic laws and explains how the government is to work. p. 135

consumer goods (kən•sōō′mər gōōdz) Products made for personal use. p. 203

continent (kon′tə•nent) One of the main areas of land on Earth. p. 22

convention (kən•ven′shən) A special meeting or assembly held for a certain purpose. p. 135

cooperate (kō•op′ə•rāt) To work together as a team. p. 59

Corn Belt (kôrn belt) A region in the Middle West that grows more corn than any other region in the world. p. 245

council (koun′səl) A group of advisers. p. 68

county commissioner (koun′tē kə•mish′ən•ər) One of the people who govern a county by making ordinances, or laws, for the county and by making sure that laws are obeyed. p. 268

county council (koun′tē koun′səl) A group of people who decide how a county's money will be spent. p. 268

county seat (koun′tē sēt) The town or city that is the center of government for a county. p. 268

culture (kul′chər) A group of people's way of speaking, dressing, and behaving and their beliefs. p. 10

D

dam (dam) A wall built across a river or creek to help control flooding. p. 39

debt (det) The owing of money. p. 217

decade (dek′ād) A period of time lasting ten years. p. 77

Declaration of Independence (dek•lə•rā′shən əv in•di•pen′dəns) The 1776 document that announced the United States of America's break from British rule. p. 110

deed (dēd) A document that describes a piece of land and tells who owns it. p. 121

defense plant (di•fens′ plant) A factory used to make things needed to defend the country. p. 209

delegate (del′ə•git) Someone chosen by people to represent them at a meeting. p. 134

demand (di•mand′) What consumers are willing and able to buy. p. 216

depression (di•presh′ən) A time when there are few jobs and people have little money. p. 204

discrimination (dis•krim•ə•nā′shən) Unfair treatment. p. 211

diverse (di•vûrs′) Made up of distinct items; for instance, an economy with a wide variety of industries is a diverse economy. p. 220

double-bar graph (də′bəl•bär graf′) A chart or graph that uses two bars of different heights to show and compare data. p. 174

drought (drout) A long period of time with very little or no precipitation. p. 50

E

earthworks (ûrth′wûrks) Large human-made mounds of dirt. p. 61

economics (e•kə•nä′miks) The study of how people use resources to meet their needs. p. 8

economy (i•kon′ə•mē) The way people use resources to meet their needs. p. 8

effect (i•fekt′) Something that results from an earlier action or cause. p. 63

elevation (el•ə•vā′shən) The height of the land. p. 32

enabling act (in•ā′bling akt) A special law that let a territory become a state. p. 134

entrepreneur (än•trə•prə•nûr′) A person who starts and runs a business. p. 188

equator (i•kwā′tər) An imaginary line that runs east and west around the middle of Earth. p. 24

evidence (e′və•dəns) Proof. p. 2

executive branch (ig•zek′yə•tiv branch) The part of government that carries out laws. p. 264

exile (eg′zīl) A person who is forced to or decides to leave his or her country. p. 237

export (eks′pôrt) To send products out of one country to be sold in another. p. 218

extended family (ek•stend′əd fam′lē) A family group that includes the immediate family plus grand-parents, aunts, uncles, and other relatives. p. 73

extinct (ik•stingkt′) No longer existing. p. 60

F

fable (fā′bəl) A story that teaches a lesson. p. 239

fact (fakt) A statement that can be proved true. p. 115

federal (fed′ər•əl) National p. 275

fertile (fûr′təl) Good for growing crops. p. 27

flatboat (flat′bōt) A boat with a flat bottom. p. 164

flow chart (flō chärt) A drawing that shows the order in which things happen. p. 266

fork (fôrk) A branch of a river. p. 36

fort (fôrt) A building that offers protection from an enemy attack. p. 95

free enterprise (frē en′tər•prīz) An economic system in which people are free to start and run their own businesses. p. 188

free state (frē stāt) A state in which slavery was against the law. p. 176

frontier (frun•tir′) The edge of settled land. p. 112

fuel (fyōō′əl) A natural resource that is used to make heat or energy. p. 41

G

geographer (jē•og′rə•fər) A person who studies Earth and the people who live on it. p. 6

geography (jē•og′rə•fē) The study of Earth and the people who live on it. p. 6

glacier (glā′shər) A large mass of ice. p. 26

government (guv′ərn•mənt) A system of leaders and laws that helps people live safely together in a community, a state, or a country. p. 9

gristmill (grist′mil) A place for grinding grain. p. 162

H

habitat (hab′ə•tat) A place where an animal naturally finds food and shelter. p. 44

headwaters (hed′wô•terz) The source of a river. p. 66

hemisphere (hem′ə•sfir) One half of Earth. p. 22

hereditary (hə•red′ə•ter•ē) Passed from one generation of family members to another. p. 68

heritage (her′ə•tij) Ways of life that have been passed down through history. p. 12

high-tech (hī•tek′) Having to do with the technology of computers and electronics. p. 220

Hispanic (his•pan′ik) A person whose ancestors come from a Spanish-speaking country in North America, Central America, or South America. p. 237

historian (hi•stōr′ē•ən) A person who studies the past. p. 2

historical map (his•tôr′i•kəl map) A map that gives information about places at certain times in the past. p. 132

history (his′tə•rē) The study of the past. p. 2

hub (hub) A center of transportation. p. 168

human feature (hyōō′mən fē′chər) A characteristic of Earth created by people. p. 6

human resource (hyōō′mən rē′sôrs) A worker and the knowledge and skills brought to the job. p. 251

humid (hyōō′mid) Having a lot of moisture. p. 50

hydrosphere (hī′drə•sfir) All the water on Earth's surface. p. 34

I

immediate family (i•mē′dē•ət fam′lē) A family group that consists of a father, a mother, and their children. p. 73

immigrant (im′ə•grənt) A person who moves to one country from another country. p. 187

import (im•pôrt′) To bring products from one country into another. p. 218

industry (in′dəs•trē) A business that makes one kind of product. p. 163

infantry (in′fən•trē) A group of foot soldiers. p. 179

interact (in•ter•akt′) To affect one another. p. 6

interstate highway (in′tər•stāt hī′wā) A road that links major cities across the country. p. 210

interurban rail (in′tər•ər•bən rāl) A network of rail lines connecting rural areas with nearby cities and towns. p. 197

invest (in•vest′) To put money and other resources into companies in order to make money. p. 218

isolated (ī′sə•lāt•əd) Separated from all others. p. 160

J

judicial branch (jōō•dish′əl branch) The part of government that makes sure that laws are fair. p. 265

jury trial (jŏŏr′ē trī′əl) A trial in which a group of citizens decides whether a person accused of a crime is guilty or not guilty. p. 265

L

labor union (lā′bər yōōn′yən) An organization of workers who do the same kinds of jobs. p. 196

lake effect (lāk i•fekt′) The effect of a lake on the weather in places near it. p. 50

landform (land′fôrm) A shape that makes up part of Earth's surface. p. 21

legislative branch (lej′əs•lā′tiv branch) The part of government that makes, or passes, laws. p. 263

leisure time (lē′zhər tīm) Time away from work. p. 211

line graph (līn graf) A graph that shows how data changes over a period of time. p. 140

lines of latitude (līnz av la′tə•tōod) Imaginary lines that circle the globe from east to west. p. 24

lines of longitude (līnz uv lahn′jə•tōod) Imaginary lines that circle the globe from the North Pole to the South Pole. p. 25

lithosphere (lith′ə•sfir) The soil and rock that form Earth's surface. p. 28

location (lō•kā′shən) The place where something can be found. p. 6

locomotive (lō•kə•mō′tiv) A train engine. p. 168

longhouse (long′hous) A long wooden building. p. 67

M

majority (mə•jôr′ə•tē) More than half. p. 264

manufacturing (man•yə•fak′chər•ing) The making of finished products out of raw materials. p. 184

marsh (märsh) A lowland area with wet soil and tall grasses. p. 28

metropolitan area (me•trə•pä′lə•tən âr′ē•ə) A large city plus all smaller cities around it. p. 252

migrate (mī′grāt) To move from place to place. p. 58

mineral (min′ə•rəl) A natural substance found in the ground. p. 41

missionary (mish′ə•ner•ē) A person who teaches religious beliefs to others. p. 94

GLOSSARY

moraine (mə•rān´) A hill formed of stony soil carried by a glacier and left behind when it melts. p. 28

mouth (mouth) The place where a river empties into a larger body of water. p. 35

natural region (nach´ər•əl rē´jən) A part of Earth that has one major kind of natural feature, such as mountains, hills, or plains. p. 27

natural resource (nach´ər•əl rē´sôrs) Something found in nature that people can use. p. 21

naturalized citizen (nach´ər•əl•īzd sit´ə•zən) An immigrant who has become a citizen of the United States. p. 280

navigable (nav´ə•gə•bəl) Wide and deep enough for ships to travel; describes some rivers. p. 165

nominate (nä´mə•nāt) To name as a candidate to run in an election. p. 276

nonrenewable resource (non´rē•nōo•ə•bəl rē´sôrs) A resource that cannot be made again. p. 41

opinion (ə•pin´yən) What a person thinks. p. 115

oral history (or´əl his´tə•rē) A story told aloud about an event. p. 2

orbit (ôr´bit) To circle. p. 212

ordinance (ôr´də•nəns) An order or law. p. 121

parallel (par´ə•lel) A line of latitude. p. 25

permanent (pûr´mə•nənt) Lasting a long time. p. 98

physical feature (fi´zi•kəl fē´chər) A characteristic of Earth formed by nature. p. 6

pioneer (pī•ə•nir´) An early settler in a place. p. 111

plain (plān) A flat area of land. p. 27

point of view (point uv vyōo) The way a person sees things. p. 3

pollute (pə•lōot´) To harm the environment. p. 41

population (pä•pyə•lā´shən) The number of people who live in a place. p. 140

population density (pä•pyə•lā´shən den´sə•tē) The number of people living in an area of a certain size. p. 242

portage (pôr´tij) An overland route between two bodies of water. p. 66

prairie (prâr´ē) A flat grassland. p. 45

precipitation (pri•sip•ə•tā´shən) Water that falls to Earth as rain, snow, sleet, or hail. p. 46

prediction (prē•dik´shən) An educated guess. p. 256

primary source (prī´mer•ē sôrs) A record made by a person who saw or took part in an event. p. 4

prime meridian (prīm mə•rid´ē•ən) The starting point for labeling the lines of longitude. p. 25

proclamation (prä•klə•mā´shən) An order from a leader to the citizens of a place. p. 106

product (prä´dəkt) Something that people make or grow. p. 40

productivity (prō•dək•ti´və•tē) The amount of goods or services produced in a period of time. p. 170

profit (prof´it) Amount gained from selling something minus the cost of producing it. p. 189

quarry (kwô´rē) A place where stone is cut or blasted out of the ground. p. 42

reaper (rē´pər) A machine used for cutting wheat. p. 170

recession (ri•se´shən) An economic slowdown that is slightly less damaging than a depression. p. 217

reclaim (ri•klām´) To make land usable again. p. 246

refinery (ri•fī´nər•ē) A factory in which resources such as oil are made into products people can use. p. 185

region (rē´jən) An area with at least one feature that makes it different from other areas. pp. 6, 20

register (rej´is•tər) To sign up in writing. p. 281

relative location (re´lə•tiv lō•kā´•shən) The position of a place in relation to other places. p. 21

relief (ri•lēf´) Differences in elevation. p. 32

renewable resource (ri•nōo´ə•bəl rē´sôrs) A resource that can be made again by nature or people. p. 43

represent (rep•ri•zent´) To speak for people. p. 134

representative (rep•ri•zent´ə•tiv) A person who speaks for a group of people. p. 109

reservoir (re´zər•vwär) A lake that stores water held back by a dam. p. 39

resolve (ri•zolv´) To settle a conflict. p. 206

responsibility (ri•spon•sə•bil´ə•tē) A duty. p. 280

retreat (ri•trēt´) To turn away from battle. p. 123

revolution (rev•ə•lōo´shən) A sudden, great change. p. 110

rights (rīts) Freedoms or legal claims. p. 99

river system (ri´vər sis´təm) A river and all its tributaries. p. 36

route (rōot) A path that a person takes to get from one place to another. p. 214

rural (rur´əl) Related to farmlands, forests, and other parts of the countryside. p. 236

sand dune (sand dōon) A hill built up from sand that the wind has swept from beaches. p. 28

savings plan (sāv´ings plan) A long-term plan for how a person or business will use money. p. 274

scarce (skârs) Hard to find. p. 96

school board (skōōl bôrd) A group of people elected by voters in a school district to make decisions about running the schools. p. 271

sea level (sē lev´əl) The same height as the surface of the oceans. p. 29

secede (si•sēd´) To leave a group of states. p. 179

secondary source (se´kən•der•ē sôrs) A record written by a person who was not at an event. p. 5

section (sek´shən) A part of a township 1 mile (about 2 km) square. p. 121

segregation (seg•rə•gā´shən) Keeping people in separate groups because of race or culture. p. 211

self-sufficient (self´ sə•fish´ənt) Able to produce everything needed to live. p. 160

service industry (sûr´vis in´dəs•trē) An industry that provides services but does not make goods. p. 221

sharecropper (shâr´krop•ər) Someone who rents land and pays with a share of the crops raised. p. 187

shortage (shôr´tij) A low supply of something. p. 201

slave (slāv) A person who is owned by another. p. 122

slave state (slāv stāt) A state that allowed slavery. p. 176

society (sə•sī´ə•tē) A group of people. p. 11

sod (sod) Soil held together by grass and roots. p. 171

source (sôrs) The place where a river begins. p. 35

space shuttle (spās shu´təl) A vehicle that orbits Earth carrying astronauts. p. 212

special district (spesh´əl dis´trikt) An area in which a certain problem needs to be solved. p. 271

specialize (spesh´əl•īz) To work at only one job. p. 61

stagecoach (stāj´kōch) A wagon with an enclosed carriage, pulled by horses. p. 166

steamboat (stēm´bōt) A type of boat with a large paddle wheel, powered by steam. p. 165

subsistence farming (sub•sis´təns färm´ing) Growing crops and raising animals for one's needs. p. 169

suburb (sub´ərb) A smaller town near a large city. p. 210

suffrage (suf´rij) The right to vote. p. 203

supply (sə•plī´) What producers are willing and able to sell. p. 216

surplus (sər´pləs) An extra supply. p. 169

surrender (sə•ren´dər) To give up. p. 114

tax (taks) The money that a government collects to pay for the services it provides. p. 109

temperance (tem´pə•rəns) Drinking little or no alcohol. p. 202

territory (ter´ə•tôr•ē) Land that is owned by a country but is not part of any state. p. 114

thresher (thresh´ər) A steam-powered farm machine used for separating wheat grains from stalks. p. 171

till (til) A layer of soil left behind by glaciers. p. 28

time line (tīm līn) A diagram that shows the order in which events took place. p. 76

tornado (tôr•nā´dō) A funnel-shaped column of spinning air. p. 51

tourism (tŏŏr´i•zəm) The industry that offers services to people who travel. p. 245

town board (toun bôrd) The legislative branch for a town. p. 269

township (toun´ship) A piece of land 6 miles (about 10 km) square. p. 121

township board (toun´ship bôrd) The legislative branch of a township. p. 269

township trustee (toun´ship trus•tē´) The head of each township government. p. 269

trace (trās) A trail made by animals. p. 165

treaty (trē´tē) A written agreement among nations or groups of people. p. 103

tribe (trīb) A group of bands of people who share land and ways of life. p. 61

tributary (trib´yə•ter•ē) A river or creek that flows into a larger river or creek. p. 35

turning point (tûrn´ing point) An event that causes an important change to take place. p. 124

Underground Railroad (un´dər•ground rāl´rōd) A route along which runaway slaves could find help in gaining freedom. p. 178

unemployment (un•im•ploi´mənt) The number of people without jobs. p. 205

unite (yōō•nīt´) To bring together. p. 105

urban (ûrb´ən) Related to cities or towns. p. 236

veteran (vet´ə•rən) A former soldier. p. 276

veto (vē´tō) To stop a bill by refusing to sign it. p. 264

voyageur (voi´•ə•zhûr) A French word meaning "traveler." p. 97

volunteer (vol•ən•tir´) A person who chooses to work without receiving payment. p. 282

GLOSSARY

Index

Page references for illustrations are set in italic type. An italic *m* indicates a map. Page references set in boldface type indicate the pages on which vocabulary terms are defined.

A

Abolitionists, **176**, 176–178
Absolute location, **24**, 24–25
Achrey, Oatess, 11
Adams, John, 126
Ade, George, 239
Africa, *22*, 23, *m24*
African American Indiana
    Black Expo, 237
African Americans
    civil rights and, *211*,
        211–212
    in Civil War, 180
    community of, 152, 202,
        237, 238
    Constitution of 1851 and,
        177
    festivals of, 237
    in government, 212,
        278–279
    in industry, 188, *188*
    migration to North, 187,
        202
    in military, 180
    population of, 202, 237
    right to vote, 203
    as sharecroppers, 187
    in sports, *211*, 240
    voting right of, 136
    See also Slaves and slavery
*African Repository and
    Colonial Journal*, 177
Agencies, **264**, *271*
Agriculture. *See* Farming
Airplanes, 204, 247, *247*
Allen, Thomas B., 152
Allen County, *231*
Allied Powers, 209
Ally, **103**
Amendment, **202**, 203
American Railway Union, 196
American Revolution, 109–114,
    144–145
Amish, 10, 239, *239*
Ancestor, **74**
Anderson, 186
Angel Mounds Historic Site,
    m56, 56, *61*
Animals
    early, 58–59, 60
    extinction of, 60
    as natural resource, 44–45,
        59, 67
Antarctica, 22, *m24*
Antonyms, 229
Appeals, **265**
Arrowheads, 64, *64*
Artifacts, 64–65
Artists, 240
Asia, 22

Asian Americans, 58, *m59*, 237,
    238
Assemble, **262**
Astronauts, 212–213
Atlatl (throwing stick), 60
Auburn Cord Duesenberg
    Museum, 198–199, *198–199*
Auburn Automobile
    Company, 198–199, *198–199*
Australia, 22
Automobile, *151*, **194**, 194–196,
    198–199, *199*, 203, 210, 216
Aviation, **204**, 247

B

Baby boom, 210
Bacon, Lydia, 157
Ball brothers, 185, 189, 203
Ball State University, 189, 251
Bands, **59**
Banks, depression and, 204,
    207
Barges, *21*, 218, **247**
Basketball, 211, 240–241
Bass Lake, 38
Battleships, 130, *130*, 208–209
Bayh, Birch, 277
Bayh, Evan, 277, *278*
Bean Blossom Bluegrass
    Festival, 238, *238*
Beaver hats, 96, 100
Bedford, 31, 42, 246, 272
Bell, Alexander Graham, 172
Berne, 12
Beste, J. Richard, 43
Big Clifty Creek, 37
Big House, 72
Bill, **264**, 266–267, *267*
Bill of Rights, **262**, 264, 281
Biosphere, **44**, 44–45
Bird, Larry, 241
Birds, 44–45, *45*
Birkbeck, Morris, 158
Bituminous coal, *m41*, **41**, 246,
    248, *m249*
Black Expo, 11
Blane, William, 162
Bloody Shirt law, 181
Bloomington, 15, *m31*, 137, 246
Blue Jacket (Native American
    leader), 123, 124
Blue River, *m35*
Bluegrass music, 238
Bluespring Caverns, *m31*
Board of Agriculture, 172
Boats and ships
    barges, 218, **247**
    battleships, 130, *130*,
        208–209

canal boats, 166–167, *167*
canoes, 36, *66*, 95, 164
flatboats, 36, *126*, **164**
keelboat, 164
oceangoing, 218
on Ohio River, 37
steamboats, 36, *151*, **165**, *165*
submarines, 200
in War of 1812, 130, *130*
Bolton, Sarah Knowles, 229,
    239
Bonds, **201**, 201
Border states, *m180*
Borman, Frank, 212
Boundary, **126**, 126–127, *m127*
Bread Dance, 74
Bridges, 164, *164*, 216, 253
Britain
    in American Revolution,
        111–114
    exploration and settlement
        by, 102–107, *m103*, *m107*
    forts of, *m105*, 111, 123, 131
    in French and Indian War,
        103–105
    trade with Native
        Americans, 102–103, 105,
        122
    treaty with Native
        Americans, 103
    in War of 1812, 130–131
    in World War II, 208–209
Broadleaf trees, 44
Buddhists, 239
Budget, **264**
Buell, Dorothy, *282*, 284
Buggies and Bad Times
    (McCullough), 193
Burns Harbor, 218
Bush, George, 277

C

Cabins, *158*, 159–160, *160*, *176*
Cahokia, 62, 112
Calumet region, 185, 186, 244
Camp Morton, 181
Canada, 22, 94, 104, 179, 219
Canal, **166**, 166–167, *m167*, *167*
Canal boats, 166–167, *167*
Canoe, 36, *66*, 95, 164
Capital, *m86*, 135, 137–139
Capital resources, 189
Capitol
    in Corydon, *135*
    government and, 263
    of Indiana, *139*, *231*,
        288–289, *288–289*
    of U.S., 42, *131*, *278*
Cardinal (state bird), 45

Cargo, **247**
Carmel, 236
Carmichael, Hoagy, 240
Carson, Julia, 278–279, *279*
Cattle, 40, 170
Cause, **63**, 93
Cavalry, **179**, 180
Cavelier, René-Robert, 95
Caverns, 30–31
Caves, 30–31
Cecil M. Harden Reservoir, 39,
    53
Celebrations, 197, 237–238
Céloron, Pierre Joseph, 103
Census, **127**, 134, 236–237, 252,
    277
Centennial, **197**
Central Till Plain, *m27*, **27**,
    28–29, *29*
Century, **77**
Character traits, 178, 209, 282
Charlestown, 134
Charlestown State Park, *30*
Chilled-iron plow, 171, *171*
Christians, *238*
Cities
    government of, 269–270
    growth of, 185, 186, 270
    immigrants in, 187
    industries in, 184–185, 186,
        194–195, 196
    leaving, for suburbs, 236
    manufacturing in, 184–185
    metropolitan area of,
        252–253
    problems of, 252–253
    services provided by, 252,
        253, *253*
Citizen
    acting responsibly, 284
    informed, 251
    naturalized, **280**
    responsibilities of, 280,
        282–283, *283*
    rights of, 281–282
    savings plans of, 274
Citizenship Day, *281*
City Council, 269
City-County Council, 270, *271*
Civic virtues, 282, **283**
Civil chiefs, 68, 69
Civil rights, **211**
Civil Rights movement, 211
Civil War, **179**, 179–181, *m180*,
    m183
Civilian Conservation Corps
    (CCC) camps, 205, *205*
Claim, 159
Clan, **69**, 74
Clark, George Rogers
    in American Revolution, *87*,
        93, 111–114, *115*, 250

For permission to reprint copyrighted material, grateful acknowledgment is made to the following sources:

Atheneum Books for Young Readers, an imprint of Simon & Schuster Children's Publishing Division: *A Place Called Freedom* by Scott Russell Sanders, illustrated by Thomas B. Allen. Text copyright © 1997 by Scott Russell Sanders; illustrations copyright © 1997 by Thomas B. Allen.

Barron's Educational Series, Inc.: Cover illustration by Pam Tanzey from *How the U.S. Government Works* by Syl Sobel. Illustration copyright © 1999 by Barron's Educational Series, Inc.

Curtis Brown, Ltd.: From "This Is Indiana" by Rebecca Kai Dotlich. Text copyright © 2000 by Rebecca Kai Dotlich.

Candlewick Press, Inc., Cambridge, MA: Cover illustration by Nneka Bennett from *Vision of Beauty: The Story of Sarah Breedlove Walker* by Kathryn Lasky. Illustration copyright © 2000 by Nneka Bennett.

Chelsea House Publishers, a subsidiary of Haights Cross Communications: Cover illustration from *George Rogers Clark* by Michael Burgan. Copyright © 2002 by Chelsea House Publishers, a subsidiary of Haights Cross Communications.

Clarion Books/Houghton Mifflin Company: Cover illustration by Ronald Himler from *Train to Somewhere* by Eve Bunting. Illustration copyright © 1996 by Ronald Himler.

Crestmont Publishing: Cover illustration by Delton Gerdes from *Sir Johnny's Recycling Adventure* by Rachael Peterpaul Paulson.

Robert and Katheryn Hessong: From *Ollie's Cabin in the Woods* by Robert and Katheryn Hessong, cover illustration by Carolyn Hessong Hickman. Text and cover illustration copyright © 1999 by Robert and Katheryn Hessong. Published by Guild Press of Indiana, Inc.

Hyperion: Cover illustration by Bryan Collier from *Freedom River* by Doreen Rappaport. Illustration copyright © 2000 by Bryan Collier.

Hal Leonard Corporation: From "Small Town" by John Cougar Mellencamp. Lyrics © 1985 by EMI FULL KEEL MUSIC. International copyright secured.

Metropolitan Teaching and Learning Company: Cover illustration by Peter Fiore from *These Lands Are Ours: Tecumseh's Fight for the Old Northwest* by Kate Connell. Copyright © 2001 by Metropolitan Teaching and Learning Company.

The Millbrook Press, Inc., Brookfield, CT: Cover illustration from *The Shawnees: People of the Eastern Woodlands* by Laurie A. O'Neill. Copyright © 1995 by Laurie A. O'Neill.

Patria Press, Inc.: Cover illustration by Cathy Morrison from *Young Patriots Series: William Henry Harrison, Young Tippecanoe* by Howard Peckham. Cover illustration © 2000 by Patria Press, Inc.

Random House Children's Books, a division of Random House, Inc.: Cover illustration by Dave Kramer from *Ruthie's Gift* by Kimberly Brubaker Bradley. Illustration copyright © 1998 by Dave Kramer.

Scholastic Inc.: Cover illustration by Robert Andrew Parker from *The Year of No More Corn* by Helen Ketteman. Illustration copyright © 1993 by Robert Andrew Parker. Published by Orchard Books, an imprint of Scholastic Inc.

Sleeping Bear Press: Cover illustration by Bruce Langdon from *H is for Hoosier: An Indiana Alphabet* by Cynthia Furlong Reynolds.

ILLUSTRATION CREDITS:

UNIT 1

15 (br) Shannon Stirnweis; 15 (br) Shannon Stirnweis; 15 (cr) Shannon Stirnweis; 15 (tr) Shannon Stirnweis; 15 (tr) Shannon Stirnweis; 16 (c) Dave Henderson; 47 (t) Studio Liddell; 48 (b) Studio Liddell; 49 (t) Studio Liddell; 59 (br) Dave Henderson; 60 (tr) Dave Henderson; 69 (t) Dave Henderson; 73 (b) Dave Henderson; 76 (bl) Craig Attebery; 76 (br) Craig Attebery; 77 (bc) Craig Attebery; 83 (br) Shannon Stirnweis; 83 (br) Shannon Stirnweis; 83 (cr) Shannon Stirnweis; 83 (tr) Shannon Stirnweis; 83 (tr) Shannon Stirnweis.

UNIT 2

87 (br) Domenick D'Andrea; 87 (br) Domenick D'Andrea; 87 (cr) Domenick D'Andrea; 87 (tr) Domenick D'Andrea; 87 (tr) Domenick D'Andrea; 97 (b) Craig Attebery; 147 (br) Domenick D'Andrea; 147 (br) Domenick D'Andrea; 147 (cr) Domenick D'Andrea; 147 (tr) Domenick D'Andrea; 147 (tr) Domenick D'Andrea; 88-89 (c) Bill Maughan; 90-91 (c) Bill Maughan.

UNIT 3

151 (br) Keith Batcheller; 151 (br) Keith Batcheller; 151 (cr) Keith Batcheller; 151 (tr) Keith Batcheller; 151 (tr) Keith Batcheller; 160 (t) Ralph Canaday; 179 (t) Ralph Canaday; 227 (br) Keith Batcheller; 227 (br) Keith Batcheller; 227 (cr) Keith Batcheller; 227 (tr) Keith Batcheller; 227 (tr) Keith Batcheller.

UNIT 4

246 (b) Craig Attebery; 267 (c) Patrick Gnan.

All maps by MapQuest

PHOTO CREDITS

Cover: Stephen Sellers, Indiana Department of Natural Resources (capitol); Cleveland Enterprises (map); Harcourt (flag); Tom Till Photography (waterfall); Harcourt (basketball); Jim Millay/Panoramic Images (dunes).

PLACEMENT KEY: (t) top; (b) bottom; (l) left; (r) right; (c) center; (bg) background; (fg) foreground; (I) inset.

POSTER INSERT

Flag: Don Mason/Corbis Stock Market, Eagle: Minden Pictures

TITLE PAGE AND TABLE OF CONTENTS

i, (bg) Joseph Sohm; Visions of America/Corbis; i (fg) Doug Roush/Harcourt; ii Doug Roush/Harcourt; iv (l) Ron Slenzak/Corbis; v (l) Indiana Historical Society; vi (l) Sal Dimarco/Black Star/Harcourt; vii (l) U.S. Mint Press Office.

INTRODUCTION

1 (bg) Joseph Sohm; Visions of America/Corbis; 1 (object) Doug Roush/Harcourt; 2 (b) Indiana State Museum; 2 (tr) Richard Cummins/The Viesti Collection; 3 (tr) Stone; 3 (bl) Indiana State Museum; 3 (bc) IFA/eStock Photography/PictureQuest; 3 (br) Curt Maas/AGStockUSA; 3 (tcr) Mark E. Gibson; 4 (b) J. C. Allen & Son, Inc.; 4 (br) Manuscript Section, Indiana State Library; 5 (br) James P. Rowan; 7 (tl) Larry Mishkar/Dembinsky Photo Associates; 7 (tr) Richard Cummins/Corbis; 7 (bl) J. C. Allen & Son, Inc.; 7 (br) Rich Baker/Unicorn Stock Photos; 7 (cr) Mark E. Gibson; 7 (cl) Karen Roush; 8 (bl) Superstock; 8 (br) S & S Fire Apparatus Co.; 9 (b) D. & I. MacDonald/Unicorn Stock Photos; 9 (inset) Lake County Museum/Corbis; 10 (b) Indiana State Fair; 10 (tr) Earthwatch Photography; 11 (tr) Associated Press, AP; 11 (bl) Berne Chamber of Commerce; 11 (cr) Jessie Walker; 12 (tr) Valparaiso Community Festivals & Events, Inc.; 12 (bl),(br) Joe Harpring/Columbus Scottish Festival.

UNIT 1

Opener (fg) Ron Slenzak/Corbis; (bg) Darryl Jones Photography; 13 (spread) Darryl Jones Photography; 13 (t) Ron Slenzak/Corbis; 18 (c) Indianapolis Museum of Art; 20 (bl) Bob Krist/Corbis; 21 (br) Bruce Forster/Stone; 23 (cr) Jack Olson; 23 (cr) Bill Lea/Dembinsky Photo Associates; 26 (bc) Hans Strand/Stone; 28 (tc) James P. Rowen; 29 (bl) Inga Spence/Visuals Unlimited; 29 (tr) Tom Till/ Photographer; 30 (bc) Michael Hubrich/Dembinsky Photo Associates; 30 (inset) Department of Natural Resources/ Indiana; 31 (tr) Bluespring Caverns Park; 34 (b) Richard Fields-IDNR; 35 (tl) Jack Holtel/ Photographik Co.; 36 (b) Department of Natural Resources/Indiana; 37 (t) Tom Till/ Photographer; 38 (b) Jeff Greenburg/PhotoEdit; 39 (tc) Aneal Vohra/Unicorn Stock Photos; 40 (bl) Robert Brenner/PhotoEdit; 41 (cr) Andrew Sacks/Stone; 41 (tr) Superstock; 42 (t) J. Bruce Baumann/National Geographic Image Collection; 42 (tr) Pete Seaward/Stone; 43 (b) David Muench/Corbis; 44 (bc) Robin Rudd/Unicorn Stock; 44 (tr) Gene Stratton-Porter Memorial Society, Inc.; 45 (c) Bill Banaszewski/ Visuals Unlimited; 45 (tc) Maslowski/Photo Researchers; 46 (bl) Myrleen Ferguson/ PhotoEdit; 50 (br) Image State; 51 (tr) Alan R. Moller/Stone; 52 (b) Jack Holtel/Photographik Co.; 52 (cr) Dan Dempster/Dembinsky Photo Associates; 56 (c) ; 58 (b) Jonathan Blair/Corbis; 61 (b) Courtesy of The Friends of Angel Mounds, Inc.; 61 (tc) Mark Gulezian/Quick Silver Photographers; 62 (tc) Ohio Historical Society; 64 (br) Ball State University/Feldman & Associates; 64 (cl) Tim Wright/Corbis/Feldman & Associates; 65 (bl) Indiana State Museum/ Feldman & Associates; 65 (cl) Ball State University/Feldman & Associates; 65 (cr) Ball State University/Feldman & Associates; 65 (tr) Indiana State Museum/Feldman & Associates; 66 (bl) H. Schmeiser/Unicorn Stock Photos; 67 (bc) Ohio Historical Society; 67 (t) Don Voelker/Voelker Enterprises, Inc.; 68 (tr) Library of Congress; 71 (br) Hulton /Getty ; 72 (bc) Ohio Historical Society; 72 (t) L. Johnstone/Eye Ubiquitous; 73 (inset) National Museum of the American Indian, Smithsonian Institution/ Carmelo Guadagno ; 75 (inset) Department of Ethnography/The British Museum; 75 (tr) University of Notre Dame Sports Information Dept.; 80-81 (c) Jeff Greenberg/Unicorn Stock Photos; 81 (cl) Lawrence Williams/Williams Photography; 81 (cr) Ellen Skye/Indiana Dunes National Lakeshore; 81 (tl) James P. Rowan photography; 81 (tr) R. & S. Day/Academy of Natural Sciences, Philadelphia/Visual Resources for Ornithology.; 84 (bl) Jack Holtel/ Photographik Co.; 84 (b) *The Shawnees: People of the Eastern Woodlands* © 1995 by Laurie A. O'Neill, Reprinted with permission of the Millbrook Press, Inc., Brookfield, CT.; 84 (cr) Scholastic Inc./Photo Researchers; 84 (tr) Orchard Books/Scholastic Inc.

UNIT 2

Unit Opener, (bg) Balthazar Korab, Ltd.; (fg) Indiana Historical Society; (spread) Balthazar Korab, Ltd.; 85 (t) Indiana Historical Society; 88 (tl) Robert and Katheryn Hessong/Guild Press of Indiana, Inc.; 92 (both) Darryl Jones Photography; 94 (bl) Silvio/Superstock; 96 (bl) Stock Montage; 98 (b) Louis S. Glanzman/ National Geographic Image Collection; 99 (c) Minnesota Historical Society; 100 (bl) Museum of the Fur Trade, Chadron Nebraska; 100 (cr) Marilyn "Angel" Wynn/Native Stock.com; 101 (bl) Indiana State Museum/Feldman & Associates; 101 (cr) Tippecanoe County Historical Association/Feldman & Associates; 101 (tl) Indiana State Museum/Feldman & Associates; 102

(bl) Patrick Ward/Corbis; 102 (c) The Granger Collection, New York; 104 (b) Wisconsin Historical Society; 105 (tl) The Granger Collection, New York; 106 (bl) Antique Postcards/Al Hoffman; 109 (bc) Larry Stevens/Nawrocki Stock Photos, Inc.; 109 (br) Johnston, DC/Corbis; 110 (b) Art Resource, NY; 111 (t) Indiana Historical Bureau, State of Indiana; 112 (bc) James P. Rowen; 113 (bc) George Rogers Clark National Historical Park, National Park Service; 114 (middle right) Stock Montage; 115 (br) The Granger Collection, New York; 118 (both) The Granger Collection, New York; 120 (b) Indiana Historical Society/Color added to this photo; 121 (br) Independence National Historical Park; 122 (tr) Joseph H. Balley/National Geographic Image Collection; 123 (b) The Granger Collection, New York; 124 (bc) North Wind Picture Archives; 124 (tr) The Granger Collection, New York; 125 (tr) Ohio Historical Society; 126 (b) Bettman/Corbis; 127 (cl) The Granger Collection, New York; 128 (bl) National Portrait Gallery, Smithsonian Institution/Art Resource/NY; 128 (br) Indiana Historical Society; 128 (tl) The Granger Collection; 129 (b) Indiana Division/Indiana State Library; 129 (b) Bettman/Corbis; 130 (b) Hulton/Getty ; 131 (t) Architect of the Capitol; 132 (bl) Richard T. Nowitz/Corbis; 132 (br) Jeff Greenburg/Visuals Unlimited; 134 (bl) Charles E. Schmidt/Unicorn Stock Photos; 135 (b) Charles Schmidt/Unicorn Stock Photos; 135 (inset) Charles Schmidt/ Unicorn Stock Photos; 136 (tl) Indianapolis Museum of Art, Gift of Mrs. Addison Bybee; 136 (tr) Indiana State Archives; 137 (br) Joseph Sohm/Corbis; 137 (tc) Governors' Portraits Collection, Indiana Historical Society, State of Indiana; 138 (br) Indiana State Archives; 139 (middle) North Winds Picture Library; 140 (b) Private Collection/Bridgeman Art Library; 145 (bl) Karen Roush/Pictyour Stock; 145 (cl) National Park Service; 145 (tl) National Park Service; 145 (tr) National Park Service; 144-145 (c) Karen Roush/Pictyour Stock; 148 (bl) Jack Holtel/Photographik Co.; 148 (cl) Patria Press; 148 (cr) George Rodgers Clark: American General (Dec 2001) by Michael Burgan, Arthur M. Schlesinger (Ed.); 148 (tr) These Lands Are Ours: Tecumseh's Fight for the Old North West (Jan. 1993) by Kate Connell, Jon Naiimo Jones (Illustrator).

UNIT 3

Unit Opener, (bg) Darryl Jones Photography; (fg) Sal Dimarco/Black Star/Harcourt; (spread) Darryl Jones Photography; 149 (t) Sal Dimarco/Black Star/Harcourt; ; 152 (cl) Scott Russell Sanders/Thomas B. Allen/Anthem Books; 152 (tl) Scott Russell Sanders/Thomas B. Allen/Anthem Books; 153 (b) Scott Russell Sanders/Thomas B. Allen/Anthem Books; 154 (bc) Scott Russell Sanders/Thomas B. Allen/ Anthem Books; 155 (cl) Scott Russell Sanders/ Thomas B. Allen/Anthem Books; 158 (b) James P. Rowen; 158 (bl) The Granger Collection, New York; 161 (b) William A. Allard/National Geographic Image Collection; 162 (b) Superstock; 162 (tr) The Granger Collection, New York; 163 (tr) Aneal Vohra/Unicorn Stock Photos; 164 (b) Darryl Jones Photography; 165 (bc) Indiana Historical Society; 165 (tl) Medford Taylor/ National Geographic Image Collection; 166 (t) Superstock; 167 (bl) Luis Marden/National Geographic Image Collection; 168 (tr) The Granger Collection, New York; 169 (br) Shawn Spence/Conner Praire; 170 (br) Courtesy of Conner Praire; 170 (cl) Courtesy of Conner Praire; 170 (c) Conner Praire; 171 (tr) Indiana Division, Indiana State Library; 172 (br) Indiana State Fair; 173 (tr) The Granger Collection, New York; 174 (b) Corbis; 176 (bl) The Granger Collection, New York; 177 (bl) Levi Coffin House Association & Waynet.org; 178 (b) Cincinnati Art Museum, Subscription Fund Purchase; 178 (c) Levi Coffin House Association & Waynet.org; 181 (tc) Library

of Congress/Corbis; 184 (b) Library of Congress; 185 (b) The Ball Corporation; 186 (br) Mark Rykoff/Corbis; 186 (tr) Lowell Georgia/Corbis; 187 (b) Hulton Archive/Getty Images; 188 (tr) A'Lelia Bundles/Walker Family Collection; 189 (cl) Eli Lilly Photo Archives; 189 (cr) Eli Lilly Photo Archives; 192 Tim Bath; 194 (bl) Image donated by Nancy Beaver Kennedy/Photo by John Ryan; 195 (cl) Indianapolis Motor Speedway; 195 (cr) Corbis/Bettman Archives; 195 (t) Indianapolis Motor Speedway; 196 (br) T.L. Florek/Indiana Transportation Museum; 196 (c) J.C. Allen & Sons, Inc.; 196 (tr) Scott Molloy Labor Archives; 197 (tl) Indiana Historical Society; 198 (bl) Michael Sharp/Mira Media Image Resource Alliance; 198 (br) Auburn Cord Duesenberg Museum/Feldman & Associates; 198 (tl) Auburn Cord Duesenberg Museum/Feldman & Associates; 198 (tr) Auburn Cord Duesenberg Museum/Feldman & Associates; 199 (cl) Auburn Cord Duesenberg Museum/Feldman & Associates; 199 (tr) Auburn Cord Duesenberg Museum/Feldman & Associates; 200 (b) Bettman/Corbis; 201 (br) Corbis; 201 (t) Corbis; 201 (tl) The Granger Collection, New York; 202 (bl) Joseph H. Bailey/National Geographic Image Collection; 202 (br) Huntington Library; 203 (br) The Granger Collection, New York; 204 (b) Stock Montage, Inc.; 204 (t) Lee Maxwell; 206 (bl) Bettman/Corbis; 208 (b) Bettman/Corbis; 209 (bc) Corbis; 209 (tr) Underwood & Underwood/ Corbis; 210 (b) AP/Wide World Photos; 210 (tl) Indiana State Archives; 211 (br) AP/Wide World Photos; 211 (tl) Bob Doeppers/Indianapolis Star; 212 (bc) Kansas Cosmosphere and Space Center; 212 (br) NASA; 212 (tl) Bettman/Corbis; 213 (c) NASA; 213 (cl) NASA/Science Photo Library/ Photo Researchers; 213 (tr) WPI Archives & Special Collections, George C. Gordon Library; 216 (b) Fort Wayne Journal Gazette; 217 (cr) Farm Aid; 217 (t) Reuters New Media Inc./CORBIS; 219 (b) Michael Newman/PhotoEdit; 220 (br) Indiana State University; 220 (tr) Courtesy of Toyota Motor Manufacturing; 221 (tr) T. Wathen/ Quandrant Fine Photographic Images; 224 (br) Historic New Harmony; 225 (bl) Historic New Harmony; 225 (br) Historic New Harmony; 225 (cr) Historic New Harmony; 225 (tr) Historic New Harmony; 228 (bl) Jack Holtel/ Photographik Co.; 228 (cl) Doreen Rappaport/ Bryan Collier/Hyperion Books for Children; 228 (cr) VISION OF BEAUTY: THE STORY OF SARAH BREEDLOVE WALKER. Text Copyright © 2000 by Katheryn Lasky, Illustrations Copyright © 2000 by Nneka Bennett. Reproduction by permission of the publisher Candlewick Press, Inc., Cambridge, MA.; 228 (tr) Cover, from TRAIN TO SOMEWHERE by Eve Bunting. Jacket illustration copyright © 1996 by Ronald Himler. Reprinted by permission of Clarion Books/Houghton Mifflin Company. All Rights Reserved.; 156-157 Dale J. Travis; 224-225 (c) Historic New Harmony.

UNIT 4

Unit Opener, (bg) Matthew Stockman/Allsport; (fg) U.S. Mint Press Office; (spread) Matthew Stockman/Allsport; 229 (t) U.S. Mint Press Office; 231 (br) Spencer Grant/Photo Edit; 231 (br) National Park Service; 231 (c) Cathlyn Melloan/GettyImages; 231 (tr) Mary Kate Denny/PhotoEdit; 231 (tr) Bioanalytical Systems; 232 (bl) Gary Randall/Visuals Unlimited; 232 (c) Darryl Jones/Darryl Jones Photography; 232 (tr) Maslowski/Photo Researchers, Inc.; 234 Dan Dempster/Dembinsky Photo Assoc.; 236 (br) Michael Conroy/AP/Wide World Photos; 237 (tr) David Young-Wolff/PhotoEdit; 238 (bc) B. Seitz/ Photo Researchers; 238 (bl) M-Bio's Archive; 238 (br) /Superstock; 238 (tl) Bean Blossom Bluegrass Festival; 239 (bl) Indiana Area United Methodist Church Communications; 239 (tr) Bachmann/ Uniphoto Picture Agency; 240 (br) PAWS, Inc.; 240

(c) Indianapolis Museum of Art, James E. Roberts Fund; 240 (cr) PAWS, Inc.; 240 (tl) Bettman/Corbis; 241 (c) Andrew Ritchie; 241 (tr) Courtesy of the Major Taylor Velodrome, Photo by John Giles; 242 (b) Kent Whitehead/ White Light Photo; 242 (cr) Indiana Department of Tourism; 244 (bl) Robert Brenner/ PhotoEdit; 245 (b) Pictor/Uniphoto; 245 (c) David Sieren/ Visuals Unlimited; 245 (cr) Gary D. Lansman/ The Stock Market; 245 (tl) Superstock; 245 (tr) David Simson/Stock Boston Inc./PictureQuest; 247 (t) Eric Curry/Tecmap Corporation/Corbis; 247 (tr) /PhotoEdit; 248 (b) Tom Pantages/ Phototake/PictureQuest; 248 (b) Rink/ Schoenberger/Grant Heilman Photography, Inc.; 248 (b) Mark A. Schneider/ Visuals Unlimited, Inc.; 250 (b) Indiana Division, Indiana State Library; 251 (br) Varnau Creative Group/Tony Clevenger; 252 (bl) Aneal Vohra/ Unicorn Stock Photography; 252 (br) Michael Vaughn Photography; 253 (br) Associated Press, AP; 253 (cl) Mark Mellet/ PictureQuest; 253 (t) Indianapolis Water Company; 254 (tr) Teena Ligman/Hoosier National Forest; 255 (br) Stone; 255 (tr) Mike McGovern/USDA Natural Resource Conservation Service (Indiana); 256 (b) Mike McGovern/USDA Natural Resource Conservation Service (Indiana); 257 (bc) Robert Falls Sr./Bruce Coleman Inc.; 262 (b) Associated Press, AP; 263 (br) Don Farrall/Getty Images; 263 (br) National Park Service/Dennis Latta; 263 (r) Superstock; 264 (br) National Park Service/ Dennis Latta; 264 (tr) Associated Press, AP; 265 (tr) Indiana Supreme Court/Division of State Court Administration; 268 (bl) Will Counts; 270 (bl) Michael Vaughn Photography; 270 (tr) Nathaniel Good; 272 (bl) Photo Dyenamics/Ron Dye/Feldman & Associates; 272 (cr) Larry DeBoer; 273 (bl) Photo Dyenamics; 273 (cr) Darryl Jones Photography; 273 (tl) Ron Dye/ Photo Dyenamics; 274 (br) Ryan McVay/ PhotoDisc/PictureQuest; 275 (b) John Neubauer/PhotoEdit; 275 (cr) President Benjamin Harrison Home; 276 (bc) Indiana Historical Society Library; 276 (bl) Indiana Historical Society Library; 276 (br) Indiana Historical Society Library; 276 (cl) Uniphoto, Inc./John Neubauer; 276 (cr) Indiana Historical Society Library (Neg. No. C5861); 277 (cr) Varnau Creative Group/Michael Vaughn Photography; 277 (tr) David Young-Wolff/PhotoEdit; 278 (b) Uniphoto, Inc.; 278 (tc) Uniphoto, Inc./Mark Reinstein; 278 (tc) Library of Congress; 278 (tl) Uniphoto Picture Agency; 278 (tr) Ron Edmonds/AP/Wide World Photos; 279 (tl) Denis Ryan Kelly Jr.; 280 (bl) Kendall Reeves; 281 (br) Associated Press, AP; 281 (tr) The Promotion Company/Indianapolis, IN.; 282 (b) Dembinsky Photo Associates; 282 (br) Calumet Regional Archives/Indiana University Northwest; 283 (tr) Mpozi Mshale Tolbert/Indianapolis Star; 284 (b) David Young-Wolf/PhotoEdit; 285 (br) Michael Newman/PhotoEdit; 288 (c) Richard Fields/ Department of Natural Resources; 289 (cr) Steven Sellers/Indiana Department of Natural Resources; 289 (tl) Richard Fields/Department of Natural Resources; 289 (tr) Richard Fields/ Department of Natural Resources; 291 (br) Spencer Grant/Photo Edit; 291 (br) National Park Service; 291 (cr) Cathlyn Melloan/GettyImages; 291 (tr) Bioanalytical Systems; 291 (tr) Mary Kate Denny/PhotoEdit; 292 (bl) Jack Holtel/ Photographik Co.; 292 (cl) Syl Sobel/Pam Tanzey/Barron's Educational Series, Inc.; 292 (cr) Crestmont Publishing; 292 (tr) H is for Hoosier: An Indiana Alphabet (Sept 2001) by Cynthia Furlong Reynolds, Bruce Langdon (Illustrator); 228-229 (c) ; 260-261 Will Counts/Southern Indiana Clark & Floyd Counties Convention & Tourism Bureau; 288-289 (c) Richard Cummins/ The Viesti Collection, Inc.

All other photos by Harcourt Photographers.